W9-DIH-914

MEDIEVALIA ET HUMANISTICA

MEDIEVALIA ET HUMANISTICA
New Series
Edited by Paul Maurice Clogan

Number 3: Social Dimensions in Medieval and Renaissance Studies

The Social Significance of Twelfth-Century Chivalric Romance *Robert W. Hanning* • Nature and the Aesthetic Social Theory of Leon Battista Alberti *Andrea di Tommaso* • Pierre de Langtoft's Chronicle: An Essay in Medieval Historiography *Robert Stepsis* • Clerical Judges in English Secular Courts: The Ideal Versus the Reality *Ralph V. Turner* • Medieval Poems and Medieval Society *Donald R. Howard* • "Bachelor" and Retainer *J. M. W. Bean* • The Medieval Lyric and Its Public *Stephen G. Nichols, Jr.* • Simon of Saint-Quentin as Historian of the Mongols and Seljuk Turks *Gregory G. Guzman* • Quest and Query in the *Chastelaine de Vergi Emilie P. Kostoroski* • The Illustrations of the Cædmonian *Genesis:* Literary Criticism Through Art *Thomas H. Ohlgren* • The Figural Style and Meaning of *The Second Nun's Prologue and Tale Paul M. Clogan* • Caxton's Two Choices: "Modern" and "Medieval" Rhetoric in Traversagni's *Nova Rhetorica* and the Anonymous *Court of Sapience James J. Murphy* • Cynewulf's Multiple Revelations *Jackson J. Campbell* • The Fair Field of Anglo-Norman: Recent Cultivation *Ruth J. Dean* • Must We Abandon the Concept of Courtly Love? *Francis L. Utley.*

Number 4: Medieval and Renaissance Spirituality

Spirituality of Regular Canons in the Twelfth Century: A New Approach *Caroline W. Bynum* • Some Unorthodox Popular Ideas of the Thirteenth Century *Walter L. Wakefield* • The Heresy of the Free Spirit and Late Medieval Mysticism *Eleanor McLaughlin* • Popular Devotion in the Vernacular Drama of Medieval England *E. Catherine Dunn* • Drama and Spirituality in the Middle Ages *Sandro Sticca* • Spirituality and Poverty: Angelo da Clareno and Ubertino da Casale *E. Randolph Daniel* • History and Eschatology: Medieval and Early Protestant Thought in Some English and Scottish Writings *Marjorie Reeves* • Ritual Behavior in Renaissance Florence: The Setting *Richard C. Trexler* • Fruitful Business: Medieval and Renaissance Elements in the Devotional Method of St. John Fisher *Thomas M. C. Lawler* • Predentius and Sixteenth-Century Antiquarian Scholarship *Robert W. Gaston* • Wyclif's Political Theory: A Century of Study *Lowrie J. Daly* • Classical and Medieval Rhetoric: Three Recent Studies *John Conley* • Mimesis from Aristotle through the Eighteenth Century: Some Recent Studies *P. Albert Duhamel* • Shakespeare's History Plays: The Romantic or the Heroic View *Irving Ribner* • Government and Culture in the Renaissance City-State: Three Recent Studies *Julius Kirshner* • From Complaint to Satire: The Art of the *Confessio Amantis Paul M. Clogan.*

MEDIEVALIA ET HUMANISTICA

STUDIES IN MEDIEVAL & RENAISSANCE CULTURE

Founded in 1943 by S. Harrison Thomson

NEW SERIES
NUMBER 5

MEDIEVAL HISTORIOGRAPHY

Edited by Paul Maurice Clogan

North Texas State University
Denton, Texas
1974

FERNALD LIBRARY
COLBY-SAWYER COLLEGE
NEW LONDON, N. H. 03257

D
111
M5
no. 5

57477

Copyright © 1974 by The Medieval and Renaissance Society.
All rights reserved.
Printed in the United States of America.
P. O. Box 13348, North Texas State University, Denton, Texas 76203.
International Standard Book Number: 0-913904-01-5.
International Standard Serial Number: 0076-6127.
Library of Congress Catalogue Card Number: 70-99227.

To the memory of
AGNES JOSEPHINE CLOGAN

Editorial Note

FOUNDED IN 1943 by S. Harrison Thomson and now under new editorship and management, *Medievalia et Humanistica* continues to publish, in a series of annual volumes, significant scholarship, criticism, and reviews in all areas of medieval and Renaissance culture: literature, art, history, law, music, philosophy, science, social and economic institutions. *Medievalia et Humanistica* encourages the individual scholar to examine the relationship of his discipline to other disciplines and to relate his study in a theoretical or practical way to its cultural and historical context. Review articles examine significant recent publications, and contributing editors report on the progress of medieval and Renaissance studies in the United States and Canada.

Medievalia et Humanistica is sponsored by the Medieval Interdepartmental Section of the Modern Language Association of America, and publication in the series is open to contributions from all sources. The editorial board welcomes interdisciplinary critical and historical studies by young or established scholars and urges contributors to communicate in an attractive, clear, and concise style the larger implications in addition to the precise material of their research, with documentation held to a minimum. Texts, maps, illustrations, and diagrams will be published when they are essential to the argument of the article.

Individuals, institutions, and libraries may enter standing orders for the new series and receive a 10% discount. Future volumes will be sent to them automatically, and they will be billed when each volume is shipped. Such standing orders may, of course, be canceled at any time. Books for review, manuscripts (which should be prepared in conformity with the *MLA Style Sheet* and accompanied by a stamped, self-addressed manuscript envelope), and all inquires regarding both *Fasciculi* I-XVII in the original series and standing and individual orders to the New Series should addressed to the Editor, *Medievalia et Humanistica* P.O. Box 13348, North Texas State University, Denton, Texas 76203.

Preface

The first five articles on historiography are based upon papers which were presented at the Conference on Medieval Historiography, held at Harvard University, November 13-14, 1972, under the direction of Professors Morton W. Bloomfield, Giles Constable, and Isadore Twersky. These articles cover the subject of medieval historiography both chronologically and geographically and are interdisciplinary (literature as well as history) and cross-cultural (Jewish, Moslem, Christian) in approach. They were originally written for a reading public and distributed to the participants in advance of the conference which was a discussion and defense of the papers in terms of the broad problems of medieval and early modern historiography. In preparing the articles for publication, the authors have made some revisions in the light of their own second thoughts and of the discussion at the conference. Amos Funkenstein identifies what he calls the principle of accommodation in medieval historical thought, the realization that God's plan for mankind is revealed in stages determined by the evolution of mankind. Though medieval thinkers understood history primarily as the work of God, Professor Funkenstein argues that man's development could play an important part in this understanding. He demonstrates his thesis by a profound analysis of ancient, patristic, medieval, and modern philosophics of history from Irenaeus to Hegel. Donald R. Kelley's article explores the character of historical consciousness in medieval jurisprudence from Justinian to Baldus and shows that the law was the main vehicle of secular and socially based historical consciousness in the Latin West. "History and Prophecy in Medieval Thought" is an important article by the most distinguished scholar of medieval and Renaissance prophecy. Marjorie E. Reeves displays her great knowledge of her subject and places the idea of the future in the later Middle Ages in proper perspective. Robert W. Hanning examines the medieval epic and in particular *Beowulf* for an understanding of medieval attitudes to history, of the heroic element in history, and of the sense of history in the Middle Ages. Finally, Edward L. Keenan, Jr., considers the historiography of Muscovy and the mentality of those who shaped the historical consciousness of Muscovy at a time when she began to play a prominent role in Eastern Europe. *Medievalia et Humanistica* is pleased to publish these original and important articles.

Among the other articles in this volume, Joseph H. Lynch's study makes a significant contribution to the understanding of monastic regulation and discipline in the Middle Ages by attributing the origin of the prohibition against payment for entry into a monastery to the influence of Byzantine Christianity upon the Frankish Church. Margaret Jennings reveals how a thirteenth-century homily recounting a dramatic episode in the life of a favorite medieval saint is a good example of *modus antiquus* in sermon writing. James R. Banker proposes an interesting link between *ars dictaminis* and the pseudo-Ciceronian *Rhetorica ad Herennium* by establishing Giovanni di Bonandrea as the first to lecture on both at the University of Bologna, 1293–1321. Bennett A. Brockman offers not only a critical review and interpretation of a dramatic moment in the Chester Cycle but also a comprehensive prospectus of exegetic and literary texts bearing upon that critical interpretation. A. Compton Reeves, who studies Thomas Hoccleve's own comments in his poetry on his position as clerk of the Privy Seal, paints a revealing portrait of a functioning bureaucrat. Kenneth J. Oberembt contributes a stylistic analysis of Lord Berners' translations with implications for the study of late medieval prose, a subject which is only beginning to be explored. Finally, Ronald E. McFarland establishes the physics and metaphysics of optics in Lord Herbert's six poems to Diana Cecil concerning the color black.

In addition, this volume also contains five review articles and six review notices of significant recent publications. The next volume in the new series of *Medievalia et Humanistica* will explore from different perspectives the subject of hagiography and romance and will also include other articles on varied subjects. Review articles will examine significant recent publications, and contributing editors will report on the progress of medieval and Renaissance studies in the United States and Canada.

P. M. C.

MEDIEVALIA ET HUMANISTICA

Paul Maurice Clogan, Editor
NORTH TEXAS STATE UNIVERSITY
Julie Sydney Davis, Managing Editor

EDITORIAL BOARD

Michael Altschul
Case Western Reserve University

Bernhard Bischoff
University of Munich

Curt F. Bühler
The Pierpont Morgan Library

Marvin L. Colker
University of Virginia

John Conley
*University of Illinois at
    Chicago Circle*

Giles Constable
Harvard University

Charles T. Davis
Tulane University

Peter Dronke
University of Cambridge

Stanley E. Fish
*University of California at
    Berkeley*

Astrik L. Gabriel
University of Notre Dame

J. H. Hexter
Yale University

Richard W. Hunt
Bodleian Library

W. T. H. Jackson
Columbia University

Berthe M. Marti
*University of North Carolina at
    Chapel Hill*

Millard Meiss
The Institute for Advanced Study

Charles Mitchell
Bryn Mawr College

Heiko A. Oberman
*Institut für Spätmittelalter und
    Reformation
University of Tübingen*

Laurence K. Shook
*Pontifical Institute of Mediaeval
    Studies*

Jerome Taylor
*University of Wisconsin at
    Madison*

Charles Trinkaus
*University of Michigan at
    Ann Arbor*

Charles Witke
*University of Michigan at
    Ann Arbor*

Contents

MEDIEVALIA ET HUMANISTICA

Periodization and Self-Understanding in the Middle Ages and Early Modern Times

Amos Funkenstein

OUR AIM is threefold. We want (1) to examine medieval periodizations (in contraposition to their early modern counterparts) in their anthropological presuppositions, inasmuch as they convey a sense of man's role in history. We want (2) to elicit from them the method by which medieval historical reasoning determined the importance of the immediate present in the course of history without resorting to new prophecies. And (3) we shall try to answer a more fundamental question, with which we shall find ourselves confronted all along our discussion: what characterizes a period as a period bare of chronographical conveniences or unquestioned traditions? Were the various medieval constructs of periods conceived merely as an interval between important events? Can different traditions or ideal types be discerned?

I

A new concept of historical periods—how to determine that which the middle ages sometimes called the "qualitas temporum" [1]—arises in the seventeenth century, and finds its first systematic expression in the *raisonnement* of Giambattista Vico. It consists in the demand and in a serious attempt to determine periods so to speak from within: through some internal, integrating principle rather than, as hitherto, in contraposition to other segments of the historical time. Vico's methodological key words in this respect are "harmony," "correspondence," or "accommodation." All human affairs *(cose umani)* of a society in a given phase correspond to and reflect one another; they all form a harmonious whole and are shaped by the very same "mode of the time." [2] Each of the ideal successive ages of every society—the divine, the heroic, and

3

the human times—brings forth its own significations and achievements, its own language, its own jurisprudence, its own religious imagery. Vico's periods are *topoi* going back to Varro and beyond; new are the ways to determine them.

A period is thus the context of events and institutions without which no historical fact is understandable. This was not Vico's discovery; ever since the sixteenth-century philologists, legal historians, and biblical critics discovered the *context* as a critical if not relativizing argument. By the time of Vico it was a truism to warn against those who mold their notion of past affairs after their resemblance to the present *(de rebus antiquissimis secundum sui temporis conditionem notiones forment).*[3] Contrary to the classical and medieval view of the historical fact as simple and self-explanatory, and therefore of the eye witness (only if sincere) as the best historian,[4] the sixteenth and seventeenth centuries developed a method of understanding through alienation and reconstruction; past monuments and institutions can be understood only if severed from actual connotations and restored to their remote original setting.[5] History became *eo ipso* interpretation.

The awareness that no fact and no piece of historical evidence is self-explanatory in itself was as revolutionary as the simultaneous revolution in natural science, and for precisely the same reasons. The analogy between the new approaches was drawn already by contemporaries. In a well-known passage of his *Tractatus Theologico-Politicus,* Spinoza explains why "the method of interpreting the Scriptures is the same as the method of interpreting nature" *(methodum interpretandi Scripturae idem est methodum interpretandi Naturae).* His remarks may be interpreted to suggest that much as the historian must reconstruct the sense of the author *(mens auctorum)*—say, the ancient Israelite image of God (which, later chapters reveal, fitted into only one definite form of political government)—out of scattered and seemingly contradicting hints until it becomes, under the hand of the interpreter, clearer than it *could* ever have been to its bearers, so also the natural philosopher, who follows the (Galilean) *metodo risolutivo e compositivo,* does not rely on nature (induction, generalized sense-data) to explain itself, but operates with mental constructs of his own—or even with counterfactual conditional idealizations such as the principle of inertia—constructs which cannot be demonstrated through immediate reference to nature.[6]

Yet Vico's periods express more than an insight into the necessity of immanent contextual interpretation; they became an almost aestheti-

4

cal category, an "Einheit in der Mannigfaltigkeit." All manifestations of an age are facets of one and the same collective mental configuration; Vico uses, in a sense peculiar to him, the term "common sense" to name the definite mental configuration of each age,[7] the harmonic principle of each period.

Aesthetical terms describe Vico's intention best in yet another way: imagination rather than reason is the driving force of the human spirit. Periods are but the common denominator for a set of images and their objectivizations; therefore, only with the aid of his own imagination can the historian reconstruct past states of the "common sense." The human spirit, being always of the same structure, enfolds in similar patterns within the individual as within the group; introspection became for Vico the tool for historical empathy. "Imagination" in the latter, subjective sense is not the rational isolation of causes, nor the narrative revivication of the past. It is the capacity to uncover symbols and hidden structures which underly the various and disparate social phenomena of a given period, the ability to discover in Zeus a "symbol" of a class, to detect patterns of cross-references, the ability to treat institutions and events as symbols and metaphors of something else—namely the "common sense" of a time. Historical knowledge turns to a large part into *Anschauung*. It must be conceded that Vico had no use for the principle of individuality of either societies or historical constellations (periods)—but only precisely because he insisted on the basic similarity of the human collective imagination and the phases of its productivity in every society.[8] Other historians in the eighteenth century did, and came to recognize periods as "points of view" or discrete perspectives of history, much as Leibniz's monads were "points of view" or "aspects" of the totality of the world.[9]

The similarities with Leibniz reach further (even if we discard as insignificant Vico's adherence to a theory of "metaphysical points"). Leibniz presented the most comprehensive and consistent philosophical justification for the constructive aspect of the Galilean analytical-synthetical method and, with it, for the concept and postulate of contextual interpretation. Against the Cartesians, who saw the nerve of the new science in the ability (which Aristotelian physics allegedly lacked) to sever an object (or a relation) from its normal context and see it "as it is by itself" *(ut per se et sua natura est),* [10] Leibniz implies that natural laws are meaningless unless they refer to a context of physical (as against logical) possibilities. Indeed, with this distinction between possibility and compossibility [11] Leibniz already developed the logical foundation of the concept of contextual harmony and made it a corner-stone of his metaphysics. The monads are contexts of attributes if the predicate-in-notion principle *(predicatum inest subjecto)* is to be taken literally. And monads cluster into "possible worlds" inasmuch as they are, beyond their logical possibility, compossible on the grounds of the principle of sufficient reason.[12] They are a logical, epistemological, but also an aesthetical category of contextual unity.[13]

Vico's "collective mentality of an age" thus has two complementary aspects. On the one hand it secures the anonymity of historical processes; from now onwards, the founder *(ktistes)* becomes ever more dethroned from the outstanding place he had occupied in genetic accounts. "Zeitgeister" of all kinds have in common that they are imagined as force-fields mightier than the mightiest individual. On the other hand, Vico stressed time and again the spontaneity of this collective mentality of an age. By itself, though indeed "occasioned" by outer necessities (an expression borrowed from the Occasionalists), the human spirit emanates all human ideas and institutions in regular phases. Again we detect the affinity to Leibniz, whose monads represent, as do Vico's societies, a genuine unity only because they produce their perceptions and apperceptions of themselves; they "have no windows." As in his ontology, Leibniz also gave the most radical epistemological meaning to the logical postulate *praedicatum inest subjecto.* As the background for this emphasis on spontaneity, we have to understand Vico's assertion that society is a human artifact (much as nature is a divine artifact); and "verum" being "factum," understanding society is easier than the interpretation of external objects. In this sense only history is the history of ideas.[14]

In this spontaneity of the collective imagination (or *sensus communis*), or rather in his theory of occasioned spontaneity, Vico believed to have mediated between the reality of man's original brutal nature and the ideal of eternal law, between Hobbes and Grotius. Society emerged neither by nature *(physei)* nor by convention *(thesei)*, but by both, since man can and did transform his brutal nature by himself; he acquires a "historical nature." Leibniz, we remember, attempted a similar mediation between mechanical and teleological models of causation in the field of physics.[15] Vico insisted that "natural law" is based neither on social instincts nor on deliberate reasoning out of necessities (or norms), but on the very immanent, regular, "ideal" *process* through which time and again civilization emerges as man's acquired nature. This is Vico's version of a "List der Vernunft," of how private vices

6

transform into public benefits. He calls it "providence," which is nothing but the inner, immanent dynamics accounting for the regular transformation of one period to another.

Thus, in a paradoxical turn of expression, "providence" came to signify man's *emancipation* from God or nature, the autonomy and spontaneity of his social endeavors. [16] Here Vico expresses, beyond any particular correspondence we might find between his thinking and this or that contemporary theory, the sense and self-understanding of modern thought, which stressed, in endless variations, the theme of man's or nature's autonomy. Vico's periods are meant to demonstrate the gradual growth of human independence, i.e., the rational determination of man's collective fate.

II

Vico's impact was negligible. But his main themes—the contextual harmony within each period, the necessary regularity in the succession of periods (nature), and the growing spontaneity of the social endeavor (freedom)—whether accepted or challenged, maintained a regulative role in the formation of modern historical reasoning. In them we see the new content given to inherited *topoi* of historical periodizations, such as the *tria tempora* [17] or the organological equation between the *aetates mundi et hominis*. Should we, then, claim that the various medieval periodizations reflect an entirely different sense of history—even where terms and metaphors are similar to their later counterparts?

To begin with, "harmony," "correspondence" are not alien notions to the medieval historical reflection. We encounter them as technical terms in a tradition which led to the "symbolism" or "speculative biblicism" of the twelfth century. In it we identify the first ideal type of medieval periodizations. [18] Speculative analogies and exegetical *figurae* serve to reveal the structure and *mysteria* of history. The Antiochene exegetes (albeit insisting that only the events themselves, not the Old Testament itself, should be searched for a meaning transcending into the new aeon) elaborated prefigurations of events and persons systematically. Irenaeus of Lyon saw the life of Christ as a *recapitulatio* of the phases of history unto him. [19] Ambrosius found the four paradisiacal rivers corresponding to the Platonic virtues (as did Philo) and again corresponding to the world periods (*tempora mundi*); [20] a historian of the tenth century, Radulfus Glaber, later used the *topos* to interpret the history of the West to the time of the Carolingians and after

7

as a history of the political realization of *iustitia*.[21] The most potent picture of this sort inherited from the patristic literature was Augustine's detailed equation of the days of creation with the ages of the world *(aetates mundi)* and again with the ages of man *(aetates hominis)*.[22] The fascination of this image can be measured by the fact that it even entered, since Abraham bar Hija, into Jewish exegesis.[23]

The search for symbolical correspondences is rooted in the apocalyptic reading of handed-down texts, though it was often used later to refute apocalyptical expectations and to stress the relative remoteness, rather than closeness, of a new aeon. On the whole it remained in the early middle ages merely an exegetical device, a part of the transliteral understanding *(spiritualis intelligentia)* of the Scriptures. Recent history—the present—had no particular characterization: it remained as a part of the undifferentiated sixth age *(aetas sexta),* a truly middle age *(medium aevum)* between the first and the coming presence of Christ; all that could be said about it was that the world grows older. The present, in this perspective, was labeled as insignificant.

No century of medieval historical thought was as productive and innovative as the twelfth century. Its enchantment with new and richer periodizations was not an art for art's sake, nor did it simply add details to an existing frame. In an attempt to interpret the confusing complexity of recent history and with an awakened sense of the significance—or importance, if you will—of the deeds and events of recent generations, it discovered in the symbolic exegesis a method to determine the exact place of the present in the history of salvation. From Rupert of Deutz to Joachim of Fiore, the so-called "symbolists" dealt with the totality of history, including post-testamental history, in a manner reserved hitherto to scriptural exegesis only. Recent history became as worthy of exegesis as that of the *nascens ecclesia* or before. The symbolic interpreter justified his knowledge with the often-quoted verse (Daniel 12:4): "many shall pass, and knowledge will multiply" *(pertransibunt plurimi, et multiplex erit scientia).*[24] He believed that history becomes gradually more transparent, that more and more of the divine plan is revealed with the approximation of the end. He did not need new prophecies or visible signs, as earlier generations did, to foretell the structure and general course of the future: in his symbolic inferences he found, so he believed, a method of prediction without divination.

The "harmony" which this pattern of thought seeks seems, then, to have nothing in common with the immanent contextual "fitting together" of which the philological, "higher" criticism since the sixteenth century speaks, to which Vico was an heir. Only on the level of mystical exegesis, not on that of the *historice* exegesis ("history" defined as a mere *narratio rei gestae ut gesta*), did the symbolist look for "concordia"—as, for example, Joachim of Fiore in his elaborate analogies between the periods of the Father, the Son, and the Holy Ghost. Yet for all the light-years separating the medieval symbolism from our historical reasoning, they share one faculty: both of them—the former always, the latter in some of its trends—are exercises in a specific kind of structuring imagination, enabling them to unearth structural analogies between disparate matters. The intense energy spent in the search for hidden significations, for *figurae,* had but to shift direction to become a *spiritualis intellegentia* not of that which is beyond history, but of history itself. Vico not only had such sense for immanent structures and significant references; he also recognized in it the very novelty of his method. We owe to this disciplined capacity some of the most inspiring instances of modern historical literature, such as Burckhardt's *Kultur der Renaissance.* Spengler, who had this sense and misused it, named it "morphology." And even if skeptical, we are still intrigued by analogies like that between "Gothic architecture and scholasticism," and look for them; analogies which do not intend to establish causal dependencies, but patterns of signification. Of course, the periods of the symbolists, as we admitted at the outset, were not *immanent* structuring principles; nor did they envision the course of history as a spontaneous unfolding of human faculties. The configurations which they unearthed within or between periods belonged to an altogether transcendant, divine plan.

Is this not true of all medieval periodizations? No matter how persistent the formal existence of medieval periodizations was—how often we find, from Bodin to Spengler, reminiscences of the *tria tempora,* of the *aetates mundi, status ecclesiae* or *translationes imperii*—it seems that they involve in the middle ages theological presuppositions alien to their modern successors. Periods come and go not in accordance with immanent principles, but as a part or a divine schedule; or, in the language of Bonaventura, "Faith moves us to believe that the three periods of law, namely that of natural law, of the Scripture, and of grace followed each other in the most harmonious order." [25] The succession of periods manifests the well-ordered divine providence, not the independence and sponaneity of human history.

9

III

But this crucial distinction, once drawn, calls again for a partial correction. The kind of reasoning subsumed under the vague name "Christian philosophy of history" (or at times, *Geschichtstheologie*) shows, since Irenaeus of Lyon, a persistent occupation with the relative autonomy of man's collective evolution. Against the apocalyptic version of divine providence which allots to man an utterly passive role in the gradual unfolding of the secret plan of history "written on the divine tablet," [26] it insists on the accommodation of God's plan of salvation to the *Lex humani generis* of slow evolution (Irenaeus), to the *mediocritas humana* (Tertullian). [27] Compared to the apocalyptic *oikonomia* the schedule of times lost its rigidity. If we isolate this principle of accommodation, we find it attached to a second, more rational ideal type of periodizations; it led to casual or teleological justifications either of periods or of their succession.

The systematic position of this figure of thought varied. Irenaeus used it in order to achieve a better definition of the continuity and discontinuity of the old and new dispensation against Marcion and the Gnosis. At times it served apocalyptic expectations; at times it served to mitigate or discard them. It was used to rebuke the objection of heathen philosophers (like Celsus or Porphyry) as to why the Saviour did not appear earlier if man was to be saved *(quare non ante venit Christus).* [28] Mixing the apocalyptic-Paulinian periodizations (six ages, three epochs) with Stoic or Epicurean accounts of the taming of man's brutal nature, Eusebius describes the gradual restitution of man's "royal nature" from Anarchy and Atheism through Polyarchy and Polytheism to Monarchy and Monotheism. [29] Such mixtures became inevitable whenever proofs were assembled that the history of the *gentes* was as much a *praeparatio evangelica* as was the history of the chosen people. Eusebius used the argument to construct a "political theology," to show the necessary correspondence of universal monotheism and universal monarchy. [30] In other instances, this principle was used, in Jewish and Christian exegesis alike, to answer the question why God permitted sacrifice and other anthropomorphistic usages; [31] Maimonides describes how God, unwilling to act *contra naturam* and change human nature which does not change suddenly *(min hahefech el hahefech pit'om)—natura non facit saltus—*allowed for some of the usages of the polytheistic universal culture of the Sa'aba to continue among the nascent Israel through changing their direction. [32] Similar interpretation can be found from Augustine through Walahfrid Strabo to Thomas Aquinas. Using a similar heuristic device, Petrus Alfunsi explains the necessary primitiveness of Islam as an accommodation to the barbarism of the early Arabs.[33] The adjustment of revelation to the "capacity" of understanding which men reached, or of sacraments to their respective times, remained a standard argument in scholastic theology.[34] Still another significant occasion for the use of the argument of accommodation was the discussion of the sense and limits of a variety of customs within the church. The outlines of a complete theory of temporal change as a sign of divine accommodation is contained in Walahfrid Strabo's *De exordiis,* one of the most interesting examples of this rich tradition of arguments concerning the *varietas.*[35]

The twelfth century's fondness for new and richer periodizations, we argued, reflected the urge to interpret the complexity of recent history and to express the sense of new achievements in the light of historical retrospection. This is particularly true of new and old periodizations based on the principle of accommodation; in them the twelfth century discovered a rational method of prediction without divination, of determining the place and role of recent events in the course of history more or less *sola ratione,* i.e. by reading the immanent "trends" of history.

Anselm of Havelberg described the operation of God as *pedagogice et medicinaliter* in words taken from Gregory of Nazianzus: between the two "revolutions of life" *(transpositiones famosae vitae),* dividing the periods *ante legem, sub lege, sub gratia* and coming together with cosmic changes *(cum attestatione terraemotus),* and again the third revolution expected to end history, humanity has been "slowly adjusted" *(paulatim usa est)* through additions, subtractions, and changes.[36] With this argument, Anselm justified to a point the diversity of the Eastern and Western churches and suggested a slow period of preparation for a reunion. Anselm extended the argument later to justify the confusing multiplicity of orders, the diversity of religious movements of his time, as a sign of rigor and a necessity at this particular stage in the development of the church. He distinguishes seven such smaller periods—later on, the Joachimites will call them *aetatunculae* [37]—corresponding to the seven seals of the Apocalypse; of these *status ecclesiae,* he sees the present church in the fourth, characterized by the strategy of indirect approach of Satan—not through heathens and heretics, but through *falsi fratres.* The accommodated strategy of the Holy Ghost must consist in an intensification of the *varietas,* in ever new incentives and

11

reforms, in ever new variants of *viri religiosi.* "This variety was not made due to the mutability of God, but rather due to the changing weakness of the human race and its change from generation to generation." [38]

His contemporary, Otto of Freising, combined the opposites: the Eusebian "Imperial theology" with the Augustinian Two Cities. Augustine, it should be emphasized, used even organological metaphors in order to separate radically the course of the *civitas dei peregrinans in terris* from that of the *civitas terrena;* the procursus of both is independent even if synchronic. [39] Otto of Freising accepts and deepens the Augustinian analysis of the origins and course of political power. The cycles of earthly politics, discernible in the four major *translationes imperii,* are promoted by the very *libido propagandae dominationis*— Augustine spoke of the *libido dominandi*—to which civil society owes its existence, expansion, but also decay. Only *terrore* could men be forced from their brutal primitive existence in solitude into societies; without it, no crafts or sciences would evolve. Will for power generated the *pax terrena* down to the formation of world monarchies (since the greed for power is insatiable). It also generates equal antagonism which will dissolve them from within; the apex of might is the beginning of its slow decline. Note the principle of heterogony of ends which already here characterizes the origin and immanent mechanism of the *civitas terrena.* These *corsi e ricorsi* of growth, maturity, and decay are as valid for the Carolingian and Salian Empire as they were true of the Persian and Roman. Note that organological metaphors are less important than the almost mechanical chain of causes which nevertheless serves a preordained goal; for the history of Israel (in the flesh and later in the spirit), the history of revelation and the history of the church are accommodated to these immanent laws of political realities. Christianity needed for its mission a world empire (Eusebius), and had to immerse itself in the dialectics of worldly power *(dominium),* which it had to acquire in ever greater measure since Constantine; each *translatio imperii* added to its might, and when it came to the summit of power (since the struggle over investitures) it entered also the path of its own decline. The accommodation of the Church to the World, albeit necessary, has its price yet to be paid.

These were some of the various uses of the idea of accommodation. At times joined with symbolic speculations and at times independent of them, it is discernible at least as an ideal type. A sense of both harmony and continuity prevails in this rational, "evolutionary" logic of periodization too. Augustine named it "temporal beauty" *(pulchritu-*

do temporalis), the beauty manifested in the "fitting together" of changing features to their proper ages. In the life of the individual as in that of the world, each single age has its own beauty *(habet. . .decorum suum. . .singula quaeque aetas).* [40] Every age in the history of salvation had the sacraments and institutions which befitted it, which were accommodated to its needs, until the beauty of the whole unravels like a great song *(velut magnum carmen).* [41] The "fitting together," the correspondence of events and institutions of sacred and profane history, the history of Israel and that of the *gentes,* had been already the *thema probandum* of Eusebius. If we look at all for a forerunner to the concept of immanent-historical "contexts," here occasionally it is to be found, elaborated in particular in the Maimonidean "reconstruction" of the alien and by necessity forgotten "Sabean" culture. [42] Such examples are relatively rare in medieval literature; and without being always able to point at direct influences, we are reminded of similarly scattered examples of Graeco-Roman historiography—the "Archeology" of Thucydides; [43] the demand to interpret Homer with Homer only; [44] theories relating laws and politics to changing temporal, regional, or climatic conditions; [45] and, of course, the numerous accounts of the slow shift from the state of nature to society and civilization. The latter, much as some versions of the medieval idea of accommodation, can be read as a footnote to Xenophanes' fragment: "Not from the beginning did the gods reveal man everything, but rather with time men find out the better." [46]

And what is more important, the relative autonomy of human history is implied or expressed wherever history is considered in the light of the principle of accommodation. It assumes that God, so to speak *de potestate eius ordinata,* does not always operate directly in history, but at times through the mediation of "laws of nature." The term "indirect guidance" is to be found in Maimonides; he also speaks of the "Cunning of God" *(talattuf 'alallah)* which consists in using (rather than transgressing) the order of nature, including human nature, to implement his education program. [47] In some versions the "accommodation" consists in a "heterogony of ends." This is the case with the historical role ascribed by Augustine and again by Otto of Freising to the *libido dominandi,* to natural aggressivity as a means of establishing human society and the motor behind the growth (and decay) of the *civitas terrena.*

The modern, secularized career of this figure of thought is better known. In some of its versions, society emerges out of (enlightened) self-interests: "private vices" become "public virtues" [48] in spite of the individual (Mandeville, Spinoza); Vico called this balancing mechanism "providence," Smith "the invisible hand," Kant spoke of the "hidden plan of nature," [49] Hegel of the "List der Vernunft." Hegel expressed better than others this dialectic of "nature" and reason in history, [50] called later by Wundt the "heterogony of ends." "Das ist die List der Vernunft zu nennen, dass sie die Leidenschaften fur sich wirken lässt." Individuals make history; their motives have to become at one and the same time means and ends in themselves if history is to be "Fortschritt in Bewusstsein der Freiheit." For the subjective freedom of every agent in history is his "unlimited right" and must be as much honored as its opposite, the objective goal of mankind. Freedom and necessity appear to the subjective consciousness as contradictory: their congruence in the objective course of history is this very "cunning of reason." Man believes he serves only himself; but he serves in reality the necessary course of events. Hegel articulated it: the "cunning of reason," this modern version of the medieval principle of accommodation, is based on the assumption of man's absolute dependence on history—and the relative freedom of the individual in it.

The cunning of God—the cunning of reason: this contraposition defines, at last, where the difference between the medieval and the modern versions of "reason in history" (and the periodizations expressing it) is to be sought. Medieval evolutionary models defied the apocalyptical insistence on the utter passivity of man in history; and, in its more rational moments, the middle ages admitted the partial autonomy of man's evolution. They did not, as the modern successors of the principle of accommodation, use the term "providence" as a cover for the absolute autonomy of the process in which "man maketh himself." "Fortschritt im Bewusstsein der Freiheit" is true of a segment in the history of historical reasoning and is true of the *historia rerum gestarum,* not of history itself, not of the *res gestae;* Hegel mistook both to be essentially the same.

Because the middle ages lacked this emphasis on the total freedom of man in history, because it regarded, even in its more subtle examples of historical reasoning, the historical world as given much more than made—it could not achieve, even where it came most near to it, a definite and all-encompassing concept of historical contexts.

IV

We did, then, find some antecedents to the harmony, regular contin-

uity, and spontaneity which Vico, and a good part of historical reasoning after him, sought in history. In their modern career, none of
these themes remained unchallenged. In the name of the principle of
individuality, or at least the insufficiency of our knowledge to establish
historical laws,[51] the concept of regular or necessary sequences of
periods was attacked; historical periods were left by Ranke and Burckhardt in their uniqueness, each of them "immediate to God." We today
feel that even the nineteenth-century concept of periods was an undue
hypostatization, that not everything happening within a period necessarily "fits together." To argue that it does is to stress hermeneutical
circles beyond tolerance, or to handle an incomplete induction as a
complete one.[52]

Did the middle ages produce a similar critical trend against its concepts of necessary harmony and regularity? Such criticism, and a more
pragmatic concept of periods, is implied in some scholastic discussions
of the fourteenth century, in a time, however, when historical reflection
lost the central role it occupied in the twelfth century. We detect, in
these discussions, the contours of a third ideal type of periodization:
the positivistic-nominalistic reduction of the concept of "periods."

Ockham in particular abolished the Thomistic-Aristotelian concept
of a relative, or hypothetical, necessity—that category of necessity (or
impossibility) which was neither logical nor merely factual, but physical, the necessary mutual order *(ordo ad invicem)* of objects. Not that
Ockham intended to abolish the Aristotelian cosmology any more than
Thomas, or that Thomas endorsed any less than Ockham that "whatever God produces by means of secondary causes, God can produce and
conserve immediately and without their aid," a maxim inherited from
Tempier's list of condemnations.[53] The difference is rather that Thomas believed in the necessity of *some* order (even where it is re-
voked)—while, for Ockham, order is simply the world as it exists, with
or without an internal structure of reference of the individuals inhabit-
ing it. In other words: *potentia dei absoluta* meant, for Thomas and for
Ockham alike, everything which does not involve logical contradiction; the realm, that is, of logical possibilities.[54] *Potentia ordinata* in
the version of Thomas accounts not merely for the universe as it is, but
encompasses an infinite number of possible perfect worlds,[55] each of
them incommensurable with the other. For Thomas, *potentia ordinata*
is thus the realm of physical (as against mere logical) necessities or
possibilities. Not without a temporary loss for natural philosophy,
Ockham abolished this distinction between logical and physical ne-

15

cessities; laws, in nature or history, were for him but contingent factual generalizations, and the ordained power of God thus was for him only a temporal index of God's absolute power.

In both the organological and symbolical periodization, the necessity of events to occur when they occurred—on teleological, analogical, mechanical, or symbolic grounds—was the very nerve of the argument. But relations, the *terministae* would argue time and again, should never be hypostatized; there is no "absolute" place in nature—the same *Locus proprius* could, if God wanted it, exist in many worlds—and there is no absolute reference point in history; had God wanted it, the Savior of the world could have been *aut lapis, aut asinus.* "Laws," "orders" of any kind are but universal statements of fact; at each moment of time, God can add or subtract, destroy or create singular things without changing anything else in the world.

"Periods" thus are contingent constellations of things and conditions alterable at any point of time. Whether Ockham analyzes the history of private property *(dominium)* or the history of the Papacy,[56] he insists on a sharp distinction of periods without any attempt to describe a succession of periods, i.e. conditions, as evolving of necessity from each other. Man was permitted to acquire dominion after the Fall—to compensate for the loss of the natural dominion he had over things in Paradise; this is a mere statement of fact, not of necessities. The very freedom of man is not a necessity, but a statement of fact; but due to this fact, no definite political order, no "ideal" state can be called a necessity.

Our classification of medieval periodizations is not the medieval one; when classifying periodizations, the middle ages did so according to subject matters.[57] But *that* we were able, with (I hope) some sense, to discern patterns from the vantage point of the various modern practices and reflections shows at least this: that for all our richer and more subtle historical understanding, our constructs, like theirs, alternated more than classical historiography between the conscious emphasis of either constructive imagination, or reason, or again the positive, contingent facts. And yet, for all the instances in which the middle ages approached our search for contexts, it never reached the methodical consciousness of placing such a search in the first order of priorities; nor could it develop throughout immanent interpretations of historical relations, for it could not really overcome its view of history as governed by transcendent structures and of historical facts as given rather than made.

NOTES

1. The phrase is taken from Hildebertus Cenomanensis, *Sermo in Septuagesima,* Migne, PL CLXXVII, 1073; a similar phrase *ratio temporum* (not in the computistic sense), e.g. Beda, *Super acta apostolorum,* Migne, PL XCII, 953. The medieval terms for "periods" and "periodizations" were manifold: *aetates; aetatunculae; tempora; intervalla, spatia, discrimina, articuli temporum; divisio temporum; status;* cf. also below no. 56.

2. Giambattista Vico, *Scienza Nuova* (1744), Praef. p. 632 "Convenolamente a tali tre sorte di natura e governi, si parlavono tre specie de lingue. . .") I, 311 *(tra loro conformi)* I, 348; IV, 979 (mode of the time), *Opere* ed. I, Nicolini (Bari 1928), IV, 1, 27 112; IV, 2 88.

3. Franz Budde, *Historia Ecclesiastica* (3rd ed., Jena, 1726), Praef.; quoted by L. Diestel, *Geschichte des Alten Testament in der Christlichen Kirche* (Jena, 1869), p. 463.

4. "Dicta autern Graece historia *apo tou historein,* id est videre vel cognoscere. Apud veteres enim nemo conscribebat historiam, nisi is qui interfuisset, et ea quae conscribenda essent vidisset:" Isidor of Seville, *Etymologiorum sive originum libri XX,* I, 41, 1 (ed. Lindsay). On the medieval concept of historical facts, see A. Funkenstein, *Heilsplan und naturliche Entwicklung* (München, 1965), pp. 70–77.

5. On the origins of the new hermeneutics in legal theories cf. J. G. A. Popcock, *The Ancient Constitution and Feudal Law,* (Cambridge, 1957), esp. Ch. I; D. R. Kelley, *Foundations of Modern Historical Scholarship, Language, Law and History in the French Renaissance* (New York, 1970). Both lack reference to the important insights of W. Dilthey, *Weltanschauung und Analyse des Menschen seit Renaissance Reformation, Werke II* (Leipzig-Berlin, 1927), pp. 110ff., 113.

6. Spinoza, *Tractatus Theologico Politicus, Opera* ed. Vloten (Haag, 1882), Ch. VII. XVII. Spinoza's method consists in the question for an immanent criterion for the permissible limits of *allegoresis:* corporeal images of God should be allegorized, but not physical, for the primitive mind conceived God as having a soul, but not a body—a *contradictio in adjecto* in (Spinoza's) philosophical terms.

7. Vico, *Scienza Nuova,* I, 141 (p. 77): "Il senso commune e un guidizio senz' alcuna riflessione, communamente sentito da tutto un ordine, da tutto un populo, da tutta una nazione o da tutto il genere umano." This, in essence, is what K. Mannheim, *Ideologie und Utopie* (4th ed., Frankfurt/Main, 1965), pp. 60–64, called *der totale Ideologiebegriff,* based on the "collective experience" of groups (pp. 153–54). The difference between Vico's *sensus communis* and Bacon's *idola foris* lies, to speak Mannheim's language, exactly in that Bacon's idols have the function of uncovering (collective) errors, that they are not universal or *wertfrei,* that they belong to the *partikulärer Ideologiebegriff* (p. 58). He does not mention Vico in his historical survey; (Vico, however, mentions the idols-theory of Bacon as a forerunner of his own inquiries). Cf. also W. Stark, "Giambattista Vico's Sociology of Knowledge," *Giambattista Vico: An International Symposium,* ed. G. Tagliacozzo and H. V. White (Baltimore, 1969: cited hereafter GVIS), pp. 297—307 (without discussion of the "common sense"), It is interesting to note the similarities and differences between Vico's "common sense" and Ibn Khaldun's *Asabiyah (The Muqaddimah,* ed. F. Rosenthal [3 vol., Princeton, 1958] I, LXXVII, 261–265, and *passim*). Both concepts occupy approximately the same positional value in their systems, but the latter indicates rather an emotional configuration, the former an intellectual.

8. In different "guises," *Scienza Nuova* I, 148. On the lack of a sense for individuality in Vico, see F. Meinecke, *Die Entstehung des Historismus, Werke* III, ed. C. Hin-

17

richs (München, 1959), pp. 63–69. This sense of individuality consists not merely in insistence on singularity, but involved at least in the view of those who tried to find a systematic formula for "historicism" an *epistemic resignation.* The concept demands historical constructs to contain "einen starken unvertilgten Rest von Anschauung" which makes them "individuelle Totalitätsbegriffe:" E. Troeltsch, *Der Historismus und seine Probleme* (Tübingen, 1922), p. 36. Meinecke recognizes a few "forerunners;" cf. also his "Klassizismus, Romantizismus und historisches Denken im 18. Jh.," *Werke* IV, ed. E. Kessel, (München, 1959), p. 264; he acknowledges the role of Leibniz in the formation of the concept of indivuduality; but does not realize the impact of the Leibnizian language on the historical thinking in eighteenth-century Germany.

9. See P. Reill, "History and Hermeneutics in the Aufklärung: The Thought of Johann Christoph Gatterer," *Journal of Modern History,* 45 (1973) 24–51, esp. 46–51.

10. E.g. Johannes Clauberg, *Differentia inter Cartesianam et in scholis vulgo usitatam philosophiam, Opera omnia Philosophica* (Amsterdam, 1691), II, 1217–1235: "Vulgaris philosophia non tam accurate considerat rem ut in se et sua natura est, sed potius prout se habet in respectu aliorum." Cf. Descartes, *Regula ad directionem ingenii* (Adam-Tannery X), pp. 382–384.

11. The best recent discussions are those of Jakko K. Hintikka, "Leibniz on Plenitude, Relations, and the Reign of Law," *Leibniz: A Collection of Critical Essays,* ed. H. G. Frankfurt (New York, 1972), pp. 155–190; N. Rescher, "Logical Difficulties in Leibniz Metaphysics," *Essays in Philosophical Analysis* (Pittsburgh, 1969), pp. 159–170. It is interesting to note that a modern interpretation suggested to read Leibniz's "Laws of Nature" as having the status of "analogies" or symbols; G. Buchdahl, *Metaphysics and the Philosophy of Science* (Cambridge, Mass. 1969), pp. 394–405; as already L. Couturat, "Sur la Metaphysique de Leibniz," *Revue de Metaphysique et de Morale* 10 (1902). Cf. also below no. 11

12. What we call context, Leibniz called harmony and compossibility. That both each possible "world" and each monad expresses the (undefinable) context of singulars respectively attributes can be shown in the following way. The difficulty in the principle *predicatum inest subjecto* is, as has frequently been pointed out since B. Russell, *A Critical Exposition of the Philosophy of Leibniz* (London, 1900), that it does not allow for relational attributes. If a monad is incompatible with another, this must be because of incompatibility of one or more of their respective attributes. But this would make these attributes merely relative. Leibniz seems to say that, if A_1, A_2, A_3 are the attributes of a_1 (a monad), and B_1, B_2, B_3 the attributes of b_1, then $A_n \neq B_n$ (incompatibility) *not* because A_n is contradictory to B_n (for this would establish a relation), but because some law in a "world" W. The totality of the idea of a monad makes A_n (c) and B_n (c) incompatible, and not anything in A_n and B_n. If this law could be known definitely, then all monads $a_1 \ldots a_m$ of W_n would be determined in *one* aspect; but laws as our finite intellect knows them are not *ominimodo* determinating, nor can we have knowledge of *all* singulars. That some substances (and attributes within substances) are incompatible is a *postulate:* more than factual, and less than logical necessity this narrower sense of compatibility is comparable to the synthetical judgments *a priori,* and is grounded on the principle of sufficient reason. It determines the existing (against all possible) worlds with the greatest number of (compatible) singulars obeying the least number of principles. Leibniz speaks of "harmony" or of a "nécessité physique" ("architectonique") as differing from the law of contradiction ("architectonique") as differing from the law of contradiction ("nécessité logique"). E.g. *Philosophische Werke* (ed. Gerhard) VI, 50, 321, 612.

13. On the various aesthetic presumptions and influences of Leibniz cf. e.g., A.

Bäumler, *Das Irationalitätsproblem in der Asthetik und Logik des 18. Jahrhunderts bis zur Kritik der Urteilskraft* (Halle, 1923), pp. 38–60 and *passim.*

14. Vico prefers to paraphrase Spinoza: "L'ordine dell'idee deve procedere secondo l'ordine delle cose." Vico, *Scienza Nuova, Opere* 4, 1. 238 (. 96); Spinoza, *Ethica* II, prop. 7; *Opera,* ed. Gebhard (Heidelberg, 1925) II, 89: "ordo et connexio idearum idem est ac ordo et connexio rerum." Vico limits the validity of the assertion to the *cose umani.* Cf. F. Nicolini, *Commento storico alla seconds Scienza Nuova* (Rome, 1949) I, 94. On the rich history and transformations of the principle *verum et factum convertuntur,* see K. Lowith, "Vicos Grundsatz: verum et factum convertuntur," *Aufsätze und Vorträge 1930–1970* (Stuttgart, 1971), pp. 157–188.

15. This interpretative possibility has been pointed out by Y. Belaval, "Vico and Anti-Cartesianism," GVIS, 90–91. On Leibniz's *conatus* as mediating between "freedom" and "necessity," see J. W. N. Watkins, *Hobbes's System of Ideas* (London, 1965), pp. 125–132; but Hönigswald, *Hobbes und die Staatsphilosophie* (Munchen, 1922), noted already the affinity to Hobbes.

16. Giving new (if not contrary) meaning to traditional terms was a characteristic usage in the seventeenth century. Spinoza, e.g., transformed the particular and general providence of medieval theology into a naturalistic connotation of "auxilium dei internum et externum," *Tractatus Theologico-Politicus,* ed. Vloten (Haag, 1882) I, 407.

17. Such similarities are easy to detect and are not necessarily superficial. Vico's three periods are reminiscent of Varro's *tria discrimina temporum (Adelon, mythicon, historicon):* Censorinus, *De die natali* XXI, 1 ed. Hulfach (Leipzig, 1897), pp. 44–45. Cf. (with reference to Vico) ed. Spranger, "Die Kulturzyklentheorie und das Problem des Kulturverfalls," *SB der Preussischen Akademie der Wissenschaften, phil. -hist. Klasse* (19 6) XXXV, 14, p. 22, no. 5. This is not merely a historiographical survey; it corresponds to Varro's famous "three theologies" (the mythical, political and natural); W. Jaeger, *Die Theologie der frühen griechischen Denker* (Stuttgart, 1964), pp. 2–3, which stands in the succession of Greek cultural theories; but they remind us equally of the Christian triadic division of times *ante legem, sub lege, sub gratia.* In the case of Vico as in that of other humanists, it is hard to determine to which tradition he owes more; precisely because the blending of categories is not new.

18. A. Dempf, *Sacrum Imperium* (Munchen, 19 9), pp. 229–268 (Symbolimus); R. Seeburg, *Lehrbuch der Dogmengeschichte* (Berlin, 1930), II, 184 ("biblizistische Spekulation"). It seems to me more adequate to speak of this tradition as an ideal type, since it is often mixed with other patterns of thought.

19. Irenaeus, *Adversus Haereses,* IV, 62 ed. W. W. Harvey (Cambridge, 1857) II, 62; Cf. II, 33,2 and F. Loofs, *Theophilus von Antiochien "Adversus Marcionem" und die anderen Quellen bei Irenaus* (Leipzig, 1930), p. 357 (Justin Martyr as a source for the idea of recapitulation; E. Scharl, *Recapitulatio mundi* (Freiburg, 1941); and our *Heiesplan* (above N. 4), 20, 136–37, 61, 63.

20. Ambrosius, *De paradiso* 3, 19ff., CSEL XXXII (Opera I), 277; Philo, *Legis Allegoriae* I, 19ff. (63–87). For a Jewish historical projection of the four paradisical rivers, though applied to the pagan history rather than that of the chosen people, cf. *Genesis Rabba* 16, 7. *(atid ha'kadosh baruch hu le'hashkot kos tar'ela le'akum etc.)*

21. Radulfus Glaber, *Historiarum sui temporis libri quinque* I, 1–3, ed. M. Prou (Paris, 1896), pp. 4–5; cf. Funkenstein, *Heilsplan,* (above n. 4), 77–84.

22. In *De Genesi contra manichaeos* A, 23–24, Migne, PL XXXIV, 190. For other reference see A. Wachtel, *Beiträge zur Geschichtstheologie des Aurelius Augustinus* (Bonn, 1960), pp. 48–78 H. Scholz, *Glaube und Unglaube in der Weltgeschichte. Ein Kommentar zu Augustins De Civitate Dei* (Leipzig, 1911), p. 154; Dempf, *ibid.,* p. 119 and below no. 41.

23. Abraham bar Hija, *Sefer megilat hamegale,* ed. Poznanski (Berlin, 1924), pp. 14–47; Ramban, *Perush hatora* to Gen. 2:3; Jitzhak Abarbanel, *Perush hatora* (Warsaw, 1862), p. 14; cf. J. Guttmann in the introduction to the quoted ed. of bar Hija, p. xiii. It is not improbable that bar Hija took the analogy directly from *De civitate Dei* rather than *via* Isidor of Sevilla, as Guttmann suggested; bar Hija's subjectivisation of the concept of time (which, against M. Wachsman, "hamahshawa hafilosofit shel avraham bar hija hanasi" *sefer hajowel le H. A. Wolfson* (Jerusalem, 1965), pp. 143ff., is far from being "original") might well have also originated in similar Augustinian teachings; A. G. Ladner, *The Idea of Reform* (New York, 1967), pp. 203–222.

24. Gregory the Great, In *Exechielem* II, 4, Migne, PL LXXVI, 980; Bernard of Clairvaux, Migne, PL CLXXXII, 1040ff., Joachim of Fiore, *Concordia Novi ac Veteris Testamenti* (Venice, 1519), Praef., Abraham bar Hija, *Sefer megillat ha' megalle,* p. 3.

25. "Nam fide credimus, aptata esse secula verbo dei; fide credimus, trium legum tempora, scilicet naturae, scripturae et gratiae sibi succedere ordinatissime decurissee; fide credimus, mundum per finale iudicium terminandum esse; in primo potentiam, in secundo providentiam, in tertio summi principii advertentes. . . ." Bonaventura, *Itenerarium mentis ad Deum* I, 12, *Opuscula varia Theologica* V (Quaracchi, 1891), p. 298 b; Augustine, *Enchiridion* ed. Scheel (Tubingen, 1930), p. 73.

26. *Aethiopian Henoch* 81, 2; *Jubilees* 1, 29; C. D. Rossler, *Gesetz und Geschichte, Untersuchungen zu Judischen Apokalyptik und der Pharisaischen Orthodoxie* (Neukirchen, 1960), p. 55: "Programm gottlicher Handlungen." On the passivity of man in the apocalyptic tradition (even the chosen 'adat kodesh, the avant-garde of the new b rit, is but in the possession of a pesher but does not act), see P. Volz, *Die Eschatologie der judischen Gemeinde im neutestamentlichen Zeitalter* (Tubingen, 1934), pp. 6, 107, 136.

27. Irenaeus of Lyon, *Adversus Haereses,* IV, 63, III, ed. W. W. Harvey (2 vol., Cambridge, 1857), II, 297. Tertullian, *De virginibus velandis* I, 4, CCSL II, 1209. K. Prunm S. T. "Göttliche Planung   menschliche Entwicklung," *Scholastik* 13 (1938) pp. 206–224, 342–366, esp. 354–361; St. Otto, *Natura und Dispositio: Untersuchungen zum Naturbegriff und Denkform Tertullians* (München, 1960), pp. 56, 210.

28. Augustine, *De civitate Dei* X, 32, CCSL 47, 311; A. Wachtel, *Beitrage zur Geschichtstheologie des Aurelius Augustinus* (Bonn, 1960), pp. 24, 48, 133. The quotation below, no. 38, answers the same question. Cf. IV Ezra 5, 4ff., ed. B. Violet, *Die Esraapokalypse* (Leipzig, 1910) I, 76; II, 79.

29. Eusebius, *Historia Ecclesiastica,* I, 2, ed. Schwartz (5th ed., Berlin, 1952), pp. 7–8; F. E. Cranz, "Kingdom and Polity in Eusebius of Caesarea" *Harvard Theological Review* 45 (1952), 51. With some modification, the following remarks are based on our *Heilsplan,* pp. 17–67.

30. E. Peterson: "Der Monotheismus als politisches Problem," *Theologische Traktate* (München, 1951), p. 88; H. Berkoff, *Die Theologie des Eusebius von Caesarea* (Amsterdam, 1939), *passim.*

31. *Vajikra rabba* 22.6 ed. Margulies (Jerusalem, 1956), III, 517; Theodoretus Cyrensis, *Questiones in Leviticum,* Migne PG LXXX, 30; Walafrid strabo, *De exordiis,* ed. A. Boretius and V. Krause, MGH *Capit.* II, 476; below no. 40 (Augustine).

32. Maimonides, *More nebuchim,* III, 26–54, esp. 32. Cf. below n. 41 and A. Funkenstein, "Gesetz und Geschichte: Zur historisierenden Hermeneutik bei Thomas von Aquin und Moses Maimonides," *Viator,* I (1970), pp. 147–178.

33. Petrus Alfunsi, *Dialogi* V, Migne, PL CLVII, 605 B; the concept of accommodation in reference to the *ratio preceptorum: ibid.,* 667 B. Cf. G. von Grunebaum, *Fischer Weltgeschichte* and our remarks in *Zion,* 33 (1968), 136.

34. Hugh of St. Victor, *De sacramentis Christianae fidei* II, 6, 4, Migne, PL CLXXVI,

450 A; on the question "An secundum mutationes temporum mutata sit fides" see *ibid.*, I. 10, 6, Migne, PL CLXXVI, 335. The history of this question since Anselm of Canterbury is dealt with by J. Beumer, S.J., "Der theoretische Beitrag der Frühscholastik zum Problem des Dogmenfortschritts," *Zeitschrift fur Katholische Theologie*, 74 (1942), pp. 205–226. On the thirteenth century, cf., e.g., E. Gossmann, *Metaphysik und Heitsgeschichte: Eine theologische Untersuchung der Summa Halensis* (München, 1964), pp. 251–256.

35. Walahfrid Strabo, *De exordiis et incrementis quarundam in observationitus ecclesiasticis rerum,* ed. A. Boretius and V. Krause, MGH *Capit.* II, 473–476, 481, 507; cf. A. Borst, *Der Turmbau von Babel. Geschichte der Meinungen uber Ursprung und Vielfalt der Sprachen und Völker* 6 vols. (Stuttgart, 1957–1963), II, pp. 513 514 and our Heilsplan (above n. 4), pp. 60–64.

36. Anselm of Havelberg, *Dialogi,* I, 5, Migne, PL CLXXXVIII, 1147; Gregor of Nazianz, *Oratio* 5.25. On this similarity, see J. de Ghellinck, *Le mouvement theologique du XIIᵉ siecle,* 2nd ed. (Bruxelles-Paris, 1948), p. 376, n. 8, with further literature. No attention was paid to this dependence in most of the vast literature on Anselm.

37. Joachim of Fiore, *Enchiridion in Apocalypsim,* ed. J. C. Huck, *Joachim von Floris und die joachimitische Literatur (Freiburg, 1938), p. 290; Du Cange s.v. Aetatunculae.* On the history of the exegesis of the Apocalypse and Anselm's place in it, see W. Kamlah, Apokalypse und Geschichtstheologie (Berlin, 1935), esp. pp. 66–70.

38. "Facta est haec varietas non propter invariabilis Dei. . .mutabilitatem, sed propter humani generis variabilem infirmitatem et temporalem mutationem de generatione in generationem." *Dialogi,* I, 13, Migne, PL CLXXXVIII, 1160 A–B. Kamlah, *Apokalypse,* p. 69; W. Berges, "Anselm von Havelberg und der Geistesgeschichte des 12ten Jahrhundert," *Jb. für die Geschichte Mittel- und Ostdeutschlands* 5 (1956), 52 compares it to Hegel's *List der Vernunft.* (Tertullian, we remember, spoke of the *mediocritas humana,* and Walahfrid Strabo of the *fragilitas carnalium*).

39. Cf. our *Heilsplan* (above n. 4), pp. 93–113.

40. The detailed elaboration of the analogy *aetates mundi-aetates hominis (infantia, pueritia*—development of the senses—ten generations; *adulescentia, iuventus, gravitas*—development of *actio* and *cognitio*—fourteen generations or years each; which is the sum of [five senses + two faculties] × [two sexes]. The last age has no definite limit) goes back, I believe, to the Stoic distinction between *logos endiathetos* and *logos prophorikos* and the numerical values attached to each age of enfoldment by the Stoa: Cf. M. Pohlenz, *Die Stoa* 2 vols. (Gottingen, 1959), I, 39; II, 21.

41. Ep. 138, I, 5th ed. Goldbacher, CSEL 44, 130: "aptum fuit primis temporibus sacrificium, quod praeceperat deus, nunc vero non ita est, aliud enim praecepit, quod huic tempori aptum esset, qui multo magis quam homo novit, quid cuique tempori accommodate adhibeatur, quid quanto impertiat, addat, detrahat, augeat minuative immutabilis mutabilium sicut creator ita moderator, donec universi saeculi pulchritudo, cuius particulae sunt, quae suis quibusque temporibus apta sunt, velut magnum carmen. . .excurrat;" cf. also L. Spitzer, *Classical and Christian Ideas of World Harmony, Prolegomena to an Interpretation of the Word "Stimmung"* (Baltimore, 1963), pp. 28–33.

42. Cf. above n. 31. Maimodides, we tried to prove, did more than to indicate that parts of the law were a measure against heathenism and "accommodated" to the mentality of the nascent Israel. Had this been his only scope, then he could hardly be said to have surpassed the previous exegetical hints of the Christian and Jewish doctrines of accommodation; and then all we could see in his detailed account of the Sabean Society would be an example of a-historical analogies. So indeed did H. Graetz, *Die Konstruktion der jüdischen Geschichte* (1846, repr. Berlin, 1936), 86

(note). But Maimonides did more inasmuch as he recognized the necessity to alienate biblical legal institutions from their present meaning and to reconstruct in detail, if they are to be understood, their original (and, due to the pedagogical success of these very laws, forgotten) context.

43. K. von Fritz, *Die Griechische Geschichtschreibung,* I (Berlin, 1967), pp. 575–617 (and nn. 263–280).

44. This postulate, often attributed to Aristarch of Samothrace, was actually formulated as a program by Porphyry. R. Pfeiffer, *Geschichte der Klassischen Philologie von den Anfängen bis zum Ende des Hellenismus,* trans. M. Arnold (Hamburg, 1970), pp. 276–278. Of the intensive philological work of antiquity, the middle ages inherited but the general rhetorical methodological device of the *accessus ad auctorea*—which later became a part of the explication of both canon and Roman law. Cf. H. Wolters, "Geschichttliche Bildung im Rahmen der Artes liberales," in *Artes Liberales. Studien und Texte zur Geistesgeschichte des Mittelalters* hg. J. Koch 5th ed. (Leiden-Koln, 1959).

45. With the reception of Aristotle, such theories became topical in medieval political thought. Cf., e.g., Marsilius of Padua, *Defensor Pacis* p.Ic.9, 210: "Hoc tamen non ignorare debemus, quod alia et altera multitudo, in alia vel diversa regione ac tempore dispositia et ad alteram et diversam policiam, aliumque aut alterum terre principatum, ut dicit Aristoteles 3° Politice, c. 9°.

46. Fragm. B. 18; Diels-Kranz, *Fragmente der Vorsokratisker* (6th ed., Berlin, 1934). The middle ages, at times, inverted the *topos;* Revelation was given in the beginning, to save man from cumbersome and at times misleading searches; see Sa'adia Ga'on, *Kitab al-amanat,* ed. Landauer (Leiden, 1880), Praef.

47. *More Nebuchim* III, 32. The similarity to Hegel's "List der Vernunft" has been noted by S. Pines, *Maimonides, the Guide of the Perplexed* (Chicago, 1963), LXXI–LXXII, n. 32.

48. On Mandeville and Vico, see M. Goretti, "Vico et l'heterogenese des fins (Vico et Mandeville)," *Les Etudes Philosophiques* 3/4 (1968), 351–359. On the importance of this principle in modern social thought, see W. Euchner, *Egoismus und Gemeinwohl. Studien zur Geschichte der burgerlichen Philosophie* (Frankfurt/Main, 1973), pp. 74–76, 104–115, and *passim.*

49. I. Kant, *Ideen zu einer allgemeinen Geschichte, Werke* ed. Weischedel (Frankfurt, 1964), pp. 37, 45, cf. J. Yovel, "The summum bonum and History in Kant" (Hebr.), *Iyyun* 16 (1965), 11–49.

50. Hegel, *Philosophie der Geschichte,* ed. F, Brunstadt (Reclam, 1961), pp. 61, 65, 69, 78. On Wundt and Weber, cf. W. Stark, "Max Weber and the heterogeny of purposes," *Social Research* 34, 2 (1967), 249–264. We argued that if Hegel's sense of "meaning in history" is to be traced backwards, it is to be found in the idea of accommodation with its teleological vocabulary rather than in other antique or medieval traditions. In his important book, K. Lowith, *Meaning in History* (Chicago, 1949) neglected to distinguish traditions and their "Sitz im Leben," and this induced some erroneous comparisons.

51. Ranke's concept of the absolute individuality of periods was traced by C. Hinrichs, *Ranke und die Geschichtstheologie der Goethëzeit* (Gottingen, 1954). Burckhardt was more pragmatic; against Lassaux (against whom the "Weltgeschichtliche Betrachtungen" are directed to a great part) he argued that "the historical sciences are "as yet" excluded from the discovery of meaningful "laws" *(Lebensgesetze): Weltgeschichtliche Betrachtungen,* ed. R. Marx (Stuttgart, 1955), p. 216.

52. This is, e.g., the point in the distinction made by G. Leff, *History and Historical Method* (New York, 1970), p. 79 between "periods" and "types."

53. Phil. Boehner, *Ockham: Philosophical Writings* (Edinburgh, 1957); cf. E. Hochstatter, *Studien zur Metaphysik und Erkenntnislehre Wilhelms von Ockham* (Berlin-

Leipzig, 1927), pp. 12–26, esp. 17f. As to Thomas, cf. *De potentia* 9, 3a. 7, ed. Marietti, *Questiones Disputatae* (Turin-Rome, 1927), I, 62: "Deus perfecte operatur ut causa prima; requiritur tamen operatio naturae ut causae secundae. Posset tamen deus effectum naturae sine natura facere; vult tamen facere mediante natura, ut serveretur ordo in rebus." The same concordance may be found, of course, in the definition of the only limit of God's omnipotence being the law of contradiction. As to the concept of relative necessity, see Thomas, *ibid.,* 9. la. 3, ed. Marietti 7–11, esp. 9; *Summa Theologica,* la. 25. 3.

54. The term *possibile logicum* was coined by Duns Scotus, though the concept was clearly present earlier. It is not identical with Aristotle's "absolute possibility," though the Middle Ages assumed this identity as a matter of course. Cf. I. Pape, *Tradition und Transformation der Modalität* I: *Möglichkeit-Unmöglichkeit* (Hamburg, 1966), pp. 35–60 and the literature mentioned there.

55. *Summa Theologica* Ia. 25. 3; cf. *De Potentia* 9. 3. 17. There he asserts the necessity of some—always perfect, always revocable—order in any of the worlds which God could create. The passage in *De Potentia* is also interesting because of its reference to Maimonides' refutation of the Kalam's arguments for utter contingency. The role of Maimonides in the medieval discussions on omnipotence and contingency has not yet received proper examination.

56. J. Miethke, *Ockhams Weg zur Sozialphilosophie* (Berlin, 1970), pp. 467–477 gives important examples for Ockham's treatment of periods. I do not agree with his interpretation of the difference between Thomas, Scotus, and Ockham as to the actual consequences of thinking in terms of the absolute sovereignty of God; both take into account changes in the *ordo rerum;* Ockham's method of annihilation serves also only negative purposes (showing what a "thing" is *not*); the difference lies merely in that Thomas insists on the necessity of *some* "ordo ad invicem" of things.

57. E.g. Hugo of St. Victor, *De Scripturis et scriptoribus sanctis* 17, Migne, PL CLXXV, 4 divides the *porrectio temporum* in *duo status, qui ad esse hominis pertinent* (the old and the new man) *tria tempora* (before and under the law, grace), "sex aetates . . .secundum communes innovationes rerum"—important event, and *quatuor successiones* (four ruling classes: patriarchs, judges, kings, priests).

Clio and the Lawyers

FORMS OF HISTORICAL CONSCIOUSNESS IN MEDIEVAL JURISPRUDENCE

Donald R. Kelley

DISCUSSING the question of historical consciousness in medieval law may seem at first to be like writing the famous work on the snakes, or the owls, in Iceland. The judgment of such authorities as Fritz Schultz on Roman legal science, Paul Koschaker on medieval civilians, and Stephan Kuttner on the canonists is that none existed.[1] Even scholars willing to concede a "sense of history" to the middle ages usually talk about Otto of Freising or Joachim of Flora or, at most, Chaucer.[2] Yet such an opinion surely needs modification unless we are satisfied to accept the narrowest and most self-congratulatory view of "history," denying it to all ages but our own, and unless we insist upon interpreting texts in the most superficial and rationalistic fashion, confounding the professed ideals of medieval scholars with their perceptions of reality. To medieval jurists in particular, as to idealists in all ages, history usually seemed more of a burden than a legacy; but it by no means follows that history did not penetrate their consciousness. On the contrary it may be suggested that they had at least as profound an understanding of the processes of history—know thy enemy!—as historians. The question remaining is just how medieval jurists perceived and tried to account for these processes.

Humanist hyperbole to the contrary notwithstanding, it is not only in the Renaissance that law and history have been conjoined: from the beginning the courses run by these disciplines were not only congruent but often contiguous. This circumstance was due above all to their situation in the western scheme of learning derived from antiquity. Both in particular were allied to— and from the standpoint of classical pedagogy practically equated with—rhetoric; so that in terms of training and public function the orator became the model both for the lawyer and for the historian. In the middle ages, with the decline of the

25

oratorical ideal (among other things), their relationship became still closer, both of them, in effect, drawn down into the *trivium* and subsumed under rhetoric, or the *ars dictaminis*.[3] Irnerius himself, the twelfth-century restorer of Roman legal science, was in fact a *magister artium*, and only his disciples, the so-called "four doctors," received professional status. Even then close ties were preserved, and as Odofredus declared, "The orator may properly be called an advocate."[4] Much the same was true for historians after receiving a measure of "professorial" standing in the sixteenth-century, and they continued to identify their function with the "office of the orator" *(munus oratoris)*. In a sense, then, the sixteenth-century "conjunction of law and history" which produced the movement modern historians call "legal humanism" was little more than an attempt to recall each to its "trivial" origins, and so it was characterized by its professional opponents.

Such academic consanguinity was reinforced by deeper and sometimes crasser coincidences. On the one hand both law and history represent the racial or public memory of a people and so express their ideals, values, and views of human nature and society; on the other hand both reflect national fears, prejudices, and myths, and so are bound up with national ideology, whether popular or official. Frequently, therefore, historians and jurists have shared not only sources and methods but also issues and political goals. Belonging to overlapping professions, they have waged similar and sometimes mutual ideological battles; committed to common causes, they were not infrequently rewarded—or punished—by the same masters. It cannot be concluded from this that lawyers and historians have always shared the same code of values, much less trusted each other completely; but they have belonged to the same world of discourse (set off by convention from the alien field of natural philosophy) and often have shared the same perspective. This was especially true in the Middle Ages—moreso in a sense than in the sixteenth century, when the war of the *mores italicus* and *gallicus* created a rift between lawyers and historians of law. If it is legitimate to speak in any sense of the "birth of history" in the twelfth century, surely the medieval jurists should not be left out of account.

Jus Civile

In the longest perspective, the medieval phase of the western legal tradition may be said to span a dozen centuries, beginning with the collections made by the Emperor Justinian in the sixth century and continuing well into what on most grounds we think of as "modern times," including the work of such philosophers as Bodin, Grotius, and even Vico, which cannot be fully appreciated apart from the structure and methods of medieval jurisprudence. In the west, however, direct knowledge of the Corpus Juris hardly existed before the "Renaissance of the twelfth century," which began to fulfill the hopes expressed by one enthusiast for the empire, that "with the ancient laws the whole world will be restored." [11] What happened, in more prosaic terms, was that the study of law was taken from its concealment in the liberal arts to the level of a science, sanctioned by the formation of its own university faculty and professional organization.

Out of this came the European "legist tradition" (as canonists referred to it), [12] beginning with the Glossators, dominant from the late eleventh to the late thirteenth century, and carried on by the Commentators, or Post-Glossators, through the sixteenth century and beyond. The distinction was established by the sixteenth century and fixed by humanist critics, who called the two schools Accursiani and Bartolisti, or Bartolo-Baldisti, respectively; [13] but it should be added that the jurists themselves were aware of a pattern of change in their ranks, and like their theological and philosophical rivals they distinguished between "ancients" and "modern"—even "ancients, more recent, and moderns" *(antiqui, noviores, modernique)* [8]—as well as between old and new law. By the thirteenth century the originally Romano-Byzantine canon had expanded in several ways, not only spilling over into ecclesiastical law but also sweeping into its own course certain later north Italian jurisprudence and imperial legislation incorporated into the so-called *Consuetudines Feudorum,* which came to be recognized as the "tenth collation" of "Roman" law. Such were the "authorities" which were technically above suspicion of error and which gave shape, sustenance, and direction to the *legista traditio* for many generations.

It would be a mistake to suppose that this tradition was monolithic in any ideological sense, of course, for there was a wide range of bitter conflicts—canonists versus civilians, Gallicans versus Italians, Germanists versus Romanists, feudists versus advocates of written law, and eventually Protestants versus Catholics. The Italian or "citramontane" jurists lamented "these ultramontane jackasses [*isti asini ultramontani*] who are never happy except when criticizing the Gloss" of Accursius, while the "ultramontanes," especially the French, condemned the servility of their rivals toward the papacy. [9] Indeed, medieval juristic method was founded on the theory and practice of dialectical conflict, and no books aside from the Bible have produced so much controversy over such an extended period. On the most controversial issues there were often not even particular resolutions, not to speak of a *communis opinio;* and well into the eighteenth century scholars were still listing their accumulated pros and cons. Nevertheless, about the manner of formulating issues and about the perception of the underlying social reality there was little disagreement. All medieval jurists, identifying directly with the *antecessores,* or *professores legum,* of Justinian's law schools, shared the same terminology, logic, formulas, apparatus, and to some degree methods. Despite varying allegiances, in short, they spoke the same language, saw the world through the same spectacles, and shared many of what Justice Holmes called "inarticulate major premises."

This consistency of outlook is particularly apparent in the field of history, and the reason for this again attaches to the juridical canon of Justinian. Many of the legists' views about the past were variations on themes found in Byzantine law, especially in the great anthology of classical jurisprudence, the Digest, and in Justinian's prefatory legislation. Here were to be found not only sophisticated conceptions of political and moral philosophy but also a deep consciousness of history—"almost fourteen hundred years" of it. In general, classical Rome had a most subtle appreciation for the workings of legal history. Despite popular notions about founding fathers, Cicero was well aware that the Roman legal tradition was the result not of a single law-giver but of many generations. [10] And despite emphasis upon the rationality of civil law, scholars were aware also of the corrupting force of time— "tempus edax rerum" is the Vergilian phrase. "For long lapse of time has rendered old works and customs obsolete," wrote Aulus Gellius, "and it is in the light of those words that the sense of the laws is to be understood." [11]

Though not publicized, such attitudes inform all the work of Justinian and his editors. The Digest itself was a great act of filial piety toward the first Rome, and the Emperor insisted upon his "reverence for antiquity" *(antquitatis reverentia).* [12] He honored the old jurists (*veteris juris conditores* he called them at one point) [13] by setting down their names in the Digest. Certain laws he included simply because they were "approved by the long usage of this revered city," and even denied that the reasons for some laws were any longer visible. He also emphasized how important it was for beginning law students—"new Justinians" he was pleased to call them—to study the "monuments of ancient learning" *(antiquae eruditionis monumenta)*.[14] In recognition of this his editor, Tribonian, placed among the very first titles of the Digest a selection from Pomponius' textbook "On the Origin of Laws" *(De Origine juris)*, which celebrated the great line of jurists from Appius Claudius down to classical times.[15]

But if Justinian could speak in glowing terms of an idealized past, he had no intention of letting its reality get in his way. "For how can antiquity interfere with our authority?" he asked rhetorically. Much as he honored the old jurists, he was careful to stipulate that their decisions (the *responsa prudentum*) no longer had the force of law, and he strictly forbade further "interpretations," permitting only "paratitles," or summaries. Nor did he hesitate to omit, modify, or even reverse what he called the "old learning" or "old laws." In particular he declared his intention of eliminating "superfluities," inequities (such as the law of escheat, derived from the "evil days" of Rome), contradictions (the famous *antinomiae* which it was improper to discuss before the Renaissance), and anachronisms (that is, laws which have fallen *in disuetudinem*).[16] Such were the guidelines for transforming the legacy of Rome into the "new law" *(jus novum)* of Byzantium.

To judge only from the Emperor's rhetoric, his goal was entirely meta-historical. He wanted his law to "prevail for all time," and his transcendent aims were inflated further by imprecations to the Holy Trinity and to his own divine office.[17] Yet behind this heaven-storming project there is apparent a very substantial awareness of the destructiveness of time, the mutability of laws, and the untrustworthiness of posterity. Internal conflicts had rendered Rome unstable for almost fourteen centuries, and the old laws were "oppressed with age." He also realized that "only divine things are perfect," that human nature was incorrigibly weak, and that only a superhuman effort could stem what he called "the vain discord of posterity." The conclusion which Justinian drew from these considerations pointed in quite the opposite direction from his will as legislator. "It is characteristic of human jurisprudence to be always indefinitely extending," he admitted, "and there is nothing in it which can endure forever, for nature is constantly hastening to bring forth new forms."[18] This statement not only illustrates Justinian's considerable "sense of history" but also embodies one of the fundamental arguments for the modern idea of progress, that is, the creativity of nature and the "plenitude of forms." And it makes articulate one of those concealed major premises of legal thought that eventually opened the way to the historical investigation of laws and institutions.

In the event, of course, Justinian's reluctant admissions proved more prophetic than his imperial program: history would not stop for him; later interpreters would not be still. It is true that the Glossators tried to avoid admitting change since Justinian's age, or rather they hoped, like Arnold of Brescia, to revive intact "the good customs and ancient laws" of Rome.[19] They seldom questioned the text of the law, therefore, and never its authority. Justinian had called his collection a "monument," but as Accursius insisted, the word really meant document (from *moneo* not *memoria*).[20] Thus the changes they did effect were largely inadvertent, due to misunderstanding or strict logical necessity. But inadvertence is a powerful force in the history of thought, especially when combined with the enthusiasm and (sometimes) cultural shock which Roman law, like Aristotelian philosophy, tended to generate.

In the Corpus Juris Civilis, furthermore, medieval jurists could not help but recognize the remnants of almost the entire life-cycle of a civilization. "It is called old," observed Azo, "because it contains the confused legislation of almost 1400 years from the founding of Rome at the time of Romulus down to the time of Justinian."[21] In their introductory "materia" they offered information of historical interest, but of course their most direct contact with history was in the *De Origine juris,* all the more because so much of it was so obviously obsolete. So Odofredus and others discussed at some length the five sources (or "species") of law, and yet they realized that four (the *plebiscita,* the *senatusconsulta,* the *responsa prudentum,* and the *lex pretoria*) were of purely antiquarian value.[22] It should be noted that it was this title which provided the point of departure for the modern field of legal history, of which, consequently, the Glossators may be regarded as the earliest pioneers—playing the role of Marco Polo if not Columbus. Among their intellectual descendents were Aymar du Rivail, who compiled the first history of civil and canon law, such historians of feudal law as Marina Freccia and Charles Dumoulin, and Thomas Diplovataccius, author of a biographical dictionary of the legist tradition—none of whom, it may be remarked, owed significant debts to humanism.[23]

But there were more significant manifestations of historical awareness. On the one hand, for example, despite the Christian facade provided by Justinian, the authors of the laws in the Digest were in fact pagans, as Accursius reminded his readers. On the other hand, while in theory admitting no fundamental changes between the time of the Caesars and that of the Hohenstaufen, the Glossators in fact recognized the "barbarous" Lombard accretions that had been given imperial sanction in the eleventh and twelfth centuries. Most interesting of all is the little known fact that Accursius (like his future humanist critics, though they took all the credit) was capable of detecting, on historical grounds, not only contradictions and interpolations but, more generally, an earlier stage of law *(media jurisprudentia)* not quite covered over by Justinian's attempt to bring everything up to date (*hodie per Justiniano* is one formula).[24] Much of the supposed credulity of the Accursians, it may be suggested, arose not so much from ignorance, as humanists charged, but rather from professional scruples.

In some ways the Commentators were more doctrinaire in their clinging to the assumption of consistency in the texts of civil law. Yet again—though again partly through inadvertence—they possessed a broad awareness of historical change even if they did not find much occasion to display it. To some extent this was a result of their dialectical method, which made them face up to difficult problems, to some extent the result of their exaggerated respect for academic authority, which underlay their compulsive tendency to accumulate *opiniones,* itself in effect a historiographical habit.[25] It was the appreciation and criticism of such a legacy of interpretation that led fourteenth-century jurists to compose bibliographical and historiographical essays not unlike modern discussions of the *états des question.* In effect the history of the legist tradition itself begins with such bibliographical notes, including the gloss of Johannes Andrea on Durandus' *Speculum* and (though not extant) Baldus' *Commemoration of the Most Famous Jurists,* which Savigny took as the antecedents of his own work.[26]

What is more striking is that by the fifteenth century the outlawed "interpretation" of legal texts had been transformed by the Commentators from a surreptitious practice into an elaborate theory; and in fact the *defensio interpretationis* sheltered not only a rubric of discussion but a legal genre. "Interpretation is a necessary part of law," declared Pietro Andrea Gammaro, going on to explain that this arose from the law of nations and especially "because laws vary."[27] This conscious mechanism of change was attached to the conventional legal topic "on the meaning of terms" *(de verborum significatione)* and was justified by reference to a number of juridical conventions, including the concept of equity, the force of custom, the conflict of laws, and the so-called "corrective laws" *(leges correctoriae)*. Nevertheless it represented another departure from Justinian's ideal. On this basis professional jurists could claim not merely a mechanical but a "creative function," as a recent historian has remarked—not merely a traditional but also an historical role.[28] It was partly because of such presumptions, it may be added, that humanist critics rejected the adaptive methods of professional lawyers in favor of the static ideals of classicism and Byzantine jurisprudence.

A more conspicuous, though less fortunate, example of the Commentators' encounter with history was their attempts to grapple with the problem of "origins." Two cases in point are the fable about the miraculous recovery of the famous Florentine manuscript of the Digest in the siege of Malfi in 1135 and the assignment of the founding of the University of Bologna to the time of Charlemagne, neither universally accepted.[29] Still more amusing examples appear in the vastly inventive etymologies devised by jurists in their best Isidorean style. But in fact such *obiter dicta* need not be taken too seriously. Some derivations were merely logical (as *jus* from *justitia* instead of the reverse); some honorific (*jus* from Justinian); and others, as Hermann Kantorowicz has remarked, were at least half-facetious.[30] But then etymologies were only incidentally historical; more often than not their purpose was legal or philosophical—to get at the *quidditas* of a term, as Seyssel put it.[31] And as for the problem of ultimate "origins," it is still located largely in the realm of myth, or mystery.

The truth is that the jurists' justification for history was mostly practical. No doubt "antiquities must be studied," in the words of Odofredus, "so that none of the ancient past should be ignored"; but the reason was that history furnished a valuable repository of examples, precedents, and explanatory models to strengthen legal argumentation.[32] For Baldus, investigating origins meant looking for "causes" of a matter—that is, the four Aristotelian causes.[33] These attitudes naturally reinforced the "scientific" rather than the "historical" character of medieval jurisprudence, emphasizing its general, rational, and explanatory basis. "Scire est per causas cognoscere. . ." is the dictum of Chasseneux. "Legista et canonista cognoscunt per causas." [34] But eventually history, too, would come to profess such an analytic concern with human behavior, especially in the political, pragmatic, and neo-Polybian writings of Machiavelli, Bodin, and other Renaissance interpreters of constitutional history.

But if jurisprudence was a "science" in the opinion of many of its practitioners, it had not for that reason lost touch with the humanities and so, in the most rudimentary sense, with history; for like grammar, as John of Salisbury pointed out, law was occupied not only with nature but also with the wills of men.[35] Though divine in origin, the study of law yet turned, in Socratic fashion, to the "human conditon itself"; and because of its public concerns *(utilitas hominum)* it was superior to other professional fields, especially (as argued in endless *quaestiones*) to medicine.[36] Although universal, jurisprudence yet encompassed the particularity of human experience. "Our science," as Baldus put it, "concerns accidents and human deeds, which are as diverse as the minds and wills of men." [37] This emphasis upon the civic and activist ideals of Roman law at the expense of the naturalistic bias of scholastic philosophy, analogous to the attitude of Leonardo Bruni toward political philosophy, also made contributions (though largely unnoticed) to the general phenomenon of "civic humanism." Like Bruni, Bartolus, Baldus, Lucas de Penna, and other classical-minded jurists were drawn toward an even greater appreciation for history, which after all was the chief souce of information about the deeds of men.[38]

It was in the area not of philosophical jurisprudence, not of natural or divine law but in a general sense of human law—*jus positivum* was the term in use from the twelfth century[39]—that medieval jurists most directly confronted problems of legal and institutional history. In a sense the ground had been prepared by discussions of the principle of equity and its function in moderating the rigors of law,[40] and by a growing willingness to question the text of civil law and even to admit the presence of "antinomies"—for as Azo remarked, "to forget nothing and never to err belongs rather to divinity than to humanity" [41]—and by the general principle, stated by Placentinus, that "Man is the author of law, God of justice." [42] But the primary lòci of thinking about history were three time-honored doctrines that had always accommodated the idea of change in laws over time. One was simply the legislative principle that "Posterior laws regularly correct prior ones." [43] Another was the doctrine of disuetude—"Leges per disuetudine possunt tolli" is the formula[44]—which Justinian had made an axiom of his legislation. The third was the concept of prescription (especially the *praescriptio longi temporis,* dating from the second century), which jurists elaborated under a varied terminology: *longa, vetera, antiqua consuetude, vetusta, inveterata mos,* and *usus longevum* are some of the terms listed by Odofredus.[45]

33

57477

FERNALD LIBRARY
COLBY-SAWYER COLLEGE
NEW LONDON, N. H. 03257

The consequences of these doctrines, or processes, were generally irreversible, and jurists were as often as not content simply to note that "today the law has been changed" *(hodie jus mutatum est)*.[46] This insidious though largely unconscious device of *hodie* was applied frequently in the Digest (not only by Tribonian and his assistants but also by classical jurists and so left by the Byzantine editors),[47] and it was very liberally resorted to by the Glossators as well as the Commentators (and also, more self-consciously, by the humanists). Examples from public law were numerous. Formerly, according to the famous *lex regia*, power rested with the people; *hodie* no longer, declared Placentinus, Cino, and others.[48] Formerly, the Roman senators; *hodie*, wrote Baldus, no longer.[49] Formerly, the Emperor had unconditional authority, argued Alberico de Rosate, but *hodie* he had his authority from the church.[50] Formerly, too, usury was accepted; *hodie*, according to Bartolus, not.[51]

Underlying these ad hoc notions of legal change was an attitude that could not help but subvert the uniform and universalist ideals of Roman law which even humanists took over intact: this was a sort of historical and geographical relativism demanding that human institutions should be interpreted in terms of conditions and environment as well as ideal and precept. "Whoever speaks the Latin language. . .is bound by Roman law" was a medieval formula that humanists like Valla could endorse with enthusiasm;[52] but it hardly struck a chord among most Europeans, even educated Europeans, who never saw a toga or a forum or perhaps even a Roman ruin. *Hodie,* things were different. "Human laws," remarked Lucas de Penna, "vary according to the disposition of the land and differences in time [*secundum dispositionum terrarum et varietates temporum*]. . ., and so from the diversity of times flow the diversity of things."[53]

Reflected in this change were the very mechanics and morphology of history, and from the standpoint of medieval law none has better represented the process than that most philosophical of jurists, Baldus. It was a process at once backward- and forward-looking, accommodating both continuity and change. On the one hand, as Ernst Kantorowicz has pointed out, the principle of the "continuity of forms" constituted a link with the past and, for Baldus, a way of preserving the sempiternal ideals of jurisprudence.[54] On the other hand Baldus provided for future change through the idea already expressed by Justinian and, in a somewhat different form, described by Arthur Lovejoy— that is, the "plenitude of forms." "New cases demand new remedies,"

Baldus once observed; and his general conclusion may be taken as one of the first premises of historical consciousness: "Nature and the acts of men always produce new forms" *(natura et actus hominum semper novas producunt formas).* [55]

Consuetudo

The ultimate, and yet in historical terms most immediate, source of these "new forms" is to be found in the realm of custom; and it is here that we enter that penumbral area where law and history overlap—where patterns of social behavior are transformed into enforceable public norms. Whatever the utility of Walter Ullmann's "ascending thesis" for political theory, it does seem to apply to medieval views of the historical process; [56] for before the great lawmaker established laws *de proprio motu,* the people had expressed themselves in their own inarticulate fashion. As Isidore of Seville declared, "Human nature is governed by two rules, namely, natural law and custom." [57] Or according to the often-cited dictum of Irnerius, "Law [*jus*] is threefold, arising from legislation [*lex*], custom [*mos*], and natural necessity [*necessitas naturae*]." [58] It is this quasi-private, sub-political, almost subconscious area of custom (*consuetudo, mos, usus,* or even *stylus*) that has nurtured historical consciousness most successfully.

In Roman law custom is described as *jus non scriptum,* but medieval lawyers also included in it barbarian laws that had been written down and even in a sense codified. "Today," as Bartolus wrote, "feudal law is nothing but custom set down in writing." [59] The justification for accepting custom as law was the alleged "tacit consent of the people," [60] and it had at least two aspects, one geographical and one temporal. The first rested ultimately upon the designation of the *jus gentium* as a recognized form of law (and indeed canonists included civil law itself in this category); the second upon the realization that all legal traditions were born out of unwritten usage, passing from a *de facto* to a *de jure* level. "Law arises out of fact" *(lex ex facto oritur)* is the formula established by later jurists, beginning with Wilhelmus de Cuneo. [61] The relationship between law and custom was endlessly complex, and Bartolus in particular offers an elaborate discussion about "when custom makes law, when it corroborates law, when it imitates law, when it repeals law, and when it is repealed by law." [62] In any case the transforming force of custom was ever present, acting, as jurists admitted, as "the founder, interpreter, and repealer of laws." *Consuetu-*

do est legum condatrix, interpretatrix, et abrogatrix: this opinion of Azo provided not only one of the heaviest counterweights to the authority of civil law but also a fundamental explanation for the process of legal and social change. [63]

Some such assumption was present from the beginning. According to one of the earliest civilian texts in the West, the *Petri Exceptiones* of the late eleventh century, "Usages approved for a long time" were granted as much authority as written law; and the Glossators, though not always the canonists, tended to agree. [64] In his *Book for Poor Scholars,* Vacarius justified customary law by remarking that "things are dissolved by the same process by which they have been created." [65] Given the "fragility of human nature," as Accursius wrote, how could "human justice" be unchanging? [66] Still worse, customs themselves were not always in accord with justice; and it became a commonplace that "evil customs are not to be followed". *(malae consuetudines servandae non sunt).* [67] The function of these flexible and sometimes ambiguous notions was to give judges a freer hand in the interpretation of civil law, but indirectly they served also, by providing a rationale for legal diversity and mutability, to open up legal perspective to problems of what we would call social and cultural history.

Customary law was a matter of some territorial pride as well as privilege for many jurists, who were prone to celebrate the excellence of local unwritten usages by seeing to it that they were given written currency. It was Bracton's proud claim that only England was ruled by customary law; [68] but in truth custom was widely accepted throughout Europe and often, as in the *pays du droit coutumier* in northern France, was dominant. According to the greatest of the early French *feudistae,* Philippe de Beaumanoir, custom had the force of law if it fulfilled two conditions, that it was general and that it had been accepted beyond living memory, and in that case it was to be preferred to written law. [69] The essential ingredient, however, was what would later be called the principle of territoriality—*Consuetudo regionis aut loci servanda est,* in the formula of Azo—which assumes that custom is the expression of and so should be administered to a particular locale or its immediate environs. [70] The idea that "Place determines behavior" *(locus regit actum)* was another premise that was to be shared by lawyers and historians.

The principal text in the discussion of customary law was the *Consuetudines Feudorum* appended to the Corpus Juris of Justinian. Although commonly regarded as authoritative, it was nevertheless often described in terms offensive to the point of scatology—"not writ but shit" *(nec lex sed faex)* would not be an unfair rendering.[71] Yet barbarous as this Italo-Lombard law seemed to classical-minded jurists like Lucas de Penna (not to speak of humanists like Petrarch), it did display conspicuous signs of—and provoked extensive research into—historical change. The redactor Girardus Niger, according to J.G.A. Pocock, "displayed a historical sense not too common at the beginning of the twelfth century"; and his introduction provided, as Ralph Giesey has pointed out, "a convenient synopsis of the historical evolution of feudal succession up to the time of its compilation (about 1125)."[72] An evolutionary pattern may be seen, too, in the glosses and commentaries which accumulated from the thirteenth century onwards, including what amounted to critical historiographical discussions by Baldus, Jacobus Alvarottus, and others from the fourteenth to the sixteenth century.[73]

Most interesting among the rubrics of the *Consuetudines Feudorum* was the one, established on the analogy of the Digest title *De Origine juris,* concerning the "origin of feudal law" *(De Origine juris feudorum).* The formal *quaestio* was that of the "authenticity" of feudal law; and the commentators divided themselves into two schools of thought. One was what I have called the Romanist position, the *communis opinio,* which linked the fief with such civil law precedents as the *precaria* or the *emphyteuma*—the argument being either that feudal law was literally *jus antiquissimum* as the text had it, or else that, in the words of Durandus, it was an "imitation" of antiquity, similar to the Romans' own imitation of the Greeks as reported by Pomponius.[74] The other was the Germanist position, which insisted that feudal vocabulary was made up of "new names" *(nova nomina),* and hence feudal institutions were post-Roman as well as non-Roman.[75] As usual it was the "ultramontane," and especially the French, jurists who followed this anti-imperialist line, and again their achievement represents a story by itself. What finally emerged from this (in a sense still continuing) debate was not only a sharper awareness of national self-consciousness but also one of the most remarkable examples of the common ground between history and jurisprudence.

Jus Canonicum

A common heritage, overlapping careers, mutual concerns, and the fact that many jurists took their degrees *utriusque* make it impossible to discuss civil law without some attention to its ecclesiastical counterpart. Canon law, too, was productive of "new forms" and significant for historical thought. Like civilians, canonists had an appreciation for antiquity, looking back with Gregory VII, for example, to an idealized *ecclesia primitiva* and likewise believing that "the ancient canons must be served." [76] They, too, distinguished between "old law" and "new law," that is, between Gratian's Decretum (c. 1140) and the papal Decretals added over the next two centuries, and were taught to interpret laws literally *(grammaticaliter et ad litteram).* [77] More important, it was the canonists who developed the rules and techniques for determining the authenticity—or exposing the forgery—of particular documents. These devices, established especially by the papal chancery of the twelfth century, were incorporated into canon law under the rubric "De Fide instrumentum," which prescribed ways of assessing a text in terms of style and script as well as seal and general condition. [78] The whole question of the *discrimen veri et falsi,* which again has civilian precedents going back at least to the third century *Lex Cornelia de falsis,* makes a very large story by itself. [79] Suffice it to say that long before the time of Lorenzo Valla the practice of historical and philological criticism had been advanced by canonists. Indeed it is possible that such precedents were known by Valla himself, since canon law was the principal source (as well as principal target) of his famous "Declamation against the Donation of Constantine."

For the most part, however, the focus of canonists was not on restoration but on continuity—not on *antiquitas* but on *traditio.* As Walter Ullmann has pointed out, "the idea of historical continuity was fully made use of in papal disputations;" [80] and this practice became widespread in the legal profession. Canonists and civilians alike shared assumptions about what may be called the morphology of legal tradition. The key to this was again the doctrine of the "continuity of forms," and the emphasis, naturally enough, was on the positive side of legal tradition—not on decline through human weakness but on preservation of nature through right (or at least legal fiction), not on unstable temporality but on idealized, often mystical endurance (represented in particular by the term *aevum,* which, as Fritz Kern pointed out, was sometimes etymologically associated with *ê,* an old Germanic word for law). [81] "When the form does not change," as Baldus argued, on behalf of the immortality of the Roman *populus,* "the thing itself is said not to change." [82] On this basis jurists were able to demonstrate, or at least to save the appearances of, continuity—of asserting various kinds of political or institutional immortality, unchangeable succession, corporate permanence, immutable sovereignty, the "mystical" yet vital body of the commonwealth,[83] and other fictions amenable to *Geistesgeschichte*. That such abstractions have been so largely the preserve of German legal historians, especially since Gierke, should not blind us to their importance in the historical consciousness of an earlier age.

The locus classicus—or should we say locus barbaricus?—of canonist thought about the general structure of human history is the famous theme of "translation of empire." [84] Despite an interesting pre-history from Carolingian times, this idea does not emerge into the full heat of controversy until its appearance in an early gloss (that of "Paucapala") on Gratian and more especially in the decretals, through Innocent III's bull Venerabilem. Thence, through such commentaries as that of Johannes Teutonicus, it made its way into historiography. This theory—tracing the course of empire westward from the Medes and Persians through the Greeks to the Romans and, by agency of the papacy, the Germans—became even more grandiose in the hands of historians, who linked world cultural leadership with world monarchy and affected to find an accompanying "translation of learning" *(translatio studii* or *sapientiae)*, including, of course, jurisprudence.[85] Associated with this formula was the legend of Charlemagne's founding of the University of Paris—"Studium de Roma Parisiis transtulit," wrote a twelfth-century grammarian, and the idea persisted until the seventeenth century. Yet beneath this apparent universalism lurked a most parochial view of history, and the idea of translation was not without its critics, especially among the "ultramontane" commentators of northern Europe. Next to the Donation of Constantine, in fact, there was no more controversial thesis in medieval historiography and law.

Perhaps the most amusing thing about this canonist idea is that the weapons ultimately turned against it were themselves canonist in origin. The issue arose from the first law, "Cunctos populos," in the Code, which designated the emperor "lord of the whole world" *(dominus totius mundi)*, and around it the "vain discord of posterity" was almost deafening. The *communis opinio*, expressed for example by Cino da Pistoia (and Petrarch), was that he held authority de jure, not de facto;[86] but many voices were raised against this view, especially those of such French jurists as Jacques de Revigny and Jason del Maino.[87] Their position was that the emperor's authority extended only to his subjects *(non ligant nisi subditos imperatoris)* and that, consequently, the law was misleading *(et sic male dicit cunctos etc.)*. The clinching argument was always the canonist proposition, again originating with Innocent III, that "the King of the French recognized no superior in temporals"—so, according to the still more notorious formula, was "emperor in his kingdom." [88] And other ultramontane jurists, especially the Spanish and English, followed suit.

But this incipient nationalism had a historical as well as a legal basis, stemming from a refusal to apply the distinction between law and fact in this case. Jason del Maino, for example, pointed out that there were numerous peoples, the Persians and Vandals as well as the French, who had never been subject to the empire; [89] and Cosmo Guymier, glossing the Pragmatic Sanction of Bourges, offered the testimony of the "old chroniclers" in support of the same conclusion. [90] By the fifteenth century, in general, the validity of historical evidence was often recognized, especially in the Gallican branch of the canonist tradition, which was particularly intent upon reestablishing privileges lost and "ancient liberties" usurped, as they saw it, by modern Romanist deviations from the "primitive church." [91] Because of this problem of "usurpation," indeed, Gallicanism was from at least the time of "the lawyers of the last Capetians" a fertile field for the cultivation of historical argumentation; and this attitude was confirmed by the practices of the Parlement of Paris in particular, which like the monarchy itself began to build a tradition out of its own precedents, thus helping to create, though inadvertently again, an interpretation of history. The pluralism implicit in such anti-universalist and anti-authoritarian opinions was another premise shared by lawyers and historians, and they owed it in no small part to canon law.

Despite the weight of tradition, the lure of sempiternal fictions, and the stasis of juridical ideals, reality could not be imprisoned. *Eppur si muove*—the human world at least, and in this case the canonists were prepared to agree. Forms may be undying, as Baldus thought, but he also added, "Nihil perpetuum sub sole." [92] Underlying the *translatio imperii*, too, was something a bit more profound than the notion of a providential succession of Four World Monarchies, or hypostasized Ages. There was also a sense—a tragic sense—of the essential mutability of human societies. The invariably cited text was from the *Liber ecclesiastici:* "God transfers kingdoms from one people to another because of injustice, injuries, blasphemies, and other evils." [93] Nature may have established the basis of political and legal order, but human nature guaranteed that disorder would finally return. In terms of the structure of history this resulted in the rise and fall of individual societies; on the level of the texture of history it involved what a recent

historian of canon law has called "a theory of the relativity and mutability of laws, or *leges*." [94] This theory was reinforced by the controversies within the canonist tradition and by the sense of the national
diversity of European society, which no universal system could
overcome or conceal.

In their attempts to bring some order out of this disorder, to find
some pattern in this mutability, canonists were led, or perhaps driven,
to a fundamental sort of relativism. "One must take into consideration," wrote one eleventh-century churchman, "geography, the nature
of the time [*qualitas temporum*], the weakness of men, and other unavoidable realities which normally change rules; for by power many
things are changed for the common good of the churches. . . .Sometimes contradictory canons are issued in one council and prohibited in
another. Yet this should not frustrate those who, in terms of our temporal life, want virtue to overcome vice, and truth falsehood." [95] On the
level of policy-making such casuistry lent support to ideas of "equity,"
which offered protection against the severity of laws, or of "reason of
state," which demanded attention to circumstances as well as to principles. [96] On the level of perception, however, it confirmed a historical
view of law-making and of social order, and it further justified the
canonist assumption that laws had to be interpreted in terms of the
places, times, and persons *(locus, tempus, persona)*. [97]

Again it was the "ultramontane asses," and especially the Gallicans,
who developed most fully these views, turning them as usual against
the universalism of the church, extending them into heterodoxy and,
eventually, into historiography. "So it is not necessary for all the faithful to live in a common republic," declared John of Paris. "They may
live in different climes, regions, and conditions, according to different
ways of living and under different governments." [98] With John of Paris,
of course, we approach the arena of propaganda, where rather more
contrasting and colorful views of history tend to prevail. Yet such
protestations of national independence by publicists—which must be
counted not only among the most significant manifestations of historical consciousness but also among the most effective incentives for
further historical research—were the product most directly of the controversies defined and promoted by medieval jurists.

Jus Gentium

From the later middle ages the historical and comparative investigation of laws and institutions was carried out in a broader context than the "two laws" of professional jurisprudence, yet still in association with the traditions of Roman law. This context was that of the *jus gentium*, which according to Baldus was "applied by all nations." [99] From at least his time, of course, this "law of nations" was not merely that recognized by Justinian but the sum of the legal traditions of all nations, past, present, and to come; and this ever-expanding territory was explored by historians and philosophers as well as jurists. The focus in general was not upon the abstract or normative "source," but upon the positive and individual development of individual nations, which according to one formula of the Commentators were "established by the law of nations." It was their opinion, too, that the *jus gentium* was chronologically posterior to the *jus naturale,* and so necessarily it had to be approached historically, or at least empirically.

In the framework of the *jus gentium* certain general patterns of development were beginning to be perceived by medieval jurists. The starting point was not a bountiful Providence but prehistorical anarchy, not Eden but what amounts to a "state of nature." The basis of this was no doubt the Christian assumption that the social order was a pagan creation of dubious respectability—that the Roman Empire in particular "was built on violence not justice" and that its legitimation was a matter of providential yet *de facto* approval or subsequent rationalization. Combined with this assumption, however, was a kind of evolutionary theory of social history. [100] Formerly men lived in forests, remarked Alberico de Rosate, and only later did they build houses, live in cities, and create laws. The mechanism of this evolution likewise had a human and nonprovidential aspect. "Notice that the two pronouns 'mine' and 'thine'," remarked Lucas de Penna, "procede not from justice but from the iniquity of mortals. . ., that is, from custom." [101] Whence arose—whether through the *jus gentium* or not was debated— slavery, wars, and other evils as well as such useful devices as contracts and other civil institutions. But thereafter the story of human society was one literally of "civilization"—and that largely through the good offices of the grand tradition of professional jurisprudence.

This pattern became much clearer in the works of such modern products of the legist tradition as Jean Bodin, who took a more deliberate interest in history. Like the earlier jurists, Bodin dispensed with the notion of a "golden age" and posited instead a primitive time which, ridden with barbarism and unparalleled crime, was a veritable *bellum omnium contra omnes.* [102] The subsequent pattern, common to both law and history, was one of gradual improvement, in general terms, from oral tradition to increasingly coherent and cultivated written forms. Just as history changed from myth and annals to chronicles to more rational and explanatory narrative to the level of intellectualized and ideologized historiography, so law developed from unwritten customs to more generalized written laws to the rationalized jurisprudence of professional lawyers and judges and finally, perhaps, to a systematized "code." The progression from fact to law, implicit in medieval jurisprudence, becomes explicit in the work of certain early modern social philosophers. Of course, the change could also be interpreted as degeneration, a falling away from virtue and *boni mores,* and indeed was so interpreted by such malcontents as François Hotman; [103] but more often it was looked upon as a manifestation of civilization and enlightenment. At least one form of the modern idea of progress, it may be suggested, was a byproduct of the legist tradition.

In a number of ways the harvest time of the investigation of the *jus gentium*—"universal law" is roughly equivalent—and indeed of medieval jurisprudence in general came in the sixteenth century; and no one represents this fruition better than Jean Bodin, whose work establishes as well the most conspicuous link between the medieval art of law and the modern science of society. Bodin had full command of the methods, apparatus, and aims of professional jurisprudence and in fact, as his most acute commentator remarked, was the inheritor less of Machiavelli than of Bartolus and Beaumanoir. [104] The chief difference was that Bodin shifted emphasis from commentary on standard "authorities" to analysis of historical "sources" (though they were often the same works)—that is, from interpreting texts to interpreting history itself. In line with the assumption of earlier French legists, Bodin rejected Roman claims upon any universal tradition, not only in his famous refutation of the old theory of Four World Monarchies but even more fundamentally by denying the relevance as well as the authority of civil law. "The better part of law," he believed, "is to be found in history;" and so he launched into an empirical and comparative study of the institutions of all nations to which he had access. [105] To this enterprise he brought many of the attitudes displayed by his professional forebears, especially a fascination with "origins," a sense of temporal and geographic relativity, and an appreciation of the mutability of human institutions.

This late and transmuted phase of jurisprudence inspired by Bodin was continued by other scholars and philosophers in succeeding generations and led ultimately to the work of *philosophes* like Montesquieu and Vico, who also wanted, as Montesquieu put it, "to illuminate history through laws and laws through history." [106] The clearest connection can be seen in Vico, whose great treatise of universal law may be regarded not only as a juristic prefiguring of his "new science" but also as a kind of philosophical summing up of the legist tradition. Like Bodin and Montesquieu, Vico discussed various conventional legal topics (such as the origin of feudal law), adapted conventional methods of interpretation (such as etymology), and took as his field of operations the entire world of the *gentes*. His major point of departure (as well as his major goal) was the problem of "origins," and so he focussed upon that "image of antiquity," the Twelve Tables, which in fact inspired his basic insights about the original character of primitive society (law emerging from custom and founded upon violence), the universality of the feudal pattern ("Roman law emerged from feudal law, not feudal from Roman"), and in general about what he termed "poetic wisdom." [107] Indeed there are few aspects of Vico's historical philosophy that did not stem from, or have direct analogies with juridical conventions; and this includes his famous *corso-ricorso* thesis, the *verum ipsum factum* principle, and his ultimate aim of uncovering the most fundamental rules of human behavior (the *jus naturale gentium,* as he called it). [108] Obviously this opens up another world of inquiry altogether, but it does serve to suggest the longer perspective of the present discussion.

In conclusion, it may be said that the task of Vico and Montesquieu was to reconstruct what medieval jurists took on faith, which was the reason underlying law, the *logos* behind the letter. At first, impressed by the structure of Justinian's law (as well as his rhetoric), jurists had looked upon Roman law as itself "written reason" (*ratio scripta*); but increasingly they began to act as if this "reason" were an ideal apart from, or rather behind, the written law and that the authority rested actually in the ideal *(ratio legis est ipsa lex).* In jurisprudence, as in Biblical scholarship, the letter killed but the spirit gave life, and so jurists sought the reason, or intent, of the literal text (*ratio, sententia, voluntas,* or *mens legis* was the formula). [109] By the sixteenth century this rationale (rather than the Emperor) was itself sovereign. So scholars began to look more deliberately beyond the horizons of Roman law to other societies, past and present, and to other methods of interpretation, especially to historical and comparative techniques. The target was still the *mens legum*, but increasingly in the sense not of the meaning of particular laws but rather of the structure of human law in general. Thus a procedure of legal exegesis was, in association with historical investigation, transformed into a philosophical concept, especially by Vico (who adapts the term directly) and by Montesquieu (if one can supply the translation). It is appropriate to conclude by suggesting that, at least from one perspective, one of the major consequences of the legist tradition was the formulation of "the spirit of the laws."

NOTES

1. Schulz, *Principles of Roman Law,* trans. M. Wolff (Oxford, 1936) 98, Koschaker, *Europa und das römische Recht* (Munich, 1953) 88, and Kuttner, *Harmony from Dissonance* (Latrobe, Pa., 1960) 35.
2. Heer, *The Intellectual History of Europe,* trans. J. Steinberg (New York, 1966) 80; cf. Morton Bloomfield, "Chaucer's Sense of History," *Essays and Explorations* (Cambridge, Mass., 1960) 15. An almost unique discussion of the "Senso della Storia" in medieval law is Riccardo Orestano, *Introduzione allo studio del diritto romano* (Turin, 1963) 114, 136. See also the fascinating, if rather doctrinaire, application of structuralist theory to medieval law by Pietro Costa, *Iurisdictio, Semantico del potere publico nella pubblicistica medievale (1100–1433)* (Milan, 1969).
3. On rhetoric and law see Hastings Rashdall, *The Universities of Europe in the Middle Ages,* ed. F. M. Powicke and A. B. Emden (Oxford, 1936) I, 109; on rhetoric and history M. Schulz, *Die Lehre von der historische Methode. . .* (Berlin, 1909). There is a section "de origine juris" in Boncampagni's *Rhetorica novissima* (1226), according to Rockinger, in *Sitzungsberichte der königl. bayerischen Akademie der Wissenschaften zu München,* I (1861) 136.
4. Odofredus, *Lectura super Digesto veteri* (Lyon, 1550; repr. Bologna, 1967) f. 10ᵛ (D. I, 1, 2): "Orator proprie dicitur advocatus." Cf. Cassiodorus, *An Introduction to Divine and Human Readings,* trans. L. W. Jones (New York, 1946) 148: "The art of rhetoric. . .is expertness in discourse on civil questions."
5. Cited by Percy Ernst Schramm, *Kaiser, Rom und Renovatio* (Berlin, 1929) 286.
6. Ruffinus, *Summa Decretorum,* cited by R. W. and A. J. Carlyle, *A History of Political Theory in the West* (London, 1903–1936) II, 103.
7. The classic attack on the "Accursiani" is Guillaume Budé, *Annotationes in . . .Pandectas* (Paris, 1508), and on Bartolus, Lorenzo Valla, "In Bartoli de insignis et armis libellum," *Opera onmia* (Basel, 1546; repr. Turin, 1962) I, 633; *bartolobaldizein* is a coinage of Theodore Beza, *Correspondance,* ed. H. Aubert et al (Geneva, 1960–) I, 35. Odofredus is one who distinguished between "vetustiores" and "moderni." The standard periodization appears in Etienne Pasquier, *Les Recherches de la France* (Paris, 1621) Bk. IX, ch. 34, "les glossateurs," "les docteurs en droict" or "Bartholistes" or "scribentes," and "les docteurs humanistes." In general see my "Rise of Legal History in the Renaissance," *History and Theory,* IX (1970) 174–94.
8. By the Bartolist Claude de Seyssel, *Speculum feudorum* (Basel, 1566) 3. The designation "antiqui" is used from the eleventh century, according to Paul Vinogradoff, *Roman Law in Medieval Europe* (Oxford, 1929) 39.
9. Baldus, cited by Biagio Brugi in *L'Opera di Baldo,* per cura dell'Università di

Perugia nel V centenario della morte del grande giureconsulto (Perugia, 1901) 78. Cf. Chasseneux, *Catalogus gloriae mundi* (Paris, 1529) V, 28, and Walter Ullmann, *Medieval Papalism* (London, 1949) 45.

10. *De Republica,* II, 1, 2.
11. *Noctes Atticae,* XX, 1.
12. Justinian's constitution *Tanta.* Cf. Durandus, *Speculum* (Lyon, 1547) f. 2^r: "Antiquitas est reverenda." In general see Fritz Schulz, *History of Roman Legal Science* (Oxford, 1953).
13. *Code,* I, 14, 12, 3.
14. *Deo auctore.*
15. *Digest,* I, 2, 2.
16. *Deo auctore.* See Schulz, *Principles of Roman Law,* 14. A fundamental study is still François Baudouin, *Justinianus, sive de jure novo* (Paris, 1556).
17. Constitution *Omnem.*
18. *Tanta*: "Sed quia divinae quidem res perfectissimae sunt, humano vero juris condicio semper in infinitum decurrit est nihil in ea, quod stare perpetuo possit (multas enim formas edere natura novas deproperat), non desperamus quaedam postea emergi negotia, quae adhuc legum laqueis non sunt innodata."
19. Otto of Freising, *The Deeds of Frederick Barbarossa,* trans. C. C. Mierow (New York, 1953) 61.
20. Accursius, *Ad Digestum, in tit.*
21. Azo, *Summa* (Venice, 1566; repr. Turin, 1966) col. 29. See Hermann Fitting, *Summa Codicis des Irnerius* (Berlin, 1894) 3; also Hermann Kantorowicz, *Studies in the Glossators of the Roman Law* (Cambridge, Eng., 1938) 37, and Edwin A. Quain, "The Medieval Accessus ad Auctores," *Traditio,* III (1945) 228 ff.
22. Odofredus, *Super Digesto,* f. 8^r.
23. Aymar du Rivail, *Historia juris civilis,* followed by *Historia juris pontificalis* (Mainz, 1530); cf E. von Moeller, *Aymar du Rivail, der erste Rechtshistoriker* (Berlin, 1907). Thomas Diplovataccius, *De claris juris consultis,* ed. H. Kantorowicz and F. Schulz (Berlin, 1919).
24. Carlo Alberto Maschi, "Accursio precursore del metodo storico-critico nel studio del 'corpus iuris civilis,' " *Atti del Convegno internazionali di studi accursiani,* ed. Guido Rossi (Milan, 1968), II, 610.
25. See M. P. Gilmore, *Humanists and Jurists* (Cambridge, 1963) 158–59.
26. Karl von Savigny, *Geschichte des römischen Rechts im Mittelalter* (Heidelberg, 1834–51; 2nd ed.) III, Anhang II, "Aelteste Beyträge zur juristischen Literärgeschichte" contains the texts; and see Enrico Besta, "Baldo e la storia letteraria di diritto," in *Opera di Baldo,* 81–111.
27. Gammaro, *De Extensionibus,* in *Tractatus universi juris* (Venice, 1584) XVIII, 248.
28. Vincenzo Piano Mortari, *Ricerche sulla teoria dell'interpretazione del diritto nel secolo XVI* (Milan, 1956) 54.
29. Hermann Kantorowicz, "A Medieval Grammarian on the Sources of the Law," *Tijdschrift voor Rechtsgeschiedenis,* XV (1937) 46, and Savigny, III, 97.
30. Kantorowicz, *Studies in the Glossators,* 57.
31. Seyssel, *op. cit.,* 11.
32. Odofredus, *Super Digesto,* f. 12^r.
33. Baldus, *Super Digesto,* f. 4^r.
34. Chasseneux, *Catalogus,* X, 9.
35. John of Salisbury, *Metalogicon,* trans. D. McGarry (Berkeley, 1962) 73.
36. Cited in *Opera di Baldo,* p. 435. Some of the more formal entries in the controversy have been discussed by Lynn Thorndike, *Science and Thought in the Fifteenth Century* (New York, 1929) 24–58, and Eugenio Garin, *La Disputa delle arti nel Quattrocento* (Florence, 1947).

37. *Opera di Baldo, loc. cit.*
38. The point has been made by Peter Riesenberg, "Civism and Roman Law in Fourteenth-Century Italian Society," *Explorations in Economic History*, VII (1969–70) 252; the neglect of the jurists by historians of the Italian Renaissance is practically universal. Baldus' relation to the new idea of *civilità* was discussed by Iulio Tarducci, "Il Temp di Baldo e lo spirito della sua scuola," *Opera di Baldo*, 409–66.
39. Gabriel Lebras (ed.), *L'Histoire du droit et des institutions de l'eglise en occident*, VII (Paris, 1955) 388.
40. See Norbert Horn, *Aequitas in der Lehren des Baldus* (Cologne, 1968).
41. Azo, *Summa*, col. 29. Cf. Odofredus, *Super Digesto*, f. 3ʳ: "Jus civile an sit purgatum contrariis."
42. Placentinus, *Summa Institutionum*, cited by Orestano, *op. cit.* 131.
43. Alberico de Rosate, *Super Digesto*, f. 28ᵛ.
44. Odofredus, *Lectura super Codicem* (Lyon, 1552) f. 3ʳ.
45. Odofredus, *Super Digesto*, f. 15ʳ. In general see Noel Vilain, "Prescription et bonne foi du Décret de Gratien (1140) à Jean d'André (+ 1348), *Traditio*, XIV (1958) 129.
46. Odofredus, *Super Codicem, loc. cit.* Francesco Calasso, *I Glossatori e la teoria della sovranità* (Milan, 1951) 19.
47. Emilio Albertario, "Hodie," *Studi di diritto romano*, VI (Milan, 1953) 125–42.
48. Placentinus, *Summa Codicis* (Mainz, 1536; repr. Turin, 1962) 17; Cynus, *In Codicem. . .doctissima commentaria* (Frankfurt, 1578; repr. Turin, 1964) 17. Cf. Charles T. Davis, *Dante and the Idea of Rome* (Oxford, 1957) 17.
49. Baldus, *Super Digesto*, f. 2ʳ (prooemium).
50. Alberious de Rosato, *Super Codicem*, f. 7ʳ.
51. Cited by C. N. S. Woolf, *Bartolus of Sassoferrato* (Cambridge, Eng., 1913) 47.
52. *Summa Lipsiensis*, cited by S. Mochi Onory, *Fonti canonistiche dell'idea moderna dello stato* (Milan, 1951) 174; cf. Valla, *Elegantiae Latinae linguae*, I, praefatio, in *Opera*, I.
53. Cited by Walter Ullmann, *The Medieval Idea of Law* (London, 1946) 57.
54. Kantorowicz, *The King's Two Bodies* (Princeton, 1957) 295.
55. *Opera di Baldo*, 433.
56. *Principles of Government and Politics in the Middle Ages* (London, 1961) 19.
57. Cited by Carlyle, V, 46.
58. Cited by Carlyle, II, 53. In general see Francesco Calasso, *Medio evo del diritto*, I (Milan, 1954) 181 ff, and Horn, *Aequitas*, 82ff.
59. Bartolus, *In Primam Digesti veteris partem* (Venice, 1590) f. 17ʳ.
60. Ullmann, *Medieval Idea of Law*, 63. Cf. the discussion in Chasseneux, *Consuetudines Ducatus Burgundiae* (Frankfurt, 1574) prooemium.
61. It is commonly used in the sixteenth-century, as e. g., Ulrich Zasius, *Paratitla*, in *Operum omnium* (Lyon, 1550) I, col. 17 (on D. I, 2, 2); Francois Hotman, *Matago de Matagonibus* (s. l., 1575) 30; Thomas Smith, *De Republica Anglorum*, ed. L. Aston (Cambridge, Eng., 1906) 74. The locus is usually D. IX, 2, 52, 2; see E. Cortese, *La Norma giuridica* (Rome, 1962–64); and Charles Fried, "The *Lex Aquilia* as a Source of Law for Bartolus and Baldus," *American Journal for Legal History*, IV (1960) 142–72. Above all see the discussion of Luigi Prosdocimi, " 'Ius vetus' accursiano e 'Ius novum' postaccursiano," *Atti del Convegno internazionali di studi accursiani*, 950. There is much more to be said on this question. Special thanks to Domenico Maffei for suggestions on this matter.
62. Bartolus, *In Primam Digesti veteris partem*, f. 18ʳ.
63. Odofredus, *Super Digesto*, f. 16ʳ; cf. Azo, *Summa Codicis*, cited by Carlyle, II, 52.
64. Cited by Carlyle, *loc. cit.*
65. Cited by Vinogradoff, *Roman Law in Medieval Europe*, 57.

66. Accursius, *Ad Digestum*, I, 1, 1.
67. Baldus, cited by Horn, *Aequitas*, 85. In general see F. Olivier-Martin, *Histoire de la Coutume. . .de Paris* (Paris, 1922) I.
68. Bracton, *De Legibus et consuetudines Angliae*, ed. G. Woodbine and trans. S. Thorne (Cambridge, Mass., 1968) I, 1.
69. Carlyle, II, 42.
70. Azo, *Brocardia* (Venice, 1561) col. 123. See P. Meylan, "Les Statutes réels et personels dans la doctrine de Dumoulin," *Mélanges Paul Fournier* (Paris, 1929) 511–26, and Paul Ourliac, *Droit romain et practique méridionale au XVIe siècle, Etienne Bertrand* (Paris, 1937).
71. E. g., Lucas de Penna, cited by Ullmann, *Medieval Idea of Law*, 73.
72. Pocock, *The Ancient Constitution and the Feudal Law* (Cambridge, Eng., 1957) 74, and R. E. Giesey, *The Juristic Basis of Dynastic Right to the French*, Trans. American Philosophical Society, LI (5) (Philadelphia, 1961) 1.
73. The essential texts are in the study by Savigny's disciple, Ernst Adolph Laspeyres, *Ueber die Entstehung und älteste Bearbeitung des Libri Feudorum* (Berlin, 1830).
74. This is studied in detail in my "De Origine Feudorum: the Beginnings on an Historical Problem," *Speculum*, XXXIX (1964) 207–28.
75. Andrea de Isernia, *In Usu feudorum commentaria* (Naples, 1571) f. 6ʳ.
76. Odofredus, *Super Codicem*, f. 9ᵛ. In general see Glenn Olsen, "The Idea of the Ecclesia Primitiva in the Writings of the Twelfth-Century Canonists," *Traditio*, XXV (1969) 61–86; and Stanley Chodorow, *Christian Political Theory and Church Politics in the Mid-Twelfth-Century* (Berkeley, 1972).
77. *Sexti Decretalium*, II, t. 12, and *Extravag. Ioann. XXII*, t. 14, rubric "De Verborum significatione," in Emil Friedberg (ed.), *Corpus Iuris Canonici* (Graz, 1959) II. Cf. Lebras, *Institutions ecclesiastiques*, 105.
78. *Decr. Greg. IX*, II, t. 22; cf. V, t. 20 ("De Crimine falsi").
79. Peter Herde, "Römisches und kanonistisches Recht bei der Verfolgung des Fälschungsdelikts im Mittelalter," *Traditio*, XXI (1965) 291-362; also Horst Fuhrmann, "Die Fälschung im Mittelalter," *Historisches Zeitschrift*, CXCVII (1963) 529–601, and R. Lane Poole, *Lectures on the History of the Papal Chancery down to the Time of Innocent III* (Cambridge, Eng., 1915) 145.
80. Ullmann, *Medieval Papalism*, 9.
81. Cited by Kantorowicz, *King's Two Bodies*, 299.
82. Texts cited by Goez, *Translatio Imperii*, 11 ff. See n. 84.
83. Among recent studies see R. E. Giesey, "The French Estates and the Corpus Mysticum Regni," *Album Helen Maud Cam* (Louvain, 1960) 155–71.
84. An excellent and comprehensive study is Werner Goez, *Translatio Imperii* (Tübingen, 1958), discussing jurists as well as historians; see also Ullman, *Medieval Papalism*, 168 ff.
85. Paul Renucci, *L'Aventure de l'humanisme européen au moyen-âge* (Paris, 1953) 139; Hermann Kantorowicz, "A Medieval Grammarian," 47.
86. Summarized in Paulus Castrensis, *In Primam Codicis partem commentaria* (Venice, 1582) f. 3ᵛ. See J. Baskeiwicz, "Quelques remarques sur la conception de dominium mundi dans l'oeuvre de Bartolus," in *Bartolo da Sassoferrato, Studi e documenti per il centenario* (Milan, 1962) II, 9–25.
87. Iacobus de Ravanis (originally attributed to Petrus de Bella Pertica), *Lectura . . .super prima parte Codicis* (Paris, n. d.; repr. Bologna, 1967) f. IIʳ; Jason del Mayno, *In Primam Codicis partem commentaria* (Venice, 1589) f. 2ʳ.
88. *Per Venerabilem;* of Albericus de Rosate, *Super Codice*, f. 7ᵛ. The best recent guide to this much discussed topic is Gaines Post, *Studies in Medieval Legal Thought* (Princeton, 1964) 454 ff.
89. Jason, *op. cit.*, f. 3ʳ.

90. *Pragmatica Sanctio, glossata per Cosmam Guymier* (Lyon, 1488) f.1ʳ.
91. E. g., P. Bertrand, *De Origine jurisdictionum,* in *Tractatus universi juris* (Venice, 1584) III (part 1) f. 31ʳ. In general see Johannes Haller, *Papsttum und Kirchenreform* (Berlin, 1903) 242, passim; citing Jouvenal des Ursins (e.g.), "quod ecclesia Gallicana ad suas antiquas libertates reduceretur." Also Victor Martin, *Les Origines du Gallicanisme* (Paris, 1939) I, and G. Mollat, "Les Origines du gallicanisme parlementaire au XIVe siècle," *Revue d'histoire ecclésiastique,* XLIII (1948) 90–147.
92. Cited by Kantorowicz, *King's Two Bodies,* 299.
93. Texts cited by Goez, *Translatio Imperii,* 11 ff.
94. Charles Duggan, *Twelfth-Century Decretal Collections* (London, 1963) 14.
95. Cited by J. M. Salgado, "La Methode d'interprétation en usage chez les canonistes," *Revue de l'Université d'Ottawa,* XXI (1951) 209.
96. Classic discussion in Post, *Studies,* p. 241 ff.
97. Lebras, *Institutions ecclésiastiques,* 116.
98. Cited by Ullmann, "The Development of the Medieval Idea of Sovereignty," *English Historical Review,* LXIV (1949) 17. See also the recent study centering on the *Somnium viridarii:* J.-P. Royer, *L'Eglise et le Royaume de France au XIV siècle* (Paris, 1969).
99. Cited by Horn, *Aequitas,* 74.
100. Albericus de Rosate, *Super Codice,* f. 7ʳ, and *Super Digesto,* f. 14ʳ. Cf. Bertrand, *De Origine jurisdictionum,* f. 29ᵛ, discussing the founding of the Greek and Roman states "non per viam legitimam. . .sed per meram violentiam potentie."
101. Ullmann, *Medieval Idea of Law,* 47; Albericus de Rosate, *Super Digesto,* f. 14ʳ: "Bellum enim qui processerunt a iuregentium processerunt ab istis pronomibus meum et tuum. . . ."
102. Bodin, *Method for the Easy Comprehension of History,* trans. B. Reynolds (New York, 1945) 297 .
103. Hotman, *Antitribonian* (Paris, 1903). On this see the thesis presented by A. H. Saint-Chamaran to the Université de Droit d'Economie et de Science Sociale de Paris in 1973.
104. J. Moreau-Reibel, *Jean Bodin et le droit public comparé* (Paris, 1933) 135, and J. Brejon, *André Tiraqueau* (Paris, 1937) iii.
105. See my "Development and Context of Bodin's Method," *Jean Bodin: Verhandlungen der internationalen Bodin Tagung in München,* ed. H. Denzer (Munich, 1972) 123–50.
106. *L'Esprit des lois,* XXX, 2.
107. *De Universi juris uno principio et fine uno,* in *Opere,* I, ed. G. Gentile and F. Nicolini (Bari, 1914) 1. See my "Vico's Road," in the forthcoming *Giambattista Vico's Science of Humanity,* ed. G. Tagliacozzo and D. Verene.
108. *De Universi juris,* p. 95; of *La Scienza nuova seconda,* in *Opere,* IV, ed. F. Nicolini (Bari, 1928) 102, *passim.*
109. *De Universi juris,* 66. The term "mens legum" is common in the sixteenth-century. The best study is that of Piano Mortari (cited in n. 28).

History and Prophecy in Medieval Thought

Marjorie E. Reeves

ONE OF THE PROBLEMS for medieval thinkers was, I think, to know how to interpret the moving moments of time against an unchanging, eternal pattern of reality. Since change in itself had little meaning, the movement of history had to be understood by means of images through which men sought to discover the divine design laid up in heaven which governed the whole time-process. These images were various. The pilgrimage—one of the commonest—took the People of God through history as aliens seeking a destination outside history. Closely related to this was St. Augustine's concept of the two cities, the *civitas pellegrina* confronting the *civitas terrena* in a perpetual conflict which could never be resolved within time.[1] Jerusalem was forever juxtaposed to Babylon. This conflict image could even produce a cyclical movement in history, as the pilgrim people passed through a repeating pattern of tribulations. Surprisingly, this idea actually finds visual expression among the otherwise one-directional *figurae* of Joachim of Fiore.[2] Furthermore, the classical analogy with the natural order could still be found in terms of plotting the course of history like the cycle of the sun.[3]

On the other hand, the genealogy of Christ could give a one-way sense of direction to all history up to the First Advent, and this found natural expression in the image of the Tree. The time-process need no longer be seen as a mere succession or cycle of tribulations, but rather as embodying an organic growth, the budding, flowering and fruiting of divine seed planted secretly. The Jesse Tree expresses this idea vividly, but its climax comes mid-way in the time-process: it is completed in the Incarnation and does not become a two-tier tree growing on upwards into the future.[4] The concept of Two Dispensations is linked with the Jesse Tree, for the First is measured by the generations of Christ, and the second (rather less certainly) by some kind of parallel

51

measurement. The histories of the two chosen Peoples of God, Israel and the Church, could then be seen in concord, the persons and events of the First Dispensation being similitudes of the Church's history in the Second. But they usually stand in parallel sequence, side by side, rather than in organic continuity.

Professor Southern has pointed to one concept of meaning in history which might indeed lead to a prophetic hope in the future—that of the "saving remnant," found in the sacred history of the Jews and paralleled in the Virgilian myth of the sacred Trojan remnant destined to found Rome.[5] Although adapted and used by Franks, Britons, and others as a theme which established past glory, this could—in the hands of a Geoffrey of Monmouth, for instance—carry the overtones of a prophetic future. We shall see this concept picked up in a different form by later revolutionary groups.

Finally, the Days of Creation suggested the concept of periodisation, and this idea was, of course, popularised by St. Augustine. But it could be used with or without a notion of progression in history. The first five World Days could be viewed as having rolled by without significant differentiation. The Seventh was obviously of a different quality, but if this were pushed beyond history, the preceding six need not necessarily represent an onward progression through time.[6] It is true that the creation of the First Man on the Sixth Day gave a climactic character to the Sixth Age in which the Second Man appeared, but the First Advent, like the expected Second, represented the direct intervention of God. It need not be seen as the culmination of a progressing, discernible pattern of history, though God's messengers, the prophets, might appear as milestones pointing towards the crowning event.

Thus medieval prophecy was not necessarily concerned with the historic process, except at the points of direct divine intervention, which gave men fulfilled prophecy in the Incarnation, and a focus for future expectation in Last Things. Karl Löwith has made the point that in the orthodox prophetic tradition of Judaism and Christianity the future might indeed be predetermined, but by a personal Divine Will which could only be revealed, rather than by a natural process which could be predicted or inferred from the past, as a classical thinker such as Polybius had supposed. "And since the final fulfillment of Hebrew and Christian destiny lies in an eschatological future, the issue of which depends on man's faith and will, and not on a natural law of pragmatic history, the basic feeling in regard to the future becomes one of suspense in face of its theoretical incalculability."[7] The time interval between where men stood and the End could be interpreted according to one of the "non-progressive" images I have indicated. The immediate future was unimportant, except in so far as it might display the Signs which pointed towards its dissolution. There was nothing to do but to wait for the Last Things. In spite of Matthew XXIV, 36, however, the question *When?* continually stimulated the interpretation of prophetic "signs," whether these signs were visions, natural phenomena, number calculations, biblical, historical, or astrological clues. The standard Fifteen Signs of Last Judgement set out a succession of signs to be expected. These would be happenings in time, but extraordinary events rather than the concluding stages of a pattern built into history itself. Miss Smalley has shown how the orthodox tradition of exegesis embodied this attitude towards the future: "Scripture spiritually expounded reflected the past, the present and the end of time. The span between present and Last Things was dark." But she goes on, ". . .yet if Scripture reflected all truth. . .why should this one particular patch of the mirror be blurred?" [8] It was the desire to span this gap or clear this part of the mirror which in the twelfth century caused a certain departure from tradition in the interpretation of history itself as prophecy.

To see history itself as prophecy, I submit, there had first to be a concept of meaning within time itself towards which the whole process was moving. It must always, of course, be subordinated to the eternal unchanging purpose, but such a design in history could give significance to the movement of events and institutions from the past into the present and even on into the immediate future. By reading God's signs men could plot out this design and live in the present according to their prophetic future. These signs were chiefly found in past history, for the essence of this approach was the extrapolation of a pattern which was already partially revealed in past events. [9] The concept of Seven Ages could become such a pattern if the Seventh, the Sabbath Age, were brought back within history, thus giving a sense of direction to the whole time sequence. Support for this interpretation could be found in the fact that the World Week was an embodiment of the *created* order, which included the idea of time. It is significant that from St. Augustine onwards the Seventh Day was often distinguished from the Eighth: since the latter quite specifically represented eternity, the Seventh must then either fall within history or in some limbo between time and eternity. [10] In an alternative pattern of double sevens, based on the image of Seven Seals and Openings in history, support for the idea of a Sabbath age is found in the "silence" of the Seventh Seal opening (Apocalypse, VIII, 1). Again, the concept of progressive stages of revelation could be cast in a pattern of threes, but here also there were two different ways of reading the clues: it might be held that mankind was already in the third stage or, alternatively, that the third stage was still to be expected in the future. The division, *ante legem, sub lege, sub gratia,* halted progress in the present and gave no impetus to future history as unfulfilled prophecy. On the other hand, the concept of a Trinitarian structure to history could—though not always—provide the most powerful affirmation about the future by projecting the Dispensation of the Third Person forward into it. Besides these clues to the meaning of history in number patterns, there was one all-important sign in the Apocalypse: the strange prophecy of Satan bound for a thousand years.[11] Once again, however, the idea of the millennium could be interpreted in several senses: as the whole period from the First to the Second Advent, as an apotheosis at the end of history, or as a blessed state beyond history. Only the second of these supported the notion of a Sabbath Age within history and thus focused attention on the part of history still to come.

Two scholars in the first half of the twelfth century gave a meaning to the time-process as a whole by interpreting it as a progressive revelation of the Trinity. Rupert, abbot of Deutz, in an extensive Biblical commentary, entitled *De Trinitate et Operibus Eius,*[12] saw the three great Dispensations as the primeval state, *ex ortu primae lucis usque ad lapsum primi hominis*; the second, from the Fall to the Passion of the Second Man; the third, from the Resurrection to the *consummatio seculi.* He then connected each stage specifically with one Person: "the work of the first belongs to the Father, but that of the second to the Son and of the third to the Holy Spirit. . . .Therefore, seeking in this pilgrimage to adore the glory of the holy Trinity, we respond through our senses to the mirrored works of the Triune God." Here a structure of meaning is certainly given to history, but no promise is thrown forward into the future. Rupert also uses the pattern of seven ages, assigning five to the period before the First Advent, in the usual way, and the sixth thence to the Last Things. But the seventh—*quae veraciter sabbatum dicatur, et sit, id est requies*—occupies an ambiguous position. It appears to be an extra-temporal state, not succeeding to the sixth in the same way as the sixth to the fifth, but *conjuncta velut ex latere*; yet in a sense it falls within the time-process, for it only lasts *usque ad finem saeculi* and is distinguished from the Eighth Day. In his third part, *De*

Operibus Spiritus Sancti, Rupert seems to have come close to the idea of a culminating work of the Spirit, but he does not throw the emphasis of this third dispensation sufficiently into the future to give a prophetic thrust to his interpretation of history. He sees the original seven stages of the Creation as embodying the seven Gifts of the Spirit in an ascending scale from *timor Dei* up to *sapientia,* but in his third dispensation he plots the reverse scale, descending again to *timor Dei* in expectation of the Last Judgement. Thus he remains ambivalent about the end of history, seeing it, in one sense, as a descent into tribulation, although, in another, culminating in a Sabbath Age to come.

The second writer to give a Trinitarian meaning to history was Anselm of Havelberg. His is clearly a philosophy of progressive revelation. Although the Deity is invariable and immutable, on account of the *variabilem infirmitatem et temporalem mutationem* of the human race, there must be progressive stages in revelation[13] because in the process of time signs of the spiritual graces must increase which more and more declare the truth itself. Thus the knowledge of truth will grow in course of time from what is good to what is better and so at last to what is best. Yet once again Anselm does not carry the stages of illumination into an historical future. His three divisions are the accepted *ante legem, sub lege, sub gratia.* His use of the pattern of sevens is based on the Book with Seven Seals, with its symbol of the Sabbath Age as the silence in heaven at the opening of the Seventh Seal. But Anselm, more unequivocally than Rupert, places this, not as a culmination to history, but after the Last Judgement. Thus, although these two writers advanced to the point of affirming a developing meaning in the time-process, they did not clearly project its final fruition into the last stage of history.

It was left to Joachim of Fiore to throw the third age (or state) decisively forward into the period between his own day and the *consummatio seculi,* thus seeking to "clear the blurred patch" in the mirror of history. It was neither on a given vision, nor on an interpretation of other types of "sign," but pre-eminently on the construction of an original design of history that Joachim based his claim to give a prophetic view of the future. Although one can point to certain obvious religious and political aspects of his milieu which must have shaped Joachim's general outlook, it is difficult to identify any specific sources for his distinctive ideas or to explain his emergence at precisely this point of time. Speculation on prophecies of the future was certainly current, as witness the discussion initiated by Lucius III on a Sibylline prophecy at Joachim's first interview with the Pope, but Joachim was a mystic and his distinctive philosophy of history was, I believe, the fruit of vision and thought in his Calabrian retreat, rather than learned study and communication. The originality of his structure lay chiefly in the fact that whereas others had seen the three stages in time in simple progression, Joachim believed that the very inner relations of the Trinity were at work in the time-process. Thus the third age must not simply follow the second, but proceed equally from both the first and the second. This entailed giving the second a time span parallel to the first, so that the concords between them could be drawn out, not in two parallel lines running to a horizon of Last Judgement, but in two converging lines meeting in the third *status*. I have argued elsewhere that Joachim did indeed use the well-known pattern of parallel twos in certain contexts—the *Diffinitio ω*, as he called it—but, by emphasising the middle *virgula* as the One proceeding from the Two—*ω*—this symbol was continually being transformed into the *Diffinitio A,* the triangle which symbolised the pattern of threes. [14]

In searching the sacred history of the Scriptures Joachim naturally thought in terms of the traditional four senses, and his writings contain many sequences of fours in which these occur. Yet it is clear that these categories did not fit his thought adequately. [15] His "literal sense" contained two elements: the actual visual form of the letters making up the text, and the actual events in time which they recorded. From these "letters" of the Old and New Testaments proceeded the *spiritualis intellectus* (or *intelligentia*). Here, in the first place, Joachim used an adapted form of the traditional spiritual senses which he called historical (to be distinguished from literal history), moral, and allegorical, subdividing the last into tropological, [16] contemplative and anagogical. These were all spiritual senses in that through them human souls passed from things visible to things invisible, reaching their culmination in the anagogical sense which led the soul to the after-life. But all these concerned meaning for the individual soul. Joachim needed another—a "prophetic" sense of Scripture—through which to express the inner meaning of the time-process itself, that is, the working of the Trinity within the concrete events of the past, always pointing to a completion in the corresponding events of the future.

His passionate faith that the smallest concrete happenings of history might carry the profoundest significance is strikingly illustrated in the fact that he found one of his chief clues both to the extra sense of Scripture and to the pattern of history itself in a curious episode of

Israel's history, when five tribes received their inheritance first and seven afterwards. Joachim found he could match this in the New Testament with groups of five "earlier" and seven "later" churches. [17] This division of the twelve into five prior and seven posterior came to him as a revelation about time and its promise for the future. He then applied the five/seven divisions to the senses of Scripture. The five were the historical, moral, tropological, contemplative, and anagogical through which the individual soul here and now passed from things material to things spiritual and eternal. For the prophetic meaning of time which could only be completely fulfilled hereafter, he postulated another sense—the *sensus typica*—which he sub-divided into seven species. These represented the seven aspects of the Trinity at work in the whole process of history: Father; Son; Spirit; Father and Son; Father and Spirit; Son and Spirit; Three Persons in One. In this "sense," meaning could not be completed until the end of time, for the prior things waited on the posterior yet to be revealed and the history so far completed always pointed to the future. The difference between the lowest of the five, the *sensus historica,* in which individual souls learnt from the lessons of history, and the *sensus typica,* in which the operation of the three Persons and their relationships were sought in temporal happenings, points up the distinction between the category of five senses and that of seven. Sometimes Joachim designates all the five/seven senses as spiritual, but occasionally he applies this term only to the five, leaving the whole range of the *sensus typica* apart. This is curious, since otherwise seven symbolises for Joachim that which is more spiritual, for example the seven Gifts of the Holy Spirit as against the five physical senses. His hesitation in calling the *sensus typica* spiritual derives, I think, from the fact that all its seven species (or *modi*) are concerned with this-worldly meanings, that is, within the time-process, and in this respect are more "material" than those meanings through which the individual soul passes beyond the flesh. Yet, on the other hand, the overtones of the mystic number seven invest history itself with a spiritual meaning which will reach its climax in the third *status ad instar superne Hierusalem.* [18]

Expounding this system of meanings in Book V of the *Liber Concordie,* Joachim illustrates with the example of two women, one, a "virgin" or woman dedicated to God and the other married or a bondwoman. The *intelligentia historica* teaches us that one is free and the other a bondwoman; the moral, that one signifies spiritual affection, the other carnal. At this point the two women become Sarah and Hagar. Under the tropological sense Sarah represents the Spiritual Intelligence, Hagar, the Letter. Under the contemplative sense, Sarah signifies the contemplative life, Hagar, the active, while anagogically Sarah points to the future life, where Hagar is bound to this present life. The seven species of the *intelligentia typica* give a set of meanings on quite a different plane. Under the first, Hagar signifies the general people of Jerusalem, Sarah, the tribe of Levi set apart by God; in the second, the two women represent the *ecclesia secularium* and *ecclesia clericorum* of the second *status*; in the third, the *ecclesia conversorum* and *ecclesia monachorum* of the third *status*. These three senses pertain successively to Father, Son, and Spirit in their appropriate *status*. In the fourth (Father and Son), Hagar signifies the Synagogue, Sarah the Latin Church. In the fifth (Father and Spirit), Hagar is again the Synagogue, but Sarah the "spiritual church which flourished from the beginning in the monastic religion of the Greeks, until at last this venerable institution reached the Latins." The sixth, belonging to Son and Spirit, reveals Hagar as the church of the sixth *etas,* Sarah as the spiritual church of the Sabbath Age. In the seventh species, pertaining to all three Persons and therefore covering the whole of history, Hagar represents the church of the first and second *status,* Sarah *felicem illam ecclesiam . . . in illa septima etate seculi.*

Joachim works out his prophetic interpretation of history, that is, his *intelligentia typica,* through a number of historical symbols, although his ingenuity is not always equal to expounding them in terms of all seven species. Thus, taking the Seven Days of Creation, he can apply the Acts of the seven separate Days to the first *status,* then to the second, more tentatively to the third, and, in the seventh species of the *intelligentia,* to the over-all time span of all three *status,* pertaining to the unity of three Persons in one Godhead. But he realises that he has omitted three species and falls into considerable complications in trying to work out these relationships.

In the *Psalterium decem chordarum* Joachim turns again to Abraham and his family. He demonstrates the five senses in a series of twos: Abraham and Lot can be interpreted in the historical sense, the two wives of Abraham in the moral, the two sons of Isaac in the tropological (with Esau signifying the *doctrina carnalis,* Jacob the *doctrina spiritualis*). In the contemplative sense, Jacob's two wives, Leah and Rachel, stand for the conventual and the eremitical life, and anagogically, of the two sons of Joseph, Manasseh symbolises the temporal life and Ephraim the celestial. For the seven species of the *intelligentia typica*

Joachim takes a group of three: Abraham and his two wives. In the first, Abraham signifies the Jewish priests, Hagar, the people of Israel, Sarah, the tribe of Levi; in the second, Abraham stands for the bishops, Hagar for the church of the laity, Sarah, for the church of the clergy; in the third, Abraham figures the *prelatos cenobiorum,* Hagar the *ecclesiam conversorum,* Sarah the *ecclesiam monachorum.* In the fourth species, Abraham represents the Jewish priests and Greek bishops, Hagar the Jewish synagogue, Sarah, the Greek Church. In the fifth, Abraham symbolises the Jewish priests and Latin bishops, Hagar the Synagogue, Sarah the Latin Church. In the sixth, Abraham embodies the prelates of the second and third *status,* Hagar the *ecclesiam laborantium que presens est,* and Sarah the *ecclesiam quiescentium que futura est in tertio statu.* In the seventh—*in qua finis est omnium*—Abraham signifies God the Father with all prelates from the beginning to the end of time, Hagar, the whole church of the elect from the beginning to the end, Sarah, *illa que sursum est Hyerusalem que est mater nostra.* Joachim does further expositions, according to this system, of the three chief patriarchs and the twelve sons of Jacob and, finally, of the three great women, Sarah, Rebecca, and Rachel. All these show consistently his fundamental distinction between the senses designed for individual edification and the *intelligentia typica* which is the clue to the meaning of history itself and in which the past always points forward to the future.

Joachim's system, I believe, had a decisive influence on the whole idea of history as prophecy. There already existed, on the one hand, concepts of patterns in history, and, on the other, a mythology of its End, with a Last World Emperor, Antichrist, sometimes in multiple form, divine agencies of intervention and a millennium after the Last Judgement. But, I have suggested, for previous thinkers the patterns offered no further stages within history, and the order of this world must dissolve under the pressures of the final drama. Joachim's belief in the Trinitarian structure of history demanded that time should not collapse until the *intelligentia typica* had been worked out to its completion. Thus he brought together pattern and mythology by extrapolating the pattern of history and drawing most of the final act of the drama back into time. The greatest Antichrist must arise and be defeated at such a point in history as to leave a significant "moment" of time for the third *status* (or sabbath of history, or millennium) before the *consummatio seculi.* The agencies and institutions to triumph over Antichrist and rule the third *status* always remained hazy in Joachim's prophetic view, except for his famous two orders of spiritual men to lead the way over Jordan into the Promised Land, and his *Ecclesia Spiritualis* which, he insisted, would still be the Latin Church. But it was of the essence of his philosophy of history that they should be *human* agencies. Thus the older myth of the Last World Emperor was easily brought within the programme by later followers, and future history could be peopled with figures that were human indeed, although, since they would enact the final triumph of righteousness, they acquired enhanced human stature. In particular, Joachim's prophetic expectation threw up the concepts of new orders and the Angelic Pope, at once symbols of continuity and revolution. Like Marxism, Joachim's interpretation of history was both deterministic and a stimulant to revolutionary action. On the one hand, the divinely ordained pattern was immutable, but, on the other, change was now seen as part of the very fabric of meaning in history, challenging men to revolutionise their lives and seek an "active part" in the last act of the drama. *Opus ergo mutare vitam,* writes Joachim, *quia mutari necesse est statum mundi* (*Lib. Conc.,* f. 21ᵛ).

Professor E. Randolph Daniel has examined an immediate contemporary reaction to Joachim the prophet in the conversation between Joachim and the English crusaders led by Richard I, recorded by Roger Howden at Messina in 1191.[19] Here it is at once evident that Joachim made his first impact through the deterministic pattern of twos, that is, the pattern of the two Dispensations, running in parallel to the First and Second Advents respectively, rather than through his revolutionary pattern of threes. In terms of the Seven Seals and Openings, the Saracens stood in concord with the Assyrians who persecuted the Jews under the fourth seal and again (according to Joachim) under the sixth.[20] So the fourth age of the Church had seen the rise of Mohammedanism and the onslaught of the Saracens. Using the figure of Apocalypse 13:1, the Beast with seven heads and ten horns that rises from the sea, Joachim saw in the fourth head, wounded unto death, the initial victories of the Crusaders when "in the time of Pope Urban they gathered from all the occidental parts to go overseas and liberate the Holy City." But the deadly wound must be healed, the head must recover, and in the sixth age now approaching the "new Assyrians" must burst forth in greater fury. In 1191 Joachim seems uncertain as to where exactly he is standing in the foreordained programme. He expounds the passage on the seven-headed Dragon, identifying Saladin as the sixth head and, according to Howden's first version (i.e. Benedict of Peterborough), predicting his overthrow. In the second version, the prophesied victory becomes vaguer and more distant, so that Richard asks: Why then have we come too soon? These different versions, of course, probably represent Howden's adjustment of the conversation, but from Joachim's writings we can detect the ambivalence of his attitude towards the effort of the Third Crusade. In the text of the Dragon figure he says that the sixth head will be Saladin, if still alive, or another who will gather a general army against the elect of God. Once he hints that the period in which the head is *"quasi mortuum"* may be lasting until now, in which case there could be momentary victory for the crusaders. But all the time his attention is concentrated on the full sixth storm yet to break, and then the seventh and worst head "yet to come"—Antichrist. He gathers up the presages of evil. The Roman *Imperium,* the barrier against the heathen ordained by God, must collapse when the Sixth Angel pours his phial on the River Euphrates:[21] this has already been foreshadowed in the destruction of Frederick I's great and powerful army, an event which he views with grief, but regards as inevitable. The Beast from the sea and the Beast from the land must join in deadly alliance against the Church: this is coming to pass in the terrible alliance between the Saracens and the Patarin heretics of which he collected a rumour at Messina in 1195 from a man recently imprisoned in Alexandria. Joachim's real attention is concentrated on the inevitable crisis of evil which must be imminent according to all his calculations and concords. He can have given little prophetic strengthening to crusaders fighting outside the pattern, as it were, and after his death the legend of the famous prophecy at Messina settles into a heavy menacing pronouncement that the time for the recovery of Jerusalem has not yet come. Thus until the mid-thirteenth-century Joachim's doctrine adds little new or exciting to the prevailing attitude towards the future.

It is interesting to speculate whether, had Joachimism not passed through the crucible of Spiritual Franciscan thought, the revolutionary implications of his doctrine of history would ever have been widely grasped. One writer in the early thirteenth-century, Werner of Rochefort, appears to use his pattern of threes, but not applied to the meaning of history.[22] Otherwise Joachim remains the prophet of Antichrist and the expounder of a pattern of twos in history, until in the mid-thirteenth-century a group of Franciscans let off a charge of his buried dynamite. What made them develop an interest in Joachim's prophetic future? It was not simply the convincing fulfillment of his prophecy concerning the two new orders, for the Dominicans, on the whole, accepted the prophecy without assuming the great role it offered for the future. Just how the Spiritual Franciscan group which gathered round John of Parma and Hugh de Digne made the transition, as it were, from the pattern of twos to that of threes in Joachim's philosophy of history still remains unclear. Did they fasten on Joachim's scheme of Scriptural senses and start from the Trinitarian structure of history expounded as the *intelligentia typica?* There is no evidence for such an approach. The conversations with Hugh de Digne recorded by Salimbene concern the application of specific prophecies, especially those on Frederick II. The pseudo-Joachimist works circulating in the mid-thirteenth century (from whatever source they emanated) began to proclaim the future third *status* but with little systematic exposition of the Trinitarian theory of history on which this was founded.

The Spiritual Franciscans, I think, started from their own overwhelming experience of the significance of St. Francis, a significance which seemed to initiate a new era of history and endow his followers with a new cosmic role. They then found the justification of their experience in Joachim's theory, with its prophetic thrust forward into the future. Without paying much attention to the exegetical basis of his doctrine, they responded to the ongoing drama of the second *status* now moving into the third, as Joachim depicted it. The argument that Joachim's system as such played little part in this process of assimilation finds support in the work of the later Joachite, Pierre Jean d'Olivi. His exegesis in his commentary on St. Matthew seldom draws on Joachim's system of senses, yet there are enough hints of belief in a Joachimist future to suggest that this work is consistent in outlook with the more overtly Joachimist *Postilla in Apocalypsim.*[23] It was not, I think, Joachim's doctrine of history which captured the attention of these Franciscans, but the dramatic thrust of his imagination towards the future which offered an interpretation of their own experience. Thus they transformed Joachim's system into a drama shaped by the clues he had given and leading towards a final act which would embody his expectation. A moderate example of this outlook is seen in Salimbene's *Chronica,* which is not a straight chronicle but, in part at least, an interpretation of history moulded by the Joachimist themes through which he reads the "signs" of the times. As Professor Delno West is working on this subject, I shall not elaborate further. Fra Angelo Clareno shapes the past, present, and future experience of the persecuted Spirituals into a drama of seven tribulations which carries overtones of the Seven Seal-Openings.[24] At the moment of writing he believes himself to be standing at the end of the sixth tribulation and on the threshold of the seventh and worst which must follow quickly, according to the Joachimist pattern of a double persecution under the sixth seal, so that the seventh seal remains for the Sabbath which Clareno so fervently expects. The pattern of seven *tempora* of the Church, worked out by Olivi and adopted by Ubertino da Casale, shapes the whole of history between the First and Second Advents into a cosmic drama rising to a double climax in the final triumph of good over evil and the Sabbath Age to follow at the Seventh Seal-Opening. Thus the gap between the present and the End is prophetically bridged, the blurred patch in the mirror hopefully cleared. The Spiritual Franciscans added another pattern for the understanding of history, one born out of their deep conviction that they really had experienced a new Coming of Christ in the person of St. Francis. Thus Olivi, and after him Ubertino, used the concept of three Advents. Their sense of novelty and expectation belied the orthodox view that the climax of history lay behind them in the First Advent. There must be another climax, an intermediary Advent, before the winding up of history at the final Advent. Their experience demanded a pattern of threes to supplement that of two Dispensations. The same type of experience in the Reformation period led to similar concepts of three advents or three Resurrections. I have only selected a few examples from the thought of well-known Spiritual Franciscans. The subject of St. Bonaventura's philosophy of history is too vast to deal with here. The point I am suggesting is that the Franciscan use of Joachimism was largely responsible for the growth of a dramatic view of history which focused attention on the immediate future and gradually peopled it with a variety of *dramatis personae*.

In the last part of this paper I want to examine a few further examples to show the hold which a pattern of history which linked past, present, and future could have over the imagination. First, let us return to attitudes towards the crusading enterprise and the infidel. Joachim's third *status* certainly embraced the conversion of the Jews,[25] but, so far as I have discovered, he gives only two hints that the infidel might also be gathered into the one sheepfold: first, when he says that Christians will prevail *praedicando magis quam preliando,*[26] and secondly, in the text to the Dragon figure of the *Liber Figurarum,* where he prophesies along with the conversion of the Jews that of *multi gentes infideles.*[27] Professor Daniel has collected evidence to suggest that mid-thirteenth-century Joachites, accepting the inevitability of Joachim's sixth and seventh tribulations which could only be endured, abandoned belief in crusading and moved over to an active hope in conversion as part of the programme for the third *status*. Thus the pseudo-Joachimist *Super Hieremiam* criticises attempts to stimulate further crusades as being against the divine plan.[28] But I think what Randolph Daniel calls the Joachite alternative to the Crusade only emerged slowly. In Roger Bacon's *Opus Majus,* for example, he directly invokes the prophets for guidance on how to prepare for the approaching menace, but there is no hint of conversion in a third *status*.[29] In his late tracts, on the other hand, the *Opus Tertium* (1267/8) and the *Compendium studii philosophiae* (1272), he looks forward to a world united in one sheepfold and expects the Tartars to be converted, but the Saracens are still to be destroyed.[30] It is true that the *Super Hieremiam* prophesies that God will convert the *gentes incredulas* through the two new orders,[31] and that the *Super Esaiam* expects many—both Tartar and Mohammedan—to be called to the faith,[32] yet, in the *Praemissiones* preceding the latter, the Mohammedan people are expected to disappear from the earth. Again, a prophetic verse, dated after 1268, expects Mohammedans to be brought into the *unum ovile,*[33] but Arnold of Villanova in 1297 believes this sect will be destroyed, although he looks forward to the enjoyment of terrestrial Jerusalem in the *tempus plenitudinis gentium*.[34] Olivi, however, is quite clear about the prophetic pattern to be worked out: as St. Francis set out to convert the Saracens in the sixth year after his conversion, so in the sixth age of the Church this conversion must be accomplished by the Order.[35] This is a striking example of the method of extrapolating number patterns.

In the fourteenth century, universal conversion as the logical end to history was being widely propagated and, as I have tried to show elsewhere, remained a powerful dream down to the seventeenth century. By this time a prophecy—the conversion of the Jews—which had begun as a sign of the imminent End, had been extended to all peoples and transformed into a feature of an apotheosis of history which included universal peace and brotherhood. Leaving aside some obvious late-medieval examples, let me jump to the sixteenth century and cite only Wolfgang Lazius, who writes: *infra tempus 1548 annorum saeculum congregabitur in unum ovile,*[36] and Paolo Angelo, who believes that in the idealized situation of that blessed time men will build three bridges to go dry-foot between Europe and Asia.[37]

One of the problems in seeking to spell out a pattern for the future in relation to the past was that of continuity or discontinuity in institutions. Would the crossing of Jordan from the second to the third *status* constitute a divinely ordained revolution? Joachim himself clearly saw continuity in the most fundamental institution of all, the Latin Church, the rock of St. Peter, although expecting the active life designated in Peter to be superseded by the contemplative life pertaining to John. By the end of the thirteenth-century, when the group of the Spirituals was under fierce persecution by authority, the pressure to hope for a sharp break must have been great. When the idea of the Angelic Pope mysteriously emerges to meet this need for a new authority, it seems a revolutionary concept—a direct divine intervention. Yet in the famous series of Pope Prophecies, first perpetrated according to Grundmann in 1305, continuity and revolution are skillfully joined.[38] The idea of an historical series linking past, present, and future came, it would seem, from the Greek model of the Leo Oracle on which the Pope Prophecies were based. In this model a historic series of emperors culminated in the immediate intervention of God directing officials to a hidden emperor, even in some versions a buried one, who must be resurrected to fill the empty throne. This chosen ruler then initiates an angelic series. The authors of the first series of Pope Prophecies adapted the Leo pictures and texts to depict a sequence of popes starting from Nicholas III. By ascribing them to Joachim the whole series could be claimed as prophecy, but, in fact, down to a certain point, each picture and text represents an historical judgement in veiled oracular form. The exact moment of transition to real prophecy is not quite certain, but the visionary future begins to take shape clearly when God summons the electors to seek a hermit among the rocks to become the next pope. From this point onwards, the angelic quality of the new life in the third *status* is apparent in captions and in figures of angels associated with the popes. Thus the continuity of the institution is preserved, yet a radical break with an evil past is brought about by divine intervention.

The fascination exercised by this particular type of prophecy is shown in the production of a second series of fifteen, c. 1356, probably by a group of Florentine Fraticelli. Here a more gloomy view of the papal future was taken, and the series culminated, not in angelic popes, but in a representation of evil, probably Antichrist. It is significant, therefore, that when, before the end of the fourteenth century, the two series were put together, the earlier one was placed second, so that the whole thirty still culminated in the visionary angelic sequence. As such it continued to fascinate many down to the seventeenth century, treated by some as fulfilled prophecy and by others as yet to be completed. As late as the end of the sixteenth century there was a fresh outburst of interest in this "papal history." Printed editions with interpretations appeared and manuscript anthologies were produced, while a crop of imitative series suggests in unfilled spaces at the end of each sequence that the idea of projecting the history of a great institution into a visionary or revolutionary future still had power to hold the imagination.

When the Angelic sequence of popes did not supervene at the expected time, the remnant of the Spiritual Franciscan party, scattered in small groups, could only wait and hope for the apotheosis of history they never ceased to believe in. Ubertino da Casale describes the little flock—*quendam populum novum et humilem in hac novissima hora, qui esset dissimilis . . . ab omnibus aliis*[39]—as they wait, mentioning in particular a group which has retired to Asia, until the day of their salvation. Here we meet in a new form (religious instead of political) the response of the "saving remnant" to prophecy, and this becomes increasingly the attitude of the hunted Fraticelli in Italy and Beguins in Provence and Catalonia. As their criticism of Papacy and Church grows sharper, they identify both more closely with the great whore of Babylon. By a significant shift of interpretation, Constantine, who, with Pope Silvester, had embodied for Joachim a great moment of blessedness in the Church,[40] becomes for the Fraticelli the author of the disastrous Donation which was the beginning of corruption in the Church. Since that day the official Church has been gradually transformed into the Babylonish Woman, but always the pure remnant of the true Church has been hidden away in her midst, and always it has been persecuted: *senpre gli molti hanno gli pochi fedeli de Christo perseguitati.*[41] Some Italian Fraticelli see their experience in terms of Noah's Ark. They are the true seed of the future; buffeted by all the tempests of hostility, they must yet be saved to bring in the new age. Their navigators are St. Francis, Olivi, and the Abbot Joachim himself whose *Liber Concordie* they cite:[42]

> where in the fifth book . . . he says that the five hundred years of Noah before he constructed the ark signify the fifth *status* of the Church of Christ, finishing with himself (Joachim), and that as in the first year of the sixth hundred Noah was commanded to build the ark, so at the beginning of the sixth *status*, Christ had sent a man into the world who would construct another ark . . . in which once again the seed of the elect would be saved from the deluge [to fall on] the faithless . . . And this man was the venerable patriarch *messer sancto Franciescho.*

A similar reading of history inspired the Provencal followers of Olivi. They distinguished two churches—a carnal, *quam dicunt esse ecclesiam Romanam quantum as multitudinem reproborum,* and a spiritual, *quantum ad viros quos vocant spirituales et evangelicos.* At the end of the sixth age the carnal church will be rejected, while from the surviving third part of the Franciscan Order will be drawn the handful of chosen men who will found the *ecclesia spiritualis que erit humilis et benigna in septimo et ultimo statu Ecclesie.*[43]

For those who were too impatient to wait for divine intervention to reshape the authority of the Church the revolutionary implications of Joachimism offered an opportunity to cast themselves in the key roles of the final age. Thus we meet quite a different response to prophetic history in the sect of Apostolic Brethren.[44] Their origins in the mid-thirteenth century are not clear, but I have argued elsewhere that their roots probably lay in Joachimism. Certainly their chief leader, Fra Dolcino, appears to have worked out a theory of history on which he based his expectation for the future and therefore his incitement to revolution. It is interesting that this theory of history was not Trinitarian and did not, in its periodisation, owe much to Joachim. Yet it led unmistakeably to a climax within time which is an apotheosis of history. Dolcino believed that there were four *status* of history: the first belonged to the patriarchs and other just men of the Old Testament; the second was initiated by Christ and the Apostles; the third, beginning with St. Silvester, had reached its climax in the way of life initiated by St. Francis and St. Dominic. But each of these was destined to decline in virtue, until the fourth *status* now being initiated in the *Apostoli* themselves. The Roman Church was now *illa meretrix magna,* and the spiritual power of St. Peter had descended on the Apostolic Brethren. The evil order of Babylon would shortly be destroyed by Frederick, King of Sicily, and then the perfect order of the new Apostles would reign throughout the world until the end of the age.

There were, of course, other scattered manifestations of revolutionary aspirations in the later Middle Ages. A curious pictorial expression of such hopes is found in the *Breviloquium,* a mid-fourteenth-century version of Joachimism emanating from Catalonia.[45] The three *status* are represented in little pictures of patriarchs, apostles, and new spiritual men. The ecclesiastical authority of the final age is also shown in terms of the *novus ordo.*[46] Revolution is, however, most clearly expressed in the conclusion of *Tables of Concords,* based on Joachim's. In the *Liber Figurarum*[47] these clearly represent Joachim's pattern of twos: they set out in parallel tables the generations and concords of the two Dispensations, from Adam to the First Advent, from the Incarnation to the Second Advent, with only a little hint of a spiritual revolution in a third *status*. The *Breviloquium,* continuing the tables for a further century and a half, introduces towards the end a violent overthrow of papal authority, with mitre, keys, and sceptre cast down, followed by a further visionary list of leaders before the end of the age.[48] This is the most vivid expression I have found of continuity suddenly shattered by prophetic expectation.

There is a veritable jungle of late medieval political prophecy. These represent the marriage of an old mythology about the *Imperium* with what I will now call the Joachimist drama of the seven ages or the seven *tempora* of the Church. The old tradition, as I have said, contained a myth of a Last World Emperor who would reign gloriously for a space, but basically it expressed a pessimistic view of history. The Roman *Imperium* had been ordained to hold back the barbarian hordes as long as God willed. When this barrier broke, Antichrist would be at hand. Even the Last World Emperor would resign his crown in despair at the onslaught of Antichrist, and, with the divine intervention necessary to destroy the great enemy, the temporal order would dissolve. Thus a negative function and a defeated end were assigned to the *Imperium*. Joachim had not questioned the political myth—since his third *status* was conceived entirely in religious terms—but his great innovation in staging the fiercest conflict with evil at the end of the sixth age (or sixth *tempus* of the Church), followed by the climax of the seventh age before Last Judgement, brought the whole drama within the temporal order and made possible a politico/religious apotheosis of history in which human agencies triumphed over evil. It was natural, therefore, to people the stage for the last two acts with prophetic figures of good and evil according to political loyalties. The history of the *Imperium* could be viewed from the perspective of a new Imperial role belonging to the *renovatio mundi*. Thus Alexander von Roes included a prophecy of a world emperor in his *De Translatione Imperii,*[49] and Pierre Dubois, claiming a cosmic role for the French monarchy in his *De recuperatione Terre Sancte,* believed that the *Imperium* must return to France, for only from the heirs of Charlemagne could universal peace flow.[50] It was the role of a French Emperor to recover the Holy Land and rule a federation of nations from Jerusalem. A political programme of what may be termed French Joachimism developed in the fourteenth century. The strange Franciscan, Jean de Roquetaillade, read history virtually in terms of two dynasties, the evil and the good.[51] The source of all political evil lay in the accursed seed of the Hohenstaufen, the *serpens antiquus*. In contrast stood the blessed race of the French princes, the New Maccabees, who would protect the true Angelic Pope in the days of the evil onslaught and finally, with him, bring in the new age, when the Holy Spirit would be poured out anew on a world united in peace under the two great heads. Roquetaillade varied the details of his political programme, as events overtook the writing of his various tracts (c. 1345–56), but the different manifestations of Antichrist usually wore a Hohenstaufen countenance, while—as French fortunes sank in the Hundred Years' War—Roquetaillade became more convinced that the *Imperium* must be transferred to the French monarch and the whole world eventually be ruled by him.

In the final confrontation of good and evil forces which was to be the climax of tribulation in history, there were now two leading figures on each side: a benign Emperor and Angelic Pope against Antichrist in two forms, political tyrant and pseudo-pope. Thus the drama naturally took the form of Schism. It was a curious coincidence that this prophetic drama was put into its final and most popular form at a moment just preceding the Great Schism. Whoever the mysterious Telesphorus of Cosenza was, politically he was a French Joachite.[52] His pattern of wicked German tyrant in collusion with pseudo-pope making schism in the Church is mainly an elaboration of Roquetaillade's programme, leading, of course, to the recovery of initiative by the French monarchy and the installation of a series of Angelic Popes. In some copies this political future is vividly conveyed in a series of little pictures which enhance the dramatic excitement. In a final holy partnership Emperor and Pope will reform the Church and recover the Holy Land. Then will follow the age of beatitude which Telesphorus identifies with the millennium of Satan bound. The popularity of Telesphorus' little tract, even after the Great Schism was ended, bears witness to a continuing preoccupation with the idea of a dramatic and final confrontation between the forces of good (political and religious) and those of evil (political and pseudo-religious) shortly to be manifested in this world.

Equally fascinating was the dream of the *renovatio mundi* in the seventh act, as worked out in the fourteenth and fifteenth centuries in terms of both a German and a French world regime.[53] By the end of the fifteenth century the vision of world peace and beatitude had taken on a colour which was a subtle mixture of medieval and Renaissance

69

aspirations. In its expectation of a single universal politico/religious world order it was medieval, but in its excitement over the new vistas of learning and of lands, it expressed the Renaissance sense of novelty. Change had now become something positive and good. But the clues to its meaning were still sought within the old prophetic framework. A Joachimist reading of history could feed an incipient belief in progress.

An idea of history in which the greatest age lay just ahead, or was already beginning, captured the imagination of influential Renaissance thinkers as well as the more unstable. Thus Giles of Viterbo, Cardinal and General of the Augustinian Friars, humanist scholar and student of the Cabbala, read history in terms of two great peaks to which all events led, the first, the coming of Christianity and the second, the great spiritual unfolding now just ahead of humanity. He worked out this philosophy of history in his great work, *De Historia Viginti Saeculorum,* where by harmonising classical and Christian history he attempted to establish a universal pattern of concords. [54] Now all the signs—the overseas discoveries of new lands, the new learning, the appearance of the greatest emperor in Charles V, who united the prophecies of the Eagle and the Lily—pointed to the imminence of the second climax of universal history, a golden age which he envisaged in terms at once humanist and mystical, political and religious. [55]

Guillaume Postel, a French scholar learned in languages, stands in contrast to Giles in the instability of his personality and career, yet he also read Renaissance signs in terms of a new age already prophesied. [56] Religiously he expected the Jesuits to be the agents of the *renovatio mundi;* politically, he looked to the French monarchy except for a short period when, in frustration, he turned to the Emperor Ferdinand. He, too, saw history as the master-plan of Providence which was now moving to its climax, and interpreted all the new discoveries and achievements of Man as tokens of its imminence: [57]

> Today we see clearly that, quite suddenly, Greek, Latin and Hebrew letters, along with all learning, divine and human, have made more progress in fifty years than in the previous thousand. . . . And we see another great change and marvel when we consider how . . . the new world, which is greater than our own, has not only been discovered and conquered, but also converted to the Christian religion . . . I do not mention the arts of artillery and printing, discovered among the Latin Christians . . .

His prophetic new age, preceded by world-wide conquest and mission—had a splendid ecumenical structure: a trinity of sovereign pope, sovereign king, and supreme judge, with twelve sees and their rulers under them; one synthesized world religion; social and cultural unity, based on abolition of private property and separate languages.

Finally, we see the experience of change in the sixteenth century calling forth among some Protestants a radical response in some respects analogous to that of the Spiritual Franciscans in the thirteenth and fourteenth centuries. Unlike Postel, these Protestants necessarily postulated an institutional break, yet they, too, drew on medieval prophecy, they used the dramatic pattern of the seven ages of the Church, and, most significantly, they sometimes found their own experience of blinding new illumination fittingly embodied in Joachim's concept of a third age of history, or—with a more Christological emphasis—in the second of three Advents or Resurrections. Giacopo Brocardo gives us an example of a Protestant Joachite who re-interprets the Joachimist patterns of threes and sevens in a thorough-going way.[58] The third *status* of the Holy Spirit in which Brocardo believes himself to be already living, is that of "opened prophecy." Like the preceding *status,* the third will have seven divisions. Of these, the first was from Luther's preaching to that of the Swiss reformers, the second and third covered the preaching elsewhere, such as England and Denmark, and the fourth "commeth to the French troubles." The fifth ran "even unto the universal slaughter of the Gospellers." In the sixth, the second (intermediary) Advent of Christ would mark the vanishing of Antichrist and the seventh would be the full Sabbath. Thus the complete peace of the third *status* would not be achieved until its seventh sub-division. Then, Brocardo believed, there must be a General Council which would guide men into open prophecy and erect a Church of all Christian people. The diffusion of the Gospel throughout the world is symbolised in the bells and pomegranites adorning Aaron's robe:[59]

> [These] signify the last age of the worlde, wherein Christes Garment is more inlarged and comprehendeth the whole world, when everywhere there shal be little Belles and Pomegarnates, that is, Churches, and the preaching of the Gosple shalbe in the whole worlde. No other religion, no other lawe, and rule to heare then that of the Gosple shall be heard. Then shall be the kyngdom of God in the state of the Holy Ghost untyll that when the Saboth is fynished in this worlde, hee bryngeth us in his thyrde comming to Heaven.

The political counterpart to this Protestant religious dream—and equally rooted in the medieval prophetic tradition of history—is the concept of a Providential role for the chosen nation which, in its English manifestation, has received attention lately in studies by Haller, Lamont, Hill and others.[60] A little known example of this outlook is provided by James Maxwell, who, in 1615, brought together a remarkable medieval collection of *Admirable and notable Prophesies* by twenty-four Catholic witnesses.[61] The strong influence of tradition appears in the two leading figures of his expected *renovatio mundi*—last holy emperor and angelic pope—but his interpretation of his medieval sources hints cautiously at a new political quarter from which the new pope and the saviour/ruler will arise:

> The Good Bishop or Pope that should thus reforme the Church is commonly called Pastor Angelicus, Angelicall Pope, and who knoweth but that he may even be a Pastor Anglicus, a Pastor or Bishop sent forth from the Countrie of England. The English have been more fertile converters of Nations . . . then any other Land else . . .

And—commenting on a medieval prophecy about red flowers—he expects the ruler to be a "rosie Prince" and hopes that he will spring from the Rose of England.[62] To support his claim that England may be the true heir to the prophecies, he traces the British royal house back to Constantine and announces *A Discourse of Gods especiall providence for . . . the Monarchie of great Brittaine: wherein is shewed by divers probabilities, olde Predictions and Prophecies, that from thence is likely to spring the last Imperiall Monarchie . . . .* Prophetic aspiration has now been turned into national channels.

Tracking down this theme of prophetic history obviously gives a one-sided notion of the way history was viewed. By the end of the period I have taken, the writing of "real history" has made great strides, and its development is rightly regarded as a significant intellectual advance. But in tracing the Renaissance beginnings of what we should call true historical study, let us not forget that belief in prophetic history was continuing side by side, and mingling with it. Wolfgang Lazius, after writing four books of Viennese history, twelve on the Roman Empire and two on the genealogy of the Hapsburgs, turned to the compilation of an exhaustive anthology of prophetic history to show that Charles V must be the great emperor of the *renovatio mundi*.[63] Another important anthology of prophecies, the *Mirabilis Liber*,[64] proves the universality of the French monarchy. Symphoriano Campeggio in his *De Monarchia Gallorum*[65] argues for the prophetic destiny of the French monarchy, and Tommaso Campanella, on a similar theme, uses the same arguments in the seventeenth century as Pierre Dubois had done in the thirteenth.[66] The significant point about this type of prophetic history which developed out of Joachimism in the later Middle Ages and continued to flourish until the seventeenth century is that in its thrust towards future history it gradually accommodated the notion of change as meaningful because the whole temporal order was progressing towards its golden age. Thus it finds a certain place in the history of the idea of progress. The ironical point about it is that it continued to enshrine an ecumenical dream in an age when western unity was finally falling apart into nation states.

NOTES

1. See P.R. Brown, *Augustine of Hippo* (London, 1967), pp. 315–322.
2. *Liber Figurarum,* ed. L. Tondelli, M. Reeves, B. Hirsch-Reich, *Il Libro delle Figure dell'Abate Gioacchino da Fiore,* vol. II, 2nd edn., Turin, 1954), Pls. XV, XVI (edn. hereinafter cited *Lib. Fig.*) In the Dresden MS. of the *Lib. Fig.* the figures actually look like wheels of fortune.
3. In the *Breviloquium* (full ref. below, n. 45), *Distinctio* 1, ff. 10ʳ, 11ʳ, 12ᵛ–13ᵛ, each of the three *status* has a dawn, mid-day, and sunset, although in many respects this is clearly a Joachimist tract.
4. See M. Reeves, 'The *Arbores* of Joachim of Fiore,' *Studies in Italian History presented to Miss E.M. Jamison, being Papers of the British School at Rome,* xxiv (1956), 126.
5. See R.L. Southern, Presidential Address, *Transactions of the Royal Historical Society* (1970), 179, 194.
6. Thus P.R. Brown describes Augustine's mood in these terms: "Augustine thought of himself as living in the Sixth, the last, the Old Age of the World. He thought of this . . . with the sadness of one for whom nothing new could happen," *op. cit.,* p. 296.
7. K. Löwith, *Meaning in History* (Chicago, 1957), p. 9.
8. B. Smalley, *The Study of the Bible in the Middle Ages* (Oxford, 1952), pp. 286–287.
9. See Löwith, *op. cit.,* p. 6: 'The past is a promise to the future: consequently the interpretation of the past becomes a prophecy in reverse, demonstrating the past as a meaningful preparation for the future.'
10. There seems to me to be an ambiguity here even in the thought of St. Augustine who, while placing the seventh age so definitely beyond history, yet distinguishes it from the Eighth Day, see *De Civ. Dei,* xx, capp. vi–xvii (edn. J. Welldon, London, 1924), ii, pp. 458–484.
11. Apocalypse, 20, vv. 1, 2.
12. Migne, *Patrologia Latina,* clxvii (Paris, 1854), cols. 198, 199, 1567, 1808. I have not attempted in this paper to consider the visions of Hildegarde of Bingen, since these seem to be more concerned with a cosmic order than with patterns of time.
13. Migne, *Patrologia Latina,* clxxxviii (Paris, 1855), cols. 1159, 1160.
14. This symbolism is expounded early in the *Liber Concordie novi ac veteris testamenti* (edn. Venice, 1519, hereinafter cited *Lib. Conc.*), ff. 10ʳ, 13ᵛ, 19ʳ. See M. Reeves, *The Influence of Prophecy in the Later Middle Ages* (Oxford, 1969), hereinafter cited *Prophecy,* pp. 19–20, 23.
15. The following account of Joachim's use of the senses of Scripture is based mainly on the following passages in his writings: *Lib. Conc.,* ff. 60ᵛ–73ʳ; *Psalterium decem chordarum* (edn. Venice, 1527, hereinafter cited *Psalt.*), ff. 262ᵛ–271ᵛ.
16. Joachim takes the tropological sense according to the meaning of the word, see *Lib. Conc.,* f 60ᵛ: *Tropologica quoque intelligentia illa est que agitur de diversis modis sermonum Dei; Psalt.,* f. 264ʳ: *Tropos enim grece: latine modus dicitur logos, id est*

73

sermo. The best study of Joachim's exegetical method is by H. de Lubac, *Exegèse Médiévale: Les Quatres Sens de l'Écriture* (Paris, 1961), pp. 438 *seq.*

17. See *Lib. Conc.*, ff. 31ᵛ, 39ʳ, 57ʳ *seq.*; *Expositio in Apocalypsim* (edn. Venice, 1527, hereinafter cited *Expos.*), ff. 16ᵛ seq., 28ʳ, 48ʳ *seq.* The five churches are Jerusalem, Antioch, Constantinople, Alexandria, Rome. The seven are the seven churches of Asia in Apocalypse, chs. 2–3.

18. See *Lib. Fig.*, Pl. XII.

19. E.R. Daniel, 'Apocalyptic Conversion: The Joachite Alternative to the Crusade,' *Traditio,* xxv (1969), 127–135. For Howden's double account, see 'Benedict of Peterborough,' *Gesta Henrici et Richardi* I, Rolls Series, ii, pp. 151–155; Roger Howden, *Cronica,* Rolls Series, iii, pp. 75–79.

20. Except where the source is Howden, the material in this paragraph is drawn from the following passages in Joachim's writings: *Expos.*, ff. 116ᵛ, 134ʳ–135ʳ, 162ʳ–167ᵛ, 196ʳ–197ʳ; *De Vita Sancti Benedicti,* ed. C. Baraut, *Analecta Sacra Tarraconensia,* xxiv (1951), 84–85, 92; *Lib. Fig.*, Pl. XIV.

21. Apocalypse, 16, v. 12.

22. See *Prophecy*, p. 44.

23. I am indebted for this point to Miss C. Boorman who is working on some aspects of Olivi's thought.

24. *Historia Septem Tribulationeum,* ed. F. Tocco, *Rendiconti della Reale Accademia dei Lincei,* xvii (Rome, 1908), 97–131, 221–236; F. Ehrle, *Archiv für Literatur und Kirchengeschichte des Mittelalters,* ii (1886), 125–155; 256–327.

25. On Joachim's attitude to the Jews, see B. Hirsch-Reich, 'Judentum im Mittelalter,' *Miscellanea Mediaevalia,* iv (1966), 228–263.

26. *Expos.*, f. 164ᵛ.

27. *Lib. Fig.*, Pl. XIV.

28. Daniel, *loc. cit.*, 140–145; *idem,* "Spirituality and Poverty: Angelo da Clareno and Ubertino da Casale," *Medievalia et Humanistica,* N. S. No. 4 (1973), 89–98.

29. Roger Bacon, *Opus Majus,* ed. J. Bridges (London, 1900), i, pp. 268–269.

30. Roger Bacon, *Opera Inedita,* ed. J.S. Brewer, Rolls Series, pp. 86, 402.

31. *Super Hieremiam* (ed. Venice, 1516), f. 2ʳ.

32. *Super Esaiam* (ed. Venice, 1517), f. 56ʳ.

33. Quoted *Prophecy,* p. 312.

34. See passage quoted *ibid,* p. 315.

35. See passage quoted Daniel, *loc. cit.*, 145.

36. W. Lazius, *Fragmentum vaticinii cuiusdam . . . Methodii* (Vienna, 1547), sig. Hvʳ.

37. P. Angelo, *Profetie certissime, stupende et admirabili dell'Antichristo et innumerabili mali al mondo* (Venice, 1530), f. 29ʳ.

38. See M. Reeves, 'Some Popular Prophecies from the fourteenth to the seventeenth-centuries,' *Studies in Church History,* viii, ed. G.J. Cuming and D. Baker (Cambridge, 1971), 107–134, and the references given there; *idem,* "History and Eschatology: Medieval and Early Protestant Thought in Some English and Scottish Writings," *Medievalia et Humanistica,* N. S. No. 4 (1973), 99–123.

39. Ubertino da Casale, *Arbor Vitae Crucifixae* (Venice, 1485), f. ccixʳ.

40. See *Lib. Conc.*, ff. 17ᵛ, 38ᵛ–39ᵛ, 66ᵛ, 92ᵛ, 134ᵛ; *Expos.*, ff. 62ʳ–63ʳ; *Lib. Fig.*, Pls. XV, XVI.

41. L. Oliger, 'Documenta inedita ad historiam Fraticellorum spectantia,' *Archivum Franciscanum Historicum,* iv (1911), 697.

42. F. Tocco, *Studii Francescani, Nuova biblioteca di letteratura, storia ed arte,* iii (Naples, 1909), pp. 502–503.

43. B. Gui, *Manuel de l'Inquisiteur,* ed. G. Mollat (Paris, 1926), p. 146.

44. On this sect, see B. Gui, *De Secta Illorum qui se dicunt esse de ordine Apostolorum,* Muratori, *Rerum Italicarum Scriptores,* new series, ix, Pt. v.

45. *Summula seu Breviloquium super concordie Novi et Veteris Testamenti.* This text has been edited by Dr. Harold Lee and we hope to publish it shortly in collaboration. The references here are to MS. Brit. Mus., Egerton 1150.
46. *Ibid.*, ff. 9^r, 10^r, 11^v, 34^v.
47. *Lib. Fig.*, Pls. III, IV.
48. Ms. Egerton 1150, ff. 88^v–89^r. There is a second revolution depicted on f. 92^r.
49. Alexander V. Roes, *De Translatione Imperii,* ed. H. Grundmann (Leipzig, 1930), pp. 30–31.
50. P. Dubois, *De recuperatione Terre Sancte,* ed. C. Langlois (Paris, 1891), pp. 98–99.
51. The basic work on Roquetaillade is that of J. Bignami-Odier, *Études sur Jean de Roquetaillade* (Paris, 1952).
52. *Liber de magni tribulationibus . . . compilatus a . . . Theolosphoro* (Telesphorus of Cosenza) (Venice, 1516).
53. Not that a new optimism obtained everywhere. The old belief that the world must deteriorate before the End—based on Matthew, 24, v. 12—still maintained its hold. An interesting switch from optimism to pessimism is seen in the outlook of Henry of Langenstein, see *Prophecy,* pp. 425–427.
54. Unpublished. The only two MSS. known are in the Bibl. Angelica, Rome. See the summary by L. Pélissier, *De 'Historia Viginti Saeculorum' Aegidii Viterbiensis* (Montpellier, 1896); E. Massa, 'Egidio da Viterbo e la metodologia del sapere nel Cinquecento', *Pensée humaniste et tradition chrétienne aux XVe et XVIe siècles,* ed. H. Bédarida (Paris, 1950), pp. 185–259.
55. See his *Scechina,* ed. F. Secret (Rome, 1959).
56. On Postel, see W. Bouwsma, *Concordia Mundi: The Career and Thought of Guillaume Postel (1510–1581)* (Cambridge, 1957).
57. Translated Bouwsma, *op. cit.,* p. 271.
58. G. Brocardo, *De Prophetia Libri Duo* (Lyon, 1581); *Mystica et Prophetica Libri Levitici Interpretatio* (Lyon, 1580); *Mystica et Prophetica libri Geneseos Interpretatio* (Bremen, 1585); *The Revelation of St. John reveled . . .* Englished by J. Sanford (London, 1582).
59. *The Revelation,* ff. 32^v, 153^r.
60. See, for instance, W. Haller, *Foxe's Book of Martyrs and the Elect Nation* (London, 1963); W. Lamont, *Godly Rule, Politics and Religion 1603–60* (London, 1969); C. Hill, *Antichrist in Seventeenth-Century England* (Oxford, 1971).
61. J. Maxwell, *Admirable and notable Prophesies, uttered in former times by 24 famous Romain Catholickes, concerning the Church of Rome's defection, tribulation and reformation* (London, 1615).
62. Here he refers to a pseudo-Joachimist oracle: *Flores rubei aquam odoriferam distillabunt.*
63. See n. 36 above.
64. *Mirabilis liber* (Paris, 1522).
65. S. Campeggio (or Champier), *De Monarchia Gallorum Campi Aurei: Ac Triplici Imperio, vid. Romano, Gallico, Germanico: una cum gestis heroum ac omnium Imperatorum* (Lyon, 1537).
66. On Campanella's various changes of prophetic expectation, see *Prophecy,* pp. 387–389. The case for his latest hope—in the French monarchy—is argued in *Aphorismes,* published in 1635, reprinted by L. Amabile, *Fra Tommaso Campanella ne' castelli di Napoli, in Roma, ed in Parigi* (Naples, 1887), ii, pp. 291 *seq.*

Beowulf *as Heroic History*

Robert W. Hanning

ANYONE WHO STUDIES medieval narrative in all its varieties soon discovers how difficult it is to delineate the frontier between poetry and history in the age's representations of the past. Where does the realm of *res gestae*—however exemplary, idealized, or focussed by the lens of theology—end, and the realm of imagination, with its metaphors, symbols, and literary structures, begin? I would like in this essay to examine a happy consequence of this confusion of genres. There are, I would argue, certain medieval narratives which, though usually considered literary by modern criticism on account of their artful representation of the career and fate of great heroes, are also centrally interested in how such heroes and their deeds affect the needs and destiny of the society in which they act. For these works, the interaction between individual and social careers, as it develops in time, *defines* history, and their authors frequently attempt to elucidate the complexities of the interaction using the special resources of literary composition.

The text I will use to illustrate and justify these assertions about medieval narratives which I will henceforth call "heroic histories" is *Beowulf,* the Old English epic now generally recognized as a supreme literary testament to the heroic age. Before proceeding to analyze *Beowulf* as heroic history, I will address myself briefly to several necessary preliminary questions: 1) What was the range of relationships between poetry and history within medieval culture? 2) What were the motivations for writing about the past in the Middle Ages, and for taking special account of individual achievement within the record of history? 3) What other attitudes about the relationship between individual and social destiny are preserved in medieval narratives, in addition to the attitude I have just described as defining heroic history? The answers to these questions will help us appreciate more fully *Beowulf's* masterful coalescence of poetry and history around the figure of its hero, and will thereby enhance our overall understanding of how medieval civilization developed and used its sense of history.

As far as barbarian culture at the birth of the Middle Ages is concerned, distinctions between history and poetry are distinctions without a difference. The cultural inheritance of a preliterate culture assumes poetic form for mnemonic reasons, and eventually poetic content as well, as commemorated events become assimilated to common mythic and aesthetic patterns after having been transmitted orally across a number of generations.[1] But an oral culture does not consciously or theoretically separate poetry (as a literature of entertainment or mimesis) from history, biography, or exemplary, didactic literature. The versified public utterance of an oral culture depends neither on documents nor on eyewitnesses for its material, but on a traditional body of *res gestae,* the memorable deeds of heroes which, shared and applauded, keep alive the social group's sense of identity, and of the values it shares across tribal boundaries with other heroic-age nations.[2]

Once medieval barbarian society became Christian, and *a forteriori* literate, events from the past and the present could be recorded in documents, or copied down after having been preserved in the memories of first- or second-hand witnesses. There was now, in short, a separable body of "history" with which poetry could interact. At its simplest, this interaction took the form of recounting deeds done in the recent past in the language and style of an older tradition; the result was a self-consciously antiquarian hybrid of history and literature, such as we find in the application of oral-formulaic style to post-heroic age English history in *The Battle of Brunanburh,* or of classical poetic style to a description of the Norman Conquest in Guy of Amiens' *Carmen de proelio Hastingae.*[3] More complex is the adaptation of history to poetry which recasts the events reported not only into the language and style of an earlier tradition, but also into the system of values which animated that tradition and shaped its characteristic utterance. Thus *Maldon,* a greater Old English poem than *Brunanburh,* interprets an English defeat by the Danes during an Essex campaign of 991 a.d. in terms of an entire range of inherited, by then anachronistic heroic ideals.[4]

Only in the twelfth century did an indigenous, albeit derivative culture grow out of and express the actual situation of European civilization. Within this culture, the interaction of poetry and history became for the first time not learned or archaic antiquarianism, but the mirror (however idealizing or distorting) of a society and its aspirations. The poetic histories of Gaimar and Wace, commissioned by or dedicated to leading (female) figures of a new courtly class, are perfect examples of this important evolution in the impulse to graft memory and imagination onto a single narrative stock. Since the aim of this essay is neither to chart in detail nor analyze the chronological development of the grafting process, but merely to illustrate one particular instance of it involving heroism and history, I shall let these few examples stand as a mere suggestion of the complexity of the medieval poetry-history nexus, and move on to examine briefly another relevant context for my approach to *Beowulf:* medieval motivations for writing about the past.

Each age has its own reasons for historiography. I have already alluded to the metaphysical function, as it were, of the preservation and transmission of a record of deeds done in an oral culture. If we look at the Christian Middle Ages (within which *Beowulf,* at least in its extant form, must be placed), up to and including the twelfth-century Renaissance, we can distinguish three major historiographical stimuli, each of which contains reasons for pondering the place of individual achievement within the dynamic process of history. These stimuli were religious, political, and aesthetic, or, stated differently, exegetical, practical, and cultural.

The religious or exegetical impulse reflects the dominant force of Christianity in the period, and the fact that Christianity claims to be a religion doubly anchored in history. On the one hand, God, as Jesus, entered history at a given critical moment *(kairos),* and transformed its course and meaning. On the other hand, God has guided mankind through time from the Creation until Christ's coming, and will continue to guide it providentially up to his promised return at the final judgment of men and history. The Bible is the ultimate record of God's providential rule over history; however, other kinds of history could reveal that providence in action, and were therefore to be recorded. Universal history, conversion history, ecclesiastical history—all were, at different times and places, composed by Christians who held the central conviction that human history embodied and revealed the salvific scheme which was the most important fact of men's lives.

Since, however, Christianity also depended upon individual conversion to faith in the Son of God *(Metanoia)* it had a deeply personal side, reflected from a very early date in the commemoration of Christian heroes—first martyrs, then, once Christianity was an established religion, those who rejected the comforts of the *saeculum* for the physical and spiritual trials of the desert, and still later the holy monks and hermits (and even kings!) of medieval Europe. Given the unity of

Christian thought, and especially the unity of monastic culture which dominated early medieval intellectual life,[5] attempts were inevitably made to combine hagiography, chronology, and providential history. Bede's *Historia ecclesiastica gentis anglorum* was the greatest of such early medieval syntheses,[6] the aim of which was to clarify the unity of God's design for men and nations, thereby to educate Christians, and perhaps to help in the evangelization of nations not yet converted. This is why I call the impulse behind it exegetical; whatever the nomenclature adopted, however, it was clearly a matrix within which to form a model of the relationship between the Christian hero and the movement of national or ecclesiastical history.

With this religious or exegetical impulse there coexisted within medieval society—especially its institutional sector—intensely practical motives for writing history. In the early medieval period, the most developed or literate institutions were ecclesiastical, and in a period of intermittent instability, they had to work hard at maintaining their privileges, keeping up the spirits of their members, and rendering service in return for whatever help and patronage they could get from men of real power, whose morality and trustworthiness often left much to be desired.[7] All these tasks favored the creation of an historiography of self-interest. Monasteries, the institutions of which I am particularly thinking, needed to keep records of benefactions, of the benefactors for whose souls they must regularly pray, and of the deeds of their holy founders and patron saints, whose intercession against marauding Vikings and rapacious local lords was widely regarded as crucial. The sum total of the components of this practical or political historiography, translated from charters and oral traditions to narrative form, was a document which, by preserving the historical identity of a monastery, insured its institutional continuity as a "world within a world" in the minds and hearts of its members. One of the main functions of Book Three of Orderic Vitalis' *Historia ecclesiastica* (a monastic history on its way to becoming something else) is to stand as such practical historiography.[8]

A secular parallel to this impulse is the dynastic or national history used to establish the claims, forward the political objectives, or glorify the reputation of a ruling house. The Normans were understandably much involved in the production of this type of history, owing to the energy and brilliance with which they intruded themselves into the history of other places and nations. Wace and Geraldis Cambrensis were among its prominent practitioners. Needless to say, this impulse accounted for much of the patronage of historical writing by monarchs and magnates.[9]

The place of heroic individuals within practical historiography is as founders, saviours, and benefactors. Eponymous heroes, originators of dynasties, patron saints, *exempla virtutis* like Orderic's Abbot Thierry of St. Evroul at once make history more human and more inspiring to the audience for which the history has been written.

The third type of impulse to historical writing in the Middle Ages— what I call the aesthetic or cultural impulse—is a frankly catch-all category, reflecting my belief that, aside from practical and exegetical reasons, medieval authors did not undertake to write about past (or present) happenings with a single, well-defined motive. For example, the Norman Conquest inspired equally strong moral and celebratory reactions in Anglo-Norman historians like Orderic or William of Malmesbury, and these impulses are never reconciled in their works; in his account, Orderic borrowed extensively from the *Gesta Guillelmi* of William of Poitiers, a work whose strong bias in favor of the Conqueror he allowed to stand side by side with his own conviction that the true significance historians could derive from the Conquest was the sad theme of England's ruin.[10] Categories we commonly use today, such as social, intellectual, or political history, are too narrowly analytic to describe the catholicity which marked the medieval historian's use of source materials; conversely, an all-inclusive category such as "Boethian history," to include all non-theological historiography of the Middle Ages, limits our ability to distinguish among individual historians and their special interests.[11] From the twelfth century onwards, if not earlier, a variety of such interests can be deduced from much historical writing, reflecting political developments, the intellectual self-awareness cultivated via expanded programs of higher education, and the presence of a new, elite culture in Western Europe, thriving at centers of newly strengthened secular power. R. W. Southern traces a connection between objective and critical portraits of English kings by twelfth-century English historians and the fact that the political objectives of these monarchs took them away from England frequently and prevented the growth of uncritical national identification with the ruler. (France, with its permanently resident king, produced no such critical historiography at this time.)[12]

Another critical portrait, of Abbot Samson of Bury St. Edmund's by Jocelyn of Brakelond, reflects the author's sometimes unwilling compulsion to confront the mysteries of character, while the anonymous author of *The Life of Christina of Markyate* combines with his hagio-graphical and devotional interests a novel attempt to analyze character in terms of family and social history.[13] The vogue of following classical models for the pleasure of it, such as we perceive in William of Malmesbury's Suetonian royal portraits, and the genius of Geoffrey of Monmouth in creating the derivative and exciting fictional history of a nation reveal still other facets of the culturally or aesthetically moti-vated historiography which flourished in the high Middle Ages.[14]

Within this "historiography of display," if such we may call it, the virtuoso portrayal of the singular individual, the king, the hero, or the saint played an enormous role, as the examples I have just cited would suggest. The most obvious reason for paying so much attention to individuals was the satisfaction of purely secular curiosity about the quirks and vices of the famous, but this was by no means the only motive. Involvement with great men and secular history led some historians to consider how Fortune rules heroic careers, thus opening a new line of speculation about heroes and history which might or might not be Christian in its assumptions.[15] And, as I have already suggested, a new interest in the psychology of the individual played its part as well.

Having sketched the main motives which might lead the medieval historian to consider individual achievement within the context of social experience, I will now offer a third and last context for the consideration of *Beowulf* as a medieval heroic history by arranging in a spectrum the types of narrative available to a hypothetical author who wished to weigh the relative importance of personal and group destiny in defining the human condition. I distinguish four positions in this spectrum: at the extremes are narratives in which one or the other of the two components exerts little or no influence, while in the middle are forms which consider both hero and society in exploring the meaning of history, but with opposite emphases.

The first position is occupied by works so interested in an individual life, or parts of it, that they reduce to a minimum the role of society as a protagonist having its own temporal career or destiny. This heroic-biographical approach encompasses early medieval hagiography, twelfth-century chivalric romance, and works participating in both these genres, e.g., *The Voyage of St. Brendan, Guillaume d'Angleterre.*[16] The hero-saints of early medieval hagiography are conduits of God's grace and mirrors of his power.[17] The sections of the saintly career are highly standardized—pre-natal miracles, youthful dissipation, conversion, life of monastic or eremitic struggle, holy death, posthumous miracles—and episodes illustrating each of these phases are interchangeable from one life to another, indicating how little concern the authors and their audiences had for individuals in our sense of the term. But as precise chronological indications of any kind are usually lacking, and as the Church is present largely in the antitypal relationship between the hero and Christ, history in a temporal sense can hardly be said to exist either, except insofar as its secular representatives serve as foils for the saint.[18] So it is best to see these works as Christian documents in which a completely exemplary person embodies a lesson about God's power, the relevance of which for history, though undoubtedly subscribed to by the author, is present in the text purely by implication.

Even in the twelfth century, when holy individuals came to be seen within the context of their historical moment by sophisticated biographers such as the author of Christina of Markyate's biography, history in the larger sense rarely attained a position of autonomy within a biographical or pseudo-biographical narrative. In Gautier d'Arras' *Eracle,* a fictionalized account of the life of Heraclius, a seventh-century Byzantine emperor associated with the history of the Cross after its alleged rediscovery of Helena, the hero's historical role is not as important as his usefulness to Gautier as an exemplum of the importance of humility to a Christian life, and of the pervasiveness of illusory appearance in every aspect of human life.[19]

The chivalric romance, as it developed in the twelfth century, was equally lacking in a developed view of history with which the hero could interact. Arthur's court, the great gathering place of adventurous knights, is not only presented by Chrétien de Troyes as operating according to questionable moral and social values; it is also a world whose milestones are cyclical: Pentecost, midsummer's day, the (annual?) custom of the white stag. The only linear progress in this imagined universe is the personal progress of the protagonist, whose crises of self-awareness make possible private fulfillment through love, and thus give subjective meaning to his adventures in field and forest, and ultimately to time itself.[20] In *Cligès,* Chretien's one romance apparently set in dynastic history, the poet suggests that politics exists as a foil for the game of love, the disruptive power of which will shape history when given a chance. Another pseudo-historical romance, *Partonopeu de Blois,* uses its apparatus of Trojan and Frankish history only as an illustrative background for the poet's belief that the elevation of a plebeian to a position of power over the nobility will cause social disaster. In fact, only in the thirteenth-century "Vulgate cycle" of Arthurian romance does Arthur's chivalric society come to possess a history of its own (inspired by but much different from Geoffrey of Monmouth's Arthurian Britain) that exists in complicated tension with the personal history of its stellar personages: Lancelot, Guinevere, Galahad, Arthur himself. The result is the Middle Ages' first fictional (as opposed to traditional or archaic) heroic history, a generic innovation which deserves close study, but not here.

The next space in my hypothetical spectrum contains works which, while still biographically centered, present the hero's life in a much more complex context of social organisms moving in time toward their own destiny, over which the hero does not exercise complete control. History becomes a second focus of the audience's attention, and this in turn forces author and audience to consider in what relationship the one career stands to the other. This is the form of heroic history which I will shortly illustrate in some detail using *Beowulf,* and about which I will make one other preliminary remark after I have listed the other two types of narrative option available on the spectrum.

The first of these two is the historic narrative proper (as we traditionally think of it), a connected narrative of *res gestae* centered on a dynasty or other collective entity, within whose evolution one or more great men emerge to dominate the course of action for a longer or shorter period. Works of this kind loom large in the corpus of medieval narrative, especially since secular history was so often conceived of as the aggregate of the deeds of kings. It would be the job of another essay to comment on medieval dynastic history from the viewpoint of its handling of the hero-history relationship. My amateur's opinion is that medieval authors were most at ease in this type of narrative when treating the ruler as the instrument of God, and that any attempt to arrive at a more complex understanding of how character interacts with the march of history tends to be unsatisfactory because of its inconsistencies and, one might say, paratactic portrayal of character. This is not to deny the real merits of attempts like those of the Anglo-Norman historians to analyze twelfth-century kings of England as individuals and makers of history, but only to suggest that such medieval initiatives lack the sophistication and imaginative sweep which distinguish the historiography of Thucydides and Herodotus when treating great men like Xerxes, Alcibiades, or Pericles.

Moving on to the last category, at the opposite end of the spectrum from nearly ahistoric biographical genres, I distinguish a few medieval texts in which the centrality and integrity of an historical action quite overwhelm the importance of individual contributions to it, so that we come away from the narrative with the distinct impression that it has no heroes. I am thinking here not of works whose authors lack the talent or interest to create heroes, but of history understood as *gesta Dei,* a translation into events of the idea of the *ecclesia militans.* The examples I have in mind, the anonymous *Gesta Francorum* and Villehardouin's *Conqueste de Constantinople,* are crusade memoirs in which the conviction of being part of a divinely ordained undertaking results in the suppression of authorial individualism in recounting the course of events. The author of the *Gesta,* whose narrative takes form as a series of songs of praise to God,[21] seeks to present the liberation of Jerusalem as an event illustrating the Crusaders' battle cry: *Deus vult.* In such a scheme, the meticulous delineation of individuals and their deeds would be superfluous, even subversive. (This is also true with respect to the more popular function of Crusade memoirs, to function as travel guides to the exotic Holy Land.) For Villehardouin, the communal heroism of *Deus vult* is replaced by a simple dialectical analysis showing how the great undertaking of the Crusade, deflected by providence toward the seat of the Byzantine empire, nearly founders on the rivalry between those who wished to exploit the opportunities offered them by means of vigorous, joint action, and those who wished to sunder the host, allowing each part of it to seek the Holy Land by whatever route it chose.[22] For the Marshal of Champagne, it is precisely the inviolability of the host that matters, and while he certainly had strategic reasons for this conviction, it seems also to be the case that he saw the entire crusading force as the hero of his history, and regarded its fragmentation as a kind of death by dismemberment. His austere narrative style, and refusal or inability to make any of the leaders of the army stand out as heroes, follows from his view of Crusade history. (By contrast, the account of the same campaign by Robert de Clari, another participant, shows a much greater interest in the contribution of individual lives to the movement of history; it is this difference, rather than Robert's credibility or lack of information available to Villehardouin, which accounts in large part for the difference of impact between the two works.)[23]

Obviously, a writer seriously interested in the relationship between hero and history as a problem to be solved would have to opt for one of the two middle positions in this spectrum of narrative types, for only in them are both sides of the equation fully articulated. I have suggested that historical narratives in the medieval period did not have great success in offering solutions: by contrast, I believe that heroic histories, constructed around a core of individual experience, traditional or fictional, were sometimes quite successful indeed. *Beowulf* and *La Chanson de Roland* (which I hope to discuss as heroic history in a subsequent essay) are, among other things, intensely imagined chronicles of an *intersection* between a "chosen" individual, uncompromisingly dedicated to his destiny and endowed with powers and virtues that make him unique, and a world living in time. Works embodying this intersection principle in one or another literary form gained in impact during the medieval period because, it seems to me, they profitted from the resonance between their situation and the Christian mythos, i.e., the entrance of God into history, his death, resurrection, and departure, and the fact that the effects of his life did not cease when he was no longer visibly present. I am not suggesting that all medieval heroes-in-historical-contexts are Christ figures. They are, in a sense, "displaced" Christ figures (to use Northrup Frye's term),[24] but the displacement—into mortality, narrowness of vision, even sinfulness—makes the resonance I have just mentioned an ironic one as often as not—one that serves to indicate the gap between human history, however exalted by the presence of the hero, and God's power over the events of his created universe.

The other factor in the success of medieval heroic history is the fact that it is, as I suggested at the beginning of this discussion, an intersection as well of poetry and history; it presents the past using literary structures and metaphors that clarify meaning. By offering room for meditation on, as well as reporting of, the past, and on the possibilities for human achievement, it simultaneously reports, complicates, and explains the record of history.

Having now offered several generalities about, and perspectives on, medieval heroic history, I will pass on to illustrate and defend my conception of this type of narrative by looking at its greatest medieval representative, the archaic epic *Beowulf.*

Beowulf is an epic in which a Christian author attempts to embody for his Christian audience the attraction and limits of their pre-Christian heritage.[25] The poet[26] communicates his complex attitude by focussing on crucial moments in the life of a noble hero—moments in which the hero's virtues and destiny are both fatefully intertwined with and isolated from the destiny of a nation. In this world the Gospel is unknown; the intensely public yet intensely private figure of Beowulf can become, for a brief interval, the instrument of providence, but at the moment of his death the sadness and impotence which grips the heroic world testifies that this is history as yet unillumined by the promise of redemption.

All archaic epics (whose subject matter and verse form link them to the preliterate culture of an heroic age) have an ambiguous attitude toward their subject. They are the witnesses of a society's former greatness, and the conviction that the heroic age, now irrevocably ended, was a golden age as well often underlies their testimony.[27] But they are also, in their final form, the products of a literate age distinguished from what has gone before not only by the technique of writing, but by the social consequences of literacy: new habits of mind and learning, resultant changes in social structures and values. Eventually must come a revulsion against archaic culture in favor of "modernity."[28] At any moment in the early history of a literate society, a whole range of views about the past, from nostalgia through skepticism to downright condemnation, will coexist uneasily.[29]

In the case of the early medieval period, the situation is further complicated by the fact that literacy came to the barbarian nations as an adjunct of Christianity. For the Christian Anglo-Saxons, the ideological gap between their heroic age and their present state was absolute, a fact which received its most famous statement in Alcuin's rebuke to the Bishop of Lindisfarne in a letter of 797: *quid Hinieldus cum Christo* (what has Ingeld to do with Christ? cf. *Beowulf,* l. 2024f.). The heroes of the past were pagans; their salvation was to be doubted, and, seen in that light, their deeds to be regarded with suspicion or hostility.[30]

Alcuin's remark, however, represents an extreme view which is qualified by many other facts about Anglo-Saxon England testifying to the continuing claims of the pre-Christian past on the Christian present. From Gregory's advice to Augustine that he make Christian churches out of idol fanes, to the mixture of Christian and Germanic objects in the Sutton Hoo horde, to Aldhelm's singing heroic songs after Mass to get the attention of his congregation, to the survival of beliefs and artifacts relating to Germanic kingship cults, evidence abounds to prove the conscious and unconscious continuity of culture across the Conversion.[31] It has also been shown that admiration for the deeds of pagan ancestors, combined with a profound, evangelical belief that the continental (still pagan) Saxons were kinsmen who must be saved, would have encouraged Anglo-Saxons of a certain temper to imagine that pre-conversion heroes were patriarchal figures, Christian in virtue though not in belief.[32]

There is, in short, plenty of material at hand to demonstrate continuity *and* discontinuity as characteristics of the Anglo-Saxon view of the national and heroic past. Since that past was regarded even by its critics as historical—Alcuin objects to stories of Ingeld not because they are fabulous but because they deal with real pagans—there can be no doubt that *Beowulf* is to be read as an account of history. The complexity of the poem, and the perplexity of its critics, results from the fact that, unlike *Widsith, Beowulf* is not simply recalling the past as a body of exploits, but attempting to re-create it in order to pass judgment upon it from a point of view it never knew. Anyone who does not hold that lines 175–188 of *Beowulf* are a clumsy and discordant interpolation must logically see them as distancing the audience from the poem's world via the passing of a severe judgment, even though such a condemnation clashes with the reverent evocation of history as a common heritage in the epic's opening lines, or with the admiration reserved for Hrothgar in many parts of the story. (Even if lines 175–188 do represent a textual accretion, they would still reflect a widely-held attitude toward the pagan past, here invoked by an interpolator who has contemplated the imperfect knowledge and power of the Danes up to this point in the poem, and drawn an appropriate conclusion, as I shall shortly indicate.) Fortunately, the poet achieves distance and prompts judgment more subtly elsewhere, via structural and metaphoric techniques that allow him to explore the meaning and limits of heroism, of history in a heroic age, and of the interaction between hero and history.

The best place to begin discussing how *Beowulf* functions as a post-conversion essay in pre-conversion heroic history lies not within the poem itself, but rather within Bede's *Historia ecclesiastica,* in the famous simile of the sparrow by which King Edwin's anonymous councillor "expressed his sense of the futility of life, when darkened by ignorance and unillumined by hope." [33] The point of the simile, as allegorized by the councillor, is precisely that life without Christianity is lived in ignorance of whence we come and whither we go. Implicit in the image itself are two further points: one is that the world, as intuited by the pagan spokesman, takes the form of centers of light and warmth surrounded by the dark the cold, the unknown—in short, by adversary conditions; the other is embodied in a pattern of movement, the sparrow's unexpected entry into the known and experienced world, and equally abrupt departure from it, back into the world of mystery. Bede is defining the condition of the pagan Saxons as much by the image as by its exegesis. The sparrow flying in and out of the hall illustrates the random intersection which must seem to characterize the pattern of men's relationships with each other and with society (the hall) without Christianity to explain the significance of it all. Fortified with the Christian understanding praised by the councillor, however, cannot man understand not only his own life but also salvation history as a plan organized about the intersection of time and divinity? The image of the sparrow is provocatively Janus-like in its ambiguity: comprehended from a pagan perspective (as a Christian would imagine that perspective) it equates life with the disjunction and incompleteness of the individual's encounter with experience and history. From a Christian perspective, it recalls symbolically how man's earthly experience has been given meaning from beginning to end thanks to the entry of God into history and into each Christian's life.

I have belabored what may be obvious about this celebrated passage because the opening sections of *Beowulf* are in part organized around its image and its assumptions. The epic begins by recapitulating three intersections of mighty individuals with Danish history: the founder-king Scyld, the monster Grendel, and the young warrior Beowulf. Considered cumulatively, these intersections comprise a paradigm of possible impingements upon a nation's career by heroes (or their opposites). Taken sequentially, they provide a context within which to place and judge Beowulf's expedition to Denmark. Taken metaphorically, they offer a comment on the nature of pre-Christian existence.

Scyld Scefing, the epic's first hero, is found in a boat as a child, and grows up to become a mighty king of the Danes. Through his son, Beowulf, he founds a new dynasty, and when he finally dies, he is placed in a treasure-laden boat and sent back out to sea. The analogues of this episode—in genealogies or historical works[34]—usually, if inconsistently, link Scyld (or Sceaf, when the latter appears as the seaborne foundling) to the preceding Danish king, Heremod. And none of them describes Scyld's last, posthumous voyage. The *Beowulf* poet's mention that the Danes were without a lord for a long time ("aldorlease lange hwile," 11. 15–16) and his emphasis on the parallel between Scyld's lonely arrival and lonely departure (see 11. 43–46) establish a clear pattern of intersection, sparrow-like, between scyld and Danish history. Furthermore, he suggests divine providence at work, in that God pities the Danes and sends Scyld a son, to establish a dynasty, and also receives the king into his protection at life's end (ll. 26–27). Yet not only is Scyld's origin a mystery, but mystery surrounds his death as well, as far as his retainers are concerned:

> Men ne cunnon
> secgan to sothe,   sele-rædende,
> hæleth under heofenum,   hwa thæm hlæste onfeng.
> (Men cannot say truly, hall-dwellers, heroes
> under heaven, who received the burden; ll. 50-52)[35]

The contrast between the Danes' ignorance about Scyld and the poet's (and audience's) awareness of God's hand at work through him is thematic in this part of the poem, and parallels the contrasting meanings I suggested underlie the sparrow simile.

The next intersection is that of Grendel and Heorot. The hall, symbolizing Danish heroic triumph and suggesting in its newness and joy prelapsarian Eden (see ll. 90–101, where there is no clear syntactic separation of Heorot and its occupants from the world of the *scop's* creation song), again recalls the lighted hall of Bede's simile; its unexpected visitor is no sparrow, but a murderer cast in the ironic role of antithane, seeking the forbidden share of Hrothgar's treasure—men's lives.[36] There is a grotesque symmetry between Grendel's intrusion into Danish history at its zenith, and Scyld's appearance at its nadir; again, we know more of Grendel's origin, i.e., of his place in a divinely ruled world, than do the Danes, to whom the monster's habitat is also unknown:

> . . .men ne cunnon,
> hwyder helrunan   hwyrftum scrithath.
> (Men do not know where hellish spirits go in their
> wanderings; ll. 162-163. Note the cumulative
> force of the ignorance formula from l. 50 repeated in l. 162.)

Grendel enters Heorot each night and leaves the next morning; his depredations render the hall unfit for its purpose (see ll. 145–146), and bring about the third intersection of the sequence. Beowulf arrives unexpectedly from across the sea, stays just long enough to purge the hall of its demon and his mother,[37] and leaves again, presumably never to return. In isolation, Beowulf's arrival, exploits, and departure form a common heroic pattern, familiar especially in American western adventure stories, though unique among extant archaic epics. Linked to the similar patterns of Scyld and Grendel, Beowulf's career becomes, like Bede's simile, Janus-like: it recalls Scyld's arrival, it exposes itself to Grendel's night-time world of ignorance and impotence (in which the Danes cannot fend off their mysterious attacker, nor Grendel become a part of human society or know God's love),[38] but it also brings a new heroism, fatalistic in outlook yet touched by providence, among the Scyldings.

If we examine the first two hundred lines of *Beowulf* as a prologue to the hero's appearance, we must be struck by the ideas and images of disjunction, separation, ignorance, and imbalance which predominate. Scyld separated at birth and death from his world; Grendel, the *mearc-stapa* and *an-genga*, exiled from men and hopelessly unequal to God, but in turn far too much for Hrothgar to handle (11. 191–193); the prudent Dane (11. 138–143) separating himself from his own mead-hall to save his life; even the image of Scyld forcibly taking away the mead benches of his enemies (and thus prefiguring Grendel!)—all fit into the poetic pattern. The parts of the heroic world do not coalesce, but rather encounter each other for good or ill, and move apart. Throughout *Beowulf* there will be periodic recalls of the theme of ignorance—as in the description of Grendel's mother and her haunts (11. 1233, 1331, 1355, 1377, 1410)—or of striking images of imbalance and frustration, such as the poet's observation that Beowulf is too strong for the swords that should aid him (11. 2677–2687). Their recurrence suggests to me that the poet is attempting by means of them to present a true picture of pagan life, not simply as a compendium of heroic deeds, but as life lived without the understanding, control, and, ultimately, grace to make a manageable whole out of the *disjecta membra* of experience. The poetic imagination thus serves the exegesis of history.

Nonetheless, even from the beginning of *Beowulf,* God works to give unity, continuity, and hope to a world of men who coannot perceive his providence. He sends Scyld a son so that the experience of the heroic outcast can be transformed and extended beyond itself in time and space as dynastic history. Later, when evil strikes the Danes and their ignorance (11. 175–188, continuing the pattern of heroic ignorance established in 11. 50–52 and 162–163) prevents their turning to God for aid, a hero appears who will not only rescue them, but will thereby temporarily synthesize individual heroic imperatives (the quest for fame), social needs (the purgation of Heorot and the re-establishment of Danish communal life), and the divine purpose (the defeat of Cain's kin). In Beowulf's triumph over Grendel the poet sees a temporary denial of the fragmentation of pre-conversion existence.

The poet's technique in introducing his hero is to separate him clearly from the Danes in outlook, by means of set speeches and dialogue. Then the first *kairos* of the poem follows, when Beowulf and Grendel, having both intersected Danish history, intersect each other's career within Heorot, the symbol of that history. As the antagonists lock hands in deadly combat, their grip represents as well their fateful hold on the destiny of the Danes, and God's hold on them. The poem's energy, predominantly centrifugal up to this point, is refocussed inward on the hall, and Grendel's defeat liberates that energy for the celebration of Beowulf's incorporation into the Scylding world, until the advent of Grendel's mother, who seeks revenge, isolates him again. Space does not permit the close examination of the progression here sketched; a few comments must suffice.

When Beowulf first meets Hrothgar, it is in a daylight world of formality, courtliness, and sensuous clarity which in effect, though not in fact, Beowulf has brought into the poem with him, dispelling the atmosphere of gloom and ignorance in the first two hundred lines. (See, for example, the formal speech of the Danish coast guard to the arriving Geats, 11. 235–257, which is the poem's first instance of direct discourse, and the references to shining light in 11. 303, 311, 321.) The king responds to the sudden appearance of the Geatish warrior and his *comitatus* by recalling that Beowulf's father had come to Hrothgar too, needing the young king's protection after killing a man. Hrothgar settled the feud with money, and supposes that Beowulf has now come to return the favor. This explanation seeks to domesticate Beowulf's heroic energy and ambition, placing it within a continuity of obligations passed on from generation to generation, and within a system of settling feuds which obviates the need for heroic action—except when intruders like Grendel refuse to abide by the rules and reject the *wergild* system (11. 154–158). Beowulf communicates a very different sense of the situation, couched at first in language as courtly and diplomatic as Hrothgar's, but deeply tinged with fatalism as he confronts the possibility of destruction.[39] Challenged by Unferth about a past adventure, Beowulf exults in the strength which allowed him to survive lonely sea battles with deadly monsters, and then to complete his *gylpsprec* (boasting speech), turns on his challenger and the Danes, accusing them of cowardice toward Grendel and promising that it will be a different matter when he meets the monster (11. 499–606). The hero, as he prepares to meet his doom, thinks not of social obligations and family history, but of his separateness, indeed isolation, from other men, and offers as his credentials only his great strength. The image of Beowulf as the lone swimmer, battling *wado weallende* (the raging sea) and *mihtig meredeor* (mighty sea-monsters), differs so radically from Hrothgar's analysis of the hero's motivation that we are forced to acknowledge what appears to be an unbridgeable gap between the heroic impulse and the society into whose history it thrusts itself.

The encounter with Grendel transforms the atmosphere of the epic once again, however. Beowulf's titanic handgrip makes Grendel an emblem of division, even as it destroys the monster, by tearing off his arm; [40] the expulsion from Heorot of the creature whose evil both causes and represents human isolation makes it possible for the Danes to resume an effective social existence. The forms and rituals of heroic society then reach out to embrace Beowulf in the revived communal life. The Danish *scop*, celebrating Grendel's death, places Beowulf's exploit within an exemplary continuum of good and bad deeds done by heroes and villains (11. 867–915); later, at the feast of Heorot, Wealhtheow, hearing that Hrothgar has in effect adopted Beowulf (11. 1175–1176; cf. 1.946f.), symbolically assuming him into Danish dynastic history, offers gifts to the Geatish warrior and enlists his strength in support of her young sons, after the king's eventual demise. The climax of this process of integrating heroic and dynastic destinies comes when Beowulf, in taking leave of Hrothgar, promises to aid the old monarch with all his strength if need arises, and commits his lord, Hygelac, to the same enterprise. Hrothgar, in reply, predicts peace between Geats and Danes and Beowulf's eventual selection as king of the Geats (11. 1817–1865).

Before, during, and after Beowulf's two great fights in Denmark, we are reminded that he is also God's instrument, at least for a time. In this part of the poem, in effect, God is reaffirming his control over Cain's kin, whom he long since had exiled (11. 104–114; cf. 1258–1276). Beowulf trusts in God (11. 1270–1274), who rewards him with the strength to defeat Grendel (11. 696–702, etc.). The poet is careful to remind us that his hero receives grace in ignorance: Beowulf chooses to fight Grendel without weapons out of a desire to please Hygelac and a wish to match Grendel's own contempt for them (11. 433–440), not knowing, as we are later told, that the monster is invulnerable to them (11. 794–808). Beowulf, then, by God's design rather than his own, becomes the temporary means by which providence ordains the prosperity of the nation.

The precariousness of this synthesis of personal, national, and providential activity is as important a fact for the *Beowulf* poet as its existence. He suggests its limits even as he recounts Beowulf's triumphs in Denmark. Then, in the last section of the work, recording Beowulf's death, he completely reverses all tendencies toward harmony in heroic history, and offers instead a soured, ironic version of what has gone before, embodying a final sad assessment of a world without God as a world in which time and history are themselves negative concepts. To expound and sustain his pessimism, the poet chooses the poetic strategy of illuminating history via the metaphor of treasure, which he uses as an image of flawed achievement and human limitation. In Germanic society, treasure bore a heavy weight of symbolism, representing heroic worth, historic continuity, and the socially cohesive power of the ring-giving king.[41] In *Beowulf,* such symbolic resonances lend ironic force to each occasion on which treasure serves as a focus for a negative perception about heroes and history.

Three uses of treasure in *Beowulf* have special relevance to my argument. The first concerns the necklace Wealtheow gives to the hero in Heorot after he has killed Grendel (11. 1192–1214). The energies concentrated in that mortal battle have flowed outward into social rejoicing and, with the typical expansiveness of the epic vision,[42] into the recall of another great action of the past, the fight at Finnsburh (11. 1068–1158). The Queen, her own vision expanded to include the future of the Scylding dynasty and Beowulf's role in protecting it, offers him "heals-beaga mæst / thara the ic on foldan gefrægen hæbbe (the greatest necklace ever heard of, 11. 1195–1196). Now the narrator expands *his* memory and compares the necklace to the *Brosinga mene* of Germanic legend, which Hama stole from the Gothic tyrant Eormenric; having thrust his audience backward in time from the narrative present, he then pushes forward beyond that moment (though still in the audience's remote past) to recount Hygelac's last campaign against the Frisians and Franks, on which the Geatish king wore the necklace which Beowulf had in turn given him. Hygelac is killed, and the necklace passes to the Franks—and to lesser men, the poet informs us (11. 1212–1213)—as war booty.

The necklace establishes an *ad hoc* continuum among various points in history, and thereby puts Beowulf's recent triumph into new perspective. Hama's exploit at Eormenric's expense provides, like the deeds of Sigemund and Heremod, an exemplary comparison with Beowulf's loyalty to and reward by Hrothgar; the retrospection further enhances the Geatish hero's glory. But the leap forward in time deflates the heroic present by pairing the transfer of the necklace in Heorot with its passage from Hygelac's dead body into the possession of the Franks, and by suggesting that history's tide is as likely to bring treasure to *wyrsan wigfrecan* as to unconquerable heroes. The necklace, in effect, represents in its peregrinations the movement of history, in which moments of providential guidance and happy congruence between heroism and social need are balanced by disasters like Hygelac's raid, in which discrepancies between intention and result, or desert and reward, prevail.[43] Of all this the Danes are ignorant as they applaud the treasure-giving. Their applause (1. 1214; cf. Klaeber's note), coming at the end of the poet's meditation on the necklace-as-history, must ring with hollow irony in our ears.

As a work of art and a mnemonic device, organizing and linking episodes and making possible a re-creation of the past, the necklace is also an image of the poem itself. One may go further, and say that the necklace serves as a double metaphor expressing the relationship between poetry and history in an oral culture. These facts are equally true of the next treasure artifact I shall consider, the hilt of the sword with which Beowulf kills Grendel's mother, and which, minus its blade (the latter having melted in Grendel's poisonous blood), he brings back to Hrothgar when he returns from the monsters' swampy lair. When the hero makes his presentation, the poet makes much of the fact that the hilt came to Hrothgar after the death of Grendel, God's enemy, and his mother (*Godes andsaca. . . ond his modor eac,* 11. 1682–1683); Irving notes that "the fact of transference of ownership is insistently stressed. . .even to the point of awkwardness." [44] In the underwater world of isolated heroic action, Beowulf had discovered the sword in his hour of greatest need; thanks to its appearance of being a providential gift to the hero, it assumed an emblematic status, expressing the link between heroic strength expended in a just cause (the extirpation of monsters) and the divine blessing of that strength with timely success. Now, as it changes hands, it is a relic (*ealde laf,* 1. 1688) given to Hrothgar as a souvenir of the fact that Grendel challenged the Danes and was defeated. The king starts to speak, gazing at the hilt (1. 1687), but before his speech, the poet inserts a description of the artifact, wishing, I believe, that the audience should imagine Hrothgar contemplating the hilt and speaking simultaneously, and that the audience itself should keep before it simultaneously Hrothgar's "homily" (11. 1700–1784) and the testimony of the treasure.

On the hilt is inscribed the early history of God's battle against an alien race of giants whom he destroyed by a flood. Also commemorated in runes is the name of the warrior for whom the sword was made.[45] The hilt suggests a link in history between God's wrath and the first hero to use the sword; Beowulf, its last user, is a link in the same struggle in time against monsters inimical to the eternal God (*fremde . . . ecean Dryhtne,* 11. 1691–1962). And Hrothgar, beneficiary of Beowulf's exploit, appropriately becomes possessor of the object which, by its design and its use, preserves the record of this positive bond between hero and history. Yet Hrothgar makes no mention of the hilt, nor of its testimony, in his admonitory remarks to Beowulf. He warns the hero against pride, and especially against stinginess with treasures: the ruler who arrogantly refuses to share his hoard will be overtaken by his mortality sooner or later, and after his death, another will discharge his neglected obligations and distribute the gifts. In Hrothgar's account of an heroic ruler's duty, no reference to providence or heroism intrudes. Heremod, the arch-villain of Danish history, is the negative exemplum offered, and human life is characterized by its finiteness and by its custodial obligation toward the treasure which will in any case outlive its guardian. The Scylding's speech expresses the Germanic equivalent of a Victorian sense of duty; it lacks any trace of a providential view of history such as the sword hilt (and its last user) might prompt. Is the juxtaposition of the hilt and the homily not another reminder of the limits of the Danes' knowledge of God and his providence? No indication is given that Hrothgar understands the hilt's runic message; again, I believe, the poet has deliberately opened a breach between what his audience knows and what his characters know, with the hilt as its symbol.

Like the necklace, the hilt *is* history, metaphorically. Because it is bladeless, it can no longer make history; it is useful only as a work of art, *wreothenhilt and wyrmfah* (with twisted hilt and serpentine etching, 1. 1698), and as a tool of exegesis for those who understand it. In this respect it differs from other swords in *Beowulf* which both represent and make history, in the Finn and Ingeld episodes (cf. 11. 1138–1145, 2032–2062), by prompting remembrance of past evil and offering a means of revenge. The hilt is a metaphor for the heroic poem itself: a beautifully wrought testimony to the past and its deeds, sundered from its cutting edge, and thus recalling the break in time and outlook between the heroic age and its audience. Hrothgar's imperviousness to the hilt's message exemplifies the ignorance of providence which separates the pre-Christian past from the Christian present.

The treasure horde, guarded by a dragon, which Beowulf dies attempting to secure, is the poem's last and greatest comment on heroic history. The treasure, its guardian, and its would-be plunderer form the hub of the poem's last part, and if one sees *Beowulf* as having a two-part structure (as I do for the purposes of this paper),[46] then the role of treasure certainly supports Irving's contention that the two parts exist in ironic relationship to each other.[47] In the first part, history is "redeemed" at least temporarily by the action of the hero, and there is abundant suggestion that God has, for the moment, chosen the strong, noble, and fearless man as the instrument of his providence. The giving of treasure in this part—even when, as with the necklace, it involves long-range historical irony—expresses the social cohesion of the nation. Heorot, we recall, was built as an appropriate setting for Hrothgar's treasure giving (11. 67–73). Treasure also promotes social unity by settling feuds and rewarding heroes whose strength, having been turned against society's enemies, can now be honored and, as it seems, permanently bound to the service of the nation. In the last part of *Beowulf,* however, cohesion gives way again to isolation, disjunction, and impotence. Beowulf's obligations as king come into conflict with the heroic imperatives still operating within his old frame: he leaves his dwellings to fight the dragon even without his retainers, while they in turn (except for Wiglaf) desert him in his hour of need. The last survivor of a vanished race, cut off from men and from the pleasures of society, buries a treasure he can no longer use, and a helpless father mourns the lost companionship of his son, whom he is unable to save or avenge. Figures from the early part of the epic seem to reappear in grotesquely parodied form: Hrothgar, dispensing all possible treasure in his new hall, "becomes" the dragon, a stingy king in an old barrow, ready to kill to protect the integrity of his horde.[48] Beowulf receiving treasure from Hrothgar to bring home to his beloved lord Hygelac is metamorphosed, as it were, into an anonymous slave (*niththa nathwylic,* 1.2215) who steals a cup from the dragon's horde to make a peace offering to his estranged master.

Treasure, then, becomes the occasion for Beowulf's death, through the murderous wrath of the dragon, and with the hero's demise comes the downfall of the Geats, linked to their ruler's fate in another reversal of the bond between hero's code and nation's prosperity suggested in the earlier part of the epic. Treasure in this twilight world bears a curse (11. 3069f.); it is useless to men when not actually lethal (11. 3166–3168), and can easily overcome them all (11. 2764–2766). The relationship between the curse and the dragon is not made clear in the poem (nor is a curse mentioned in the famous dragon gnome of the Exeter Book), and I believe the poet is using both to make a statement about history, with which, as we have seen, treasure is closely and symbolically linked in his mind. The horde placed in the earth by the last survivor is the legacy of his society, the monument it has assembled and which outlasts it. Put differently, it is the burden of history which brings Beowulf to his fate through the agency of the dragon.[49] As a symbol of the status quo, the dragon is ready to destroy anyone who attempts to bring his horde back into the affairs of men; his angry reaction to the slave's intrusion is a kind of travesty of the way in which, early in *Beowulf,* history is forwarded and nations saved or tested by intersecting with individual careers. Now, to become involved in the dead society (i.e., the past without a present to relate to) is to unloose forces of chaos and self-destruction. Beowulf's catastrophic intersection with the dragon and the horde is a personal version of the Geats' destruction by the weight of history—the inherited enmities of neighboring nations—which the messenger announcing Beowulf's death so confidently expects. (Or one can reverse the terms and say that the Geats' experience with history is simply the social reflex of Beowulf's losing battle against devouring Time, represented by the dragon.) In each case, men, lacking control over history, find in it only the instrument of their mortality—the extension through time of deeds done, the consequences of which are fatal.

While this dark picture of human achievements and possibilities, limning a negative relationship between the hero and national history, is susceptible of generic analysis as a feature of what Stanley Greenfield calls "epic tragedy,"[50] in this case it is also another fruit of the poet's desire to portray an unredeemed world, denied the knowledge of the true end of history which might make sense of experience and guide action. I would support this contention in one last way by contrasting the negative paradigm of history embodied in the last part of the epic with a suggestively analogous, yet completely opposite, amalgam of heroism, history, and treasure in *The Dream of the Rood,* the greatest Old English religious poem. In the *Dream,* the cross appears to the dreamer alternating in appearance between a bleeding wooden "tree" and a golden, bejeweled treasure.[51] It tells the story of how it participated in the shame and disgrace of Christ's death. When Christ is buried, so is the cross; then it is discovered, raised up, and covered with treasure (*since gegyrwed,* 1. 23), and becomes to sinful man a promise of God's grace and joy in heaven in the next life. The sequence recounted by the cross comprises a movement into history (being chosen to bear Christ), then to disgrace, burial, recovery, final triumph, and exaltation to the status of blessed treasure, symbolizing the hope implicit in Christianity's view of history, redeemed by Christ's death and resurrection. This sequence is the reverse of *Beowulf's,* in which as time passes treasure receives a curse which eventually it discharges on an unsuspecting mortal. The cross becomes man's treasure; in *Beowulf,* treasure, as it were, becomes man's cross, the burden of mortality under which he finally sinks. One can suppose, though not prove, that a contrast similar to the one I have here sketched was in the mind of the Christian poet who gave *Beowulf* the shape in which we have it, even if he did not know *The Dream of the Rood;* such an inversion of orthodox salvation history would be (and is) a devastating commentary on the hero, and the history, of an age possessed of grandeur but denied the knowledge of Christ from which alone could come understanding and control of its destiny.

A reading of *Beowulf* such as the one I have offered bears witness to a sophistication of attitude about history which we do not normally associate with the archaic epic. Perhaps we have in general underrated the seriousness with which medieval poets of a certain stripe approached and sought to elucidate the relationship between their heroes, inherited and created, and history. Implicit in such striking poetic conceits as the two hundred year old Charlemagne bemoaning his lot as he answers the angelic call to duty at the end of the *Chanson de Roland* or Galahad leading the knights of the Round table on the Quest for the Grail while Arthur bewails the end of his chivalric fellowship is a profound desire to understand and represent the complex process through which men make and are made by the history of their age and society. We have not solved the problem of heroic history ourselves, so we would do well to look carefully at the insights offered us by medieval historians generally, and by medieval poet-historians in particular.

NOTES

1. On the phenomenon of the heroic age and the characteristics of its literature, including its relationship to myth and ritual, see Lord Raglan, *The Hero* (London, 1936, repr. 1949), esp. p. 12; H. M. Chadwick, *The Heroic Age* (Cambridge, 1912, repr. 1967); C. M. Bowra, *Heroic Poetry* (London, 1953); G. R. Levy, *The Sword from the Rock* (London, 1953); and A. C. Watts, *The Lyre and the Harp* (London and New Haven, 1969).

2. See esp. Chadwick, ch. 3.
3. Orderic Vitalis, *Historia ecclesiastica*, ed. M. Chibnall (London, 1969), bk. iii, pp. 184–186, commented that Guy's poem imitated the epics of Vergil and Statius.
4. *Maldon* has often been considered a faithful account of an actual battle, but see J. B. Bessinger, "*Maldon* and the *Oláfsdrápa:* An Historical Caveat," *Studies in Old English in Honor of Arthur G. Brodeur* (Eugene, 1963), pp. 23–35.
5. On monastic culture, see J. Leclercq, *The Love of Learning and the Desire for God*, tr. C. Misrahi (New York, 1961), esp. Part Three, 'The Fruits of Monastic Culture.' Also J. Décarreaux, *Les moines et la civilisation* (Paris, 1962), chs. 4, 6–8.
6. On Bede and his *magnum opus*, see C. W. Jones, *Saints' Lives and Chronicles* (Ithaca, 1947); the chapter on Bede in J. M. Wallace-Hadrill, *Early Germanic Kingship in England and on the Continent* (London, 1971); and R. W. Hanning, *The Vision of History in Early Britain* (New York, 1966), pp. 63–90.
7. For a fine, concise statement of the practical functions and obligations of Benedictine monasteries in their 'centuries of greatness,' see R. W. Southern, *Western Society and the Church in the Middle Ages* (Harmondsworth, 1970), pp. 223–230. The practical need for consolation in distress can be understood by recalling, for example, the flight of the monks of Lindisfarne from Viking attacks in 875, carrying with them from place to place the body of St. Cuthbert, their protector.
8. See esp. bk. iii, p. 22f., on the lives and benefactions of Giroie and his family, patrons of the monastery of St. Évroul.
9. See U. Broich, "Heinrich II. als Patron der Literatur seiner Zeit," in W. F. Schirmer and U. Broich, *Studien zum literarischen Patronat im England des 12. Jahrhunderts* (Köln and Opladen, 1962), p. 27f, esp. chs. 2, 3 and 6; this study emphasizes the practical considerations underlying royal patronage of literature.
10. See Orderic, Vol. II, introd., pp. xviii–xxi, and bk. iv, p. 190: conquered England "flebile tema de sua ruina piis historiographis ad dictandum tribuit."
11. On Boethian history see F. P. Pickering, *Augustinus oder Boethius? Geschichtsschreibung und epische Dichtung im Mittelalter—und in der Neuzeit* (Berlin, 1967); *Literature and Art in the Middle Ages* (London, 1970), pt. ii, ch. 3. I owe much to Prof. Pickering's work, though I do not ultimately agree with him.
12. "England's First Entry into Europe," *Medieval Humanism* (Oxford and New York, 1970), pp. 135–157, esp. pp. 147–151.
13. My colleague, Prof. Howard Schless, first turned my attention to this aspect of Jocelyn's work. C. H. Talbot, ed., *The Life of Christina of Markyate* (Oxford, 1959), esp. pp. 66–68.
14. On William's debt to Suetonius, see M. Schütt, "The Literary Form of William of Malmesbury's *Gesta Regum*," *English Historical Review*, 46 (1931), 255–260. On Geoffrey of Monmouth, see C. Brooke, *The Twelfth Century Renaissance* (London, 1969), and Hanning, *Vision of History*, pp. 121–172.
15. See Pickering, as in n. 11, above, and, for the later Middle Ages, W. Matthews, *The Tragedy of Arthur* (Berkeley and Los Angeles, 1960), chs. 4 and 5.
16. I borrow the concept of participating in a genre from T. M. Greene, *The Descent from Heaven* (New Haven, 1963), p. 9.
17. See R. W. Southern, *Saint Anselm and his Biographer* (Cambridge, 1963), pp. 320–323. Cf. Jones, *Saints' Lives*, pp. 51–64, 73–79.
18. On this type of hagiography see R. S. Loomis, ed. *Arthurian Literature in the Middle Ages* (Oxford, 1959), pp. 25–26, 54–55, and Wallace-Hadrill, *Kingship*, pp. 59–65.
19. On Gautier's free treatment of his source materials, see A. Fourrier, *Le courant réaliste dans le roman courtois en France au moyen-âge* (Paris, 1960), pp. 207-275. I hope to discuss the themes of the *Eracle* in a forthcoming study of twelfth-century chivalric romance.
20. See R. W. Southern, *The Making of the Middle Ages* (London, 1953), ch. 5, and

R. W. Hanning, "The Social Significance of Twelfth-Century Chivalric Romance," *Medievalia et Humanistica,* N. S. 3 (1972), 3–29.

21. The ending of each section of the work is constructed like a liturgical prayer; see, e.g., pt. iv, p. 64 (ed. L. Brehier [Paris, 1924, repr. 1964]).

22. See the edition of E. Faral (Paris, 1938), pars. 60, 64, 81, 95, 113, etc., where Villehardouin invokes "ceus qui volsissent que l'ost se departist."

23. See Clari's romance-like story of the perils of the Byzantine emperor Kyrsaac, chs. 18–28, and the account of how the cleric Aliaumes de Clari, Robert's brother, was the first Crusader to get inside the walls of Constantinople, ch. 76.

24. See N. Frye, *Anatomy of Criticism* (Princeton, 1957), p. 136f.

25. This approach to the poem was first taken by J. R. R. Tolkien, "*Beowulf:* the Monsters and the Critics," *Proceedings of the British Academy,*22 (1936), pp. 245–295, and is supported by D. Whitelock, *The Audience of Beowulf* (Oxford, 1951).

26. I have avoided the question of whether or not there was one literate poet who composed *Beowulf,* though I believe there was. Cf. the different view of the poem's literacy and Christianity in R. Stevick, "Christian Elements and the Genesis of *Beowulf,* " *Modern Philology,*61 (1963), 79–89, esp. 88.

27. Such a conviction suffuses the opening lines of *Beowulf,* and underlies the discrepancy between the strength of Homeric heroes and the strength of latter-day mortals.

28. The rejection of oral culture and its habits of mind is the subject of E. Havelock's fascinating study, *A Preface to Plato* (New Haven, 1963).

29. Homer's treatment of the gods and his affectionate but satiric portrait of old Nestor are instances of ambivalence about the heroic past in the *Iliad;* cf. Achilles' speech denigrating heroism in bk. xi of the *Odyssey,* which is, in effect, a rejection of a traditional ethic.

30. For an examination of the context and significance of Alcuin's remark, and others by contemporaries which support it, see E. G. Stanley, "Haethenra Hyht in *Beowulf,* " *Brodeur Studies,* pp. 136–151.

31. Gregory's advice is in a letter in Bede's *Historia,* i. 30; on Sutton Hoo, see the British Museum *Handbook* by R. L. S. Bruce-Mitford (London, 1968); Aldhelm's strategy is known only from the late testimony of William of Malmesbury. On Cultic reminiscences surrounding kings, see W. Chaney, *The Cult of Kingship in Anglo-Saxon England* (Berkeley and Los Angeles, 1970). There is much useful material on the persistence of barbarian traditions in early medieval art in G. Henderson, *Early Medieval* (Harmondsworth, 1972).

32. See C. Donahue, "*Beowulf,* Ireland, and the Natural Good," *Traditio,*7 (1949–1951), 263–277, and L. Benson, "The Pagan Coloring of *Beowulf,* " in R. Creed, ed., *Old English Poetry* (Providence, 1967), pp. 193–214.

33. R. Girvan, *Beowulf and the Seventh Century* (London, 1935, repr. 1971), p. 56. The simile appears in the *Historia,*ii. 13. Girvan notes the parallel between the simile and *Beowulf* in terms of nostalgia only. I am not suggesting the *Beowulf* poet had to know Bede's work.

34. See G. N. Garmonsway, et al., *Beowulf and its Analogues* (London, 1968), pp. 118–123. Most of the analogues were recorded at a date later than the composition of *Beowulf.*

35. All quotations are from F. Klaeber's text of *Beowulf* (3rd ed.; Boston, 1950).

36. On the ironies of sharing and dividing up, especially as they involve Grendel, see R. W. Hanning, "Sharing, Dividing, Depriving: the Verbal Ironies of Grendel's Last Visit to Heorot," *Texas Studies in Literature and Language,*15 (1973), 203–213.

37. The word used to describe the purgation of Heorot, *fælsian,* was also used in its intensive form, *gefaelsian,* to denote the purgation of sin through confession, and may be intended to suggest moral corruption in Heorot.

38. Such I take to be the import of ll. 168–169. Cf. W. Chaney's different but equally

appropriate interpretation of these lines in "Grendel and the *gifstol:* A Legal View of Monsters," *PMLA,* 77 (1962), 513–520.

39. Beowulf announces his intention to fight Grendel as a boon which he begs of Hrothgar (see esp. ll. 426–432). Heroic fatalism sets in at l. 438f., culminating in the famous gnome of l. 455, "Gæth a wyrd swa hio scel!" (fate always goes as she wishes).

40. The key word or concept here is *gedælan,* used to describe the monster's murderous intent toward the Geats (l. 731), and also his death (l. 805). Its basic meaning is to divide. Cf. note 36, above.

41. See E. Leisi, "Gold und Manneswert im *Beowulf,* " *Anglia,*71 (1952–1953), 259–273; the sections on treasure in the unpublished Ph. D. dissertation of M. D. Cherniss, "Pre-Christian Heroic Concepts in Anglo-Saxon Christian Poetry" (University of California, Berkeley, 1966); Chaney, *Cult of Kingship,* pp. 77, 136–137 on the king's *gifstol* as an altar; and Henderson, *Early Medieval,* pp. 35–57.

42. See Greene, *Descent from Heaven,* pp. 9–12, on epic expansiveness.

43. See E. Irving, *A Reading of Beowulf* (New Haven and London, 1968), pp. 31–42, on such discrepancies throughout the poem.

44. *Reading,* p. 146.

45. See Henderson, *Early Medieval,* pp. 54, 76–78, on possible scriptural inspirations for ll. 1688–1693 (the battle of the giants with God), and an illustration of a somewhat similar Norwegian sword, without a runic narrative etched on it.

46. But see D. R. Barnes, "Folktale Morphology and the Structure of *Beowulf,* " *Speculum,*45 (1970), 416–434, which offers a convincing three-part structural analysis.

47. *Reading,* pp. 192–246; I am much indebted to this fine discussion, especially its perceptions about the contrasts of the epic's two parts, and about human limitations as a theme of Part II.

48. See *Reading,* p. 209, on the dragon as a bad king, and cf. Chaney, *Cult of Kingship,* pp. 128–130.

49. Irving, *Reading,* p. 213, stresses the heaviness of the treasure in the last survivor's speech.

50. "Beowulf and Epic Tragedy," *Brodeur Studies,* pp. 91–105.

51. There is much useful information on the Cross and treasure in the introduction to M. Swainton's edition of *The Dream of the Rood* (Manchester, 1970), esp. pp. 42–58. Cf. Henderson, pp. 204–208. In developing through several versions, this essay has profited from the advice and criticism of my wife, Prof. Barbara Hanning, and my friend and colleague, Prof. Joan Ferrante, my obligation to whom I am delighted to acknowledge.

The Trouble with Muscovy

SOME OBSERVATIONS UPON PROBLEMS OF THE COMPARATIVE STUDY OF FORM AND GENRE IN HISTORICAL WRITING

Edward L. Keenan, Jr.

GREAT-RUSSIAN HISTORIANS have had some difficulty deciding upon a periodization for what they are pleased to call "Russian" history; no conceptually helpful definition of "the Russian Middle Ages" has been put forward.[1] In view of the readily demonstrable fact that Slavic cultural history is a part of the general development of Christian European culture, it might well be a matter of some consternation to the comparativist, as well as to the historian of Russia, that repeated attempts to "align" Muscovite institutions with those of the West, or to bring her development into "phase" with Western cultural history, have been at best brilliant and appealing hypotheses, and more commonly hindrances to the progress of historical understanding.[2]

There exist several good reasons why historians have had difficulty in bringing together into a systematic frame of comparison their individual flashes of recognition. The first is that with rare exceptions, historians have been rather vague—and sometimes careless—about defining just what, in various periods, is to be understood as "Russia." Although the essential reality of East Slavic cultural community cannot be denied, it is most important to remember that before modern times there was not one, but many "Russias." Each of these regional cultures (one might conveniently associate them with towns: Kiev/Chernigov/ Pereiaslav-Volyn'/Halych; Polotsk/Novogrudok/ Vilna; Novgorod/ Pskov; Vladimir/Suzdal'/Moscow) had its own *Blütezeiten;* at different times each of them was "in phase," to a greater or lesser degree, with developments in different regions of the larger Christian world. The multifocal and episodic nature of the East Slavic cultural experience is particularly important in considering Muscovy-Suzdalia. While the latter-day predominance of Moscow and its rather distinctive amalgam of East Slavic cultural features is similar in some ways to that of London or Paris and their regional cultures, in earlier times (until the latter part of the fifteenth century) Muscovy's position with regard to the other regional centers was not comparable to that of the latter capitals within the English and Frenchspeaking worlds.

A second impediment to an understanding of "Russia's" place in the European world arises from the general neglect of a primary feature of East Slavic contact with the rest of Christendom. This contact was discontinuous and shifting; different groups of East Slavs, had, at different times, different cultural "trading partners" in the West, and each of these "trading partners" represented, at the specific time of most significant contact, a distinct local cultural "mix" within the general development of European culture. Indeed, since these "partners" (one thinks again, for brevity, of towns: Okhrid, Prague, Krakow, and a number of Baltic and Balkan towns) were themselves often peripheral and provincial centers, one might say that the various East Slavic regions were episodically influenced by a discontinuous series of rather disparate "Wests," at different stages of the latter's development.

A final factor in our inability to conceive a suitable *chronological* scale of comparison probably has to do with an underestimation of the intensity and speed with which Muscovite culture—historical thinking included—ultimately assimilated—and re-assimilated—the Western cultural "package" in the latter part of the seventeenth century.[3]

I would therefore suggest that, for matters with which this paper is concerned, the "Muscovite" period (ca. 1450–ca. 1650) is most apt for comparison to the Western Middle Ages (whose definition I leave to specialists). I would advance three justifications for this view: 1) the configuration of the sources; 2) the methods required in their study; 3) some rather striking similarities of historical writings of the "Muscovite" period to those of rather early medieval historians in the West.

Sources for the study of Muscovy before ca. 1650 represent what might be called a skewed medieval assortment; while much less historical writing seems to have disappeared since the Muscovite sixteenth century than, for example, since the Norman eleventh, less (in terms of numbers of texts, not copies) was apparently produced, and the first impression of the total source base is rather similar. Strikingly few manuscripts of any kind aside from standard liturgical and other religious texts seem to have been produced in the Muscovite culture area before the fifteenth century, and almost no works of original significance have come down to us from that time and territory. As to acts and charters, while scattered individual texts from earlier periods exist, the historian possesses—and can confidently posit the existence of—systematic series of tax, service, and diplomatic records from no earlier than the last quarter of the fifteenth century.[4] As an illustration of the quantity of information available to the modern historian—leaving aside for the moment the *Stand der Forschung*—I would say that we know no more about the family and court of Ivan the Terrible (d. 1584) than we do, for example, about the merchants of London in the thirteenth century.

The pattern and nature of our sources, then, require, strange as this may seem, that my colleagues and I employ the methods developed in Western medieval studies to study sixteenth-and even seventeenth-century Muscovite culture. Diplomatics, paleography, and philology are our constant handmaidens; reconstruction and close reading of texts, still our most fruitful device. We still await our Mabillon and Montfaucon, but we are muddling through, and as we do, it becomes increasingly clear that there is an inexorable inner logic in the fact that we confront an essentially "medieval" configuration of sources, and must rely on the tools of the medievalist. In the way it seems to have ordered its life and conceived of human affairs, in, to use the linguists' term, its "deep structures," Muscovy was a medieval society.[5]

I should point out that among specialists in Muscovite history it is widely believed, and frequently argued, that the extant sources represent but a pitiful remnant of a vanished abundance of documentary and literary sources, and that, were they but available, the lost materials would permit—nay, require—the juxtaposition of the Muscovy of Ivan IV ("The Terrible") with with Elizabethan England or Machiavelli's Italy. While I sympathize with—and have experienced—the Jungian wish that underlies such convictions, I must nonetheless point out that no sufficient evidential justification for them exists, and that to proceed within the context of such beliefs leads to the production of pernicious nonsense. Had such documentary and literary treasures ever existed, the nature and configuration of their vestigial remains would provide evidence of the fact. Indeed the extant sources do quite explicitly tell us what has been lost, and one need hardly be a skeptic to conclude that most of what has left no palpable trace probably never existed.[6]

Historians of the Muscovite "Middle Ages" are thus left in a rather paradoxical position with regard to sources and method. By contrast with historians of Minoan or Roman civilization, who must deal with rather richly elaborated cultures on the basis of obviously fragmentary information, historians of Muscovy must adjust their thinking and methods to the problems of understanding a rather archaic and fragmentarily articulated culture that is reflected in what appears to be an almost fully representative but of course not complete assortment of sources. As often as not, the silence of *our* sources is not the silence of the ages but of Muscovy itself. With specific regard to historical thought, it seems possible at present to state that there is no reason to believe that any major text of the Muscovite period has been lost, or that any significant stage or aspect of historiography is not represented in our extant sources. This being the case, one may offer the Muscovite material as a rather valuable case which permits comparative judgments concerning how a national Christian historiography develops at a very early stage, a stage nowhere else, to my knowledge, so well represented by extant sources.

I

The only historiographic tradition worthy of the name in Muscovy until the threshhold of modern times was annalistic. Sharing with Ukrainian, South Slavic, and Roumanian chronicles a striking and confining dependence upon a few limited number of late Byzantine annalistic works, Muscovite chronicle-writing had a relatively late, slow, and diffuse development.[7] Although one may follow the steady diffusion of the earlier (XII–XIV century) Kievan and Novgorodian chronicles throughout East Slavic territory, the earliest known *Muscovite* copy of the "Primary Chronicle" was made no earlier than the fourth quarter of the fourteenth century.[8] Although the next century saw the rediscovery of additional older codices and regional continuations, along with some modest annalistic jottings in Muscovite monasteries, it appears to have been not until the time of Ivan III (1462–1505) that any significant specifically Muscovite history-writing can be identified.[9] This reign was a period of unprecedented expansion and prosperity for Muscovy, capped by the conquest and partial assimilation of Novgorod and other older East Slavic cultural centers.

Historians usually associate the flurry of chronicle-writing in the latter part of Ivan III's reign with the emergence of Muscovy as a leading state in Eastern Europe, and with its new perception of itself as the only surviving seat of Orthodoxy.[10] Certainly the annals of the late fifteenth and early sixteenth centuries aspire, to a greater extent than did their predecessors, to be national—or, more precisely, dynastic chronicles. Consistent with the national-dynastic tendency of the period was the relative lack of interest on the part of Muscovite annalists in non-Muscovite history, particularly the Byzantine history which had played a more significant part in the earlier regional traditions. [11]

But while such departures from earlier tradition can be noted with regard to content, the earlier Muscovite chronicles did preserve the traditional, strictly annalistic, form. The features and limitations of this form are well known: it was characterized by a strictly year-by-year exposition, often so slavishly adhered to as to interrupt a narrative account; the seemingly haphazard inclusion of descriptions of miraculous occurrences and meteorological oddities, and the verbatim copying and conflation of earlier annalistic jottings. In this period, for example, when a chronicler had a number of annalistic or narrative sources covering a single time-span, he would break them down to the irreducible unit, the year-entry, and then introduce the fragments under the appropriate years. This procedure led, of course, to repetitions of the same entry under two different years, or even of two accounts of the same event under the same year. The result was as much a string of annalistic beads as it was a "history."

Colleagues unfamiliar with the Muscovite material might facetiously comment that certain modern historians do much the same thing. More seriously, they might wonder whether Muscovite historians, despite their retention of the traditional form, were not in fact more sophisticated in their thinking about history than the form of their writings might indicate. I think not. Form and conception seem here to have been in harmony. Muscovite annalists of the early sixteenth century inscribed their "years" without revealing any articulated conception of "history" as an abstraction, or as a systematic study distinct from the simple recording of the past. Like that of other Christian historians, of course, their view of the history of Man was millennial and providential, but neither this, nor any derivative philosophies of history was developed in any explicit way by the compilers of the annals. There was no Slavonic word equivalent to *"historia"*—the modern *"istoriia"* entered Slavonic and Russian in the late sixteenth century. [12] Nor did early sixteenth-century Muscovite annalists, by contrast with even rather early Western historians, attempt explicitly to justify their enterprise, or to comment upon the significance of the events they were recording. They had no need, apparently, for a word for "history,"

since they were not moved to comment on its purpose, its nature, or
its significance.

Let us, for illustration, recall the beginning of the prologue of Otto
of Freising's *Deeds of Frederick Barbarossa,*

> "This, I think, has been the purpose of all who have written history before us: to
> extol the famous deeds of valiant men in order to incite the hearts of mankind to
> virtue . . . etc."

and offer for comparison the beginning of one of the major Muscovite
chronicles of the period of which I speak:

> "The Slavic nation was of the tribe of Japheth called Nortsy, who settled along the
> Danube, where now are Hungarians and Bulgarians, and from there they spread
> out upon the land and were called by their own names (according to how) they
> settled in which place . . . "

Assuming that our two authors were similar in temperament, vocation, and intelligence, one must conclude that the difference between
them is not simply that Otto had read Tacitus (cf. *Annals* III, lxv) and
the Muscovite had not, but that Otto had a generalized conception of
history while the Muscovite chronicler—who never (my example may
not sufficiently reveal this) makes a single comment, or abstraction, or
generalization, about the broader significance of his material—did not.
Muscovite annalists of this period cannot be assumed to be, in terms
of their historical *Weltanschauung* and historiographical sophistication,
counterparts of any but the earliest medieval annalists of the Christian
West.

Thus the "gathering of the Russian chronicles" which followed the
"gathering of the Russian lands" under Ivan III produced a shift of
emphasis to the affairs of Muscovy and its princely house, and a rather
fuller catalogue of events, but did not immediately lead to major formal
innovations or conceptual improvements upon the preceding chronicle
tradition. In the context of later developments, however, this period of
activity can be seen as an important stage in the evolution of history-
writing in Muscovy. As a result of the rather intensive work of copyists
and compilers, a more or less common corpus of historical information
and formal models was made widely available in Muscovy, and the
simple presence of the codices begun at this time was a challenge to
later generations to write both "histories of the new times" and "new"
histories.

It should be noted that the increased interest in the past during this
period was not accompanied or immediately followed by the introduc-

tion of translations or originals of other historical literature, Western or Eastern, Latin or Greek. The brief vogue for Western, chiefly Italian, culture at the court of Ivan III, the architectural vestiges of which remain, under layers of later alteration, in his Milanese Kremlin, seems not to have involved translation, and the flirtation was in any case ended by political complications after 1500. No native historian in Muscovy in the early sixteenth century appears to have known enough Greek or Latin to translate foreign histories, a deficiency which was probably not painful, since Muscovites were by all indications unaware of their existence. [14]

II

As the sixteenth century progressed, the Muscovite state, its court, and the Great-Russian monasteries grew in power and affluence, and began to manifest that odd combination of satiety and hunger known as "growing cultural needs," including the need for bigger and better histories. In particular, the court itself seems to have begun to show greater interest in chronicles and their production, which activity had been previously exclusively the occupation of the monastic clergy.

One notes changes, towards mid-century, in the breadth of the historical material embraced by the Muscovite annals and in the nature of the sources utilized. Having "absorbed" the material of regional Great-Russian traditions, the Muscovite annalists broaden their field of vision to include other Slavic lands, and show a tendency toward the "universal history"—the "universe" being still essentially the world of Orthodoxy. [15] At approximately the same time, Muscovite annalists gain access to archival materials of the grand princely chancery, and begin rather extensive citation from documentary, particularly diplomatic, materials often without translating the latter into the Slavonic that had been *de rigueur* for annalistic texts. At the same time, chroniclers began increasingly to include portions of literary and hagiographic works in their compilations, inserting them—since everything had to *sub* one or another *anno*—wherever it was possible to associate the events described with a corresponding chronicle account.

But this expansion in size and scope seems to have been accompanied by neither formal nor conceptual change; the old annalistic frame held up, even as some "years" bulged with added material and others contained the fragments of dismembered *vitae,* scattered according to the chronicler's ability to determine when one or another event of a

109

saint's life had occurred. Indeed, of the great sixteenth-century chronicles, as of their less ambitious antecedents, one can say that their principal conceptual principle was chronology and their only formal feature the year-entry. They were, like Christian history, a seamless web of "years," stretched, in theory, from the Beginning to the End, and they had no formal or topical limits.

That chronicles grew so rapidly in size during this period was an indication of the new intellectual demands and potentialities of a rapidly developing national culture. That they became unwieldy, as scraps of *vitae,* accounts of miracles and hailstorms, martial tales and fragments of diplomatic correspondence were hung on the "years," like a shapeless pile of clothing on a coat rack, is a reflection of a lack of analytical historical imagination and of the late development of the Great-Russian system of genres. For there were, quite simply, no other forms of history in the Slavonic mode [17] and very few narrative forms in general—the *vita,* the homily, the tale—none of which was developed in the secular historical tradition. In fact, there being no firmly established narrative genres for secular prose literature, the the chronicle—though it preserved its traditional form, its essentially ecclesiastical language, and its implicit salvational message—became in effect the omnibus medium for non-religious narrative prose. No "histories," i.e. thematically limited accounts treating the development or rise and fall of separate nations, cities, races, dynasties, or individuals, were produced in Muscovite Slavonic before ca. 1600. (The fragmentary tales *(povesti)* which seem to be first efforts in such a genre were simply hung on the "coat rack" of the chronicle.) As a result, the chronicle—which was formally infinitely expandable—grew, by the second half of the sixteenth century, to utterly monstrous proportions.

Under the leadership, apparently, of the Metropolitan Macarius (1482–1563), there was organized an ambitious literary and historical enterprise which at once produced the greatest compilation of them all, revealed the *cul de sac* into which the chronicle form had been led, and generated the first native attempts to reconceptualize the writing of history.

We know very little about Macarius as a person,[18] but it is clear from the works he sponsored that he was a man of the grand, if not necessarily subtle vision, a talented organizer, and very successful fund-raiser. Having gathered scribes, illustrators, expensive materials, and manuscript sources from throughout the land, he set about producing what amounted to two great encyclopedias, one literary and the other historical. The first had as its objective the gathering and standardization of *all* texts "read in the Russian land" and their reproduction, in the form of a "Great Menology" *(Velikie chetii menei)*. In part, the accomplishment of this undertaking required that numerous *vitae* and other independent texts be detached from the earlier omnibus chronicles in which they had been embedded. Having unburdened the chronicle of this belletristic load, those engaged in Macarius' enterprise turned to the production of an historical encyclopedia which would contain every known historical account—every year-entry—organized in the traditional annalistic form. The result was the massive "Nikon Chronicle," thousands of pages in large folio, accompanied, in the best-known copy, by *16,000* illuminations. For reasons that remain obscure, the production of the illuminated version, the "Illustrated Codex," was never completed, and we see it today with some of its later illuminations cartooned but not colored, and the very last only sketched. [19]

A similarly abrupt end seems to have come to another project of the same period, which is of rather greater interest to the present discussion. At roughly the same time, apparently, as the artisans brought together by Macarius were laboring over the "Illustrated Codex," other scribes and illustrators were producing a new kind of history book, the *Book of Steps*. This work was much more modest in conception—a mere 1,400 pages in *folio*—but extremely interesting from our point of view, since it was the first major Muscovite work to break away from the annalistic form. The *Book of Steps* replaced the chronicler's chain of years with an organization by reigns, and the unit of the "year" with chapters, each of which dealt with but a single theme. That the author [20] limited himself to the description of events related in much greater detail in the antecedent omnibus chronicles, and used language rather more archaic than that of his contemporaries has led scholars to pass over the significance of the *Book of Steps*. As a historical source, it is, to be sure, not of great value, but as a specimen of historical writing its interest is immense.

At a stroke,[21] the author of the *Book of Steps* both shed the annalistic form and vague millennialism of its predecessors, and introduced a new conception of the historical process. He focused his attention not upon the record of the working-out of God's design, but upon a single development—the rise of the native dynasty— and he underscored this change of conceptualization by introducing a new organization— "steps," or generations—which supplanted the years of the Creation with a temporal frame that suited his interest in the dynasty and the unique historical process of its rise. The context and lexicon remain, of course, deeply Christian (in an Introduction, itself an innovation, it is said that the seventeen "steps" form a golden staircase which leads to Heaven). Providence and Christian exemplarism play an important, though not extensively elaborated, part. But if God is not dead, Man has here begun to come alive. Individual figures, the princes of the House of Moscow, princes of the Church, and even anonymous seers and counsellors of princes here fleetingly emerge as flesh-and-blood personalities. In portraying the deeds, psychological development, and interrelations of the princes, the author is aided immensely by his decision to discard the annalistic frame. The rigid adherence to this convention in the Slavonic chronicles had not permitted any discussion of causality that might require discussion of an event under any year other than that in which it had occurred. Now, for the first time, events that occurred in different years, but had, in the author's view, some causal or conceptual interrelationship, could be brought together in a single place and used to explain some particularly significant episode or historical process.

Now such a change in form can hardly seem to students of Western historiography a soaring leap of intellect, but it was an important innovation for Muscovite history-writing. In particular, the linkage of formal and conceptual innovation in *The Book of Steps* is noteworthy in the context of our discussion, because it illustrates a basic feature of the Muscovite material: namely, that until the ultimate abandonment of the native tradition in favor of new (Western) forms, any attempt at innovation in the conceptualization of the historical process required formal innovation, as well. In the context of the restricted Slavonic system of genres, this was an all but impossible condition.

III

There being some question as to the date of the "Illustrated Codex" and the *Book of Steps*," one can only speculate upon the circumstances which led to the abandonment of two such grandiose projects sometime around 1600. One might pause, however, to consider their significance in the development of Muscovite history-writing. The authors of these works were clearly historians whose sensibilities differed from those of their predecessors, notwithstanding their textual dependence upon the earlier chronicles. They sensed, apparently, the need to relieve the chronicle of the literary and hagiographic baggage which it had come to bear, although they were not successful in eliminating it entirely. The author of the *Book of Steps* sensed the formal impediment to historical writing created by the annalistic grid, and, while actually writing little new material, he edited his sources, within his new framework, in a radically new way.

But striking as these efforts might appear against the background of what had preceded them, they must seem "naive" or "primitive" by comparison even with early medieval European historical writing. The reasons for this are clear. Late sixteenth-century Muscovite historians were operating in a narrowly defined national framework, even more provincial than that, for example, of the early Norman historians. The context of their immediate historical experience was limited, in effect, to a single historical event—the rise of a new nation and of a vigorous new dynasty.

I should like to stress the significance of this fact for the specialist in Russian history. For these works are quite specifically Muscovite—not "Russian." Their authors clearly perceived a single, central and national historical process—the growth of their little forest principality into a vast empire. It is true, of course, that they copied the texts of the Kievan and Novgorodian chronicles, and they knew the story of the decline and fall of those two empires—but these events were remote in both time and space, and did not strike deep into their consciousness.

In the "Illustrated Codex," for example, there is little in the entry for 1241 A.D. (the year of Batu's capture of Kiev) that would indicate that the sixteenth-century chroniclers attributed any momentous historical significance to the fall of Kiev and the establishment of the Golden Horde. Nor does the text reveal that these events formed a part—even a paradoxical or asymmetrical part—of the authors' conception of the history of their own nation. It is arguable indeed, that sixteenth-century Muscovite historians did not really conceive of these events as part of their own history, and were therefore not moved to ponder the causes of the fall of Kiev or the perversities of fate—it was not their fall or their fate.[22]

There is, apparently, a second reason for the relatively naive and primitive nature of Muscovite history-writing: leaving aside the obvious biblical examples and tales of the fall of Constantinople, (which was seen in a rather limited context) Muscovite historians had never read any other nations' histories, nor any which attempted to address the more puzzling problems of the forces which shape the affairs of men and empires.

In comparing an early sixteenth-century annalist with Otto of Freising above, I mentioned that the former had not read Tacitus. He was not exceptional in this regard. Indeed, I know of no evidence that *any* Great-Russian before 1600 had read Tacitus, or Thucydides, or Herodotus, or Eusebius, or Baronius, or *any* major non-Russian history in the original, in translation, or in synopsis. And the few late Byzantine chronicles that were available in Slavonic translation were by no means replete with historical abstractions and historians' questions.

It is for these very reasons that late sixteenth-century Muscovite history-writing provides such interesting material for comparative observations. While most primitive or provincial schools of history writing in the Christian West are represented by a limited number of texts, here we have abundant material—a dozen or so different major compilations in hundreds of copies. The study of this material can lead to certain useful observations concerning the conditions which produce or foster truly historical modes of thought. In particular, it points up the importantce of the "culture of history"—that leavening, essentially scholarly, tradition which transmitted certain historical techniques of perception and analysis throughout the Christian West. The Muscovite case reveals how great was the importance of such a tradition, which, like the secret of the grape, was readily enough assimilated once introduced, but could not be spontaneously rediscovered, even in a time when great quantities of historical materials were being intensively copied and compiled. There seems to be only one possible explanation for the paradox of the production in Muscovy of such an enormous mass of annalistic writing apparently so lacking in what we would call a historical mentality. Muscovite annalists, although quite familiar with the record of the past, had never seen a history book.

IV

At the end of the sixteenth century there occurred in Muscovy a series of calamities that transformed the national historical consciousness. The catastrophic period known as the "Time of Troubles," which began with Ivan the Terrible's seizure of power from his able ministers sometime around 1560 and did not end until the establishment of the Romanov dynasty in the second decade of the seventeenth century, not only swept away the world in which Great-Russian historians could satisfy themselves and their readers by telling the tale of the rise of Muscovy, but left the small literate society of Muscovy shattered, unsure of itself, and in need of historical explanations for what had taken place.

The decades after the Time of Troubles produced the first glimmerings of what we may somewhat condescendingly call a true historical consciousness among Muscovite writers. The establishment in a ruined land of a new dynasty, about whose rise there was almost nothing to be said, the fresh recollection of a Golden Age (Ivan's reign appeared as such, in spite of later calumniation), the occupying presence of Catholic Polish and Protestant Swedish armies, tangled memories of civil war and social upheaval, a thousand inexplicable events posed for thinking Muscovites the real historians' questions—how, and why.

It is, somewhat paradoxically, precisely because the Muscovite literary culture provided few fit vessels for the bitter wine of all of this intense recent experience that Muscovite seventeenth-century history writing presents an exceedingly apt material for our discussion of form and genre. Could the shattering and chaotic events of the Time of Troubles be marshalled into the quiet and orderly ranks of the annalists' "years?" Could one continue a *Book of Steps* leading nowhere, or start a new one about a dynasty whose first representative was still on the throne?

From the very beginning of the century many of those who were writing history were asking much more sophisticated questions and finding more complex answers than had their predecessors. One perceives, in spite of their rather oblique forms of historical expression (about which more shortly), that they were addressing themselves to such questions as what it means when a dynasty comes to an end, whether a nation needs one, and how best to establish one. In particular, the figure of Ivan attracted considerable attention, and, whether to praise or to condemn him, many authors had to consider both the role of the individual in history and the influence of personal tragedy upon the affairs of state. It would not be taking interpretation too far to say that the authors of the post-crisis period also paused over such new questions as the causes of social upheaval and Muscovy's place in European culture.[23] But how were these questions to be posed and discussed? How was the story of the recent past to be told? What of form and genre? Indeed, what language to use? The ponderous Slavonic of the liturgy and the old chronicles? But it was a language few could compose in with ease, which had no developed genre for the true "history" or the political treatise. The "plain style" of the chanceries? It was, true enough, closer to the vernacular, but it was utterly lacking literary genres, and lexicon of abstractions, and poorly developed as a language of exposition (as opposed to narrative and command).

The choice of linguistic medium was inextricable from the choice of genre, since the two cultures of Muscovy, the ecclesiastical and lay, had remained remarkably isolated from each other. The notion of a chronicle, homily, or *vita* in the chancery style, or of bureaucratic paper in Slavonic was as difficult to entertain as is for English speakers say, the religous lyric in limerick form.[24] And yet the new historical consciousness of Muscovites was bursting to find expression.

It is fascinating for the specialist, and perhaps generally instructive, to observe how different authors attempted at this time to find or create forms for their historical questionings and statements. One can only be struck both by the ingenuity of the writers and the tyranny of the system of genres within which they labored. They tried everything: histories of the "troubles" written in the traditional Slavonic and in the forms of Miracle tales or even as *vitae;* vignettes in the form of false chancery letters; historical songs; and a broad range of other genres.[25]

The "plain style" and the forms of the chancery were used, for example, for a peculiar kind of history-writing—the production of spurious letters and documents of state, often attributed to Ivan the Terrible, and apparently intended both to present a certain view of that ruler's personality and to capture a moment in history with a kind of time-capsule verisimilitude. Such works were apparently produced within the chancery culture itself, by clerks who were familiar with the older diplomatic, and who had access to original documents of the time they were attempting to evoke. These authors were also, apparently, aware of the vogue for the spurious "Royal letters" among readers of the popular *Flugblätter* in the West. These spurious documentary texts can be most deceptive, and they must be studied with a scepticism not always characteristic of Great-Russian historical science. But, as is shown by the case of one such text, long thought to be a letter from the Khan of the Golden Horde, but in fact a rather sophisticated poem, they are not always to be dismissed as mere forgeries.[26] The primary objective of their authors was quite obviously not to deceive, but rather to evoke or recapture a historical moment in one of the forms—in this case a kind of court poetry in the chancery plain style—available to them.

Other, more complex literary forms were employed by writers of history at this time, and, as in the case of the spurious documentary texts, the unusual combination of form and author's purpose has been somewhat disorienting for later historians. The so-called *History of Kazan',* for example, is the first systematic history of the rise and fall of a state to be written in Muscovy. It is also, however, a kind of chivalric romance written in a rather literary Slavonic, which fact creates a difficult problem of perception and definition for the modern historian. What is one to make of this text? It is a long work—100 chapters—whose author was apparently a layman, someone at home in the grand princely archive and in the language of the chancery. But, unlike the great majority of his class, he was schooled in Slavonic as well and he knew the great chronicles of the sixteenth century. His subject was broader than the title would suggest; he was interested not only in the Muscovite conquest of the once-mighty Khanate of Kazan, but in the larger process by which Muscovy succeeded to the position of the once-glorious Golden Horde. He had a very sound historical appreciation of the magnitude of such an event, and of the significance of Muscovy's acquisition of control over the Volga. He was well-informed about the internal political structure of the Tatar khanate, and he had a good sense of the significance of various turning points in Muscovite-Kazani relations. Indeed, his periodization and conceptualization of these relations has dominated Russian interpretations of this subject for three hundred years.

But in spite of the historicity of the author's conception, the form he chose was in essence a literary one. One might even conclude that he intended his history primarily as literature, as a pleasant tale of chivalry.

For in eschewing the annalistic genre, and choosing that of the chivalric romance, the author of the *Kazanskaia istoriia* seems to have found himself bound by the conventions of his genre, and obliged to introduce principles of conceptualization and interpretation that create a dissonance with the historical modes of thought that clearly underlay his original conception. Previous annalistic accounts of the struggle between Muscovites and Tatars had treated it as primarily a Christian/pagan confrontation, and had ascribed every victory or defeat to Divine intervention. Our author is clearly more secular and pragmatic, and, while perhaps somewhat inclined to portray Christians in a more favorable light than Muslims, certainly does not view the history of Muscovite-Kazani relations exclusively in the light of confessional or racial conflict. Nor is the chief mechanism of history, for him, the Divine Providence. But he replaces the traditional view not with a system of historical forces, but with a moral universe moved by essentially chivalric principles. In his universe, the noble are everywhere victorious and the base, whether Slav or Tatar, are defeated; the brave,

Christian or Muslim, triumph, while the cowardly are destroyed; a man true to his master and to his word, whatever the other circumstances, wins out. Nor are we to consider this author a historian who, like many ancient and early Christian historians, had a notion of the mechanisms which shape human affairs that was somewhat at odds with what we are pleased to call reality, or should we see his work primarily as *belles-lettres*—a good early historical romance? I am inclined to the latter view, both by the essentially chivalric universe of the work, and by the observation that our author chose Slavonic—the literary language—but *not* the chronicle form. But perhaps it is best for the present to resolve the matter by concluding that our question is illegitimate and anachronistic. For to a Muscovite historian of the early seventeenth century, who still had not learned of most of the ancient and early Christian historians, to whom a literary system in disarray offered a single secular narrative, historical genre—that of the chronicle—who had no notion of treating history as a branch of science or learning (for there were no schools), the distinction simply did not apply. He was barber and surgeon and dentist in one, and we shall be hard put to separate his roles.[27]

V

I should like to conclude these brief remarks on Muscovite historical literature with some remarks on what might be called a pseudo-medieval history, the "History of Ivan the Terrible" apparently written by an unknown seventeenth-century author who used the pseudonym of Prince Andrei Kurbskii.[28] This text is of particular interest as a specimen of historical writing for the fact that, although it appeared rather late in the seventeenth century, at a time when one may discern the beginnings in Muscovy of modern historical writing, its author was apparently attempting to write history as Andrei Kurbskii (ca. 1528–1583) might have written it, i.e. he was imitating what he thought to be the style and genre of sixteenth-century histories.

The identification of this conscious attempt at archaism allows us some insight into its author's conceptualization of history and history-writing, and into his perception of the history-writing of the earlier time. It appears that he had hoped, by describing the reign of Ivan in the words of a contemporary, to influence public opinion in his own time—the 1670's—by relating how a strong-willed and corrupt king, whose prerogative was unchecked by the beneficent influences and

118

regulating power of a service nobility, could bring even the most glorious kingdom to ruin (and incidentally, a lot of nobles to an early grave). He hit upon the *persona* of Andrei Kurbskii, a Muscovite boyar who had defected to the Polish-Lithuanian Commonwealth in 1564. Since a number of rather varied spurious writings of the intervening century had been attributed to Kurbskii, who apparently was himself not a writer, our author had no problem of imitating any single characteristic literary style. But his choice of *persona,* together with the decision to write a "History" did create a number of very difficult problems of content and style for him, as we shall see.

The models and sources which the author had at his disposal can be established from textual comparisons, and presumed from what is known about the *milieu* in which the history seems to have appeared. He quite apparently knew some late versions of the mid-sixteenth-century Muscovite chronicles, and we may be equally confident that he knew at least some portions of a rather important "modern" Muscovite work—Andrei Lyzlov's "History of the Scythians"— since he copied roughly a sixth of his work almost verbatim from Lyzlov's. [29]

On the basis of a snippet of the then-recent translations of Guagnini's and Stryjkowski's histories and of Pamphilus Eusebius' *Chronicle,* which appear in most manuscripts that contain the *History,* and from our knowledge of the intense translation activities in Moscow in the 1670's, we may surmise that the author was also familiar with a variety of neo-Byzantine, classical, and Renaissance writings.

But while Kurbskii's *History* is obviously shaped by such readings, and reveals by its chapter form and post-Ciceronian East Slavic creole a considerable similarity to these late seventeenth-century translations, its author seems to have had a relatively primitive notion of what history is and how histories are written, and little whatsoever of how history had been written in Kurbskii's time.

Thus, for example, while "Kurbskii" quite explicitly was setting himself the kind of historical question long typical of Western histories (i.e. the fatal consequences for a nation of flaws in the character of the king), and apparently intended to write a history of Ivan's whole reign, he seems neither to have known that no Muscovite historian in Muscovy in Ivan's and Kurbskii's time had posed such questions, nor to have considered the other implications of his choice of *persona.* Indeed, it appears that the author quite simply blundered. Most of the events he wanted to describe occurred *after* Kurbskii had left Muscovy, and no special *piquance* could be added to the narrative by having "Kurbskii" recount, from a supposed distant exile, the cruel tortures of the second half of Ivan's reign. There is evidence that the author finally became aware of this contradiction half-way through the job, but decided to see it through.

When one turns to the consideration of form and genre, the contradictions of the *History* emerge even more clearly. In setting his Moscow-educated "author" in Lithuanian exile presumably around 1570,[31] the real author of the *History* gave himself two options: he could have "Kurbskii" write as a Muscovite of the period would have, in Slavonic, in annalistic or *khronograf* form, or *a la Polonaise,* in the style of the chronicles of Guagnini or Stryjkowski etc. (in Muscovite Slavonic translation, of course).

But what emerges from an examination of the form of the *History* is that its author was successful in imitating neither of these genres. His account is organized neither in the strictly chronological order of the Muscovite annals nor in the more episodic form preferred by the late sixteenth-century Polish chroniclers.[32] In fact, consideration of the form and genre of Kurbskii's *History* permits a rather startling and helpful observation—the Muscovite historical writings that most closely resemble it from the formal point of view are the late seventeenth-century accounts of *contemporary events,* like *"Sozertsanie kratkoe let 7190 i 91 i 92 v nikh chto sodeiasia vo grazhdanstve,"* sometimes attributed to Semeon (Sil'vestr) Medvedev,[33] or Andrei Artamonovich Matveev's *Istoriia s sovershennym ispytaniem i s podlinnym izvestiem o smutnom vremeni. . . "*[34] The author of Kurbskii's *History,* whoever he was, was almost certainly a contemporary of these authors, and in choosing his genre—or rather Kurbskii's—he was bound by the conventions of his *own* time. He made his putative sixteenth-century author write according to the formal conventions of a very special, ephemeral, and rather amorphous genre—the "underground" contemporary, eye-witness account of the last quarter of the seventeenth century.

VI

Historians in medieval Muscovy shared with their Western counterparts a Christian view of Man and of the universe, and knowledge of the limited portion of the Christian historical tradition that had come to Muscovy in the transmission of earlier translations from ninth-and tenth-century Byzantine chronicles. By comparison even with early

Western medieval historians, however, they worked in a limited cultural and historical environment: Muscovy's own historical experience before 1600 had been neither of long duration nor rich in variety; her historians had meagre knowledge of the historical record of other societies and scant acquaintance with the works of the major Christian historians. There was, moreover, no native tradition of formal education in the Western sense, i.e. we know nothing of regular schools, nor even of any systematically elaborated monastic scholarly traditions.

These limiting factors seem to have been responsible for two salient features of Muscovite historical writing which invite comparison with Western phenomena. The first is the striking influence of the immediate national experience, which seems not only to determine the stages at which societies are most likely to display heightened interest in history-writing, regardless of whether antecedent scholarly or literary traditions provide the techniques and forms for it, but also to establish the conceptual terms in which it will be framed. There is nothing novel about this observation, but it is perhaps worth noting that the rule applies in a marginal case, where external influences are minimal.

Evidence for such a view is provided most particularly by the profound revolution produced in Muscovite historical thinking by the traumas of the end of the sixteenth and beginning of the seventeenth century. The impressions created by the end of the only ruling dynasty the East Slavs had known, the collapse of effective political power, and the following decades of calamity produced a leap—in fact a number of leaps—of historical imagination and sophistication that are in many respects quite remarkable.

But the examination of the written records of the effervescence and inquisitive energies of the early seventeenth century leads to our second major observation: inherent limitations of the archaic Muscovite system of narrative genres and the absence of any school tradition of historical writing determined that no entirely suitable means for the expression of the statements and questionings of Muscovite historians would be found until certain other seventeenth-century processes (in particular the introduction of Western historical and scholarly traditions) had run their course. However fascinating and appealing the poems and travesties and romances and false relics of the period may be (when seen in their proper context), however emphatically we insist upon their underlying historicity and their importance as evidence of the emergence of a new Muscovite historical sense, there can be no denying that they failed their authors as forms of historical expression, and led nowhere. In later generations those Great Russians who were moved to write about history rejected these antecedents, and adopted in its entirety the cultural "package"—form, genre, and theory—of western historical writing.[35]

Many of the stages here outlined—the simple chronicle, the chivalric history, the various verse and other "oblique genre" compositions—have some interesting analogies in Western history-writing of the Middle Ages, especially of the earlier period and more northern regions. Indeed some of the cases might seem to Western medievalists somewhat banal. I would propose, however, that they are of some interest for the fact that the Muscovite case seems to be the most amply-documented example of a primitive and relatively autonomous national historiography in Christian Europe, and offers (since we also possess rather complete information about certain other features of Muscovite cultural life) the possibilitty of observations not possible in the analogous cases.

One does, however, encounter a paradox at this point. For it appears that our ability to evaluate or interpret the historical thought represented in "oblique" genres is more limited in the case of Muscovy than in other cultures. One might even posit that our ability to make confident judgements about such sources is inversely proportional to our need to rely upon them. For in dealing with a culture which provides its historians, their readers, and modern scholars a well-articulated system of forms and genres—a system that includes, in particular, a variety of forms of historical narrative and theoretical works *about* history, we, like the authors' contemporaries, can perceive their very choice of form or genre as a part of their "message," and confidently interpret that choice in the context of what they chose *not* to write. This observation seems to be true even for cases in which we might possess only fragmentary remnants of the literary-historical system in question.

But when the system of genres itself is shown on the basis of relatively complete information to be fragmentary or poorly established, no such confidence in our perception of an author's intent and the quality of his historical thought is possible. It is not clear to me, for example, that we are on firm ground in attributing to a Muscovite writer of fabulous or "oblique" accounts the kind of historical knowledge and sophistication which, as Mr. Hanning has shown, characterized the work of Geoffrey of Monmouth.[36]

One is left, then, with a problem of interpretation whose solution depends not so much upon form, or genre, or the analysis of information, but upon our knowledge and appreciation of the literary and scholarly context. It seems that ultimately it is the knowledge of this context which will establish the limits of our ability to evaluate the historiographical significance of "oblique" genres, as it has established, for example, the bases for different appreciations of primitive art, on the one hand, and modern primitivism, on the other.

And thus we come to the "trouble with Muscovy:" the fact that we simply know, and probably can know, too little of the literary and scholarly context in which most of the works we have been considering here were created to be confident of any interpretative judgment about Muscovite medieval historiography. We have determined from its general outlines the nature of the beast, but we have still to establish a positive identification. And the possibilities suggested thus far embrace an interpretative range as broad, to return to the analogy with art history, as that bound by the aurochs of Lascaux on the one hand, and Picasso's bulls on the other. While I incline, as is obvious from the remarks above, toward the former analogy as the more apt, I am not assured that we shall in this generation have an understanding of the Muscovite cultural matrix sufficiently precise and profound to permit any definite identification.

NOTES

1. Some notable suggestions and perceptive observations with regard to historians' methods and conceptions of their subject, together with particularly valuable comments on form and genre, are found in numerous works by D.S. Likhachev, particularly *Russkie letopisi i ikh kul'turno-istoricheskoe znachenie*, (Moscow, 1947), and *Chelovek v literature drevnei Rusi* (Moscow-Leningrad, 1958).

2. One may refer to almost any of the periodic controversies about periodization, (such as that conducted in various journals in the late 1950's), about feudalism (G. Vernadsky, "Feudalism in Russia," *Speculum* XIV, 302–23, and L.V. Cherepnin, *Kritika burzhuaznykh kontseptsii istorii Rossii perioda feodalizma* (Moscow, 1962), or absolutism (see the current discussion in *Voprosy istorii*), or to articles which develop aspects of comparative/synchronic treatment of Muscovite history, e.g., the original but ultimately unconvincing essay by the late Michael Cherniavsky, "Ivan the Terrible as Renaissance Prince," *Slavic Review*, vol. 27, 1968, 195–211.

3. For a summary English-language treatment of some of these processes, see, V.O. Kliuchevsky, *A Course in Russian History; the Seventeenth Century*, translated by Natalie Duddington (Chicago: Quadrangle Books, 1968).

4. The recent republication of the earliest inventories of the grand princely arhive (made in the 1570's and in 1614) makes it clear that no earlier series existed, or, more precisely, was extant in the sixteenth century. See S.O. Shmidt, *Opisi tsarskogo arkhiva i arkhiva Posol'skogo prikaza XVI–XVII vv.* (Moscow, 1960).

5. It is worth noting in this connection that although the first printing press began operations (which were soon interrupted) in Moscow in 1564, printing was a strictly controlled ecclesiastical and government monopoly until the eighteenth century,

and that with the exception of laws, military manuals etc. only religious materials were printed until the time of Peter the Great. The first Muscovite printed primer appeared in 1634; the first history in 1709; the first native *belles-lettres* in the 1730's.

6. A thorough discussion of one aspect of this problem, the mythical library of books in Greek and Latin thought to have belonged to Ivan IV, can be found in S.A. Belokurov, *O biblioteke moskovskikh gosudarei v XVI stoletii* (Moscow, 1898). Belokurov shows quite convincingly that no such library ever existed.

7. I shall for the purposes of the present paper limit myself to the discussion of chronicles in the narrow sense, leaving the so-called "Chronograph" tradition for later treatment. D. S. Likhachev has argued eloquently for consideration of the influence of the Chronograph tradition upon that of the chronicles, and points out, for example, that the Chronograph permitted the kind of lattitude of theme development and chronological cross reference which we shall discuss below. The difficulty one finds in accepting Mr. Likhachev's views on the relationship of the Chronograph to the dominant chronicle form and tradition arises from three considerations which can be briefly stated: 1) the first version of the Chronograph was written not in 1442, as Likhachev believed, but at the very end of the fifteenth century (or perhaps the beginning of the sixteenth: B.M. Kloss ("O vremeni sozdaniia russkogo Khronografa" *Trudy otdela drevnerusskoi literatury,* vol. 26, 1971, pp. 244–255) argues for 1488–1494, but one may question his latter date); 2) while the first Chronograph was clearly not composed by Pakhomii Logofet, as Likhachev thought, it does display South Slavic traits of language and editing, and in any case it remained alien to the main tradition of Muscovite history writing. (Kloss' work shows that many of the examples of stylistic "influence" of the Chronograph on Muscovite chronicles must be explained by positing the reverse relationship: the author of the Chronograph used some Muscovite chronicles.) The Chronograph form did not strike root in Muscovy until the very end of the sixteenth century (redactions of 1599 and 1601) and became dominant only at some much later time; 3) the complex relationship of the various versions of the Chronograph to one another remains for practical purposes unexplained—the pioneering work of A. Popov, *Obzor khronografov russkoi redaktsii,* 2 pts. (Moscow, 1869), having had no continuators—and until such fundamental matters as dating and textual history of the various Chronographs are explained, it is somewhat fatuous to speculate upon influences, historiographic traditions and the like.

8. G.M. Prokhorov, "Kodikologicheskii analiz Lavrent'evskoi letopisi," *Vspomoga-tel'nye istoricheskie distsipliny,* IV, Leningrad, 1972, pp. 77–104.

9. It is true that since A.A. Shakhmatov's classic works of reconstruction, scholars have assumed the existence of Muscovite compilations dating from the earliest decades of the fifteenth century, but no contemporary copies or conclusive proofs have been brought to light. The earliest indisputably Muscovite chronicles seem to have been compiled in the 1480's or 1490's. See A.N. Nasonov, *Istoriia russkogo letopisaniia XI-nachala XVIII veka* (Moscow, 1969), Chapter Ten.

10. Ia. S. Lur'e, "Novye pamiatniki russkogo letopisaniia kontsa XV veka," *Istoriia SSSR,* No. 6, 1965, 113–131.

11. I speak here only of the chronicles of the period ca. 1480-ca. 1520, i.e. the so-called "Codices" of 1479, 1495, 1497, the *Simeonovskaia, Ermolinskaia, Tipografskaia,* and associated texts. On the Chronograph, see note 7, above.

12. M. Fasmer, *Etimologicheskii Slovar' russkogo iazyka,* vol. II, p. 143.

13. The first words of the "Chronicle of 1497," *PSRL,* XXVIII, 13.

14. For information concerning Muscovite knowledge and translation of Greek and Latin works, see Belokurov as cited in note 6, above, and A.I. Sobolevskii, *Perevod-naia literatura moskovskoi Rusi-XIV-XVII vekov,* (St. Petersburg, 1903).

15. For a discussion of the contents and composition of the Nikon Chronicle and the

Litsevoi svod, see A.E. Presniakov, "Moskovskaia istoricheskaia entsiklopediia XVI veka," *Izvestiia Otdeleniia russkogo iazyka i slovesnosti imp. Akademii nauk,* vol. 5, book 3 (1900), 824–76 and O.I. Podobedova, *Miniatiury russkikh istoricheskikh rukopisei* (Moscow, 1965).

16. Likhachev, *Russkie letopisi . . . ,* 354–375, contains a useful discussion of the relationship between court records and the chronicles, but a number of fruitful lines of inquiry remain unexplored. It appears, for example, that the documents that were used in the composition of the "Letopisets nachala tsarstva" *(PSRL XIX)* are precisely those which are *missing* from the otherwise complete books of Nogai and Crimean diplomatic records, i.e., that they were removed from the archive (after the first inventory of 1575?) by the authors of the chronicle and not returned.

17. One must here again exclude the Chronograph from our generalization, for the reasons cited in note 7.

18. There is no modern biography; I.I. Smirnov's *Ocherki politicheskoi istorii Russkog gosudarstva 30–50–kh godov XVI veka* (Moscow-Leningrad, 1958) contains (pp. 194–202) a sketch of his political career.

19. Podobedova, p. 148.

20. Probably, as Vasenko thought, the deposed Mitropolitan Afanasii (D.G. Vasenko, "Kto byl avtorom 'Knigi Stepennoi tsarskogo rodosloviia'?", *Zhurnal Ministerstra narodnogo prosveshcheniia,* vol. 244, No. 12 (1902), pp. 289–306.

21. A number of authors have mentioned the possible influence of the Serbian Životi kraljeva i archiepiskopa Srpskich (Published by Dj. Daničić (Zagreb, 1866) and L. Mirković (Belgrade, 1935)); the matter merits detailed investigation.

22. The later struggle against the remnants of the "Golden Horde," was a matter of some interest to Muscovite annalists—but, of course, from a purely Muscovite point of view.

23. See in particular the collection of tales of the Time of Troubles edited by Platonov in Volume 13 of *Russkaia istoricheskaia biblioteka.*

24. One should perhaps mention the fact that correspondence which could be considered "diplomatic" was conducted in Slavonic by the Patriarch of Moscow with Mt. Athos and other Orthodox centers, while the purely administrative affairs of the Church came increasingly during this period to be conducted in plain style as, particularly under Filaret and Nikon, the administrative apparatus of the Church in general was reorganized to resemble that of the state.

25. See the varied texts published in Volume 13 of the *Russkaia istoricheskaia biblioteka* and the Cherepnin article cited in note 1.

26. Edward L. Keenan, "The *Jarlyk* of Axmed-xan to Ivan III: A New Reading," *International Journal of Slavic Linguistics and Poetics,* vol. XII, 1969, pp. 33–47.

27. I have attempted to initiate a reconsideration of the *Kazan History* in "Coming to Grips with the *Kazanskaya istoriya,* " *Annals* of the Ukrainian Academy of Arts and Sciences in the United States, Volume XI, no. 1–2, 143–183.

28. I hope to provide a detailed discussion of these matters in a study of the *Istoriia o velikom kniaze moskovskom,* now in preparation.

29. For page references, See E. L. Keenan, *The Kurbskii-Groznyi Apocrypha: The Seventeenth-century Genesis of the "Correspondence" Attributed to Prince A.M. Kurbskii and Tsar Ivan IV,* with an appendix by Daniel C. Waugh (Harvard University Press, 1971), 62, n. 212.

30. Thus, while the author explicitly states at the beginning of the History that is is his intention to describe the life and reign of Ivan (the assumption must be that he meant the whole reign), he interrupts his narrative account after the campaign of 1561, presumably because he realized that his chronicle source was continuing to describe events which took place after Kurbskii's flight to Lithuania, and that his pseudonymous account could no longer be couched, as had the earlier narra-

tive, in the first person. After this point—the middle of Chapter IV—he seems simply to have finished copying another source which described the atrocities of Ivan, added portions of two saints' lives, and written a short conclusion.

31. The best argument for a dating of the *History* within the traditional context of authenticity is by A.A. Zimin, "Kogda Kurbskii napisal 'Istoriiu o velikom kniaze Moskovskom'?" *Trudy Otdela drevnerusskoi literatury*, XVIII (1962), 305–308.

32. See, e.g., Guagnini's text in *Sbiór dziejepiśow polskich* (Krakow, 1768). Vol. IV.

33. Text in Ivan Kozlovskii, *Sil'vestr Medvedev. Ocherk iz istorii russkogo prosveshcheniia i obshchestvennoi zhizni v kontse XVII veka* (Kiev, 1895), *Prilozhenie*, 1–206. (Also in *Universitetskie izvestiia* (Kiev, 1895).) For a discussion of the attribution to Medvedev, see A. Prozorovskii, *Sil'vestr Medvedev (ego zhizn' i deiatel'nost')* (Moscow, 1896).

34. Text published in N. Sakharov, ed., *Zapiski russkikh liudei* (Saint Petersburg, 1841).

35. See S.L. Peshtich, *Russkaia istoriografiia XVIII veka*, (Leningrad, 1961).

36. Robert Hanning, *The Vision of History in Early Britain: From Gildas to Geoffrey of Monmouth* (New York, 1966).

A Carolingian Borrowing From Second Nicaea (787)

Joseph H. Lynch

THE RELATIONS between the Byzantine Empire and the Carolingians were punctuated by a series of crises of a political or religous nature. The central decision of the Second Council of Nicaea (787) was the occasion for the major Carolingian theological controversy with the Byzantines. Charlemagne and his theological advisers took great offense at what they believed to be the decision taken at that council toward images and their veneration.[1] The Carolingian theologians were hampered in their understanding of the Byzantine decision by the wretched Latin translation of the Acts of II Nicaea which they had at their disposal.[2] In spite of that handicap, during the eight years following II Nicaea, the Carolingians elaborated their objections to the Byzantine view of images. Between 791 and 794, the Carolingian church produced, in the *Libri Carolini,* a long exposition of its view of images, and a detailed refutation of the Greek view, as it was perceived by the Frankish theologians. At the council of Frankfort (794), the Frankish bishops formally condemned what they saw as errors in the Byzantine view of images.[3]

Historians have generally focused their attention on two related issues, the Frankish rejection of II Nicaea and the formulation of the Frankish response to that council in the *Libri Carolini.*[4] Because the Franks vigorously rejected the central declarations of II Nicaea concerning images, modern scholars have assessed the role of the council in Carolingian history as primarily negative.[5] Contemporary Frankish accounts of the council reenforced this view, since they were unfavorable toward it.[6] What historians have generally overlooked is that Charlemagne and his advisers apparently borrowed from II Nicaea on at least one issue, that of reception of monks or nuns in religious houses in return for money.

In addition to its long treatment of images and iconoclasm, II Nicaea

127

issued twenty-two disciplinary canons.[7] After the formal close of the council on October 23, 787, the two papal legates, both named Peter, brought back to Rome a copy of the conciliar proceedings in Greek. Pope Hadrian I ordered a translation to be made, and he sent a copy of it to Charlemagne. The translation commissioned by Hadrian has not survived, and the modern printed versions of the council derive from a second translation by Anastasius the Librarian, who completed it about 873. From all reports, the first translation was quite inadequate, apparently because it was the work of an Italian cleric who was insecure in Greek, in Latin, and in the theology of the image controversy.[8] Charlemagne received his copy of this translation in late 788 or 789, and it was on the basis of that text that the Carolingian theologians composed the *Libri Carolini.* Charlemagne also received as part of that translation the twenty-two disciplinary canons of II Nicaea.

Frankish borrowings from the canon law of the Byzantine church were rare. At least three such supposed borrowings were shown by Paul Fournier to have been adopted indirectly, through the medium of the *Penitential of Theodore,* a seventh-century text relying heavily on the church practice of the east.[9] However, I believe that the influence of the disciplinary canons of II Nicaea can be perceived in the Capitulary and in the Instruction to *Missi* of 789, and in the Council of Frankfort (794). In spite of their negative reaction to the decision on images, the Carolingians silently borrowed from the disciplinary canons of II Nicaea at least once.

There were a number of points in Charlemagne's reign when he issued major reform documents, sometimes in the aftermath of a crisis.[10] One such point was March 23, 789, when he issued the *Admonitio Generalis* (hereafter AG), a document of eighty-one chapters dealing with a variety of civil and religious matters; and the *Duplex Legationis Edictum* (hereafter DLE), which was an instruction to *missi* consisting of sixteen chapters dealing with monastic affairs and twenty-one chapters dealing with other religious and secular matters.[11]

In at least eight instances, there were similarities between the texts issued by Charlemagne in 789 and the disciplinary canons of II Nicaea. For instance, the first canon of II Nicaea reaffirmed the validity of the canons of the Apostles, the decisions of the first six general councils, and of the accepted local councils. Charlemagne's AG began in parallel fashion by reaffirming the universal councils and by citing fifty-nine excerpts from the ancient canons, as they appeared in the canonical collection *Dionysio-Hadriana,* which Charlemagne was attempting to spread in his kingdom.[12]

Aside from the fact that the documents began with a reaffirmation of the ancient canons, there were more specific ways in which the Nicene and Carolingian decisions displayed a similarity of concern. Canon VI of II Nicaea ordered, somewhat apologetically, that provincial bishops meet once a year, instead of twice as the discipline of the ancient church had required. The AG, c. 13, restated the obligation of provincial synods to meet twice annually. Canon X of II Nicaea forbade clerics to move from their dioceses to other church positions without episcopal permission. The AG, c. 3 and c. 24, likewise bound priests not to wander, and ordered them to seek episcopal permission to exchange one position for another. Canon XIII of II Nicaea ordered that all ecclesiastical buildings which had been put to secular uses during the iconoclastic strife should be restored to their original purposes. The AG, c. 31, forbade the alienation of any monastery to a secular use. Canon XVIII of II Nicaea warned against the presence of women in episcopal residences or in monasteries. The AG, c. 4, warned priests, deacons, and all members of the clergy not to allow women into their homes, except those who were above suspicion. Finally, Canon XXI of II Nicaea ordered monks and nuns to observe stability in their monasteries. The DLE, c. 1, referred to Benedict's Rule about monks who wandered about, the *gyrovagi* and sarabaites.

Thus, six of the twenty-two canons of II Nicaea found a corresponding concern in Charlemagne's AG and DLE of 789. By themselves, these similarities do not prove direct dependence of one text on the other. Both the Latin and the Greek churches gave allegiance to most of the same ancient councils. Consequently, they shared the same legal sources, and in the eighth century, they faced similar moral, educational, and disciplinary problems among their respective clergy and laity. These similar texts could therefore be explained as a result of the same canonical tradition and ecclesiastical problems at work simultaneously in Latin and Greek guise.

However, there is one further correspondence between II Nicaea and Charlemagne's DLE which cannot be explained so readily. Canon XIX of II Nicaea was directed against bribes connected with the admission of candidates to holy orders and to religious life.

> The crime of avarice has grown so great in the rulers of churches that even some of them who are called 'religious' men and women, forgetting the commands of the Lord, are deceived and they receive for gold those coming to the holy order and to the monastic life. Whence it happens, as the great Basil says, that everything is to be rejected from those whose beginning is objectionable. For it is not permissible to serve God by means of Mammon. Therefore, if anyone shall be found doing this, if indeed he is a bishop or an abbot or any member of the sacred college, either

let him stop or let him be deposed, according to the second decision of the holy council of Chalcedon. But, may an abbess be cast out of the monastery and may she be handed over to another monastery for subjection; likewise an abbot who was not a priest. However, we define that those things given to sons by parents as a dowry, or if they (the entrants) offer anything from their own property and if those who offer things as a dedication to God should profess, [the gifts] should remain in the monastery according to their promise, whether they themselves persevere or leave. This does not hold if the reason for leaving were the fault of the prelate. [13]

This canon forbade the ordination of a cleric for money, and it threatened deposition for church officials who persisted in such simony. In essence, this measure was an adaptation of the well-known second canon of Chalcedon (451), which was cited directly in the text. [14] But, the provisions of Canon XIX forbidding payment to be a monk or nun, and those prescribing penalties for guilty abbots and abbesses are not to be found in the canon of Chalcedon. Indeed, I have found no direct precedent for them in the ancient canon law. So far as I can determine, they constitute an innovation of II Nicaea.

In parallel to Canon XIX of II Nicaea, chapter 15 of the monastic section of Charlemagne's DLE declared "that no abbot should seek a reward for the reception of a monk." [15] For several reasons, it seems certain that there is a direct connection between these two texts, which were composed about seventeen months apart. The link between the texts is not verbal, that is, the Carolingian text cannot be shown to be a quotation from II Nicaea. This is not unusual for Carolingian texts. F.L. Ganshof [16] has given some useful advice for the study of the capitularies, which is germane to comprehending the link between the text of II Nicaea and that of the DLE. Many Carolingian legislative texts, as they survive, are a form of memorandum, intended to be explained and expanded orally by those who were charged to publicize them. The chapters of the DLE fit the pattern of such a memorandum, since they are brief, to the point of obscurity. For instance, chapter 8 is simply "De eulogiis"; chapter 13 is "De ordinando abbate"; and chapter 14 is merely "De fratribus in via directis." Presumably, the *missi* knew the full meaning of these jottings and explained them orally at some length during their visitations. Ganshof stressed that the legally binding moment for such texts was their oral promulgation by the king. [17] The surviving written text was not in all probability a legal or definite text. It was simply a shorthand summary of the royal promulgation. Thus, the text of chapter 15 of the DLE cannot be subjected to an overly exact exegesis, since it was never intended as a precise legal text. Because of the character of the text, if there is a link between

canon XIX of II Nicaea and the DLE, it must be sought in the realm
of ideas rather than in the realm of direct quotation.

The first argument for such a link must be that there was no precedent in the ancient canonical tradition for specifically condemning
payments for entry into religious life. The six ancient councils which
were generally recognized as ecumenical had no canons against payment for such entry. I examined the Gallic councils of the late Roman
and Frankish periods, and found no canons directed against such
payments.[18] In addition, I examined the major canonical collections
available to the Carolingians in the eighth century, and I found no
reference to such payments in them.[19] To be sure, the demand of a fee
for religous objects and actions had been condemned frequently since
apostolic times as the sin of Simon Magus, or simony. But the condemnations of simony had never, so far as I have been able to determine,
explicitly mentioned payments for admission to a religious house.[20] In
fact, the DLE did not specifically say that payments were simoniacal,
and Canon XIX of II Nicaea was ambiguous, since it cited a clear form
of simony, i.e., payment for holy orders, along with payments for
reception in a religious house. What is striking is that, although it had
not been explicitly condemned previously, payment by candidates for
the religious life was forbidden at II Nicaea in 787 and approximately
seventeen months later in the DLE of 789.

The second argument in favor of Byzantine influence on chapter 15
of the DLE is based on the Benedictine Rule. The monastic section of
the DLE had sixteen chapters, and fourteen of them were based on the
Rule. The compilers quite evidently had the Rule before them when
they worked, since the fourteen chapters of the DLE appear in the
same order as that in which they appear in the Rule.[21] There were two
chapters, fifteen and sixteen, which had no precedent in the Rule.
Chapter 16 of the DLE was an order that guilty monks were to be
chastised by religious sanctions, and not by brutal secular punish-
ments.[22] Chapter 15 of the DLE, forbidding abbots to seek gifts from
candidates, was new, with no root in the Rule. Thus, this prohibiiton,
which appeared almost simultaneously in Byzantine and Frankish
church law, was derived neither from the ancient canon law nor from
the Rule of Benedict.

The third argument in favor of a Carolingian borrowing derives from
the form in which the prohibition of gifts from entrants was restated
at the council of Frankfort (794). The *missi* of 789, in accord with their
instructions in the DLE, probably reported to Charlemagne that the

demand for payment was common in his realms. In 794, Charlemagne convoked a great council at Frankfort, and in the course of that assembly, the prohibition of payments was renewed. The form of the prohibition at Frankfort reenforces the argument that II Nicaea was its source, because the Carolingian text seems to contain a verbal correspondence. Canon XVI at Frankfort said:

> We have heard [presumably from the *missi*] that some abbots, led by greed, require payments for those entering a monastery. Therefore it pleases us and the holy synod: for receiving brethren in the holy order in no way should money be required, but they should be received according to the Rule of Saint Benedict. [23]

This text is clearly not a translation of Canon XIX of II Nicaea. However, both canons began in the same way, with a reference to greed on the part of church officials. That common reference points to the possibility that the Carolingian bishops had the now-lost first Latin translation of the Acts of II Nicaea available to them. They did not copy it, but they apparently drew some verbal inspiration from it for their much briefer conciliar canon.

In its barest outline then, the argument for a Carolingian borrowing from II Nicaea is that a canonical provision without clear precedent in the ancient canon law appeared at II Nicaea in the Fall of 787, and then at the Carolingian Court in Spring of 789. Further, the Carolingians are known to have possessed a translation of the Acts of II Nicaea, and their basic reaction to its image decrees was one of fierce rejection. In spite of this rejection, the Carolingians borrowed the prohibition of payments for entry into a religious house, and in Canon XVI at Frankfort in 794, they repeated the prohibition in a form which may contain a verbal correspondence to II Nicaea.

Charlemagne had an ambivalent relationship to the Eastern Empire. The Byzantines were a model for him, but a model disliked and resented for political and religious reasons. [24] The period from 787 to 795 was one of great tension between the two powers. Charlemagne resented his exclusion from II Nicaea, a proposed marriage was called off, there was war between Carolingian and Byzantine forces in Italy, and the Carolingian realm rejected as heretical the Byzantine view of images. [25] This strained situation readily explains the Carolingian silence about borrowing from II Nicaea. The Byzantine council had drawn the attention of Charlemagne and his advisers to the previously unrecognized problem of forced gifts for entry into religious life. The *missi* of 789 were commissioned to look into the matter and they found the practice to be common. Consequently, Charlemagne and his advisers included the matter on the agenda of the empire-wide council at Frankfort, where it was duly condemned. In all of this, Charlemagne had no motive to acknowledge the debt owed to the Byzantines and their hated council.

This borrowing from II Nicaea had a slight currency in Carolingian legislation for about a generation and then, after 819, it all but disappeared from the concerns of the Carolingian church and seems to have had no effect on admission to religious life.

Entry into religious life, as a general phenomenon, was of interest to the Frankish monarchs. Charlemagne and his son Louis were especially concerned about the entry of free men into religious life. From the tenor of their capitularies and of other texts, they and their advisers harbored a suspicion that many such entries were fictitious and/or motivated by greed on the part of the prelates who received new members. At a series of three councils in 800, it was ordered "that no bishop or abbot should dare to seek out the property of nobles, by reason of ambition, as is contained in the council of Carthage, chapter 5." [26] The capitulary of Thionville (805) ordered all free men wishing to enter religious life to seek royal permission, and in one of the rare texts in which Charlemagne stated the motives for a decision, he declared:

> [We have taken] this decision therefore, since we have heard that some of those [who enter religious life act] not so much for reason of devotion as for escaping military duty or some other royal task; we have heard that some are tricked for reason of greed by those who desire their property, and this therefore we forbid to be done. [27]

This theme, that prelates connived by fictitious or real entries into religious life to relieve free men from their public duties in order to get their property, was repeated at least seven times in the texts of the first two decades of the ninth century. [28] Indeed, the monarchs were not alone in their concern. The monks of Fulda, in a letter critical of their abbot, asked for an end to the practice of inviting men to the monastic life for the sake of their property, and purposely hiding from the prospective monks the difficulties inherent in the monastic way of life. [29]

These various texts were tangentially connected to the issue of payments for entry into religion, but, while they were critical of greed and fraud on the part of bishops and abbots, they did not attack the payment as such. The first and last time since Frankfort (794) that gifts for admission to religious life were forbidden was in the monastic legislation of Louis the Pious, issued in 818/819. Chapter 72 said: "That no one should be received in a monastery for a gift, unless he is one whom good will and probity of life recommend." [30]

This text did not appear in the monastic legislation of August 816 or of July 817, but when the two sets of capitula were combined for an imperial assembly in 818/819, the compiler apparently added this text. In it, criticism has shifted from payments as such, to payments used to secure the admission of an unqualified or unacceptable candidate. Apparently, the regulation allows a gift for a candidate who was otherwise qualified for reception. The gift on occasion of entry, called much later a dowry, was not rejected, but only its use as a bribe to gain acceptance for an unqualified person.

After Louis' considerable legislative effort, seconding the work of abbot Benedict of Aniane,[31] the measures against payment for entry to religious life disappeared from the Carolingian capitularies and councils quite as abruptly as they had appeared in 789. To my knowledge, such prohibitions did not appear again in the capitularies of the Carolingian rulers of the ninth century, nor did they appear in the numerous extant conciliar decrees of the ninth century.

I would suggest that there were at least three reasons for the failure of the Byzantine prohibition to take permanent root in the Carolingian church law. First, the gift on the occasion of entry into religious life was a customary practice in the normal functioning of Carolingian monasticism. Abbots and entrants felt no great guilt about it. Indeed, it is significant that the Carolingians avoided calling the practice simony, and perhaps they did not see it as a variety of simony. The council of Frankfort had declared that such payments were a manifestation of greed, but not of simony. The evolution of the prohibition reveals, perhaps, a drawing back from Charlemagne's initial prohibition of payments for reception of monks. In 818/819, Louis' legislation apparently forbade payments only when the entrants were unfit. After Louis the Pious' initiatives, silence reigned on the issue.

The second reason for tacit toleration of payments from entrants lay in the financial state and problems of religious houses. Because of their crucial role in the Carolingian governing system, only a relatively few houses were allowed regular elections and control of their own affairs.[32] Most others shouldered heavy obligations of money and service to the rulers. Some attempts were made to alleviate the financial woes of monasteries by fixing the number of religious relative to resources.[33]

But the worsening political situation aborted these attempts, as it did so many other Carolingian reforms. Payments from entrants were necessary and were accepted as such.

The third reason for the relative disappearance of the prohibition lay in the process by which a text became, in practical terms, a canonical authority. It was not sufficient for a canon to be enacted at a council. It had to be included in canonical collections in order to gain currency and effective authority. The second and third quarters of the ninth century were a period of canon law revival in the Carolingian realm. After the smothering embrace of Charlemagne, the Frankish episcopate under his son and grandsons sought to guarantee the legal and fiscal integrity of the church.[34] Canonical collections were a weapon in the struggle for autonomy, and one of the crucial criteria for those collections was the desire for texts with ancient authority, even if the "ancient" texts had to be forged. The prohibition of payment for entry into religious life depended for authority on recent councils, held under Charlemagne and Louis, and through them on a Byzantine council of questionable orthodoxy. Such support was perhaps inadequate to win for the texts inclusion in the canonical collections of mid-century. According to my investigation, prohibition of payment was not incorporated in the major canonical collection of the ninth century, the Pseudo-Isidorian forgeries.[35] It was included only rarely in the minor canonical collections,[36] and then only in a fossilized form, as a chapter of the monastic legislation of Louis the Pious.[37] Hence, the prohibition had only a slight chance to be a canonical authority or influence.

To use a gardening image, the opposition of II Nicaea to payments for admission to religious life was grafted into Carolingian legislation by the silent borrowings of 789 and 794. However, abbots felt little guilt about payments, monastic finances had need of the gifts, and by the criteria of the ninth century, the prohibition was not deemed worthy to be included regularly in canonical collections. These factors combined to reject the graft. It was not until the late eleventh century that such payments were classified clearly as simony. The consequences of that new view were drawn in the greatest canonical collection of the twelfth century, Gratian's *Decretum*, in *causa* I, *questio* II.[38]

NOTES

1. The proceedings of II Nicaea in the ninth-century translation by Anastasius the Librarian are printed in *PL* CXXIX, col. 195–512. For a careful treatment of the Carolingian theological reasons for rejecting II Nicaea, see Gert Haendler, *Epo-*

chen karolingischer Theologie. Eine Untersuchung über die karolingischer Gütachten zum byzantinischen Bilderstreit (Berlin, 1958), 27–43; 67–101.

2. Wolfram von den Steinen, "Entstehungsgeschichte der *Libri Carolini,*" *Quellen und Forschungen aus italienischen Archiven und Bibliotheken,* XXI, (1929–1930), 11–28. Haendler, *op. cit.,* 67–73, held that the Carolingian theologians objected to the Byzantine view of images on grounds quite independent of the imperfections of the translation.

3. The *Libri Carolini,* edited by H. Bastgen, are published in MGH, Legum sectio III, *Concilia,* II, supplementum (Hanover, 1924). The canons of Frankfort are in MGH, Legum sectio III, *Concilia,* II/I, ed. A. Werminghoff (Hanover, 1908), 165–171; and in MGH, Legum sectio II, *Capitularia regum Francorum,* I, ed. A. Boretius (Hanover, 1883), 73–78.

4. For recent additions to the continuing controversy over the authorship of the *Libri Carolini,* see A. Freeman, "Theodulph of Orléans and the *Libri Carolini,*" *Speculum,* XXXII (1957), 663–705; and "Further Studies in the *Libri Carolini*" *Speculum,* XL (1965), 203–289; and most recently "Further Studies in the *Libri Carolini,* III. The Marginal Notes in Vaticanus Latinus 7207," *Speculum,* XLVI (1971), 597–612. There is dissent from Miss Freeman's views in L. Wallach, "The Unknown Author of the *Libri Carolini:* Patristic Exegesis, Mozarabic Antiphons and the *Vetus Latina,*" *Didascaliae: Studies in Honor of Anselm M. Albareda* ed. S. Prete (New York, 1961), 469–515; and "Ambrosii Verba Retro Versa e Translatione Graeca (Libri Carolini, II, 15)," *Harvard Theological Review,* LXV (1972), 171–189.

5. For representative negative assessments, see P. Fournier, G. Le Bras, *Histoire des collections canoniques en occident depuis les Fausses Décrétales jusqu'au Décret de Gratien* (Paris, 1931), I, 80; H. von Schubert, *Geschichte der christlichen Kirche im Frühmittelalter* (Tübingen, 1921), 384–385; E. Amann, *L'époque carolingienne,* in Fliche-Martin, *Histoire de l'église,* VI (Paris, 1947), 125–126; M. D. Knowles, D. Obolensky, C. A. Bouman, *Geschichte der Kirche* II: *Früh-und Hochmittelalter* (Zurich, 1971), 86–87; Haendler, *op. cit.,* 27–43.

6. Von den Steinen, *op. cit.,* 77.

7. The disciplinary canons of II Nicaea are printed in *PL* CXXIX, col. 479–488. They are analysed in C. Hefele, H. Leclercq, *Histoire des conciles* (Paris, 1910), III, 775–794; and in G. Fritz, "Nicée (IIᵉ Concile de)," *Dictionnaire de théologie catholique* (Paris, 1931), XI/I, col. 417–441.

8. Von den Steinen, *op. cit.,* 18–23. L. Wallach, "The Greek and Latin Versions of II Nicaea and the Synodica of Hadrian I (JE 2448), " *Traditio,* XXII (1966), 103–125, dated the extant translation by Anastasius the Librarian to about 873.

9. P. Fournier, "De quelques infiltrations byzantins dans le droit canonique de l'époque carolingienne," *Mélanges offerts à M. Gustave Schlumberger* (Paris, 1924), I, 67–78.

10. F.L. Ganshof, "Observations sur le Synode de Francfort de 794," *Miscellanea historica in honorem Alberti de Meyer* (Louvain, 1946), I, 306 ff. See also C. de Clercq, *La legislation religieuse franque de Clovis à Charlemagne* (Louvain, Paris, 1936), 171–202.

11. The *Admonitio Generalis* is edited by A. Boretius in MGH, Legum sectio II, *Capitularia regum Francorum,* I (Hanover, 1883), 52–62. The *Duplex Legationis Edictum* is edited *ibid.,* 62–64. De Clercq, *op. cit.,* 171–172, noted that it is not clear from the manuscripts whether the date March 23 refers to one or both texts. He concluded that at least one was issued on that date, and the other was issued in 789 as well.

12. On Charlemagne's attempts between 789 and 802 to make the *Dionysio-Hadriana* better known north of the Alps, see De Clercq, *op. cit.,* 171 ff; and Fournier, Le Bras, *op. cit.,* 95–103.

13. See *PL* CXXIX, col. 487.
14. J. D. Mansi, ed., *Sacrorum Conciliorum Nova et Amplissima Collectio* (Florence, 1762), VII, col. 384. For a careful modern edition, see E. Schwartz, ed., *Acta Conciliorum Oecumenicorum* (Berlin, Leipzig, 1932), II, 2/2, 54.
15. "Ut nullus abbas pro susceptione monachi praemium non quaerat." *Capitularia,* I, 63. The greed of abbots was apparently a concern of Charlemagne and his advisers in 789, because c. 3 of the DLE said, "ut non parvipendentes sint pastores animarum sibi commissarum, nec maiorem curam habeant de lucris terrenis quam de animabus sibi commissis." *Ibid.*
16. F. L. Ganshof, *Recherches sur les capitulaires* (Paris, 1958), 18–29.
17. A. Dumas, "La parole et l'écriture dans les capitulaires carolingiens," *Mélanges d'histoire du moyen âge dédiés à la mémoire de Louis Halphen* (Paris, 1951), 209–216.
18. C. Munier, ed., *Concilia Galliae, A. 314- A. 506* (Turnholt, 1963), CCSL, cxlviii; and C. de Clercq, ed., *Concilia Galliae, A. 511-A. 694* (Turnholt, 1963), CCSL, cxlviiiA.
19. The *Dacheriana* in Luc D'Achery, ed., *Veterum Aliquot Scriptorum. . . Spicilegium* (Paris, 1672), XI, 1–200; and the *Dionysio-Hadriana* in *PL* LXVII, col. 39–346; C.) The *Hispana* in *PL* LXXXIV.
20. For the meaning of simony before the Investiture Contest, see A. Leinz, *Die Simonie, Eine kanonistische Studie* (Freiburg im Breisgau, 1902); N. A. Weber, *A History of Simony in the Christian Church to 814* (Baltimore, 1909); R.A. Ryder, *Simony: an Historical Synopsis and Commentary* (Washington, D.C., 1931); and H. Meier-Welcker, "Die Simonie im frühen Mittelalter," *Zeitschrift für Kirchengeschichte,* LXIV (1952–1953), 61–93. None of these authors found an explicit condemnation of entry fees as simoniacal before II Nicaea, (787).
21. Boretius, the editor of the DLE, drew attention to the correspondences between the Rule of Benedict and the DLE:

DLE 1- RB 1	DLE 7- RB 52	DLE 12- RB 59
DLE 2- RB 1	DLE 8- RB 54	DLE 13- RB 64
DLE 3- RB 2	DLE 9- RB 53	DLE 14- RB 67
DLE 4- RB 5	DLE 10- RB 55	DLE 15- no equivalent
DLE 5- RB 21	DLE 11- RB 58	DLE 16- no equivalent
DLE 6- RB 31		

Capitularia, I, 62–63. See also de Clercq, *La législation,* 176–177.
22. "Ut disciplina monachis regularis imponatur non secularis, id est non orbentur nec mancationes alias habeant nisi ex auctoritate regulae," *Capitularia,* I, 63.
23. "Audivimus enim, quod quidam abbates cupiditate ducti praemia pro introeuntibus in monasterio requirunt. Ideo placuit nobis et sancta synodo: pro suscipiendis in sancto ordine fratribus nequaquam pecunia requirantur, sed secundum regulam sancti Benedicti suscipiantur." *Capitularia,* I, 76.
24. W. Ullmann, *The Growth of Papal Government in the Middle Ages,* 3rd ed. (London, 1970), 104–105.
25. Haendler, *op. cit.,* 27–30; Knowles, *op. cit.,* 86–87.
26. "Ut nullus episcopus vel abbas atrahere audeat res nobilium causa ambitionis, sicut in canone Cartaginensi continetur cap. V." *Concilia* II/I, 209, canon XI.
27. "Hoc ideo, quia audivimus aliquos ex illis non tam causa devotionis quam exercitu seu alia funccione regali fugiendo, quosdam vero cupiditatis causa ab his qui res illorum concupiscant circumventos audivimus, et hoc ideo fieri prohibemus." *Capitularia,* I, 125, c. 15.
28. In addition to the citations in notes 26 and 27, see Concilia Rispacense, Frisingense, Salisburgense (800), canon XLIIII, *Concilia* II/I, 212; Capitulare Missorum in Theodonis Villa Datum Primum (805), c. 11, *Capitularia,* I, 122; Concilium Cabillonense (813), canons VI, VII, *Concilia* II/I, 275; Capitulare Ecclesiasticum (818, 819), c. 8, *Capitularia,* I, 277.

29. *Supplex Libellus Monachorum Fuldensium Carolo Imperatori Porrectus*, c. 8 in J. Semmler, ed., *Corpus Consuetudinum Monasticarum* (Siegberg, 1963), I, 323. For the background to the *Supplex Libellus*, see J. Semmler, "Studien zum Supplex Libellus und zur anianischen Reform in Fulda," *Zeitschrift für Kirchengeschichte*, LXIX (1958), 268–298.

30. "Ut nullus pro munere recipiatur in monasterio nisi quem bona voluntas et merita commendat." *Legislatio Aquisgranensis* in Semmler, *Corpus*, I, 533. For an account of the origins of this text, see J. Semmler, "Zur Uberlieferung der monastischen Gesetzgebung Ludwigs des Frommen," *Deutsches Archiv für Erforschung des Mittelalters*, XVI (1960), 309–388, and especially 341–369.

31. S. Dulcy, *La règle de saint Benoît d'Aniane et la réforme monastique a l'époque carolingienne* (Nîmes, 1933), 68–90. Benedict of Aniane had been at the Council of Frankfort in 794, and so presumably had heard the original Carolingian conciliar prohibition of payments for entry into religious life.

32. Louis the Pious attempted to exempt some monasteries from external control; see E. Lesne, "Les ordonnances monastiques de Louis le Pieux et la Notitia de Servitio monasteriorum," *Revue d'histoire de l'église de France*, VI (1920), 161–175; 321–338; 449–493.

33. Kings and bishops sought to balance resources and numbers in religious houses: Pippini Capitulare Papiense (787), c. 11, *Capitularia*, I, 199; Capitulare Missorum in Theodonis Villa Datum (805), c. 12, *ibid.*, 122; Capitula de Causis (811), c. 11, *ibid.*, 164; Concilium Arelatense (813), canon VIII, *Concilia*, II/I, 251; Concilium Remense (813), canon XXVII, *ibid.*, 256.

34. Le Bras has a useful essay on the reform sentiment of the mid-ninth-century canonical forgers in Fournier, Le Bras, *op. cit.*, 120–137. See also Ullmann, *op. cit.*, 167–189.

35. P. Hinschius, ed., *Decretales Pseudo-Isidorianae et Capitula Angilramni* (Leipzig, 1883). On the reluctance of reformers to use recent texts as authorities, see Fournier, Le Bras, *op. cit.*, 93.

36. There was no canon against monastic simony in A.) H. Mordek, "Die Rechtssammlungen der Handschrift von Bonneval- ein Werk der karolingischen Reform," *Deutsches Archiv für Erforschung des Mittelalters*, XXIV (1968), 339–434; B.) P. Fournier, "Le ms H 137 de l'école de medicine de Montpellier," *Annales de l'Université de Grenoble*, IX (1897), 357–389; C.) J. Rambaud-Buhot, "Une collection canonique de la réforme carolingienne (ms lat. de la Bibliothèque nationale n. 4278, ff. 128–167)," *Revue historique de droit français et étranger*, XXXIV (1956), 50–73; D.) J. Rambaud-Buhot, "Un corpus inédit de droit canonique de la réforme carolingienne à la réforme grégorienne," *Humanisme actif. Mélanges d'art et de littérature offerts à Julien Cain* (paris, 1968), II, 271–281.

37. The legislation of Aix (818/819) was included as *Additio* I of the False Capitularies of Benedict the Levite, ed. F. Knust, MGH, *Leges*, II/2 (Hanover, 1837), 17–158; see also V. Krause, "Die Münchener Handschriften 3851, 3853 mit einer Compilation von 181 Wormser Schlüssen," *Neues Archiv*, XIX (1894), 116, in which most of the DLE was copied as part of a complex canonical collection.

38. The twelfth-century assimilation of payment for entry to simony, and the prohibition of such payments, is treated in an unpublished doctoral dissertation by Joseph H. Lynch, "Simony in Entrance to Religious Houses, 1050–1215," Harvard University, 1971.

The Art of the Pseudo-Origen Homily

DE MARIA MAGDALENA

Margaret Jennings, C.S.J.

THE IMPORTANCE of the Pseudo-Origen homily *De Maria Magdalena* has been variously ascribed to its connection with Geoffrey Chaucer, to its relationship with several mediaeval rhetorical traditions, or to its rise from anonymity of authorship to a place of undisputed influence.[1] Although valuable analyses of its structure, sources, and stylistics have appeared, there has been no effort to explore the synthesis of homiletic, scriptural, rhetorical, dramatic, and mystical patterns which comprise Pseudo-Origen's masterpiece. Such a study is necessary for an appreciation of the homily's literary excellence.

A product of the late twelfth or early thirteenth century, the *De Maria Magdalena* stands at the pinnacle of the *modus antiquus* in sermon construction.[2] Dramatic, moving, and memorable, it is the perfect exemplar of pre-thematic homiletics where, as Robert of Basevorn says, a preacher like St. Bernard operates seemingly "without method,"

> exceeding the style and capability of almost all men of genius. He more than all the rest stresses Scripture in all his sayings. . .his procedure is always devout, always artful. He takes a certain theme. . .divides it into two, three, or many members, confirms it and ends it using every rhetorical color so that the whole work shines with a double glow, earthly and heavenly, and this, it seems to me, invites to devotion those who understand more feelingly. . . .[3]

Basevorn's emphasis on devotion and artistry is well illustrated in the *De Maria Magdalena*, where those terms are translated into a style both innovative and sophisticated. Innovation first appears in the anonymous author's choice of the text "Maria stabat ad monumentum foris plorans" from John 20:11—a verse rarely encountered as a homily theme. Perhaps because Augustine and Gregory the Great had written at length about Mary Magdalen's actions on that first Easter, later homilists and commentators concentrated on other aspects of her Biblical life, namely, her great act of penitence in the house of Simon and her association with Martha and Lazarus.[4] In the centuries immediate-

139

ly preceding Pseudo-Origen only Alcuin and Odo of Cluny wrote in the homiletic vein about her Paschal prominence, and their treatises were largely derivative.[5] While it is demonstrable that other contributions to the Magdalen cult, particularly the writings of Pseudo-Rhabanus, numerous hymns, and exercises like Anselm's "Oratio XVI" [6] did concentrate on Mary's loving Easter services to Christ, nevertheless, the effect of these elements is felt in homiletics only with the advent of Pseudo-Origen.

Yet the literary sophistication and compositional superiority of the *De Maria Magdalena* are even more noteworthy than its departure from conventional depictions of this favorite of mediaeval saints.[7] In addition to the structural disposition of Biblical quotations, allusions, and cadences, the homilist makes impressive use of facets of characterization, narration, and language which are infrequently encountered in the earlier homily tradition. So effective, however, is the piece's artistry that it achieves an absolute coordination of both style and drama, and the twin pitfalls of obstrusive rhetoric and excessive emotionalism are avoided.

The most apparent stylistic feature of this homily is its widespread use of Biblical quotation and allusion; no less that sixty separate citations are easily discernible. Six of these passages (all from John 20), according to the skillful analysis of Hans Hansel, divide the work into points for meditation.[8] But the Biblical material does more than simply delineate the architectonics of the homily; employed in defining the narrative characterizations of Christ and Mary, in extending her importance through the accommodation of texts referring to others, and in deepening the emotional appeal of the whole by clever allusion, it shapes a kind of poetic backbone for the text. Three short sentences, in fact, bound together only by the adverb *olim* ("once") [9] provide in capsule form the entire lifetime of the Magdalen:

> Once he loved you; once from the pharisee defended you (Luke 7:44), and to your sister diligently excused you (Luke 10:41). Once he praised you, when with ointment you anointed his feet, washed them with tears, covered them with your hair; he diminished your sorrow; he took away your sins (Luke 7:47). Once he sought you when you were not present; he called you when you were away (John 11:28). [10]

She had, of course, come to the sepulchre to anoint the dead body "as before with precious ointment she had anointed the feet of the living" (John 12:3), and the Lord is counselled by the author to remember what he had said to Martha: that Mary had indeed chosen the "better part which would not be taken from her" (Luke 10:42).[11] Scriptural quotations constantly associate Christ and Mary in the homily; grief causes her to forget that he had said how he would die (John 2:19) while the depiction of this grief echoes Christ's parting discourse to his Apostles (John 16:6) and prepares the reader for a later definition of Mary as a *discipula*. Mary knows that there is ample justification for her actions in Christ's own self-description: I will love those who love me, and those who wait for me will find me (John 14:21), and she laments her obedience to the law in leaving the tomb. [12] To have remained with Christ was not to transgress the law for he, in death, would not defile the clean; rather he would cleanse the defiled (I Tim. 4:7). The Pasch would not be contaminated by him, but be renewed (I Cor. 5:7), for he healed all who touched him and illuminated all who approached him (Matt. 8:15). [13]

Mary's importance in the homily is further stressed by the accommodation of texts to her which describe others in actual Biblical narratives. One of the most interesting uses of this device employs Christ's praise of the Canaanite woman of Matthew 15:28 but ends with his assurances to the penitent sinner of Luke 7:50: "O woman, great is your faith. . .Be it done to you as you wish, and believe, because your faith has saved you." [14] Unlike the Peter of Mark 14:66, Mary would have bravely answered the questioning servant girl, yet like him she might also ask, "What shall I do? Where shall I go?" (John 6:69), for Christ is her beloved. With Jeremiah (Lam. 1:12) she knows that there is no sorrow like her sorrow, though with Paul she believes that neither death nor life shall be able to separate her from Jesus (Rom. 8:38); and with the Virgin herself, Mary Magdalen keeps Christ's word carefully in her heart and delights in it (Luke 2:51). [15] Her love is so great that finally the magnificent consolation which Christ promised to his disciples (John 16:20) is hers: "Great sorrow is converted into great joy; tears of grief are changed into tears of love."

Though the homily displays traditional allusions and commentary, its author manages to preserve his special turn of phrase. Consequently, he surprises the reader by describing Magdalen in terms similar to those Christ had used for the "slow of heart" in Matthew 13, and he delights him by extending Christ's spiritual planting to the hearts of the faithful. [16] Mary's disparagement of the angels as *consolatores* in the manner of Job 2:11, her Pauline descriptions of the body, the spirit, and the rest of death (Rom. 7:24, I Cor. 12, Heb. 4:3), her Psalmistic wish, "ostende mihi faciem tuam," her need for the living bread of Matthew 14:20 and 15:32, her seeking "in simplicitate cordis" (Wis.

141

1:1)—all these unexpected scriptural patterns breathe a kind of life into the text which is simply not evident in the moralizations made by earlier Latin commentators on the actions of Mary Magdalen.[17]

The style of the homily is also affected by echoes of scriptural and liturgical cadences in places where there is no direct quotation. The plaintive question, "How has she sinned against you or in what manner offended you?" reminds the reader strongly of the Reproaches of the Good Friday liturgy: "What have I done to you, or in what manner have I offended you?"[18] The conditional description, "If this is sin, we are not able to deny it. . .if, however, this is not sin. . .why do you withdraw from her?" can be compared to the response of Jesus in the house of Annas: "If I have spoken badly, give testimony of the evil; if I have spoken well, however, why do you strike me?" (John 18:23). Again, the "you do not cease to weep" directly addressed to the Magdalen strikes the same chord as the Lord's own description of her act of penitence: "she has not ceased to kiss my feet" (Luke 7:45). The angels whom Mary finds at the sepulchre bear a witness to Christ remarkably like that of the Spirit-filled apostles of John 15:27, and the homilist's concluding advice "and again look into the monument of God which is in you" is similar to Paul's declaration of the inner dwelling of the Holy Spirit in the first epistle to the Corinthians (6:19).[19]

Despite numerous interwoven Biblical quotations and allusions, so skillful is its artistry that the homily's prose seems disarmingly simple and rhythmical. Simplicity and rhythm are also maintained through a sophisticated blending of narrative patterns, the most obvious being the repetition of key words and phrases. A heavy accent upon the verbs *plorare* and *dolere* and upon the nouns *amor* and *dolor* succeeds in setting both tone and theme.[20] Explanations of the *dolor* lead to a strong emphasis upon forms of *diligere* and later *errare*, while the antithetical movements of *quaero* and *invenio* appear regularly.[21] Repetition of such questions as "Why do you withdraw from her?" and "Whom do you seek? Why do you weep?" constantly engage the reader's attention, while the real importance of the *monumentum* which is stressed in the opening sections becomes clear only at the end when it is specified as the "monument of the heart."

Closely associated with repeated words and phrases is the artfully contrived and balanced construction of certain key passages in the homily. Initially, the very movement of the prose seems dependent upon a series of verbs in the imperfect tense, and the balancing is so delicate that it creates the illusion of internal rhyme:

Et iste dolor maior erat, quia nullam consolationem habebat. . .sed de hoc dolore aliquantulum consolationem habebat, quia mortuum se retinere credebat. [22]

A more subtle structural balancing is achieved in the counterpoint established between the imperatives of Matthew 7:7 ("Ask and you will receive," etc.), the declarative statement of Mary's plight ("You call him and he does not hear. . .you seek him and do not find him; you knock and he does not open"), and the narrative description shortly following it, "The Master is here and calls for you" (John 11:28). [23] The effect is startling because Mary is commanded to ask for and to seek the Lord who does not always hear and answer; yet when the Magdalen herself is called, "O how quickly Mary arose when she heard, how urgently she came, and according to her custom cast herself at your feet." [24] The last clause intricately supports two other points of balance: *solito more* in Mary implies love, quick action, and surrender; when it is repeated with regard to Christ, the frame of love remains the same though the picture changes: "For if *according to your custom* you love her, why do you so long delay her desire?" [25] Balance is also observable in the oxymoronic constructions which are strategically located in the text. "Desperando sperans" is set immediately against "sperando perseverans" and "quam scienter nescit" seems to demand its counterpart "quam docte errat." [26] Even the personification into Christ of the "optima pars" which Mary has chosen contributes to the homily's resonating balance.

By far the most facinating feature of his Latin prose style is the author's intricate playing with common words. *Cognoscere*, for example, conveys two very different ways of knowing in the contiguous sentences: "So unmindful was she that even him [i.e. Christ] she did not know. Believe me, if she had known him, she would not have sought him in the sepulchre." [27] This verbal teasing is repeated later in a similar fashion: "O Mary, if you seek Jesus, why do you not know Jesus? And if you know Jesus, why do you seek Jesus?"—a context which both points to and comments on the earlier passage. [28] The apt usage of *facere* and *ponere* is likewise noted in Mary's questioning of the "gardener" because Christ himself had "made" his own resurrection though like Lazarus he had been "placed" in the tomb; and although familiar from earlier Latin works, the varied significances of *verbum* and the exclamation "o mulier, non mulier" achieve here a maximum in dramatic placement. [29] A concluding verbal play between Mary's loving disposition *(affectum)* and its effect on the congregation [30] *(effectum)* epitomizes the homily's literary power: both listener and reader are caught up by Biblical allusion, familiar cadence, and rhythmical style into the subject matter of the text; once drawn in through this type of narration, they inevitably perceive its affective qualities.

Ultimately, the stylistics of the homily are directed towards a more effective characterization of its central figure, Mary of Magdala. From the outset she is presented favorably, since it is as lover that Mary is first perceived by the homilist who, extending Gregory's indefinite "ignis amoris," maintains that her devotion exemplifies the consuming fire of a *true* love.[31] The hearer is not compelled to investigate lengthy etymologies nor is he commanded to observe the Magdalen's perseverance or the triumph of penitence; rather he is invited simply "to see if he is able why she stands, why she weeps" because "it is good for us."[32] In a deceptively simple manner also he is told: "love makes her stand there and sorrow forces her to weep," but the consequences of this statement are complicated and conflicting because it is not an hysterical woman who is contemplated but one weighed down with a double sorrow. She had lost the living Christ, a sorrow slightly lessened through her belief in his return; but she had lost his body too and now she feared that her loving belief might grow cold.[33] Mary had come to the tomb to perform for Christ's dead body the services she had performed for the living—to anoint and to weep—and her sorrow increased as this expression of her love was denied. Peter and John had come to the tomb and, being afraid, had not remained. For Mary, however, there was nothing external to be feared; in losing him whom alone she had loved she had lost the "life of her spirit," and now perhaps *(forsitan)* it would be better for her to die than to live, perhaps in dying she might find him whom living she was not able to find.[34] Death could not worsen her state: she was already *exanimis, insensibilis,* so totally she had lost herself in the loss of her Master.[35] Only "as if hoping in despairing and persevering in hoping" did she remain standing solitary and weeping outside the sepulchre.

The exclamation "O Mary, what hope, what counsel, what heart was in you" which follows her description in the text seems to escape spontaneously from the author. To be overwhelmed with the sorrow of deprivation, to be frustrated in her great love, to be abandoned even by the chosen disciples. . .and still to remain.[36] Forgetting fear, joy, all things, herself included, so that she no longer recognized the Lord whom she loved—thus was she afflicted and thus we see her. The deadening effect of her grief is so convincingly portrayed that one fully understands why she was only able to stand and weep. Unlike the Magdalen who is chided and sometimes derided by earlier Latin writers, Pseudo-Origen's Mary is a human being whom the drama of living and loving has rendered vulnerable and fallible. [37]

A further insight into the nature of Mary's grief is provided when she discovers the two angels at the tomb. Avoiding at this point both allegorical speculation and moralization, the author merely advises Mary that perhaps she has found consolation: "You have come upon those who seem to care about you and who wish to lighten your sorrow." [38] But the narrator immediately sets up a prolonged contrast between these and Jesus, questioning, countering with Christ's recorded testimony, pleading that the love which he bore Mary during his earthly life would now insure that she be truly comforted. Finally, however, the preacher in him can keep silent no longer and he exorts Mary to accept the consolation of the angels lest the Master be displeased, and to remember Christ's admonition "Do not weep over me" lest she herself offend him. [39] "For if he loves your tears, it is perhaps not possible, as it was before, to keep back his tears." [40] But as surely as the angels have come to console, so surely is Mary too much affected by grief to hear and to heed, and in her long interior monologue, which forms the central section of the homily, the reader is admitted into the deepest recesses of both her love and her sorrow.

A psychological consistency fully in accord with her previous depiction characterizes Magdalen's self-analysis, and its first person narration is superbly effective. Mary reasons that all living creatures only make more heavy the sorrowful burden of one who seeks their dead creator; she fears that the angels will not be able to lessen her sorrow and might impede her love; besides, she seeks not angels but the Lord and Maker of both herself and the angels. Perhaps she should arise, search, be without rest until she finds the place where they have carried the Lord? But no, it is better for her to remain and guard the sepulchre lest it be destroyed in her absence; it is better, too, that she remain there so that she may be buried with the Lord. [41] How unhappy she is that she had ever left the tomb, that she had ever thought observing the law meant leaving the Lord of the law. She goes over in her mind the events of the day and arrives back at the puzzle of the angels' behavior. Why did they question her about her sadness? Did they wish to forbid her weeping? [42] At this point the reader remembers that the only thing left to Mary is her mourning, and the resolution she makes is completely plausible: "I will not obey them and as long as I live I will not cease to weep until I find my Lord." [43] Nor does one react badly to her bewilderment ("Where shall I turn?"), or to her cry of sorrow ("Tell him that I languish for love, I beg you"), or to her piercing plea: "O my hope, do not confound me in my expectation." [44] Because they are part of the stream of consciousness in a bereaved, abandoned woman, these emotional outbursts do not seem excessive. Their placement here at a distance from the climactic recognition scene is further evidence of Pseudo-Origen's consummate artistry.

Having raised his narrative tension to such a pitch, the author proceeds to normalize the situation of his characters by switching immediately from first to third person. Now he too permits chiding, but his complaint is not against Mary but against Christ's seemingly ironic "reward" for her great love and sorrow: "She saw you breathing forth her spirit, that is, your spirit, and you say, 'What do you weep for?' " [45] Magdalen's absolute devotion is declared without either derogation or explanation: "She depends totally on you; she abides totally within you; she hopes totally in you; and she despairs totally about you." [46] Certainly, the reader has been well prepared for the ensuing, tentative explanation: "because she is not in herself, but because of you is outside herself," and languishing with love, her eyes darkened, she will think him to be the gardener who is, in truth, the dayspring. [47] Having sought someone dead, Mary does not perceive the sun "who rising early shone through her windows and beamed through the ears of her body." [48] Though the author cannot excuse her for this error, he can explain it:

> So much sorrow swept upon her because of your death, that she was not able to hope about your life; so much sorrow invaded her because of your sepulchre, that she was not able to think of anything concerning your resurrection. [49]

By means of an apologia parallel to Bernard's interpretation of Christ's mother beneath the Cross, [50] the reader comes to see how "the spirit of Mary was more in your body than in hers," and he understands fully that when "she sought your body she sought equally her spirit; and when she lost your body, she lost with it her spirit." [51] What wonder is it, asks the narrator of Christ, that she does not know you, what wonder "if she has not sense who has lost the spirit?" [52] Obviously, if the Magdalen errs, "such an error proceeds not from delusion but from love and sorrow." O merciful and just judge, begs the author, if perhaps this is wrong, do not regard the error of the woman but the love of the disciple. [53]

The great power of Mary's love is finally manifested in her courageous promise to the person she thinks a gardener: tell me where you have laid him and I will take him away. Again, the narrator cannot refrain from chiding the Lord: "Why, therefore, do you not tell her where you have placed yourself?" She has eaten nothing for three days and she will not be able to satisfy her spirit unless the Lord, revealing himself, offers her the bread of his body and from the fragments fills up the basket of her heart. [54] The contrapuntal emphases on flesh and spirit, earthly and divine love, life and death, which have been intermittently observable in the homily are joined lyrically now as the narrator defines this food: "You are the living bread indeed which has in it all delight and every flavor of sweetness." [55] In the wake of this definition, the homily's climax follows simply: "Jesus said to her, 'Mary'." When Magdalen heard her name (so, we are told, was the Master accustomed to address her) she recognized the sweetness of its pronouncement and knew that her Lord has spoken. "Then her spirit was revivified" and her strong, impatient love moved her to be joined to Jesus, to touch him. Fortunately, the author's consistent emphasis on Mary's warm human characteristics allows him to bypass the dry, neatly packaged explanations of faith conventionally demanded by the words "noli me tangere." Instead, he stresses the loving kindness of the Lord to all the humble and right of heart who hope in him. And the Magdalen, "the beloved one," sought you simply and found you truly, says the homilist. Through all her sorrows she had kept hope in you, not in herself, and she was not ultimately abandoned; rather she "attained more through you than she hoped from you." [56]

Undoubtedly, the experience of this homily might also be expressed in similar terms. The great insight one gains into the Magdalen's character is paramount, but one also comes to know another figure whom I have deliberately called preacher, narrator, and author, because so he appears during the course of the treatise. Initially, the accents of the preacher are dominant: "Most beloved brothers, let us see. . . ." Nevertheless, he quickly assumes the posture of "narrator of the Magdalen" and steps into the foreground only occasionally to point out the implications of knowing the Lord, to advise Mary to accept the consolation of the angels, to place emphasis on the nature of Mary's grief. In describing her long interior monologue, however, the narrator takes on the role of omniscient author and extends to us a striking dramatic experience that is unparalleled in Latin homiletic literature. Through his virtuoso performance, a further literary dimension has been explored: the reader has not only seen Mary and heard her speak, he has actually touched her inmost being.

When the preacher begins his final "peroratio," he again takes a different tack from that of his progenitors and contemporaries. Yes, one is to learn from the formerly sinful woman how to love, seek, and desire Jesus always; but one is also to learn, as the homilist himself has learned, to accept no consolation except Jesus, and to search him out "in the monument of the heart." [57] This is, of course, to be a spiritual seeking: to remove all obstacles to faith, to beg for the Lord's appearance, to convert stiff-necked pride into true humility, to recognize the angels of activity and contemplation, [58] and never to be satisfied until one has seen, questioned, and made certain of the presence of the Lord. In the preacher's conclusion is perhaps the best explanation of his purpose and meaning:

> I dare to promise you with confidence that if you stand in faith at the monument of your heart, if in sorrow you seek Jesus and persevere in seeking, if you assume a humble posture, if by the example of Mary you will accept no consolation unless it be Jesus himself, then he is one whom, having revealed himself, you will find and know, and thus it will not be necessary to ask others where Jesus is, but you will more often point him out, announcing to others: "Because I have seen the Lord, and this he said to me!" To him is honor and glory with the Father and the Holy Spirit forever. Amen. [59]

The final admonition of the *De Maria Magdalena* makes quite obvious the homily's connection with the vocabulary and expression of mediaeval mysticism. The first hint of mystic inspiration in the text is the heavy accent on love and its effects in the opening sections, an accent which is strengthened by steady allusion to that handbook of the contemplative soul, *The Song of Songs*. In addition, the love-longing of *amore langueo* can be readily associated with similar experiences in the mystical life as described in the tracts of Hugh and Richard of St. Victor, Bernard, Bonaventure, and several English mystics. [60] Strong resemblances to Bernard's works in the apology for Mary Magdalen's actions, the reason for her learning of the Resurrection ("that she might bear you upon her heart and carry you in her body" [61]), and loving descriptions of the Eucharist continue this narrative "inwardness." Mysticism is further explicated by the preacher who develops the active and contemplative significance of the angels as a kind of prelude to the goal: "Seek Jesus whence you find him in yourself"—a goal admirably suited to the active/contemplative vocation of the homily's Benedictine author. [62]

An analysis of its literary style reveals the *De Maria Magdalena* as a magnificent expression of the Christian humanism of the Middle Ages.[63] Its major character is fully and humanly drawn with a consistent personality, adequate motivation, and plausible response. In addition, the Magdalen's Gospel-documented love for Christ is balanced in the homily by many references to his love for her—a method of treatment which allows one to meditate on Christ's humanity, "de rendre sensible au coeur la présence du Christ souffrant et glorifié et de s'unir à sa passion et son triomphe par la pensée et le sentiment."[64] Contributing also to the text's humanistic bias is a de-emphasis of the practical, theological, and allegorical considerations found in other authors.[65] Indeed, Pseudo-Origen's unique synthesis of several traditions into one artfully constructed whole "shines," in Basevorn's words, "with a double glow, earthly and heavenly, and this, it seems to me, invites to devotion those who understand more feelingly."[65]

NOTES

1. The most recent study of this homily is John McCall, "Chaucer and the Pseudo-Origen *De Maria Magdalena*," *Speculum*, 46 (1971), 491–509. Also noteworthy are Victor Saxer, *Le Culte de Marie Madeleine en Occident*, Cahiers d'archéologie et d'histoire, No. 3 (Paris: Société des fouilles archéologiques, 1959), pp. 346–48, and Hans Hansel, "Die Quellen der bayerischen *Magdalenklage*," *Zeitschrift für deutsche Philologie*, 62 (1937), 363–88.

2. Sermon theorists of the late thirteenth and fourteenth centuries oppose the *modus antiquus* to the *modus modernorum;* the latter includes only those sermons constructed according to the thematic or university schema of theme, protheme, division, subdivision, and dilation. Sermons preceding 1230 A.D. were generally not reducible to such a strict formulaic pattern. See Charles Smyth, *The Art of Preaching* (London: S.P.C.K., 1940), pp. 20–34 and Th. M. Charland, *Artes Praedicandi* (Ottawa: Institut d'Etudes Medievales d'Ottawa, 1936), pp. 102 ff.

4. For example, Peter of Celles (*PL* 202:822); Godfrey Abbot (*PL* 174:933); Peter Damien (*PL* 144:660); Peter Blescé (*PL* 207:650); Guerricus of Clairvaux (*PL* 185:213); Ratherius (*PL* 136:749); Hildebert (*PL* 171:671); "Honorius of Autun" (*PL* 172:979). Perhaps the most influential Patristic studies of Mary Magdalen were Augustine's *Tractatus CXXI* (*PL* 35:1955–58) and Gregory the Great's *Homilia XXV* (*PL* 76:1192 ff.).

5. Both Alcuin (*PL* 100:989) and Odo (*PL* 133:713) depend heavily on Augustine and Gregory. Odo, however, does discuss at length Mary Magdalen's tearful vigil at the sepulchre.

6. Anselm's prayer to Mary Magdalen appears in *PL* 158:1010. The Magdalen cult is treated extensively by Saxer *(Le Culte)*, and briefly but pointedly by Josef Szoverffy, "*Peccatrix Quondam Femina*: A Survey of the Mary Magdalen Hymns," *Traditio*, 19 (1963), 80–83. Extensive bibliography is available in Helen Meredith Garth, *Saint Mary Magdalen in Medieval Literature*, Johns Hopkins University Studies in Historical and Political Science 67, No. 3 (Baltimore: Johns Hopkins Univ. Press, 1950), pp. 12–16 and 98 ff.

7. Mary's favored position is demonstrable through both liturgical and popular devotional material. In addition to Garth, *ibid.*, see Hans Hansel, *Die Maria Magdalena*

Legende (Griefswald: H. Dallmayer, 1937) and Rossell Hope Robbins, "A Middle English Prayer to St. Mary Magdalen," *Traditio,* 24 (1968), 458.

8. This citation is an example of rhetorical anaphora, and it would be entirely possible to analyze the homily through identifying its various rhetorical tropes and figures. I have chosen, however, to limit my discussion to those uses of rhetoric which extend the dramatic and psychological features of this text.

10. "Olim te diligebat, olim a pharisaeo defendebat, et a sorore tua diligenter excusabat. Olim laudabat te, quando unguento pedes ipsius ungebas, lachrymis rigabas, et capillis tergebas, dolorem tuum mulcebat, peccata dimittebat. Olim quaerebat te cum non adesses, vocabat te cum abesses." All citations from the text here will be to the *Origenis Opera* (Hieronymo et Ruffino interpretibus), ed. J. Merlinus (Paris: J. Parvus et J. Badius, 1512), III, fols. 129^r–131^v. The "olim" section appears on fol. 129^{v}I. For the textual history of the homily, see McCall, pp. 492–497.

11. Fol. 130^{r}B: "Vere optimam partem elegit Maria, quia elegit stare ad pedes tuos, et audire sermones tuos. Vere optimam partem elegit, quia te elegit."

12. Fol. 130^{v}G: "Sed pro dolor ego volui observare legem et dimisi dominum legis. Lego obedivi, et eum cui lex obedit non custodivi: quamvis cum Christo manere non fuisset legem transgredi sed adimplere."

13. Fol. 130^{v}H: "Pascha enim ab isto defuncto non contaminatur, sed renovatur. Mortuus iste non polluit mundos, sed mundat immundos. Sanat omnes tangentes se, et illuminat ad se accedentes."

14. Fol. 131^{r}E: "O mulier magna est fides tua, magna est constantia tua. . .fiat tibi sicut vis et confide, quia fides tua te salvam fecit."

15. Fols. 130^{v}G and 131^{r}D. Paralleling the Virgin Mary and Mary Magdalen was common mediaeval practice. Hildebert and Odo both indulged in it, following in the tradition which was already well-established by the time of Isidore of Seville (*PL* 75:791).

16. Fol. 131^{r}A: ". . .ipse omne holus plantat bonum, et rigat in animabus sanctorum." The homilist makes more personal the "gardens" of Mary's heart and of the Church which were mentioned by Augustine, Alcuin, and Odo; he thus effectively draws the reader into the drama of the Magdalen's story.

17. References are to fols. 130^{r}D, 130^{v}G, 131^{r}I, 131^{v}F, and 131^{v}G.

18. Fol. 131^{r}A: "Quid post haec peccavit in te. . .aut in quo postea offendit." Cf. *Daily Missal,* ed. Maryknoll Fathers (New York: P. J. Kennedy & Sons, 1957), p. 354 for the text of the pre-Vatican II Good Friday liturgy.

19. Both the Gospel and the Homily use the words *testimonium* and *perhibeo* in their respective descriptions of the apostles and the angels; other references are to fols. 130^{r}C and 131^{v}H.

20. McCall, pp. 498–502, analyzes this text through emphasis on Mary's standing and weeping and their equivalents, love and sorrow. Love and sorrow, however, are only one set of qualities which describe the Magdalen, and the author synthesizes several other themes throughout the course of his homily.

21. The "grief in love" which defines Mary's *dolor* leads logically to loving still *(diligere)* with the possibility of erring *(errare)* when relief from grief is sought *(quaere)* and not found *(invenire).*

22. Fol. 129^{v}E; the reference is to Mary's double sorrow, first in Christ's death and secondly in the disappearance of his body. But the latter *(iste dolor)* is far worse than the former because no physical consolation or ministration is possible.

23. Fol. 129^{v}I: "Vocas eum et non audit; oras et non exaudit; quaeris illum et non invenis; pulsas et non aperit; tu sequeris illum, et fugit."

24. *Ibid:* "O quam cito surrexit Maria ut audivit, quam sollicite venit et solito more cecedit ad pedes tuos."

25. Fol. 130^{r}B: "Si enim solito more eam diligis, cur desiderium eius tandiu protrahis."

26. In fols. 129ᵛG and 131ʳC.
27. Fol. 129ᵛH: ". . .sic erat oblita ut etiam ipsum non cognosceret. Credite mihi, si ipsum cognosceret, in monumento eum non quaereret."
28. Fol. 130ᵛK: "O Maria si quaeris Iesum, cur non cognoscis Iesum? Et si cognoscis Iesum, quid quaeris Iesum?"
29. Fols. 131ʳD, 131ᵛF, and 131ʳE.
30. Fol. 131ᵛG: "Sequamur igitur fratres huius milieris affectum, ut perveniamus ad effectum."
31. Fol. 129ʳC: ". . .ac veri amoris igne succensa, nimis ardens desiderio indesinenter plorans a monumento non recedebat."
32. Fol. 129ʳC: "videamus si possumus cur staret, videamus et cur ploraret. Prosit nobis."
33. The text conveys Mary's continuing mistrust of herself: "Metuebat ne amor magistri sui in pectore suo frigesceret, si corpus non inveniret, quo viso recalesceret" (fol. 129ᵛE). The use of *metuere* with regard to Mary and of *timere* with regard to the fear of the Apostles indicates careful composition.
34. Fol. 129ᵛG.
35. *Ibid.* "Fortis est ut mors dilectio. Quid enim aliud faceret mors in Maria? Facta erat exanimis, facta insensibilis, sentiens non sentiebat, videns non videbat, audiens non audiebat."
36. Fol. 129ᵛH.
37. Augustine emphasized Mary's seeking the living among the dead (*PL* 38:1154 ff.), and mediaeval homilists followed his example with the exception of Haymo of Auxerre (*PL* 118:479), who claimed that Mary wept only because the body of Christ had been stolen away. McCall, p. 498, calls Mary a "vulnerable, fallible woman in love."
38. The angels were variously regarded as symbolic of either Old and New Testaments or as personifications of the theological virtues; see Gregory (*PL* 76:1191), Odo (*PL* 133:719), and Alcuin (*PL* 100:990). Pseudo-Origen remarks only: "Reperisti eos qui de te curam videntur habere, et qui volunt dolorem tuum lenire" (fol. 129ᵛI).
39. Fol. 130ʳC.
40. Fol. 130ʳD: "Nam et ipse amaret lachrymas tuas, non posset forsitan ut olim tenere lachrymas suas."
41. Fol. 130ᵛG: "Stabo igitur et hic moriar, ut saltem iuxta sepulcrum domini mei sepeliar."
42. Fol. 130ᵛH.
43. *Ibid:* "Ego illis non obediam; et dum vivo, plorare non desinam, donec dominum meum inveniam."
44. Fol. 130ᵛI: "O spes mea, ne confundas me ab expectatione mea."
45. Fol. 130ᵛK. In contrast with Mary's lengthy self-revelation, Christ's appearance in the homily is treated starkly: "Dum Maria sic doleret, et sic fleret, cum haec dixisset, conversa est retrorsum, et vidit Iesum stantem, et nesciebat quia Iesus est. Dixit ei Iesus: Mulier, quid ploras et quem quaeris?"
46. *Ibid:* "Tota pendet in te, tota maneret in te, tota sperat de te, et tota desperat de se."
47. Pseudo-Origen's description is in marked contrast with that of Odo, who declares (*loc. cit.*): "Tunc vero in eius mente sol ortus est, quando non solum resurrexisse vidit, sed etiam credidit."
48. Fol. 130ᵛK: "Mulier ista, quia densa nube doloris obtecta non videbat solem, qui mane surgens radiabat per fenestras eius, et per aures corporis sui."
49. Fol. 131ʳB: ". . .tantusque dolor invaserat eam de morte tua, ut non posset sperare de vita tua; et tantus dolar invaserat eam de sepultura tua ut nihil posset cogitare de resurrectione tua."

50. Bernard's *Sermo in Dominica infra Octavam Assumptionis B. V. Mariae (PL* 183:437–38) uses a similar matter-spirit transference to explain Mary the Virgin's participation in the sufferings of Calvary: "Vere tuam, o beata mater, animam gladius pertransivit. Alioquin nonnisi eam pertransiens, carnem Filii tui penetraret. Et quidem posteaquam emisit spiritum tuus ille Jesus (omnium quidem sed specialiter tuus), ipsius plane non attigit animam crudelis lancea, quae ipsius (nec mortuo parcens, cui nocere non posset) aperuit latus, sed tuam utique animam pertransivit. Ipsius nimirum anima jam ibi non erat; sed tua plane inde nequibat avelli."
51. Fol. 131ʳC.
52. *Ibid:* "Quid igitur mirum si sensum non habebat, quae spiritum amiserat."
53. The grammatically parallel constructions which are frequently found in the latter sections of the homily are reminiscent of Anselm's *Orationes,* particularly "Oratio XVI ad Mariam Magdalenam." But the resemblances are only linguistic because in context Anselm's prayers are "tensely emotional and completely intellectual effusions which seem to oppress the spirit with their excess of feeling" (R. W. Southern, *Saint Anselm and His Biographer* [Cambridge: Cambridge Univ. Press, 1963], pp. 45–47.)
54. Fol. 131ʳE. This reference marks the author's first departure from the literal explication of events which has occupied him throughout the homily. The effect is striking and prepares the reader well for the narrative and metaphoric climax which follows shortly.
55. Fol. 131ᵛF.
56. Fol. 131ᵛG: ". . .sed plus est consecuta per te quam expectaret a te."
57. This, of course, is what Mary has done in her self-searching monologue. Although several earlier homilists had probed Mary's mind and Bishop Fulgentius (*PL* 65:908 ff.) had even posited a series of unspoken questions which might have tormented her, no homilist before Pseudo-Origen exposes us to so moving a probe of character and motive.
58. The transfer of active-contemplative significances to the angels in not usual. Inspired by Luke 10:38–42 and common since Augustine, Mary and Martha were used to signify the two "lives" of the Church—the life of action and the life of contemplation (Garth, pp. 85–87). In the context of this homily, however, neither the active nor the contemplative is given preference; union with Jesus remains the "unum necessarium."
59. Fol. 131ᵛH.
60. Mystical theology readily accepted the meaning of "amore langueo;" for a discussion of pertinent materials, see Dom David Knowles, *The English Mystical Tradition* (London: Burns & Oates, 1961), pp. 26 ff. The use of "Jesus" rather than "Lord" or "Christ" might also indicate a belief in the mystic efficacy of the holy name but it might also be related to exposure to such hymns as the "Jesu dulcis memoria."
61. Fol. 131ʳE: ". . .ut ipsa tollat te super cor suum et portet in corpore suo."
62. McCall, p. 497.
63. Saxer, p. 347.
64. *Ibid.*
65. "Mira res! Hominem perfectae aetatis" and a hundred pounds of spices are, in Peter Damien's experiences, not movable; yet, the practical-minded theologian marvels at Mary's devotion and concludes that love can conquer all difficulties (*PL* 144:666). Most homilists favored an investigation of the implications of "noli me tangere" (Thomas Aquinas provides a sampling of the arguments in his *Catena Aurea* [Savoy, 1889], IV, 601–2) or towards allegorical explanations like Odo's (*PL* 133:715–16).

The Ars dictaminis *and Rhetorical Textbooks at the Bolognese University in the Fourteenth Century*

James R. Banker

THE LATE ROMAN and medieval practice of conveying by epistle the counsels and decrees of emperors, popes, kings, and other officials led in the eleventh century to instruction in the art of composing epistles. The first treatise on this art was written at Monte Cassino, but early in the twelfth century Bologna became the center of instruction and retained its European-wide preeminence into the fourteenth century. Epistolary instruction was not limited to Italy; by the middle of the twelfth century French masters, Bernard Silvester for example, as well as German masters were teaching the art, and in the 1180's Peter of Blois brought epistolary instruction to England.[1]

Throughout Europe the masters employed the term *ars dictaminis* or *dictamen* to identify their instruction in the art of writing persuasive epistles. Students were taught that their epistles should be marked by a discourse, the *cursus,* that achieved distinction from common patterns of speech through the use of *sententiae* and stately caldences at the end of phrases and clauses. While accepting rhythmical and metrical epistles as within the province of *dictamen,* the Italian masters restricted themselves to the art of composing prose epistles. Their students entered the chancelleries of the popes, emperors, bishops, and princes where their primary task was to write epistles of a practical nature, and a prose discourse was essential for communicating quotidian affairs. To assure that the epistles written for and to the princes and prelates were persuasive, the masters were compelled to adapt their art to the values of hierarchical society.[2]

At the University in Bologna *dictamen* treatises were composed and taught by a succession of masters from Ugo da Bologna early in the twelfth century through the most renowned—Boncompagno da Signa,

Guido Faba, and Bene da Firenze—to Bono da Lucca late in the thirteenth century.[3] I shall contend here that this practice of each master writing his own *dictamen* treatise, or students copying the lectures of the master, was abandoned after 1325 in Bologna when one treatise, *Brevis introductio ad dictamen,* became the standard text and was taught in conjunction with lectures upon the pseudo-Ciceronian *Rhetorica ad Herennium* for the remainder of the fourteenth century. The lectures on the two texts were initiated by Giovanni di Bonandrea, the author of the *dictamen* text and the foremost *dictator* of the fourteenth century, and were perpetuated by Bolognese masters until the end of that century.[4] In this paper, then, rhetorical and *dictamen* instruction at the Bolognese University in the fourteenth century will be examined with the purpose of defining Giovanni di Bonandrea's role and analyzing the subsequent fortunes of his dual instruction at the University.

The Master who lectured upon these textbooks received notarial and university training that prepared him for his long tenure in the chair of rhetoric at the Bolognese University. Giovanni was born into a noble family of Bologna and matriculated in the Guild of Notaries in 1265.[5] After studying at an unknown university he became the personal notary of the Lord Captain of Verona, Alberto della Scala.[6] In 1292 the Rectors of the University in Bologna requested the communal government to invest Giovanni with a professorship of rhetoric. They appointed Giovanni to teach rhetoric due to ". . .his great sufficiency in philosophy and especially in the faculty of rhetoric" and their belief that his instruction would confer great honor and utility upon the University and the Commune of Bologna.[7]

Evidence concerning rhetorical instruction in Bologna prior to the 1290's is sparse. Heretofore the men who taught *ars dictaminis* received professorships in grammar and were usually described as masters of grammar.[8] In the French Cathedral schools, however, the *Rhetorica ad Herennium* and Cicero's *De inventione* were commented upon by Thierry of Chartres and other masters in the preceding centuries.[9] Late in the thirteenth century Northern European masters brought this practice to Italy. Jacques de Dinant may have taught both *dictamen* and rhetoric in Bologna in the 1260's and 1270's though no known document of appointment substantiates the manuscript evidence. Guidotto da Bologna translated the *Rhetorica ad Herennium* into the vernacular in the 1260's, but the attempts to locate him at the University have not been unqualified successes.[10] The first document citing a professor of rhetoric in Bologna relates that in 1291 the communal representatives requested that Jacob of Liège be admitted to the College of Masters since he was, they stated, the only one in Bologna who could teach rhetoric.[11] In the next year Giovanni di Bonandrea received his lectureship in rhetoric, and thereafter the documentation, while not overwhelming, is noteworthy, perhaps because Giovanni served as the overseer of the Bolognese Chancellery in the first two decades of the fourteenth century.

Giovanni returned to Bologna in 1302 after a second sojourn in Verona, and from that year retained his professorship in rhetoric until his death in 1321.[12] Though no manuscripts containing his lectures on rhetoric have been identified, Giovanni did lecture upon the *Rhetorica ad Herennium,* and after his death his successors taught from this classical treatise for the following two centuries.

While already commenting upon this classical rhetorical text, Giovanni informed the Bolognese officials in 1303 that he wished to teach "another science" which had great usefulness to the city. His suggestion was implemented in 1304 when Giovanni was given the title, "perpetuus informator et promotor cancellariorum," and the Commune charged him with the task of instructing the prospective chancellors of Bologna. This was instruction on writing persuasive epistles and on constructing convincing orations.[14] In conjunction with this instruction to notaries and chancellors Giovanni wrote his *Brevis introductio ad dictamen,* the treatise that became the *dictamen* textbook in Bologna throughout the fourteenth century.

This treatise contained most of the traditional topics of *ars dictaminis* of the thirteenth century. Giovanni followed his predecessors in organizing the first book of his treatise around the parts of the epistle: the salutation, exordium, narration of facts, petition, and conclusion. In addition he repeated the admonition that the addressee was to be greeted initially with a salutation that included a correct recitation of the names and dignities of the correspondents.[15] Giovanni and the earlier writers devoted a large portion of their treatises to the salutation, indicating their belief that it played a necessary role in the epistle and its persuasion. In the discussion of the exordium and the narration of facts Giovanni taught that any recounting of human behavior required adaptation of the common opinion of the relationship between character and events.[16] In the second half of the treatise he discussed the doctrine of style appropriating the traditional doctrines of the art of punctuation, the *cursus,* and the epistle as a literary and public

155

document of persuasion. The earlier writers had viewed the figures of speech and thought as an essential element because it gave the epistle a metaphoric and grave quality unlike everyday speech. Giovanni ignored these figures, and his lectures in general show less interest in an artificial discourse that was so valued by the thirteenth-century *dictatores,* though his discussion of the *cursus* would aid a writer in constructing an elevated discourse.[17]

In the first two parts of the epistle Giovanni made substantial innovations in adapting the *dictamen* precepts to his audience of unlearned notaries. Giovanni retained his predecessors' practice of constructing model salutations that were organized according to the hierarchical orders of medieval society. But to these categories of model salutations for popes, emperors, bishops, and feudatories, he added the novel one of men "distinguished by a quality." [18] This group of men did not have an inherited position in the hierarchy or a conferred office; rather, Giovanni conceived of a social group who achieved distinction by their own efforts, thereby ennobling themselves with an acquired quality. Using the term *" habitus"* to denote a "perfect" quality resulting from training and industry, Giovanni directed attention to acquired knowledge and skills, on what is achieved by human effort. These are the skills of the merchants, notaries, and money changers of the Italian cities, and the model salutations of Giovanni single out these groups.[19] The citizens were distinctive because through education and their effort they had acquired qualities beyond what nature and other men could grant to them. By associating the guildsmen with men of inherited and conferred offices, Giovanni endowed those who achieved a distinctive quality with an equal honor.

Giovanni, moreover, abandoned the practice of placing a sententious statement after the salutation as the exordium; he advocated an exordium that moved the mind of the recipient by recounting an historical event or by narrating the exploits of a great personage.[20] The nature of the orator's or writer's case and the psychological state of the listeners determined the type of narrative exordium that he would construct. Giovanni borrowed this conception of the exordium from Cicero, but he initiated the practice of teaching through paradigmatic exordiums that were constructed according to the quality of the case and the mental state of the listeners.[21] This technique of teaching the exordium through models organized by Ciceronian categories was continued by fourteenth-century *dictatores* and later humanists.[22] In his *Brevis introductio ad dictamen,* then, Giovanni di Bonandrea elevated the merchants and artisans of the Italian communes by constructing persuasive methods that honored their preference for a literature and a history which bound together man's efforts and accomplishments. Indicating the citizens' widespread interest in Giovanni's innovative teaching is the existence of thirteen manuscripts containing his *Brevis introductio ad dictamen.*[23]

The *dictamen* treatise of Giovanni was undoubtedly intended for the Bolognese citizens. It was taught in a public place, the Palace of Notaries, and in the middle of the city rather than in the *Porta nova* quarter where the liberal arts courses were most often taught.[24] Giovanni's treatise is brief, straightforward, and organized for men who had been unable to devote a lifetime to the study of Latin. Within the treatise, his innovative instruction upon the salutation of an earned quality and the model exordiums legitimized values most congenial to the guildsmen of Bologna. While emperors and popes are found in his salutations, the overwhelming number of model exordiums are drawn from the civic ambiance. Furthermore, within Giovanni's instruction on *dictamen* he taught *ars oratoria,* the art of constructing and delivering persuasive orations. To complement the models for epistles, his *Brevis introductio ad dictamen* contains model speeches addressed to the men of the city.[25] The instruction of *ars dictaminis* and *ars oratoria* was initiated by the Council of Bologna in order ". . .to teach the unlearned as well as the lettered. . . ," and Giovanni's treatise was an "introduction" to these arts, well-suited for the notaries.[26] Though the treatise does not include any orations in the Bolognese dialect, Giovanni's student and successor, who vowed to follow his deceased master's example, gave instruction in the art of oral persuasion in the vernacular.[27] Giovanni's inclusion of model orations in Latin and his successor's instruction in the *ars oratoria* make it impossible to conclude that the lectures on the *Rhetorica ad Herennium* were instruction in *ars oratoria* and the lectures on the *Brevis introductio ad dictamen* were instruction in *ars dictaminis.* Giovanni's instruction, rather, was divided on the social status and educational achievement of the audience. The lectures on the *dictamen* text were practical, brief, and directed to men of the notarial guild, while lectures on the classical rhetorical text were directed in the University to students who were committed to a lengthy period of study.[28]

The exact nature of Giovanni's dual instruction in *dictamen* and rhetoric emerges from a Bolognese Chancellery document of 1321. In that year Giovanni died and the Council of the People of Bologna appointed his student and *repetitor,* Bartolino di Benincasa da Canulo, to succeed him. In the act of appointment the notary of the Council composed a panegyric to Giovanni that demonstrated the Bolognese citizens' evaluation of their deceased Professor and the art of rhetoric. Without rhetoric, the art of speaking eloquently, the city and other human organizations cannot exist. Rhetoric, the eulogy continues, has become moribund in Bologna since the death of the "famous and glorious Giovanni di Bonandrea." Since Bologna is known throughout the world as the mother of all arts this loss must be rectified lest the city suffer detriment and damage.[29]

Having established the incomparable value of rhetoric and Giovanni's instruction, the document then conveys the communal officials' conception of the practices of their deceased Master and their wish for his student to maintain his program of *dictamen* and rhetorical studies. The document records Giovanni's practice of reading the *Rhetorica ad Herennium* twice a year. In the years prior to his death Giovanni would begin lecturing after the Feast of St. Luke (18 October) and finish in the Easter season. After Easter he lectured again upon the *Rhetorica ad Herennium* and finished this second reading prior to the Feast of St. Michael on 29 September. These readings of the classical rhetorical text undoubtedly were "ordinary," that is, read in the morning by the established scholar while the lectures of Giovanni's *repetitor,* Bartolino, were "extraordinary," an extra reading of his Master's lectures on the *Ad Herennium* in the afternoons.[30]

Each year Giovanni also taught his *Brevis introductio ad dictamen* twice. The first lectures were given every day during the season of Lent. This *ars dictaminis* treatise was read again at an unspecified time after Easter, but Giovanni was to finish before the Feast of St. Michael. Inasmuch as the first instruction of *dictamen* extended through the six weeks of Lent, Giovanni, robably had the freedom to choose when he would give the second series of lectures on *dictamen* from Easter to September.[31] If the second lectures were given late in the period from March or April to September, which we may assume since there would be little purpose in teaching the courses of *dictamen* consecutively, the two series of lectures would be approximately six months apart. In 1303 the communal officials had appointed Giovanni to impart to their notaries the epistolary skills necessary in the chancellery. The chancellors and many of the notaries were appointed for six-month terms of office.[32] Therefore, the two series a year of *dictamen* instruction had their origin in the 1303 appointment of Giovanni di Bonandrea to instruct the chancellors and notaries of Bologna.

The dual instruction of Giovanni di Bonandrea became the pattern at the Bolognese University and was retained for the remainder of the fourteenth century. His *Brevis introductio ad dictamen* was established as the *dictamen* textbook of that century and the *Ad Herennium* achieved the preeminent position in rhetorical instruction. Several *ars dictaminis* treatises were written in or just after Giovanni's lifetime, but thereafter others have not been noted in Bologna in the fourteenth century. While he yet lived, Giovanni del Virgilio, Giovanni Battista, Pietro de'Boattieri, and possibly Lorenzo d'Aquilegia wrote *dictamen* treatises for the notaries of Bologna,[33] but in the next half century Giovanni di Bonandrea's text held a singular place in the arts curriculum of the University.

In Bologna, Bartolino di Benincasa da Canulo continued the dual instruction of Giovanni. Since neither Bartolino's comments upon Giovanni's *Brevis introductio ad dictamen* nor Giovanni's comments upon the *Rhetorica ad Herennium* are known to be extant, Bartolino's debt to his Master cannot be established, but inasmuch as Bartolino repeated Giovanni's lectures, it can be asserted that he transmitted the rhetorical knowledge of his Master. After serving as Giovanni's *repetitor,* Bartolino taught rhetoric and *ars dictaminis* at the Bolognese University from 1321 to 1338 and perhaps beyond.

In writing his *History of Bologna,* Ghirardacci, who examined and cited documents in the sixteenth century that have not survived, drew an outline of Bartolino's career in the University. Bartolino began lecturing upon rhetoric in the University and *dictamen* at the Palace of Notaries in 1321. In 1323 the Rectors of the University, "greatly content and satisfied" with Bartolino's lectures on rhetoric, appealed to the "Senate" of Bologna asking the Senators to confirm their lecturer Bartolino and increase his salary. And the Senate of Bologna complied. Ghirardacci also noted that in 1328 at the insistence of the students, Master Benincasa da Canulo was elected to read rhetoric.[34] This was probably a new appointment for Bartolino, as Pasquali-Alidosi, who also had access to nonextant documents, recorded that Bartolino read in the University from 1321 to 1326.[35] However, Ghirardacci did not record Bartolino's name in a list of lecturers in the University for 1324. He listed only one doctor of grammar, Master Vitale, who read Cicero and commented upon Ovid's *Metamorphoses.*[36] After the two, or possibly four, years had elapsed, the students requested the return of Bartolino, and he was again made lecturer in 1328.

In the decade from 1327 to 1337, Bologna underwent two political changes with the imposition of papal dominance in the person of

Cardinal Beltrando dal Pogetto followed by the *signoria* of Taddeo Pepoli. Bartolino is mentioned as a lecturer in the University in 1329, and probably continued to teach at least until 1338. In that year, several masters were compelled to vow not to teach their science outside the city of Bologna without the expressed consent of the communal government. This measure of requiring masters to swear to teach exclusively at Bologna was a tactic frequently employed to retain the services of the doctors of law, more valued than doctors of the arts. The only other grammarian or rhetorician of Bologna for whom we have evidence of such a vow is Bene da Firenze in 1218.[37] Moreover, the importance of Bartolino's rhetorical instruction is attested to by the large number of copies of his commentary to the *Rhetorica ad Herennium*.[38]

The existence of Bolognese manuscripts containing commentaries to the *Ad Herennium* after the 1340's confirms that this classical text continued to be lectured upon in Bologna and provided the basis for rhetorical instruction. The Latin manuscript numbered 2461 in Bologna in the Biblioteca Universitaria, for example, contains a lengthy commentary to the *Rhetorica ad Herennium* which begins "Negotium triplex est, silicet yconomicum, politicum et monasticum. . . ." The length of the commentary and the citation of classical authors denote the significance of this classical rhetorical text in the arts curriculum in Bologna at mid-century.[39]

No scholar has found *ars dictaminis* treatises written or notices of teachers of *dictamen* at the Bolognese University in the middle of the fourteenth century. Certainly, Pietro da Muglio taught rhetoric to Coluccio Salutati among others though probably in a private school, but there is no mention of *dictamen*.[40] Despite the lack of notices of masters teaching *dictamen* or writing new treatises, however, several mid-fourteenth-century manuscripts with commentaries to the *Rhetorica ad Herennium* also contain commentaries to the *Brevis introductio ad dictamen* of Giovanni di Bonandrea. Eight of the thirteen manuscripts containing the *dictamen* treatise have accompanying commentaries, six of which have a format suggesting that they are notes taken from the lectures of university masters.[41] These commentaries are anonymous excepting the one authored by an unknown Giovanni Dati. In his *accessus* to the commentary, Dati wrote an encomium to Giovanni di Bonandrea, praising him as the most learned man of his age and as the restorer of the rhetorical works of Cicero.[42] In the main, however, the commentators ignored the author of the *dictamen* text and directed their attention to definitions, etymologies, explanations, and elaborations of rhetorical theory, the usual material of the commentaries of university masters.

The commentators were most concerned with Giovanni's instruction on the salutation and the exordium. In several manuscripts the commentators establish historical distance between themselves and Giovanni di Bonandrea by stating that "today" the salutation required a different construction.[43] They advocated minor modifications, but the salutation was retained as a persuasive technique that gained the goodwill of the recipient by an accurate statement of his place in the social hierarchy. In their glosses of Giovanni's discussion of the exordium, the commentators elaborated his innovative exordium, particularly the model exordiums. For example, the commentator to a Bolognese manuscript explained how a model exordium in praise of Giovanni's brother, Simone, was used in Verona to win goodwill for Simone's son whom the Della Scala accused of betraying their city.[44] The remainder of Giovanni's treatise, including his treatment of the other parts of the epistle and the *cursus,* was of lesser interest to the university professors. In their discussions throughout the treatises the commentators cited an extensive number of classical and medieval authors that range from Aristotle, Lucan, Seneca, Victorinus to Peter of Blois and the earlier *dictator,* Bene da Firenze.[45] These commentaries confirm the hypothesis that the rhetorical and *dictamen* instruction begun by Giovanni continued unchanged through the middle of the fourteenth century.

This is corroborated by the comments of Giovanni Conversino da Ravenna. The early humanist has left notices of rhetorical instruction in the Bolognese University in the year 1359. Conversino stated that Pietro da Forlì, who held the chair of rhetoric at the University in Bologna, presented a course on the *Bononianti,* a title given to Giovanni di Bonandrea's *Brevis introductio ad dictamen* because of the first two words - *Bononia natus* - in the hexameter poem that precedes the treatise. Conversino stated that he had finished his studies in grammar and dialectic and was prepared to progress to the higher study of rhetoric. He completed his attendance at the lectures of Pietro da Forlì on the *Rhetorica ad Herennium* at Easter, 1359. The date of completion is significant as it represents a continuation of the semester sequence established by Giovanni di Bonandrea a half century earlier. Lectures upon the *Brevis introductio ad dictamen* were frequent; Pietro lectured upon the early fourteenth-century treatise sometime in or prior to 1359 and then was succeeded in this lectureship by Dino della Valle da

Reggio. Moreover, Giovanni Conversino himself commented upon the *Brevis introductio ad dictamen* and lectured to the law students on the *Ad Herennium.*[46]

Interest in the *dictamen* treatise of Bonandrea remained high through the end of the fourteenth century. In 1372 the treatise was copied in Bologna; the style of writing, *littera bononiensis,* as well as the blue and red capitals suggest that the manuscript was written near the Bolognese University.[47] Bartolomeo del Regno, a correspondent of Coluccio Salutati, held the chair of rhetoric at the University in Bologna in 1383, and well into the fifteenth century. In this position, he lectured upon the *Brevis introductio ad dictamen.* The manuscript which preserves a portion of his commentary to the *dictamen* treatise states that Bartolomeo also wrote upon Cicero. Given the Bolognese tradition of joined *dictamen* and rhetorical lectures and his appointment to teach rhetoric, it is assured that Bartolomeo's writing upon Cicero was his commentary to the pseudo-Ciceronian *Rhetorica ad Herennium.*[48]

The near century-long instruction on the *Brevis introductio ad dictamen* linked with lectures on the *Ad Herennium* appears to have ended near 1400. In this period manuscripts or documents do not exist, or have not been discovered, indicating that the Bolognese masters continued to lecture on Giovanni di Bonandrea's treatise. Perhaps *ars dictaminis* was no longer taught in Bologna, though in Pisa Francesco da Buti, lecturer on the *Divine Comedy,* wrote his *Regule rhetorice,* ca. 1370, in which he discussed the epistolary art.[49]

Despite the probable ending of the dual instruction, rhetoric was studied at the University in Bologna in a varied form through the fifteenth century. Already Pietro da Muglio had lectured upon the *De inventione* of Cicero and the *Rhetorica ad Herennium,* probably when he held the chair of rhetoric in Bologna from 1368 to 1383.[50] The Statutes of the College of Medicine and Arts at the beginning of the fifteenth century required the arts students to hear lectures upon the *Rhetorica ad Herennium* and Cicero's *De inventione.* Commentaries upon both classical texts are numerous from Bologna and elsewhere during the Renaissance. Guarino da Verona, for example, lectured upon the *Rhetorica ad Herennium,* and his commentary received wide circulation.[51] Moreover, Giovanni di Bonandrea's practice of composing model exordiums according to the Ciceronian "quality" of the case and the mental state of the listener, having been taught to three generations of students, was continued by the humanists. Francesco da Buti in the previously mentioned *Regule rhetorice* taught his students to employ Ciceronian categories for model exordiums and asserted that this was "the modern practice." [52] Gasparino Barzizza, from whose instruction emerged so many eminent humanists, wrote a lengthy work of model exordiums organized by the qualities of the case and the state of the audience. His *Exempla exordiorum* survives in several scores of manuscripts, attesting to the permanent influence and applicability of Giovanni di Bonandrea's teaching methods. [53]

The evidence presented in this paper demonstrates that the pattern of instruction begun by Giovanni di Bonandrea in Bologna persisted throughout the fourteenth century. His lectures and those of his successors upon the *Brevis introductio ad dictamen* and the *Rhetorica ad Herennium* established these two treatises as the standard texts of *dictamen* and rhetoric in the Bolognese University. The commentaries to these two texts were the most important repositories of rhetorical knowledge in the fourteenth century. [54] By 1400, the dual instruction had split, with the commentary to the classical text remaining as a prominent feature of renaissance rhetorical studies.

NOTES

1. See the discussions of J. de Ghellinck, *L'Essor de la littérature latine au XIIᵉ siècle* (Brussels and Paris), II, 54–68; J. J. Murphy, "Alberic of Monte Cassino: Father of the Medieval *Ars dictaminis,*" *The American Benedictine Review*, XXII (1971), 129–46; N. Denholm-Young, "The Cursus in England," in *Oxford Essays in Medieval History Presented to Herbert Edward Salter* (Oxford, 1934), pp. 68–103, reprinted in his *Collected Papers on Medieval Subjects* (Oxford, 1946), pp. 170–92; M. Brini Savorelli, "Il *Dictamen* di Bernardo Silvestre," *Rivista critica di storia della filosofia,* XX (1965), 182–230. Alberic's and Bernard's authorship of treatises on *ars dictaminis* has been debated; see the comments and citations of Murphy and Brini Savorelli as well as those of G. Vecchi, *Il magistero delle 'artes' latine a Bologna nel medioevo,* in *Pubblicazioni della Facoltà di Magistero della Università di Bologna,* 2 (Bologna, n.d.), 9–12.

2. The bibliography of texts and discussions of *ars dictaminis* is immense; see now, however, the valuable work of J. J. Murphy, *Medieval Rhetoric: A Select Bibliography* (Toronto, 1971), items Dl ff. For an understanding of the *cursus,* I have found the following discussions most valuable: R. L. Poole, *Lectures on the Papal Chancery* (Cambridge, 1915), pp. 76–97; F. Di Capua, *Scritti Minori* (Rome, 1959), I, 495–528. L. Rockinger's edition of *dictamen* texts always deserves special mention: *Briefsteller und Formelbücher des elften bis vierzehnten Jahrhunderts,* in *Quellen und Erörterungen zur Bayerischen und Deutschen Geschichte,* IX (Munich, 1863).

3. See the discussions of A. Gaudenzi, "Sulla cronologia delle opere dei dettatori bolognesi da Buoncompagni a Bene di Lucca," *Bollettino dell'Istituto Storico Italiano,* XIV (1895), 85–174; L. Paetow, *The Arts Course at Medieval Universities with Special Reference to Grammar and Rhetoric* (Champaign, 1910), pp. 70–94; and H. Wieruszowski, "*Ars dictaminis* in the Time of Dante," *Medievalia et Humanistica,* I (1943), 95–108, now reprinted in her *Politics and Culture in Medieval Spain and Italy,* in *Storia e letteratura, Raccolta di studi e testi,* 121 (Rome, 1971), 359–378.

For general discussions of the University in Bologna in the fourteenth century, see, Vecchi, *op. cit.*; H. Rashdall, *The Universities of Europe in the Middle Ages,* rev. and ed., F. Powicke and A. Emden (Oxford, 1936), I, 233–68; F. Cavazza, *Le scuole dell'antico Studio Bolognese* (Milan, 1896); G. Zaccagnini, *La vita dei maestri e degli scolari nello Studio di Bologna nei secoli XIII e XIV,* in *Biblioteca dell'Archivum Romanicum,* V (Geneva, 1926). Examples of the individual treatises: in the early twelfth century, Ugo da Bologna, *Rationes dictandi prosaice,* ed. Rockinger, *op. cit.,* pp. 53–94; in the late twelfth century, Goffredo, *Summa de arte dictandi,* ed. V. Licitra, "La 'Summa de arte dictandi' di Maestro Goffredo," *Studi medievali,* Ser. 3, VII (1966), 885–913; of the numerous treatises early in the thirteenth century, see Guido Faba, *Summa dictaminis,* ed. A. Gaudenzi, *Il propugnatore* N.S. III, 1 (1890), 287–338 and III, 2 (1890), 345–93; and Boncompagno da Signa, *Palma,* ed. C. Sutter, in his *Aus Leben und Schriften des Magisters Boncompagno* (Freiburg, 1894), pp. 105–27. G. Vecchi has edited the fifth book of Bene da Firenze's *Candelabrum* in his "Temi e momenti d'arte dettatoria nel 'Candelabrum' di Bene da Firenze," *Atti e memorie della Deputazione di storia patria per le province di Romagna,* X (1958/1959), 148–68. And near the middle of the thirteenth century, Bono da Lucca, *Cedrus Libani,* ed. G. Vecchi, in *Testi e manuali del Instituto di filologia romanza dell'Universita di Roma,* XLVI (Modena, 1963). See below, note 33, for a list of fourteenth century *artes dictaminis* treatises of Bolognese masters.

4. Future research may turn up *dictamen* treatises at Bologna in the period after 1325, thereby mediating the importance of the *Brevis introductio ad dictamen,* but the contention of this paper is based on the present state of knowledge. The most complete studies of Giovanni di Bonandrea are: G. Zaccagnini, "Giovanni di Bonandrea dettatore e rimatore e altri grammatici e dottori in arte dello Studio bolognese," *Studi e memorie per la storia dell'Università di Bologna,* V (1920), 154–204; L. Frati, "Grammatici bolognesi del trecento," *Studi e memorie per la storia dell'Università di Bologna,* IV (1920), 39–41; E. Orioli, *La cancelleria pepolesca: Atti e formule* (Bologna, 1910). The Zaccagnini article contains selections from Giovanni's *Brevis introductio ad dictamen.* A fourteenth-century anonymous translation into Italian has been edited by F. Zambrini, *Brieve introductione a dictare* (Bologna, 1854). See also the comments of G. Fantuzzi, *Notizie degli scritti bolognesi* (Bologna, 1782), II, 375–6; G. N. Pasquali-Aliodosi, *I dottori bolognesi di teologia, filosofia, medicina, e d'arti liberale, dall'anno 1000 per tutto Marzo del 1623* (Bologna, 1623), p. 79; C. Ghirardacci, *Della historia di Bologna* (Bologna, 1596 and 1654), I, 561 and II, 17–8; A. Corradi, "Notizie sui professori di latinità nello Studio di Bologna sin dalle prime memorie," *Documenti e studi pubblicati per cura della Reale deputazione di storia patria per le province di Romagna* (Bologna, 1887), II, pp. 1, 41.

5. Bologna, Archivio di Stato, *Matricola dei notai 1219–1296,* fol. 25ᵛ, and *Matricola dei notai 1218–1299,* fol. 78ʳ. For a discussion of these documents, see A. Pini, *"I libri matricularum societatum Bononiensis" e il loro riordinamento archivistico,* in *Quaderni della paleografia ed archivistica,* XV (Bologna, 1967).

6. *Documenti per la storia delle relazioni diplomatiche fra Verona e Mantova nel secolo XIII,* ed. C. Cipolla (Milan, 1905), pp. 240–3.

7. The document of appointment has been printed by Zaccagnini, "Giovanni di Bonandrea," 188–9.

8. Despite the instruction of persuasive methods in his *Candelabrum,* Bene da Firenze was appointed Professor of Grammar, see "Registro Grosso," *Chartularium Studii Bononiensis* (Bologna, 1909), I, 23–4. See the reference to Mino da Colle as a Professor of Grammar, H. Wieruszowski, "Mino da Colle di Val d'Elsa rimatore e dettatore al tempo di Dante," *Miscellanea storica della Val d'Elsa,* XLVIII (1940),

164

155, rpt. in her *Politics and Culture,* pp. 347–57, and the reference to Bono da Lucca as a Professor of Grammar noted by G. Vecchi in his introduction to the *Cedrus Libani,* p. vii, n.6.

9. See the discussion of N. Haring, "Thierry of Chartres and Dominicus Gundissalinus," *Mediaeval Studies,* XXVI (1964), 271–86; K. M. Fredborg, *The Commentary of Thierry of Chartres on Cicero's " De inventione,"* in *Cahiers de l'Institut du moyen-âge grec et latin,* 7 (Copenhagen, 1971); M. Dickey, "Some Commentaries on the 'De inventione' and 'Ad Herennium' of the Eleventh and Early Twelfth Centuries," *Medieval and Renaissance Studies,* (1968), 1–41; J. O. Ward, "The Date of the Commentary on Cicero's 'De inventione' by Thierry of Chartres (ca. 1095–1160?) and the Cornifician Attack on the Liberal Arts," *Viator,* III (1972), 219–73.

10. See A. Wilmart, "L 'Ars arengandi' de Jacques de Dinant avec un appendice sur ses ouvrages 'De dictamine'," in his *Analecta Reginensia,* in *Studi e Testi,* LIX (Vatican City, 1933), 113–51. The forthcoming study by Emil Polak will shed light on Jacques' work and relationship to the University in Bologna. For Guidotto, see the comments of G. Fantuzzi, *Notizie degli scritti bolognesi* (Bologna, 1784), IV, 344.

11. Zaccagnini has published this document; see his "Giovanni di Bonandrea," 198–9.

12. See the documents and the discussion of Zaccagnini, *ibid.,* 150–5, 189–91 and Orioli, *op. cit.,* pp. 20–4, 63–4. As Zaccagnini noted, Giovanni probably did not teach in 1305 or 1306, but then taught rhetoric until his death in 1321.

13. The document that records the appointment of his successor states that this lecturer should follow the practices of Giovanni di Bonandrea which included lecturing upon the *Rhetorica ad Herennium.* See the document in Orioli, *op. cit.,* pp. 65–7.

14. Giovanni and his family had been banished from Verona in 1301, and their goods had been seized. To better his economic situation the Master offered to read "another science," *ars dictaminis.* See the documents in Orioli, *op. cit.,* pp. 63–4 and Zaccagnini, "Giovanni di Bonandrea," 189–91.

15. There are at least thirteen manuscripts of Giovanni di Bonandrea's treatise, *Brevis introductio ad dictamen,* in Italian libraries. In this study I shall draw from one of the earliest manuscripts, the Latin manuscript numbered 2461 in Bologna's Biblioteca Universitaria and shall cite it as *Brevis introductio* with folio numbers. See L. Frati, "Indice dei codici latini conservati nella R. Biblioteca Universitaria di Bologna," *Studi italiani di filologna classica,* XVII (1909), 48. The *Brevis introductio ad dictamen* also appears in the following manuscripts: Bologna, Biblioteca Universitaria, Cod. lat. 313, Frati, *op. cit.,* XVI (1908), 192; Bologna, Biblioteca Universitaria, Cod. lat. 1754, Frati, *ibid.,* 338; Perugia, Biblioteca Comunale Augusta, Fondo Vecchio, Cod. lat. B 56, G. Mazzatinti, *Inventari dei manoscritti Biblioteche d'Italia* (Forlì, 1895), V, 80–1; Milaù, Biblioteca Ambrosiana, Cod. lat. S 2 Sup., P. O. Kristeller, *Iter Italicum* (London, 1963), I, 312; Modena, Biblioteca Estense, Fondo Campori, Cod. lat. 167 (Gamma R 2 22), R. Vandini, *Appendice prima (secunda) al catalog dei codici e manoscritti del Marchese Campori* (Modena, 1886), pp. 67–8; Venice, Biblioteca Nazionale Marciana, Fondo Antico, Cod. lat. 478 (1661), Kristeller, *Iter Italicum* (London, 1967), II, 314; Florence, Biblioteca Laurenziana, Cod. lat. Plut. 90 Sup. 87, A. M. Bandinius, *Catalogus codicum latinorum Bibliotecae Mediceae Laurentianae* (Florence, 1778), II, columns 673–4; Florence, Biblioteca Laurenziana, Cod. lat. Plut. 91 Sup. 4, *ibid.,* cols. 745–8; Naples, Biblioteca Nazionale, Cod. lat. V E 46, Kristeller, *op. cit.,* I, 417; Naples, Biblioteca Nazionale, Cod. lat. XIII G 33, *ibid.,* I, 432 and see *idem,* "Un' *Ars dictaminis* di Giovanni del Virgilio," *Italia medioevale e umanistica,* IV (1961), 181–200; Vatican City, Biblioteca Vaticana, Cod. Urb. lat. 393, C. Stornaiolo, *Codices Urbinates*

165

Latini (Rome, 1902), I, 373–5; Florence, Biblioteca Riccardiana, Cod. 2323 (S III 27), G. Lami, *Catalogus codicum manuscriptorum qui in Biblioteca Florentiae* . . . .(Livorno, 1756), pp. 79, 212.

16. See the discussion of Giovanni in which he narrates that a certain city languished due to the tyrannical rule of Ezzelino da Romano, and then explains that common opinion holds that tyranny leads to warfare. *Brevis introductio,* fols. 83ᵛ–84ʳ.

17. As an example of the masters' preoccupation with the figures of speech and thought, see Guido Faba, *Summa dictaminis,* 356–70.

18. "De adiectivatione personarum habitu precellentium." *Brevis introductio,* fol. 77ʳ.

19. *Brevis introductio,* fol. 77ʳ. Giovanni borrowed this phrasing from Cicero, *De inventione,* I. xxv. 36.

20. Evidence of the thirteenth-century practice of placing lists of *sententiae* for the epistles' exordiums can be found in Guido Faba's *Summa dictaminis,* 370–7 and in his *Summa de vitiis et virtutibus,* edited by V. Pini, "La 'Summa de vitiis et virtutibus' di Guido Faba," *Quadrivium, Rivista di filologia e musicologia medievale,* I (1956), 97–151. Giovanni borrowed Cicero's definition of the exordium: "Exordium est oratio ad reliquam dictionem idonee preparans animum auditoris; preparatur autem duobus modis, aperte et occulte." *Brevis introductio,* fols. 79ʳ–79ᵛ. Giovanni would be most familiar with Cicero's discussion of the exordium in the *De inventione,* I. xiv. 20–xviii. 26.

21. One of these forms is entitled "Forma brevis commemorationis factorum et officiorum scribentis." *Brevis introductio,* fol. 80ʳ.

22. See below, notes 52 and 53.

23. See above, note 15.

24. The document cited above in note 13 records the intention of Giovanni's successor to follow his master's practice of teaching in a public place. On the arts instruction, see Cavazza, *op. cit.,* pp. 122–3.

25. *Brevis introductio,* fols. 80ʳ–82ᵛ.

26. Orioli, *op. cit.,* pp. 65–7.

27. *Ibid.*

28. By the 1350's Giovanni's treatise was probably being taught in the University to the law students; see below, note 46.

29. See the document cited above in note 13.

30. *Ibid.,* and see Rashdall, *op. cit.,* I, 207 ff.

31. Orioli, *op. cit.,* pp. 65–7.

32. *Ibid.,* p. 67ff.

33. Giovanni del Virgilio's fragmentary treatise has been edited by Kristeller, "Un *Ars dictaminis* "; the treatise of Giovanni Battista (Giovanni Odonetti di San Giovanni di Moriana), *Illuminarium sive introductorium in arte dictaminis,* is found in Florence, Biblioteca Nazionale Centrale, Magliabechiana VIII 1412, fols. 2ʳ–18ʳ. See comments on Giovanni Battista by F. Novati, "Di un' *Ars punctandi* erroneamente attribuita a Francesco Petrarca," *Rendiconti del R. Instituto Lombardo di Scienze e Lettere,* Ser. 2, XLII (1909), 92–3. Lorenzo d'Aquilegia's *Practica dictaminis* has been published by S. Capdevila, "La 'Pratica dictaminis' de Lorens de Aquilegia en un codex de Tarragona," *Analecta Sacra Tarraconensia,* VI (1930), 210–29; Pietro de'Boattieri's *Rosa novella super arte dictaminis* is found in Florence, Biblioteca Nazionale Centrale, II IV 312, G. Mazzatinti, *Inventari dei manoscritti biblioteche d'Italia* (Forlì, 1901), XI, 21–2, and Milan, Biblioteca Ambrosiana, Cod. B 132 Sup., Kristeller, *Iter Italicum,* I, 296. On Pietro see Zaccagnini, "Giovanni di Bonandrea," 163–6 and *idem,* "Le epistole in latino e in volgare di Pietro de'Boattieri," *Studi e memorie per la storia dell'Università di Bologna,* VIII (1924), 213–48.

34. Ghirardacci, *op. cit.,* II, 49, 83.

35. Pasquali-Alidosi, *op. cit.,* p. 26.

36. Ghirardacci, *op. cit.*, II, 56.
37. Bologna, Archivio di Stato, *Provvisioni*, Ser. II, 1329, fol. 13^v, quoted in Zaccagnini, "Giovanni di Bonandrea," 170–1. For the document of 1338, see N. Rodolico, *Dal comune alla signoria, saggio sul governo di Taddeo Pepoli in Bologna* (Bologna, 1898), pp. 287–9. For Bene's vow see above, note 8.
38. For an example of this commentary, see Modena, Biblioteca Estense, Fondo Campori, Lat. 1295 (Alpha T 3 13), Vandini, *op. cit.*, II, 420. S. Wertis' forthcoming study of Bartolino will demonstrate the significance of this Bolognese master.
39. See the Bolognese ms. 2461, cited above in note 15, fols. 1^r–75^r. Its *littera bononiensis* as well as red and blue capital letters indicate its Bolognese provenance. For a discussion of the *littera bononiensis* see B. Pagnin, "La *littera bononiensis:* Studio paleografico," *Atti del Reale Instituto Veneto*, XCIII, P. II (1933–34), 1593–1665. In this manuscript the commentator to the *dictamen* treatise substituted the names of his contemporaries in order to keep his model salutations current. From the dates of the personages (King John of France, 1350–64; Emperor Charles, 1347–78) mentioned, it is evident that the commentary was written in the middle of the fourteenth century. Also see the Laurenziana Cod., Plut. 90 Sup. 87 cited above in note 15, fols. 1^r–59^v; on fol. 59^v the commentator praises the University in Bologna.
40. F. Novati, *La giovinezza di Coluccio Salutati (1331–1353)* (Turin, 1888), pp. 32–9; B. Ullman, *The Humanism of Coluccio Salutati* (Padua, 1963), pp. 4–6.
41. The following mss. cited above in note 15 have commentaries: Biblioteca Universitaria, 2416 and 313; Biblioteca Comunale Augusta, B 56; Laurenziana, Plut. 91 Sup. 4; Biblioteca Nazionale of Naples, V E 46; Biblioteca Vaticana, Urb. lat. 393; Biblioteca Universitaria, 1754; Riccardiana 2323. The first six of these mss. appear to be the glosses taken from a university lecturer.
42. See Giovanni Dati's *Recollectiones* in ms. V E 46 of the Biblioteca Nazionale of Naples, fols. 64^r–73^v.
43. For example, see the Vatican ms. Urb. lat. 393, fol. 24^r cited above in note 15.
44. See the Universitaria ms. 2461, fol. 82^r cited above in note 15.
45. *Ibid.*, fols. 79^v, 76^v, 77^r, 79^r, 76^r.
46. R. Sabbadini, *Giovanni da Ravenna, insigne figura d'umanista (1343–1408)* (Como, 1924), pp. 23–4, and see the extract by Sabbadini from Conversino's *Rationarum vite*, pp. 139–40, 209. In these selections Conversino employed the title "Bononianti," and in the explicit to the *Brevis introductio* in ms. 313, fol. 37^v (see above, note 15) the scribe uses the title "Liber bononianti."
47. See the Ambrosiana ms. S 2 Sup. cited above in note 15. In the explicit on fol. 47^v it is stated that the treatise was copied in 1372. For Bolognese characteristics of manuscripts, see Pagnin, *op. cit.*
48. Bartolomeo del Regno is listed on the *Rotuli* of the University in Bologna 1384–5, and 1407–8; see *I rotuli dei letteri legisti ed artisti dello studio bolognese dal 1384 al 1799*, ed. U. Dallari (Bologna, 1888), I, 7, 10. Ghirardacci noted that Bartolomeo taught rhetoric in 1390, *op. cit.*, II 451 while G. N. Pasquali-Alidosi asserted that the Master lectured from 1383 to 1419, *Li dottori forestieri che in Bologna hanno letto teologia, filosofia, medicina et arti liberali* (Bologna, 1623), p. 13. Coluccio Salutati's epistle to Bartolomeo has been edited by F. Novati, *Epistolario di Coluccio Salutati*, in *Fonti per la Storia d'Italia* (Rome, 1893), II, 343–54. See Also the comments of R. Sabbadini, *Le scoperte dei codici latini e greci nei secoli XIV e XV* (Florence, 1914), p. 152. Bartolomeo also lectured upon Cicero's *De officiis;* these lectures are found in Modena, Biblioteca Estense, Fondo Estense, Alpha, V I 19, Kristeller, *Iter Italicum*, I, 370.
49. See Francesco da Buti, *Regule retorice*, Florence, Biblioteca Riccardiana, 674 (N iii 24), fols. 138^v–148^v, Lami, *op. cit.*, p. 199.
50. See the discussion of G. Billanovich, "Giovanni del Virgilio, Pietro da Muglio,

Francesco da Fiano," *Italia medioevale e umanistica,* VI (1963), 203–34; VII (1964), 279–324.

51. *Statuti delle Università e dei Collegi dello Studio Bolognese,* ed. Carlo Malagola (Bologna, 1888), p. 488. For an example of Guarino's commentary, see Venice, Biblioteca Marciana, Lat., Cl. XIII, Cod. 84 (3997), fols. 1ʳ–111ᵛ, Kristeller, *Iter Italicum,* II, 245.

52. See the manuscript cited above, note 49, fol. 143ᵛ for rubric "Incipit de exordio moderno usu." Fols. 144⁴–147ᵛ follow with exordiums organized by Ciceronian categories.

53. For an example of Gasparino Barzizza's manuscripts on the exordium, see *Exempla exordiorum,* Venice, Biblioteca Marciana, Lat. Cl. XIV, 68 (4735), fols. 65ʳ–76ʳ, Kristeller, *Iter Italicum,* II, 264.

54. I have not discussed a third aspect of the rhetorical tradition in the Bolognese University in the fourteenth century. From Giovanni del Virgilio's commentary to Ovid's *Metamorphoses* through Pietro da Muglio's commentaries to the poetry of Petrarca, rhetorical analysis of classical and fourteenth-century literature was an innovative and substantive part of the rhetorical tradition in Bologna. For Giovanni del Virgilio, see F. Ghisalberti, "Giovanni del Virgilio espositore delle 'Metamorfosi'," *Giornale Dantesco,* XXXIV (1933), 1–110. Rhetorical analysis of classical literature at Bologna remains to be studied; however, see the authoritative study of Billanovich, *op. cit.,* 203–34; 279–324.

Cain and Abel in the Chester Creation

NARRATIVE TRADITION AND DRAMATIC POTENTIAL

Bennett A. Brockman

THE BIBLICAL STORY of Cain and Abel (Genesis 4: 1–15) presented the medieval dramatist a structural outline remarkably appropriate for the creation of a play tragic in ancient, medieval, and modern understandings of the term. The basic conflict in fact conforms to one of Aristotle's central prescriptions for plots which arouse the tragic emotions. The play's "tragic action is against a member of the family . . .a brother either kills or intends to kill a brother, a son a father, a mother a son. . ." [1] The medieval dramatists realized the story's dramatic potential to varying degrees, however. Two of the cycles produced in England, the Cornish *Ordinalia* and the Hegge plays, treat the story with minimal success, and the merit of the fragmentary York version is at best debatable. The Chester play reveals a talented playwright in search of, though not always discovering, the most effective dramatic vehicle for a story familiar in theological analysis, pulpit homily, and narrative verse. Since it is not as brilliant a play as that of the Wakefield Master, it is not subject to the controversy which that greater play produces. [2] It consequently exposes more clearly than its counterparts the essential dramatic quest of the cycle playwright. Responding to the human, tragic potential latent in the inherited narrative, the Chester playwright effectively unites the basic human meaning of the plot with doctrinal implications and emotional overtones derived from traditional popular and ecclesiastical interpretations of the story.

The Cain and Abel episode begins smoothly in a transition stanza as Adam, expelled from Paradise, thanks God for the sons who lighten his sorrow. [3] He determines to prevent his sons' fall into sin by describing the dream he experienced during Eve's creation. Outlining crucial moments of history, the dream emphasizes two points of dramatic and thematic significance. First, in anticipating Christ's Atonement for the world he lost, Adam invites the audience to view the ensuing murder of Abel as a prefiguration of that ultimate sacrifice, just as theologians had explained since the time of Irenaeus, who died ca. 200.[4] And second, looking ahead to the Flood and the Last Judgment, he advises his sons to obey divine commands such as tithing if they would escape drowning and torment in Hell (433–472). The device of the dream, unparalleled in extant plays, thus establishes both a thematic framework and—something the Cornish, Hegge, and York playwrights sought in vain—a dramatically credible basis for Adam's instruction in tithing and earning a living in the postlapsarian world. The playwright may have found the suggestion for the device in the ancient legend of Eve's foreboding dream of Cain drinking Abel's blood, current in two late fourteenth-century Middle English derivatives of the eighth-century *Vita Adae et Evae,* which had an especially wide European circulation from 1300–1600.[5] And he may have been aware that exegetes had long theorized that Adam and Eve taught their sons to tithe, although some authorities supposed that the brothers simply followed natural law innate in their consciences.[6] In any case, the dream may be regarded as the dramatist's thoughtful solution to a theological as well as a dramaturgical problem.

Adam then directs Cain to become a husbandman and, with pointed irony, specifies that he shall offer corn "fayre and cleane. . .with good hart. . .and full devotion" (477–488). His admonition echoes countless popular and ecclesiastical discussions of God's preference for Abel's sacrifice.[7] Eve's monologue follows, and although it awkwardly restates other consequences of the fall, it reinforces Adam's instructions and carries his lesson to its logical conclusion by reminding the brothers that the wages of sin is suffering (497–512). The entire moment prepares, in ways which seem doctrinally valid and dramatically effective, for the second fall of mankind which the audience knows must ensue.

Cain then speaks for the first time, assuring his mother that he will follow Adam's instructions. But as his parents leave the stage, he addresses the audience and reveals that his motive for offering his corn is to see whether God "will send me any more" (517–520). His attitude hardly manifests the willing heart which Adam had prescribed, which the theologians insisted was of highest importance, and which Abel evinces. And shortly the dramatist shows not only that his motive is wrong but that he also leaves unfilled even the letter of the law by offering inferior grain. Like the Cornish dramatist, the Chester play-

170

wright elects to make Cain the hypocrite who pays lip-service to his father's command. But to reveal Cain's true character, the dramatist gives him a speech which shows him not simply a tight-fisted farmer but a confirmed reprobate, as relentlessly acquisitive as the Cain whose name the theologians glossed *possessio*.[8] He decides that earless stalks are good enough to offer and declares, "God thou gets non better of me, / be thou never so grim"(535f). He continues this arrogant presumption as he adds a particularly outrageous prayer:

> Loe, god, here may thou see
> such corne as grew to me;
> part of it I bring to thee
> anon, withoutten let.   (545–548)

Perhaps the playwright and members of his audience as well perceived in Cain's "anon, withoutten let" an ironic echo of St. Ambrose's explanation that God rejected his offering partly because he made it tardily, "after many days," according to Gen. 4:3.[9] This Cain is not going to be caught on a technicality.

Regarded from this perspective, the evocation of Cain's hypocrisy seems delightfully precise and suggests, in conjunction with the ironic admonitions of his parents and his own astounding taunts, that a complex humor which Prosser failed to perceive accompanies the play's serious implications. Secure in its faith, unthreatened by Cain's posturings, the medieval audience may well have laughed at him without interrupting the play's movement or disrupting its mood, without losing sight of its didactic point, and, perhaps most important, without simply ridiculing or simply pitying Cain. They may well have been drawn to his whimsical, devil-may-care attitude; after all, they likely had not seen God any more than Cain had, and at this point in the play, before any concrete inkling of the murder and its devastating consequences—the inescapable manifestations of God's immanence, Cain's defiance of a remote authority seems broadly similar to Lucky Jim's face-making behind Professor Welch's back. Yet the audience must have harbored a certain bated fear, for, knowing the biblical story well, they knew that Cain was taunting a God who only apparently failed to take offense at his impiousness. The final stanza of his prayer unites presumption and greed to evoke further this tonal coalescence:

> I hope thou wilt quite me this,
> and sende me more of worldlie blisse,
> els, forsooth, thou doest amisse,
> and thou be in my debte.   (549–552)

The audience probably did not need Peter Comestor's analysis, nor that of the early Middle English *Vices and Virtues* (ca. 1200),[10] to tell them that as Cain pretended to give his goods to God he gave his heart to the devil. Thus even though his presumption is amusing, the levity of the moment does not obscure the fact of his approaching damnation. A current of somber dread must underlie the scene as well.

Abel, in contrast, echoes Cain's words but follows them with a reverent sacrifice which conforms to their spirit. And at the traditional sign of fire signifying the acceptance of his sacrifice, he humbly thanks God for His grace (553–568).

Cain's reaction to this development is another master stroke of characterization. Unquestionably it reflects St. Augustine's belief that Cain's subsequent fear that all men shall slay him reveals his habitual concern with the carnal; he did not dread the wrath of God, but feared only that he should be slain (*Contra Faustum,* col. 260). Thus Cain regrets not displeasing almighty God but losing his investment: "Out! out! how have I spend my good! / to se this sight I wax nere wodd!" (569f). His exclamation expresses exactly the priorities of his values. He immediately resents his younger brother's election over him, just as he earlier had insisted that he make his offering first: "my semblant for shame shakes, / for envie of this thinge" (575f). The medieval audience would have noted especially his use of the word *envie.* It is the Demon's motive for tempting Eve earlier in the *Creation,* and it of course is charged with dire doctrinal implications. Perhaps the playwright and a few of the audience would have remembered sermons based on Augustine's belief that Cain's envy represented the peculiar envy which the evil hold for the good simply because of their holiness (*De Civitate Dei,* XV.vii). Perhaps others would have recalled sermons as fearsome as the discussions of envy in the English translations of the *Somme le Roi,* which consider envy, the "modre of deeth," to be an unforgivable sin against the Holy Ghost since the envious person attempts, "like to the deuel his fadre," to destroy the good which the righteous person does.[11]

At this critical moment, as Cain smarts with shame and rages in deadly sin, God appears and admonishes him in words which are close to those of the Bible but effectively combine the Vulgate reading with that of the Septuagint. Following the Vulgate, the playwright has God reprove Cain's wrath, reminding him that good deeds are rewarded and bad deeds punished, and that he has the capacity to do good; at the same time He reassures him that, as the Septuagint translated the seventh verse, he should retain precedence over Abel. Like most theologians, the playwright resolves the discrepancy between the Vulgate and Septuagint readings by accepting both as complementary. But of greater import is the dramatic use to which he puts the admonition. Its concluding words call to mind patristic commentary which provides both a theological framework and a dramatic rationale for the action that ensues; God assures Cain of his capacity to resist sin, but threatens him should he not repent and amend his ways: "the lust therof pertaines to thee; / advise thee of thy deede" (591f). Augustine's interpretation of the warning, likely based on Jerome's explication of the difficult seventh verse, was standard in medieval commentary and was probably familiar to the playwright if not his audience. To Augustine the warning was crucial, for it offered Cain assurance that he could resist sin. The moment was thus one of high suspense; man was to be tested a second time. [12] The discourse must have served this same purpose in the Chester play; the dramatic requirement and the doctrinal tradition are identical. Perhaps Cain paused before replying, and then pensively prolonged the first line of his response: "Ah, well! well then it is soe. . ." as he contemplated the first murder.

But possibly Ambrose and Cyril of Alexandria—even though his commentary was almost certainly unknown to medieval England—point out how the playwright and the actor playing the role would have understood Cain's progression from jealous anger to fratricide despite God's warning. They observe that the admonition shamed Cain in such a way that it prompted defiance rather than penitence. [13] Regarded in this way, Cain's "Ah, well! well then it is soe" becomes a defiant growl which leads quickly to his determination to kill Abel. But however it is taken, the line shows the dramatist's careful attention to the interaction of character and situation.

Abel, ever dutiful, readily agrees to Cain's request and humbly defers to Cain's seniority, thus manifesting God's assurance that he would remain "buxom" to Cain (597–600). But Cain assails him and accuses him of attempting "to passe me of renowne." He regards Abel's reverence as a design to gain "maystry," and he declares that Abel will pay dearly for God's "fowle" rebuke. Then, ironically supposing thus to prevent Abel's attaining "suche grace" as the acceptance of his offering implies, he slays him on the spot. Cain's diatribe is a creditable accomplishment for any dramatist; it proceeds naturally from the character already established, and it gathers momentum from itself as it

173

springs from accusation to accusation—each contradicted by Abel's behavior and God's own affirmation—until its climax in the murder (601–612). As he strikes his brother, Cain's rage propels him into a final presumptuous defiance of God Himself:

> Thoughe God stode here in this place
> for to helpe the in this case,
> thou shold dye before his face.   (613–615)

The irony of his presumption would be humorous here as it had been earlier in the play, but this time the bluff is called and God's immanence is manifested beyond doubt as God challenges him with the biblical words, "Cayne, where is thy brother Abell?" Cain responds with abrupt lies to compensate for his astonishment. One can almost see him quickly kicking loose straw over the body, which must have remained an obtrusive contradiction to his story, just as some narrative accounts suggest: [14] "I wott nere; I can not tell / Of my brother." Only when he has had a moment to recover can he resume his wonted arrogance sufficiently to construct the considered denial recorded in Genesis: "wottes thou not wel / that I of him had no keepinge?" But God of course is not deceived. Perhaps pointing dramatically to the ill-concealed body, He gives Cain the lie and pronounces upon him a curse which blights the ground he inhabits and sentences him to the exile and vagabondage specified in the Bible. The curse further implies that he will be considered, in terms familiar to the medieval Englishman, an outlaw in society (621–632). God's words could well remind the audience of explanations in many vernacular narratives that the exiled Cain either suffered the shame of being loathed by all mankind or confirmed his evil nature by assembling other scoundrels into a band of roving outlaws who pillaged the countryside. Interestingly enough, the former conception, characteristic of the earlier vernacular narratives, seems implied here in preference to Josephus' explanation, prevalent later, that Cain became an active outlaw who preyed upon and corrupted his pious neighbors. [15] The vernacular poets, perhaps more sympathetic than the theologians to Cain's suffering, regarded the sentence to exile and outlawry as a legal punishment, tantamount to the capital penalty, familiar in their own society. But in this case the offender is allowed to live in disgrace as one who has murdered a kinsman whom he owed protection and in terror that as an outlaw he would be hunted down like an animal. [16] The playwright seems to have chosen popular traditions over the more authoritative interpretation of

Josephus echoed in the *Polychronicon* of Higden, Chester's celebrated man of letters, once thought to have written the plays. Josephus and Higden make much of Cain's subsequent obliteration of the vestiges of the prelapsarian world. Ignoring their view—which he must have known, since the *Polychronicon* was a major school-text until the sixteenth century—the playwright uses the sentence to exile to establish Cain's character as a pitiable human being suffering exile. The theologian's horror at Cain's spiritual death gives way to the dramatist's sympathy for Cain the man, whose punishment has simply overwhelmed him.

Cain's emotional recognition of his folly seems to confirm that the dramatist is trying to evoke the peculiarly human dimensions of Cain's tragedy: "Out! alas! where may I be? / sorrow on each syde I se; . . .I must be bound and nothing free, / and all for my follie" (633–640). Even though he remains the archetypal egoist, a note of genuine pathos infuses his grief and indeed rises to a more intense pitch as he confesses his sin and anticipates the death he will likely meet when banished from the protection of kin and friend: "vnworthy I am, I wis, / forgevenes to attayne. / well I wot, wherever I goe, who so meetes me will me sloe . . ." (643–646).

Undoubtedly Cain's lament would remind the medieval audience that he, like Judas, succumbed to the unforgivable sin of despair.[17] But the playwright emphasizes the personal horror of Cain's isolation. According to numerous theological accounts, Cain would suffer the incomparable misery of separation from God.[18] Yet the playwright omits Cain's lament that he would be hidden from God's face, the biblical clause on which the allegorical interpretation was based. The emphasis is on the human more than the theological meaning of his folly.

But doctrine and legend come equally into play as God assures Cain that he will be protected by a seven-fold curse against any slayer. The playwright has God offer two reasons for protecting Cain. The first, that it is not Abel's wish to shed his brother's blood, reconfirms Abel's piety and unassuming deference to Cain's primogeniture (649–652). The second, however, derives from and implicitly repeats two exegetical comments on the moral significance of the biblical passage. God's words to Cain, "and great pennance [one MS group reads *payne*] thou may not flee / for thy wicked deede" (655f), reflect the theologians' opinion that while Cain would have preferred for death to release him from the torment of a prolonged life, God made certain that he would suffer extensively on earth before going to his eternal punishment in

175

Hell.[19] If the word *pennance* is taken in its more familiar technical meaning rather than as a synonym for imposed suffering, the pronouncement implies Ambrose's belief, reflected in an anonymous sermon of the early fifteenth century, that Cain is mercifully granted a long life so that the imposed penance might lead him to contrition and salvation.[20] Yet it appears likely that once more the playwright has in mind the human rather than the doctrinal import of Cain's position, for the pronouncement concludes with the declaration, derived from the Septuagint translation of Gen. 4:15, that Cain's children would suffer "pennance" unto the seventh generation and affirms that Cain will receive his earthly suffering.

The playwright at this point reasserts Cain's human predicament by giving him another lament which is a product not of the biblical account but of the dramatic context in which Cain's suffering is central; for the biblical "And Cain went out from the face of the Lord, and dwelt as a fugitive on the earth, at the East side of Eden," the Chester playwright interpolates:

> Out! out! alas! alas!
> I am damned without grace,
> therfore I will from place to place,
> and loke where is the best.
>
> Well I wot and witterlye,
> into what place that come I,
> eache man will loth my company;
> so shall I never have rest.
>
> Fowle happ is me befall:
> wheither I be in howse or hall,
> cursed Cayne men will me call,
> from sorrow may non me save. (665–676)

Heading this passage "Cayne lamentat," the dramatist seems deliberately to emphasize the Old English conception of Cain's exile as an expulsion from the solace and protection of human company. His despair is a human reality, not simply a theological abstraction; and his recognition that the consequence of his misdeed is unremitted isolation merits the term tragic.

Probably because the Cain and Abel episode is part of the broad second pageant of the *Creation,* the playwright does not end the play with Cain's lament, as the other dramatists do. Instead, vitiating the effect of Cain's despair, he returns Adam and Eve to the stage by having Cain decide to seek their curses before departing into exile. The laments of Adam and Eve, which follow Cain's confession to them, suggest that the playwright is trying to maintain the focus of the larger action on them in order to unify the basically discrete events surrounding the Fall and the murder. The consequences of their original sin do include the tragedy of the murder. Their recognition that their lives must continue joyless ironically fulfills Adam's belief that God sent him "twoo soones my harte to glade" (432), and it is doubly ironic that he now finds "no more ioye. . .save onely Eve, my wife" (687f). Eve in fact understands that this present disaster derives from her initial disobedience, and she apparently believes that this new catastrophe will characterize the future (689–696). Her lament is an appropriate theological note on which to end the play; the bitter consequences of man's fall have been graphically displayed as inescapable, and Adam and Eve anticipate the harsh lot of all mankind until, the audience understands, the redemptive sacrifice which Abel's death prefigures. Unlike the French *Mystère du Viel Testament* and the *Passion* of Arnoul Gréban, the Chester playwright chooses not to follow the legendary sequence of the life of Adam and Eve and report the joy attendant on the birth of Seth.[21] Instead he leaves the impression that Eve's despondency characterizes the period before the Incarnation,[22] and he moves directly to the play of the Deluge, which figurally signifies the final destruction of the world as well as salvation through baptism and the Church.[23]

Yet for all the thematic propriety of the sequence of events beginning with Cain's decision to seek his parents' curse, a real dramatic problem remains: his decision seems not only unmotivated but incredible, given the character established for him. Cain is hardly so penitent that he craves another curse. In contrast, the introductory transition presented no real dramatic problem; the course of events from Adam's exile to his instructing his sons in tithing involves merely a telescoping of time made easily acceptable by a device such as the minstrels' playing, suggested in a marginal note in MS B. But the inclusion of the murder within the larger framework of the Fall produces difficulties which the dramatist barely surmounts. In this respect the Chester play is like the *Mystère d'Adam:* the Adam-Cain sections are theologically but not dramatically continuous.[24] Why the Chester play attempts to unify the two actions is clear, I believe, when certain dramatic and narrative analogues are recognized. Four Middle English narratives, based ultimately on the *Legenda Aurea,* the *Vita Adae et Evae,* and the *Revelations* of Pseudo-Methodius, point out at varying length the grief of Adam and Eve; these four narratives are probably representative of a tradition with which the Chester playwright would have been familiar: the *South English Legendary* (I. 167f), the Vernon MS prose *Lyff of Adam and Eve* (p. 225), and the *Polychronicon* (II.221) devote only a few lines to the moment, but the *Cursor Mundi* treats it in two longer, separate passages (lines 1084–1108 and 1183–1202) which the Chester play in effect conflates. The parents' grief is inherently pathetic and seems an inevitable subject for dramatic exploitation. It is in fact developed at length in Gréban's *Passion* and in the *Mystère du Viel Testament,* both thought to have influenced the Chester plays, though the latter in an earlier, simpler version than that which has come down to us.[25] One suspects, therefore, that the Chester dramatist found persuasive precedent for including Cain's confrontation with his parents; indeed, it is more surprising that the other English playwrights omitted it than that he included it.

Yet there are crucial differences between the French and English dramatic presentations. The *Viel Testament* and the *Passion* first show Adam and Eve's anxiety over their sons' prolonged absence, and both plays devise stratagems for having them discover the murder and Cain's curse. Gréban has them go out in search of their sons, find Abel's body, and, surmising Cain's guilt and curse, add their malediction to God's. The more elaborate *Viel Testament* has Cain confess to his sisters, one of whom reports to their parents. Both sequences are credible enough. The English play in contrast relies upon Cain to initiate the confrontation, and if we accept his professed motive at all it is with the kind of credulity we accord comparable moments in the folk ballads. Even more telling, neither French play allows Cain to be in his parents' presence when they make their discoveries, thus avoiding a scene difficult to realize, while the English play demands an encounter which would tax the resourcefulness of any playwright or actor. We more readily accept the profession of Cain in the *Viel Testament:* "De revertir envers mon pére? / Jamais il ne me reverra" (lines 2925f).

We would err, though, to depreciate the Chester playwright for failing to meet later French standards. But we can legitimately criticize his handling of the scene by comparison with the narrative but latently dramatic *Cursor Mundi,* which offers a potentially more successful, easily stageable scenario—it even provides dialogue—by manipulating the biblical account more boldly. The *Cursor Mundi* Cain apparently has no intention of confessing when he returns home. Adam immediately has misgivings when he sees Cain's face (just as Delbora does in the *Viel Testament,* lines 2915–18), and it is he who asks about Abel, initiating the biblical denial, "Quen was i keper of thi child?" (1085–1098). Fearing the worst yet believing "that kynd him mond for-bede / To haf don suilk a nogli dede," Adam and Eve go out to look for Abel, apparently leaving Cain behind. God then challenges Cain and pronounces His curse upon him. Adam discovers Abel's body, which he and Eve, weeping bitterly, take away for burial (1099–1192).

Yet since the Chester playwright does not conclude the play with Eve's lament, but rather grants Cain the final words, one may venture that he, after all, felt in part what the other English dramatists felt more compellingly: that Cain is the real center of dramatic interest and that to return to Adam and Eve, however moving or doctrinally appropriate the scene might be, destroys the play's momentum and deep emotion without compensatory gain. Indeed, Cain's emphatic concluding speech (697–704) does compensate in some measure for the disruption caused by introducing Adam and Eve, since it returns the dramatic focus to him and concentrates rather than diffuses the emotions attendant on the outcome of his attempts to deceive God. Here the playwright exhibits the same concern for the integrity of Cain's dramatic, human personality which had marked his treatment in the body of the play. This may be particularly true in the problematic last two lines of Cain's farewell. Conceivably, Cain turns to the audience and bestows on them an ironic curse.[26] But "A lurrell alway I must be" (699)—the *OED* defines *lurrell* s.v. *losscell* as a worthless person, a profligate, one who is lost, "a son of perdition"—may suggest that like the Cain of the *Viel Testament* (3122–25) he is anticipating now the life of active banditry in exile ascribed to him in legend. If so, the progression of his character from resigned, pathetic despair to defiant despair is both a credible manifestation of personality and an effective conclusion for the play.

In sum, then, the Chester play, in its own right and especially in comparison to the Hegge play and the Cornish *Origo Mundi,* seems skillfully constructed and dramatically effective. Its characters are convincingly differentiated, and when traditional commonplaces such as Abel's figural role and Cain's acquisitiveness, envy of Abel's goodness, outlawry, and despair are understood, the plot appears, with but one exception, to develop as a function of the interaction of character and situation. Thus the play's movement has an air of tragic inevitability within the framework of its inherited biblical design and its basic doctrinal meaning, so that it becomes not merely a homily against envy, an exhortation to tithe willingly, or a demonstration of the immanence of a retributive God, but rather a vivid evocation of man's misery after the Fall, a glimpse of the sacrifice which—looking forward and backward in time—redeems him; and, perhaps most important, it becomes a moving depiction of the essential tragedy, in both theological and personal terms, of a murderer whose fratricide, according to Hebrews 11:4,[27] is equatable to fideicide. But the dramatist does not forget the human consequences of the murder, expressed in Cain's despair and in his parents' grief; this awareness indeed is an indication of the play's dramatic merit and underlying strategy. The doctrinal, the thematic, the ideational never outweigh the human, the personal, the emotional: the everyday, familiar mimetic situation is the dominant interest. To be sure, the human is presented as contingent on the divine, and from this complementary dual focus not only this play but the medieval drama in general derives its unique range and depth of meaning. But even though the human-divine nexus is vital, it is not paramount, at least in dramatic terms and at least in this play. If anything about this play is clear, it is that Cain is of compelling interest as a man caught up in a predicament which he has devised but scarcely understands, and which destroys him utterly. His suffering and the suffering that he causes—those human realities which cannot be negated by appeal to abstract realities—form the play's irreducible center.

NOTES

1. Poetics, 14, trans. Preston H. Epps (Chapel Hill: Univ. of North Carolina, 1942); see further G. F. Else, *Aristotle's Poetics: The Argument* (Cambridge: Harvard Univ., 1957), pp. 413ff.
2. See discussions of these plays in Eleanor Prosser's *Drama and Religion in the English Mystery Plays* (Stanford: Stanford Univ., 1961), pp. 67–88; and in Rosemary Woolf's *The English Mystery Plays* (Berkeley: Univ. of California, 1972), pp. 124–131.
3. *The Chester Plays,* Part I, ed. Hermann Deimling, EETS ES 62 (1892), lines 425–432. This edition is quoted hereafter; line references are cited parenthetically.
4. See Irenaeus, *Contra Haereses,* IV.xxxiv.4 (*PG,* 7.1086); Augustine, *De Civitate Dei,* XV.i–viii (*PL,* 41.437–447), *Contra Faustum Manichaeum,* XII.ix–xiii (*PL,* 42.258–261), *Enarratio in Ps.* 39:9, 58:12–14, 61:5 (*PL,* 36.442, 705, 733f); Isidore, *Allegoriae Quaedam Sac. Script.,* 6, and *Mysticorum Expositiones Sacramentorum . . .in Gen.,* vi (*PL,* 83.100, 223f); Bede, *In Principium Gen.,* II (*Corpus Christianorum, Series Latina,* 118A, pars II, i, pp. 81–85); Rabanus, *Comm. in Gen.,* II.i (*PL,* 107.503). See especially three Middle English works which reflect these theological commonplaces: the early thirteenth-century *Ormulum,* ed. R. M. White and Robert Holt (Oxford: Clarendon, 1878), lines 14456–505; the widely-known early fourteenth-century *Cursor Mundi,* ed. Richard Morris, EETS 57 (1874), lines 1045–

1182; and John of Trevisa's popular translation (1387) of Ranulf Higden's *Polychronicon* (1327), II.iv, ed. Churchill Babington (London: Public Record Office, 1869), II, 218–230.

5. See L. S. A. Wells, editor of the *Vita* in R. H. Charles's *Apocrypha and Pseudepigrapha of the Old Testament in English* (Oxford: Clarendon, 1913), II, 124. Cf. the 1375 Middle English *Canticum de Creatione* in *Sammlung Altenglischer Legenden,* ed. Carl Horstmann (Heilbronn: Henninger, 1878), lines 469–473; and the *Life of Adam and Eve* in *The Wheatley Manuscript,* ed. Mabel Day, EETS 155 (1922), p. 86.

6. See, e.g., Hugo of St. Victor, *Adnotationes Elucidatioriae in Pentateuchon (PL,* 175.44); Peter Comestor, *Historia Scholastica,* Lib. Gen., xxv (*PL,* 198.1077); Chrysostom, *Homiliae XII de Statuis ad Populum Antiochenum,* xii, 4 (*PG,* 49.132); and Thomas Aquinas, *Summa Theologiae,* I–II, q. 103, a. 1.

7. The *Cursor Mundi* poet declares simply that God rejected Cain's offering because he "gaf him wit iuel will" (line 1065). The Vernon MS *Lyff of Adam and Eve,* ascribed to the decade 1370–80, echoes the theologians more exactly: "Abel was tither good of alle thinges & thonked god swithe wel; / and Caym tithed falslich, and brak godes hestes, for he withheold alwey the beste dole & yaf god of the worste" (Horstmann, p. 224). See further Josephus, *Antiquities,* I.ii.1–2; Irenaeus, IV. xviii.3f (col. 1025); Ambrose, *De Cain et Abel,* I (*PL,* 14.350); Augustine, *De Civ. Dei,* XV.vi (*PL,* 41.443–445); Alcuin, *Opuscula Exegetica,* I, inter. 15 (*PL,* 100.515); Bernard of Clairvaux, *Sermones in Cantica Canticorum,* xxiv.7 (*PL,* 183. 897f); and Peter Comestor, col. 1077.

8. See, e.g., Josephus, I.ii.1; the *Glossa Ordinaria,* Lib. Gen., iv (*PL,* 113.98); and two sermons in *The English Works of Wyclif,* ed. F. D. Matthew, EETS 74 (rev. ed. 1902), pp. 211, 374.

9. See John E. Bernbrock, S. J., "Notes on the Towneley Cycle *Slaying of Abel,*" *JEGP,* 62 (1963), 317–322.

10. Ed. Ferdinand Holthausen, EETS 89 (1888), p. 37.

11. See *The Book of Vices and Virtues,* ed. W. Nelson Francis, EETS 217 (1942), pp. 22, 24. Cf. *The South English Legendary,* ed. Charlotte D'Evelyn and Anna J. Mill, EETS 235 (1956); and the *Mystère de la Passion* of Arnoul Gréban, ed. Omer Jodogne in *Memoires,* Classe des lettres, 2ᵉ ser., XII (Bruxelles: Académie Royale de Belgique, 1965), lines 722–738.

12. See Jerome, *Liber Hebraicarum Quaestionum in Genesim,* (*PL,* 23.944); Augustine, *De Civ. Dei,* XV.vii (*PL,* 41.433–445), and Peter Comestor, col. 1077.

13. Cyril, *Glaphyra in Gen.,* I, "De Cain et Abel," and "In Johan. Evang.," VI (*PG,* 69.35 and 73.898); Ambrose, "De Cain," col.354f.

14. See *Cusor Mundi,* lines 1075–85 and 1129–32; Peter Comestor, col. 1077; and Josephus, I.ii.1.

15. See John of Trevisa's translation of the *Polychronicon,* II, 227 (Bk. II, cap. iv).

16. See the Old English *Genesis A,* ed. George Philip Krapp in *The Junius Manuscript* (New York: Columbia Univ. Press, 1931), lines 1010–21; *Beowulf,* lines 107–110, 1261–65; AElfric's early eleventh-century *Heptateuch,* ed. S. J. Crawford, EETS 160 (1922), pp. 91–93; the Middle English *Lyff of Adam and Eve* (p. 224); *Cursor Mundi,* lines 1109–1174; and the Middle English *Genesis and Exodus,* ed. Richard Morris, 2nd ed. EETS 7 (1873), lines 429–440. See further the discussions of exile and outlawry in Naomi D. Hurnard's *The King's Pardon for Homicide before A. D. 1307* (Oxford: Clarendon, 1969).

17. See the *De Institutis Coenobiorum* of John Cassian (ca. 370– ca. 435), ed. Jean-Claude Guy (Paris: Editions du Cerf, 1965), IX.ix, p. 376. Cf. Gregory the Great, *In Septem Psalmos Poenitentiales,* 4, 14 (*PL,* 79.591). After Bede (ca. 672–735) Cain becomes the foremost example of the peril of despair. See further Susan B Snyder,

"The Left Hand of God: Despair in Medieval and Renaissance Tradition," *SRen,* 12 (1965), 18–59.

18. See, e.g., Basil the Great, *Epistolae,* II. 260 (*PG,* 32.962); Ambrose, col. 376; Peter Chrysologus, Sermo 147, "De Incarnationis Sacramento," (*PL,* 52.594); Gregory the Great, col. 591; and the "Meditatio in Ps. *Miserere,*" attributed dubiously to Anselm, *PL,* 158.841.

19. E.g., Bede, *In Principium Gen.,* p. 79; Peter Comestor, col. 1077f; and *Cursor Mundi,* lines 1181f.

20. Ambrose, col. 377f, 380; without mentioning Cain, the English sermon (ca. 1400) emphasizes that temporal pain releases the sufferer from pain in purgatory, in the ratio of twenty to one (*Middle English Sermons,* ed. Woodburn O. Ross, EETS 209 [1940], pp. 41f). The fourteenth-century *Postilla, seu Expos. Aurea in Lib. Gen.,* once attributed to Thomas Aquinas and included in the Parma edition of his works (rptd. New York: Musurgia, 1948–50; 23.1–133) echoes Ambrose's view (cap. iv, p. 28).

21. *Mystère du Viel Testament,* ed. James de Rothschild, I (Paris: SATF, 1878), 129; and the *Passion,* cited in fn. 1 above, lines 1080–1104.

22. Cf. Peter Chrysologus' sermon, cited in fn. 18 above, which employs Cain's abandonment by God as the major example of the hopeless misery of life before the Incarnation.

23. V. A. Kolve, *The Play Called Corpus Christi* (Stanford: Stanford Univ. Press, 1966), pp. 67–69.

24. O. B. Hardison, Jr., discusses the *Mystère d'Adam* in *Christian Rite and Christian Drama* (Baltimore: Johns Hopkins, 1965), p. 260. But cf. R. A. Brawer, "Dramatic Technique in the Corpus Christi Creation and Fall," *MLQ,* 32 (1971), 362.

25. A. C. Baugh, "The Chester Plays and French Influence," in *Schelling Anniv. Papers* (New York: Century, 1923), pp. 35–63; Hardin Craig, *English Religious Drama* (Oxford: Clarendon, 1955), pp. 171–178; and Woolf, pp. 336–338.

26. F. M. Salter, *Mediaeval Drama in Chester* (Toronto: Univ. of Toronto, 1955), p. 96. Cf. Cain's words at the end of the York fragment: "Sethen I am sette thus out of seill, / That curse that I haue for to feill, / I giffe you the same"; *York Plays,* ed. Lucy Toulmin Smity (Oxford: Clarendon, 1865). There is an intriguing possibility that the Chester playwright, working from a possibly corrupt MS of Greban's *Passion,* transferred the ideas of *repos* and wandering to the earlier lament (Chester, lines 666–672) and mistook *randiray,* which Godefroy defines "parcourir rapidement," for *rendrai,* thus producing Cain's curious bestowal of his "gifte": "A haulte voix huche la mort / et si n'en puis venir a bout; / je randiray tant tout partout / que j'arar ung peu de repos." (lines 1076–79).

27. Cf. Bernard of Clairvaux, *Sermones in Cantica Canticorum,* 24 (*PL,* 183.897f).

The Textual Reliability of Chaucer's Lyrics

A COMPLAINT TO HIS LADY

Paul M. Clogan

THE QUESTION of what constitutes a reliable Chaucer text, as posed by Professor Ruggiers, is one which every editor and reader of Chaucer must face and one upon which much depends.[1] Is the textual reliability of a Chaucer text the same as asking the question what constitues a reliable Shakespeare, Milton, Keats or Emerson text? Can a text indeed have reliability, and, if so, what is its duration? Does a reliable text necessarily depend upon either or both the authority of the manuscripts used or the authority of an editor and his editorial principles? Who or what determines a reliable text: a dusty old manuscript forgotten or neglected for years and discovered one fine day in the Midlands or Wales, or a dusty but genteel professor who after years of teaching his students what his author did not say, one day discovers for himself what his author did say.

There are no ready and easy answers to these questions. A reliable Chaucer text is in a sense the same as a reliable Shakespeare text, but the means and principles may be different. A reliable text is a true text with its own integrity despite good and bad manuscripts and good and bad editors. A reliable text does not have to represent the author's final intention, whatever that may have been, but it does bring the reader as close as possible to the true text of the author's work. Yet a reliable text can survive only as long as the market will support it; when it disappears, it has to await the arrival of a young Turk to rediscover it and dress it up for a new audience. To illustrate my observations and to help focus, if not directly answer, the question of what constitutes a reliable Chaucer text, I would like to consider the textual editing of Chaucer's lyrics and in particular one of his neglected but important lyrics, *A Complaint to his Lady*.

The textual editing of Chaucer's twenty short poems or lyrics presents certain problems and challenges which are not to be found in the
textual editing of his longer works.[2] There is no modern critical edition
and there have been few textual examinations of his lyrics as a whole
and their relationship to his longer works. The critical commentary of
Felix Schelling early in the century "that there are few authentic lyrics
in Chaucer" has been echoed in the recent judgment of Rossell Hope
Robbins that Chaucer's lyrics are "minor not only in comparison to his
great works; they are just minor poems."[3] The study of Chaucer's
lyrics for the most part has been subsumed under the study of the
medeival lyric as a whole and, in certain cases, subjected to nineteenth-
century romantic notions of a lyric as the subjective expression of a
poet's emotions or "spontaneous overflow of powerful feelings recol-
lected in tranquility." Schelling looked for the true "lyric cry," "the
passionate throbbing of the human heart seeking artistic expression."[4]
Arthur K. Moore characterized Chaucer's lyrics with the statement
that his "lyrical exclamation seldom rings true and clear," and his "love
lyrics, a genre by nature autobiographical, reveal virtually nothing
about the man."[5] Original and personal diction rather than conventional language and style have been stressed, and only certain subjects
could be included in the lyric. As a result, Chaucer's lyrics have generally been dismissed as minor short poems, and most modern editions
of Chaucer, which were designed as schooltexts, provide only a sampling—usually a handful—of his lyrics bunched together at the tail end
of the volume just before the editor's notes or commentary and classified as Short Poems.

It is well known that Chaucer's lyrics are formal in character, conventional in language and style, and concerned with such "unlyrical"
subjects as Fortune, Truth, Gentillesse, and complaints to a scribe and
to his purse. The order and chronology of these short poems, which
belong to different periods of Chaucer's life, still remain only approximate. Moreover, the textual authorities for his lyrics are generally
miscellaneous manuscript collections which contain various non-
Chaucerian works, and they often depart from the orthographical practice of the "best" Chaucer manuscripts, as we know them. There is no
Ellesmere or Hengwrt MS. for the lyrics, and we have to accept the fact
that Chaucer's lyrics have apparently never been collected completely
into one manuscript. It is true that many of the lyrics can be found in
MS. Fairfax 16 in the Bodleian Library, but its text is not to be very
much relied upon, and this has been clearly shown by a comparison

with those pieces which are also extant in older and better manuscripts. The Cambridge University Library MS. Gg.4.27 also contains several, but it is often disfigured by clerical errors and dialectical peculiarities. Shirley's own manuscripts, especially British Museum Additional 161 65 and Cambridge Trinity College MS. R.3.20, are corrupted by Shirley's habit, when collecting Chaucer's poems which he evidently knew well, of relying too much on his frequently failing memory. While the textual value of Shirley's collections is negligible, his notes about Chaucerian authorship of certain poems provide important evidence for the final establishment of Chaucer's canon.

The preservation of Chaucer's lyrics has also be haphazard, ranging from many copies of the moralizing poems to single manuscripts of the love lyrics: 23 MSS of *Truth*, 14 MSS of *Lak of Stedfastnesse*, 12 MSS of *ABC*, but only one manuscript *To Rosemund* and *Womanly Noblesse*. Furthermore, the peculiar habits of fifteenth-century scribes are especially noticeable in manuscript collections of short poems and prose pieces; in these commonplace books the dilettante personality of the scribe is evident in the arrangement of the books and the selection of the content. We know that it was a late fifteenth-century custom to have several scribes copy short poems separately and later combine them haphazardly into one splendid collection.

A Complaint to his Lady has been preserved in Shirley's MS. Harley 78, MS. Additional 34360, and in Stowe's edition of 1561.[6] In the two MSS. the lyric is written as if it were a continuation of *The Complaint unto Pity*, which immediately precedes and which contains two close verbal parallels. Shirley apparently transcribed the lyric with the running title "Balade of pite by Chaucier." While the text of the *Complaint unto Pity* was copied in several other manuscripts as a separate poem without any note about the authorship, the text of *A Complaint to his Lady* does not occur elsewhere. Shirley distinguished between the two poems and ascribed both to Chaucer. The authenticity of *Lady* was questioned by ten Brink and rejected by Furnivall who later, however, accepted it as well as Skeat, Koch, Pollard and all modern editors. Shirley's ascription, moreover, is supported by internal evidence, for the two complaints are very similar in thought and spirit and show Italian influence. The copy of the text in MS. Additional 34360 seems to be derived from Shirley's copy in Harley 78, but it contains an additional stanza at the end.

Unlike the completed *Pity*, however, *Lady* is a series of experiments in rhyme which Chaucer apparently left unfinished, but from which he later borrowed individual lines for the composition of *Anelida and Arcite.*[7] *Lady* is divided into four sections which are distinguished by the use of three distinct meters. The first section (1–14) consists of two stanzas in rime royal, a form which Chaucer used again in *the Parliament of Fouls, Man of Law's Tale, Clerk's Tale,* and *Troilus and Criseyde* and one which he apparently found suitable to his best descriptive and narrative poetry. The second and third sections (15–39) comprise two incomplete stanzas in *terza rima,* which is the first time this meter appears in English, long before it was adopted by Wyatt and Surrey. The fourth section (40–127) is written in ten-line stanzas—also appearing in English for the first time—and resembling in form the nine-line stanza of the Complaint in *Anelida and Arcite.* The two experiments in *terza rima* have attracted the greatest attention, and most editors agree with Skeat that the rhyme scheme was "obviously copied from Dante" and therefore date the poem shortly after Chaucer's first Italian journey in 1374.[8] Since there are a number of parallels in *Lady, Pity,* and *Anelida and Arcite, Lady* may well be the earliest in composition and represent the poet's draft of experiments in three distinct rhymes from which he later borrowed individual lines and phrases. We know that Chaucer could, if he wanted to, copy Dante's *terza rima* perfectly, and we may have to accept the two incomplete stanzas in *terza rima* as an independent and original experiment in alternating rhyme which developed naturally and resembled the lyric practice of the time.

In view of the experimental and unfinished quality of *Lady,* it is questionable whether editorial emendations to perfect rhyme or meter are justified. Yet the textual editing of this lyric has been subjected to extensive emendation, even when the sense remains unaltered. The spelling, which appears to be very bad in all three copies, has been normalized throughout without indicating the variant readings, and several verbal corrections and line restorations have been freely introduced. In his search for metrical regularity, Skeat, in some cases followed by Koch, Pollard, and Robinson, repeated line 14 at the beginning of the first *terza rima* stanza in order to get a rhyme for *fulfille* in line 16. After line 22, Skeat supplied line 189 from the *Complaint of Mars* to provide a rhyme for line 21; before the beginning of the second series in *terza rima,* he further supplied lines 22 and 17 from the *Complaint unto Pity* and line 307 from *Anelida and Arcite;* and again after lines 51 and 53, Skeat supplied lines 181 and 182 from *Anelida and Arcite.* This search for metrical regularity has deprived the lyric of its distinctive style and versification. Like French poetry of the fourteenth century, the lyric represented a series of variations on a theme, with no attempt at continuous development or logical connections. *Lady* is an exercise in different keys on the conventional theme of unrequited love, and this is clearly indicated by the contrast achieved through the use of a different meter for each section. In structure and theme, *Lady* follows the French school of *complaints*. The lament of unrequited love is awkwardly presented and directly addressed to the lady herself; and there is the traditional contrast between the lover's unworthiness and the lady's praise. Yet there is a noted absence of the rhetorical figures which marked the style of the French complaints of the thirteenth and fourteenth century. Instead. Chaucer's diction seems to approximate the style of natural speech. There is no pause at the end of each line, as in Mauchaut, and the sentences, although controlled by the meter, are more fluent and less limited to the verse line as a unit of thought. Furthermore, the new verse forms of *terza rima* and the ten-line stanza, which Chaucer uses here for the first time under Italian influence, encouraged a more natural and fluent style and versification.

It is true that an editor has the right to improve upon the meter of his authorities if the difficulty is not with the sense or meaning. The metrical irregularity in this case is usually attributed to a scribe, and the editor assumes that the emendations are justified because the poet would not write or intend to write irregular metrical lines. But this editorial reasoning, which underlies the emendations in *Lady*, does not apply in the case of this lyric. The value and significance of the metrical experiments and innovations are severely undercut by editorial emendations to perfect rhyme or meter. The interlocking rhyming technique in both the *terza rima* and the ten-line stanzas allowed Chaucer to develop the effect of an interweaving pattern as well as continuous movement in the stanza. Moreover, the poet's characteristic use of conjunctions to point up a connection or contrast or to serve as a transition from one point to the next begins to emerge in this fragmentary and experimental lyric. "And yit," "though," "For," "And therfor" are used here not so much to support, limit or contradict, but to introduce for the sake of dialogue another argument or explanation. The reader becomes more aware than he was in *Pity* of an antithetic style often in the form of a dialogue. As the argument rises or falls, especially in the fourth part of *Lady*, the reader begins to hear for the first time the poet's so-called "speaking voice" which later becomes the voice of the narrator in his major works.[9]

In short, I submit that the extensive emendations in the text of *Lady* are unjustified. The poem is a series of unfinished metrical innovations, showing Chaucer experimenting and practising his art, and any emendation to perfect or improve rhyme or meter when the sense remains unaltered is unwarranted. Emendation of an unrevised text is a violation of the authorial right of revision. The search for metrical regularity has in the case of this lyric deprived the poem of its distinctive style and versification. The emendations have damaged the poem's innovative quality and contributed only a theoretical metrical improvement. Furthermore, there is evidence to suggest that the manuscripts of this lyric actually represent the poet's unrevised copy—fragments of metrical inventions copied from one of Chaucer's drafts. The unfinished appearance of the lyric as shown by incomplete stanzas and unmetrical lines are ordinarily not the work of a scribe but of a poet experimenting and practising his art before publication. While it is true that the manuscripts could not conceivably represent the poet's final intention, the unrevised text of *Lady* in the two so-called "bad" manuscripts is more trustworthy than the emended copy in modern editions. In the end, the editing of Chaucer's lyrics requires a more flexible editorial policy than that required for his longer works. Analysis of style and meaning of the individual poem on the part of the editor assumes greater importance than conformity to the practice of the best Chaucer manuscripts.

NOTES

1. This article is based upon a paper delivered at the Chaucer Group, with Professor Paul G. Ruggiers in charge, of The Eighty-Eighth Annual Convention of the Modern Language Association of America in Chicago, Illinois.
2. For editions of Chaucer's Short Poems, see J. Koch, *A Critical Edition of some of Chaucer's "Minor Poems"* (Berlin, 1883); idem, *Kleinere Dichtungen* (Heidelberg, 1928); W. W. Skeat, ed., *The Complete Works of Geoffrey Chaucer*, vol. 1 (Oxford, 1889); H. F. Heath, ed., *Minor Poems* in *The Globe Chaucer* (London, 1895); and F. N. Robinson, ed., *The Works of Geoffrey Chaucer*, 2nd ed. (Boston, 1957). For textual criticism, see Aage Brusendorff, *The Chaucer Tradition* (Oxford, 1925); Wolfgang Clemen, *Chaucer's Early Poetry*, trans. C. A. M. Sym (London, 1963); George B. Pace, "Four Unpublished Chaucer Manuscripts," *MLN*, LXIII (1948), 457–462; idem, "Chaucer's *Lak of Stedfastnesse, SB*, IV (1951–52), 105–122; idem, "The text of Chaucer's *Purse*," *PBSUV*, I (1948), 105–121; idem, "The True Text of *The Former Age*," *MS*, XXIII (1961), 363–367.
3. Felix Schelling, *The English Lyric* (Boston, 1913), p. 28: and R. H. Robbins, "The Lyrics," *Companion to Chaucer Studies*, ed. Beryl Rowland (Toronto, 1968), p. 313.
4. Schelling, p. 1.
5. *The Secular Lyric in Middle English* (Lexington, Ky., 1951), pp. 124–130.
6. On the manuscripts of *A Complaint to his Lady*, see R. Nares, *A Catalogue of the*

Harleian Manuscripts in the British Museum, vol. 1 (London, 1808); and *Catalogue of Additions to the Manuscripts in the British Museum in the Years 1888–1893* (London, 1894), pp. 317–321; J. Koch, *Kleinere Dichtungen,* p. 22; E. P. Hammond, *Chaucer: A Biographical Manual* (New York, 1908), pp. 411–412; and Brusendorff, pp. 268–273.
7. Clemen, p. 186.
8. See Skeat, I, 76; and Robinson, pp. 520, 856.
9. Clemen, p. 187.

Lord Berners' Translation of

ARTUS DE LA PETITE BRETAGNE

Kenneth J. Oberembt

I**F THE CLAIM** that Sir John Bourchier, second Lord Berners, was "the first to write modern English prose"[1] is a just one, then whatever more we can learn of his five extant works, translations all, will indeed be worthwhile. Such knowledge will not only elucidate his own achievement as a prose stylist but will also clarify the evolution of English prose during the late fifteenth and early sixteenth centuries. Yet "the work of Lord Berners," as we have recently been reminded, "has never been studied in depth."[2] What follows here is a study of his method of translating a French romance, *Artus de la Petite Bretagne*, which will reveal his attachment to the principles of the Caxtonian school, especially its abiding concern with literalism and with courtly style. *Arthur of Lytell Brytayne* is a useful point of departure: since it is probably the earliest of Berners' extant translations,[3] it will help define his theory and practice at the outset of his career.

In the prologue to *Arthur* Berners announces that it was his goal to produce a close rendering of the French: "I truste my symple reason hath ledde me to the vnderstandinge of the true sentence of the mater, accordinge to the whiche I haue folowed as nere as I coude. . . ."[4] Allowance must be made for the humility formula here as well as for the fact that statements of translation theory in medieval and early sixteenth-century prologues tend to be inaccurate and misleading.[5] In any case, the proof of Berners' achievement is not in any explicit statement of intent, but rather in his practice. And his practice reveals that *Arthur* is, at root, a fairly literal translation of *Artus*. This is no more evident than in a simple juxtaposition of corresponding English and French passages. The following example illustrates Berners' frequent clause-by-clause transformation of *Artus* and even, *mutatis mutandis,* his reconstruction of the sentence structure peculiar to his source.[6]

191

Apres la mort du bon Roy Artus qui tant fut noble roy & gentil & ensuyuit & exaulsa toute la noblesse de toute la cheualerie de tout le monde. Si comme furent Gauuain & Lancelot & maint autre cheualier ainsi comme plus a plain est contenu en pleusieurs croniques anciennes. Il est vray que en Bretaigne eut vng duc preudomme: & sur tous aultres vertueux riche & puissant et fort dauoir & damis lequel fut extrait du noble & hault lignaige du vaillant cheualier Lancelot du Lac, qui tant fist de haultes proesses ainsi comme plus a plain est contenu aux liures qui font mencion de sa cheualerie. (sig. a^r)

After the death of good Kynge Arthur who was ryght noble and gentyll, specyally in cherysshynge and enhaunsynge of nobylnesse, and mayntaynyng of the chyualrous knyghtes of the worlde. As was Gawyn and Lancelotte and many other noble knightes as it is more plainly conteyned in dyuers auncyent cronycles. It is of trouth that in tho dayes in Brytayne there was a duke ryghte prudente & aboue all other ryghte vertuous, ryche and puyssaunte bothe of hauyour and frendes who was come and extraughte of the noble hygh lygnage of the valyaunt knyght Launcelot du Lake who was in his dayes of right hyghe & noble prowesse as it is more at large comprised in the bokes makynge mencyon of his chyualrye. (fol. i^r)

The most notable structural change appears in the English rendering of the initial French clauses. First, Berners has changed French coordination into English subordination ("specyally in cherysshynge and enhaunsynge. . .and mayntaynyng") and, second, he has integrated the "As" clause (the counterpart to the French "Si comme" clause) somewhat differently by supplying an explicit referent ("chyualrous knyghtes") for the plural subject ("Gawyn and Lancelotte and many other noble knightes"), in place of the singular French referent ("cheualerie"). Otherwise, English and French sentence structures are identical. Even the English word order imitates the French, save for the few instances where Berners preferred normal English position of the adverb ("as it is more plainly conteyned" for "comme plus a plain est contenu") and adjective-noun order ("auncyent cronycles" for "croniques anciennes"). To be sure, French syntax is so much like normal English syntax that Berners would have been unwise to do other than reproduce it, but the point stands that he did so—almost in stencil fashion.[7] Yet he was not always so slavish:

Et quant le conte fut mort & enterre demy an apres vint le duc a la duchesse & luy demanda Aliz sa fille. Mais la dame le suspeconnoit de la mort de son seigneur si ne la luy donnast pour rien & la fille ne leust pas prins pour mourir. (sig. f3^r)
And whan that the Erle was thus myscheuously slayne, he was brought home to his wyfe whiche was ryght sorowful for his deth, & made hym to be honourably buryed. But this sorowfull lady in noo wyse coulde veryly tell how that he was slayne, but she had grete suspecte to the duke. And soo within halfe a yere after, the duke came vnto this countesse and demaunded of her Dame Alyce her doughter, but the countesse bycause she had hym in suspecte of the Dethe of the erle her husbonde wolde in no maner of wyse graunte therto, nor also this fayre mayden Alyce wolde in noo wyse haue hym to dye therfore. (fol. xxxiiii^r)

He has introduced here specific details about (1) the manner of the Count of Brewle's death ("myscheuously slayne"), (2) the transportation of his corpse back to the city, (3) the sorrow and suspicion of his widow, and (4) the manner of his burial ("honourably"). Berners' amplification of the Little Arthur story is continual, if not always quite so concentrated and patent; nonetheless, it never obscures the reliance of *Arthur* upon *Artus*.

Moreover, Berners' fidelity to the French text is evident in the paucity of changes he originated in the Little Arthur plot. The 348 pages of Black Letter English text give evidence of only one substantial addition—in chapter 14 in the conversation between Arthur and Jehannet. It consists of two parts: (1) Jehannet's justification for replacing Arthur's wife Perron in bed on the wedding night and (2) Arthur's approval of her action because by it he has learned for certain that his wife had not come to marriage a virgin. None other of Berners' additions is so lengthy nor so pronounced in its effect as this one. However, even this addition is short and has only local impact. Like the additions, so too deletions from the plot are infrequent and brief. On the other hand, a change of some importance because of its effect upon point of view is Berners' modification of patriotic references in *Artus*. It is the habit of the French narrator to identify himself and his audience with Arthur and the Frenchmen who accompany him on his journey East and with all Frenchmen in the story. He does this by often using the first person plural possessive adjective when referring to them—as, for instance, when he numbers Arthur's troops and those of his opponents: "car ilz estoyent bien.iii.cens & noz gens nestoyent que.xiiii. . . ." (sig. k5ᵛ). The "noz" was not translated by Berners: "how be it he and his company were but.xiiii.in nombre, & his enemyes were well to the nombre of .ccc. . . ." (fol. lxʳ). In fact, he systematically deleted this adjective. Although such revision does not essentially change the Little Arthur story, it does indicate a real shift in the narrator's attitude toward the characters, for it makes a small but consistent contribution to the withdrawal of the narrator from the action and to a reduction in his immediate involvement with Arthur and his compatriots. Berners, in brief, made the subjective narrator of his source slightly more objective.

Sometimes, then, *Arthur* resembles the work of the fifteenth-century English translators who, as Samuel K. Workman described them, kept "as close as the syntax and grammar of English permitted—and sometimes closer than it permitted—to the sentence structure of the composition under translation," [8] but most often Berners wrote a prose that is clearly English, not macaronic, a prose that tends to be more expansive and concrete than the French.

Although his method of reproducing in English the French romance is fairly conservative, Berners introduced into his adaptation a totally different style of direct discourse for its characters: he substituted a formal style for the casual style he found in his source. [9] This departure from *Artus* has no little significance and it is by far Berners' most notable change. The ensuing passages, excerpts from an argument between Hector and Governar, well exhibit the nature and effects of his stylistic adjustment. It is the morning after Arthur, Hector, and Governar's sojourn with an elderly knight and his young wife. Arthur and Governar had noticed the more than courteous attention Hector paid their hostess, and, upon being questioned about his intentions, Hector has admitted that he really desired to spend the night in bed with her. At that Governar charges Hector with baseness—that he would even think such a thought. Thereupon Hector replies and the quarrel that develops is settled only by Arthur's intervention.

Or Gouuernau, dist Hector, vous estes moult sage en sapience. Ne feries vne folie. He Dieu quel preudomme ce chat ne gouteroit mye du lait. Par Dieu, dist Gouuernau, encor dis ie que ce ne seroit mye bien fait de gentil homme. Ains seroit trayson de ce faire. Comment, dist Hector, dictes vous doncques que ie suis traitre, qui seschaufa. Vous mentez. Ie ne le fus oncques. Lors se trait pres de Gouuernau & mist la main a lespee. Sire ne me frappez point car se mait Dieu vous ne seres estre si gentil homs ne si hault quil ne men poise. (sig. d4^v)
A syr Gouernar, quod Hector, I am sure ye be so sage in scyence that ye wyl do no foly. Wysdome is greate if the cat neuer touched mylke, as much to say as whan loue toucheth, wysedome is than oftentymes ouercome. Well as for al that, quod Gouernar, it maketh no mater, but yet I say as I sayde that it should not haue ben wel done of a gentylman to haue doone as ye saye for it were rather treason so to do. Wherwith Hector began to be sore chafed & sayde, what Gouernar sayst thou that I am a traytour. Thou liest falsely. I was neuer none. And drew nere to Gouernour and layd his hand on his swerde. Than sayd Gouernar, stryke me not. I saye not that ye be a traytoure nor ye be not so great a man that youre noblenesse forthynketh me for I wolde ye were greater than ye are. . . . (fol. xxii^v)

Berners has retained, in some measure, the French style—for instance, he has Hector say "what Gouernar sayst thou that I am a traytour. Thou liest falsely. I was neuer none" which almost exactly imitates the paratactic French sentences "Comment. . . .dictes vous doncques que ie suis traitre. . . . Vous mentez. Ie ne le fus oncques"—but, in the main, he has made the dialogue between the two characters much more formal. (1) He has yoked the two independent French clauses ("vous estes moult sage en sapience. Ne feries vne folie") into one ("I am sure ye be so sage in scyence that ye wyl do no foly") and so has transformed French parataxis into English hypotaxis. Moreover, the tone of Hector's declaration has, through the subordination of the second clause to the first, been changed: the teeth-clenched threat of the French becomes a flat statement of Hector's confidence that Governar will do nothing untoward. A similar mitigation of the threatening tone is evident in Berners' rendering of the French Governar's "vous ne seres estre si gentil homs ne si hault quil ne men poise" as "ye be not so great a man that youre noblenesse forthynketh me for I wolde ye were greater than ye are," though it is here the result of change in sense rather than reconstruction of French syntax. (2) Berners has retained the French proverb ("Wysdome is greate if the cat neuer touched mylke" for "quel preudomme ce chat ne gouteroit mye du lait"), [10] but he has had Hector go on to articulate its application, "as much to say as whan loue toucheth, wysedome is than oftentymes ouercome." Such explication is not a feature of the casual style, for it would be expected that the auditor, Governar, would be able to formulate the meaning for himself. (3) Berners has added clarifying phrases "but yet I say *as I sayde*" and "it should not haue ben wel done of a gentylman *to haue doone as ye saye*" (italics mine) where the French reads merely "encor dis ie" and "ce ne seroit mye bien fait de gentil homme," and he has also substituted for the oaths uttered by Governar ("Par Dieu" and "se mait Dieu") non-blasphemous and patently connective phrases ("Well as for al that. . .it maketh no mater" and "I saye not that ye be a traytoure"). Bowdlerization and clarification generate an English style more elevated than the French.

As the styles of the French and the English excerpts differ, so do the effects they produce. The French colloquial repartee suggests a falling-out between not just two acquaintances but two intimate acquaintances. Hector and Governar know each other so well that in their dialogue they can afford to be indirect at times and yet be confident that they will be understood. Hector's proverb is a forceful illustration of this point. In saying to Governar "quel preudomme ce chat ne gouteroit mye du lait," Hector means to tell him something like "What a bold fellow is that cat who would never taste milk! It is easy enough for him to condemn another who cannot resist the temptation to drink. You, Governar, are like that self-righteous cat!" But he does not spell out his meaning because he assumes that Governar will get his point. The

195

English translation, however, invites a different assumption about the relationship between the two men. The reader knows, after having read the romance as far as chapter 26 (in *Arthur*), that they are intimate. Yet their quarrelsome speech does not well mirror that fact, for they speak to each other as if there were not only emotional but also intellectual distance between them. They are excessively explicit in language and meaning.

Let it suffice to say here that Berners quite regularly adjusted the direct discourse of his French source to a higher register and by doing so created a substantive difference between *Arthur* and *Artus*. The pose struck by the English characters is obviously more impersonal than that of their French counterparts. Still another effect is a shift from mimetic to non-mimetic speech, a change which has an important bearing on the characters and their function in the story. By merely translating ellipsis and parataxis out of their communings Berners has made them rather more figurative and less representational. This he has done, for example, in his version of the dialogue between the Lady of Rossilon, a married woman, and Sir Delelaunde, her would-be lover:

> Sire il me conuient assentir de faire vostre voulente. Veez vous celluy grant chesne en celle forest. Madame ouy bien. Or y soyez duy en vng an a ceste heure. Vrayment ie y serai toute preste & appareillee de faire vostre voulente. Ma chiere Dame vostre mercy quant plus nen puis auoir si prendray conge & men iray. Ne plus ne me verrez iusques alors, car si demouroye empres vous ie mourroye voyant voz yeulx tout mort. (sig. d6ʳ)
>
> . . .Syr your suite is so importune that it behoueth me to assente to fulfyll your desyre & wil. How be it Syr se ye not yonder great oke standinge in the forest. Yes Madame, sayd I, right well. Well, quod she, I am content to fulfill your minde on this condicion, look that this same day twelue moneth & this same propre houre that ye fayle not to be vnder yonder oke & without fayle thyder to you wyl I come redy apparayled to acomplish your entente, and before that day loke neuer for to haue it. A myne owne dere Ladie humblye I thanke you of your good wyll. Syth I cannot haue it no soner, at the least I shall passe the tyme more ioyously in hoping of that fortunate daye. Wherfore I wyll take my leue nowe of you, for ye shall not se me agayne till that tyme become, for yf I shoulde abyde in your dayly presence, your beautiful eyen should slea me to abide so longe, for that thinge that I desyre. (fol. xxiiiiᵛ)

By formalizing the speech of his characters, Berners highlights the courtly stance that lovers and would-be lovers assume, a stance in which an ideal and distant lady is sued for her favors by a lover conscious of his own unworthiness and lowliness. Courtliness is certainly a feature of the French romance, but there is less emphasis on the relationship between the sexes as an observance subject to an established code of politeness just because lady and lover address one another in a rather light and free—that is to say, casual—style. It throws the courtly stance into relief. The formal style adopted by Berners has the opposite effect. It brings to the fore the courtly ceremony that is half-hidden in the background of *Artus,* for the lovers not only act ceremoniously but speak that way as well. In a word, Berners' elevated style puts distance between the sexes and forces the reader to focus more upon the ritual behavior of lovers than upon their love-talk or personalities.

The non-representational characterization produced by Berners' stylistic adjustment of direct discourse occurs throughout *Arthur,* and, more significantly, it helps transfer the allegiance of the Little Arthur story from the mimesis of the French original to allegoresis. The realistic characters of *Artus* become in *Arthur* almost emblematic, and for the reader of the English romance the experience is not one of participating in the actions and interactions of fictional people who imitate living men and women but rather of comprehending the ideas characters embody and illustrate.

With just what degree of deliberateness Berners adopted the formal style it is difficult to say. Much of his effort, apparently, was given to producing a clear and intelligible translation of his source, and this effort meant a general inclination to amplify the sometimes tightly written French. The language of *Artus* is rarely tighter than in passages of dialogue, and in uncompacting these by adding specific details, qualifications, transitions, and clarifications, he inevitably made them less elliptical, less colloquial, and less implicit. But Berners' change of style was probably no mere by-product of the mechanics of translation. That he was consciously aware of style is obvious enough in his prologue to *Arthur,* where he apologizes for failing to retell the Little Arthur story in "fresshe ornate polysshed Englysshe" because of his insufficiency "in the facondyous arte of rethoryke," among other things (sig. iᵛ). The reference to an embellished English prose manufactured by reliance upon the figures, colors, and levels of discourse outlined in the handbooks of rhetoric associates Berners with the fifteenth-century courtly school, of which William Caxton was one of the chief exponents and an especially influential proponent of the need to reshape English prose.[11] However, Caxton's practice (as editor and author) offers little by way of substantive clues as to what exactly he meant by courtly style:

197

. . .one of Caxton's major theses was that English prose style was at its best when it kept as close as possible to a French or Latin original. He insisted on this because it was intended that some of the fine French or Latin style would show through in the English translation. It should not, therefore, be a matter for surprise that this did in fact happen from time to time. It does not of course follow that Caxton was aware of all the places where this had taken place. And it is certainly true that his own original compositions cannot be shown to have been influenced by foreign models. No rhetorical flourishes have been pointed out in his own compositions, which are more notable for their clumsy style than for their balanced or rhythmical sentences. His style becomes very loose when he has no guide. [12]

Although his restyling of material selected for publication was generally unsystematic and his own attempts to write prose in the courtly manner were faltering, still Caxton argued unceasingly for a new English prose, imitative of French and Latin exemplars and courtly in style. Berners, surely knowledgeable about Caxton's work, [13] in his own acted upon suggestions articulated by his predecessor. He chose a presumably courtly French romance for translation and he translated rather literally large portions of *Artus* that satisfied his sense of courtly style. On the other hand, he revised, almost wholesale, the colloquial dialogue of his source, making it more elevated. This he did with a consistency and a selectiveness—clearly the products of a controlling, critical intelligence—that are not always characteristic of Caxton's work. And the prologue to *Arthur* shows that Berners, unlike Caxton, could and did write courtly prose on his own. [14] The disciple adhered to his teacher's principles and improved upon his teacher's practice.

We need to examine more intensively the origins and development of fifteenth- and sixteenth-century courtly prose, and the *sine qua non* is the detailed study of individual texts by those, like Berners, who advocated and wrote it. There is little hope that Berners' works will ever have much appeal for the modern audience, though his translations deserve better than they have so far received, but they are important documents in a particular kind of prose tradition that we are really only beginning to understand and to appreciate.

NOTES

1. N.F. Blake, "Caxton and Courtly Style," *Essays and Studies,* New Series, XXI (London: John Murray, 1968), p. 44.
2. N.F. Blake, "Lord Berners: A Survey," *Medievalia et Humanistica,* New Series, Number 2 (Cleveland: The Press of Case Western Reserve University, 1971), p. 119.
3. See my forthcoming essay in *Neuphilologische Mitteilungen* entitled "Lord Berners' *Arthur of Lytell Brytayne:* Its Date of Composition and French Source."
4. Iohan Bourghcher, trans., *Arthur of Brytayn* (London, 1555?), sig. i^v. All quotations from *Arthur* are taken from this Roberte Redborne edition—from a microfilm of

the Huntington Library copy. The English text printed here varies from that of the Redborne only in that several emendations of accidentals (spelling, punctuation, capitalization) appear without annotation.

5. See Samuel K. Workman, *Fifteenth Century Translation as an Influence on English Prose* (Princeton: Princeton University Press, 1940), p. 69.

6. Quotations from the French Little Arthur story are taken from *Le petit Artus de bretaigne* (Lyon, 1496). I rely on a microfilm of the Michel Topié (?) edition supplied by the Göttingen Universitätsbibliothek. Accidentals in French quotations here have been emended, silently, at times.

7. Other, extra-syntactic differences present in the English passage above (and elsewhere in *Arthur*) include (1) an increase in the appearance of pleonasm ("extrait" and "haultes" Berners translates "come and extraughte" and "hyghe & noble") and (2) the presence of mistranslations ("a duke ryghte prudente" and "of hauyour and frendes" instead of "a valiant duke" ["vng duc preudomme"] and "of possessions and friends" ["dauoir & damis"]). Such differences are not very important, but they do underscore obliquely the overall literalness of *Arthur*.

8. *Fifteenth Century Translation*, p. 84.

9. The terminology is that defined and discussed by Martin Joos in *The Five Clocks: a linguistic excursion into the five styles of English usage* (New York: Harcourt, Brace, & World, 1967), pp. 19–38. My analysis of styles and stylistic levels is an adaptation of his.

10. It is not cited in *Proverbs Français*, ed. Joseph Morawski, Les Classiques Français du Moyen Age (Paris: E. Champion, 1925), but see Morawski's index, s.v. "chat," for several proverbs expressing the sensuality and unwisdom of cats.

11. See Caxton's *obiter dicta* on prose style in *The Prologues and Epilogues of William Caxton*, ed. W.J.B. Crotch, EETS, O.S. 176 (London: Oxford University Press, 1928; repr. 1956).

12. Blake, "Caxton and Courtly Style," pp. 35–36.

13. See Blake, "Lord Berners: A Survey," p. 126.

14. This prose is, if anything, more mannered, more given to symmetry and pleonasm than that of the romance itself.

Thomas Hoccleve, Bureaucrat

A. Compton Reeves

THOMAS HOCCLEVE began his career as a minor figure in the English governmental bureaucracy late in the fourteenth century. Had it not been for his avocation of writing poetry, we would know little more than that for many years the office of the Privy Seal had the services of an industrious clerk named Thomas Hoccleve. As it is, his poems contain an abundance of information which has been partially used by only a few historians and literary critics. Hoccleve's poetry is a source of insights into the poet's occupation, attitudes, and the general course of his life.

Hoccleve was born about 1368 and entered the Privy Seal office as an ordinary clerk about 1387,[1] but nothing is known of the education that prepared him for his profession. His equipment was not exceptional: familiarity with basic literary works and a working knowledge of French and Latin.

This is not the place for a careful exposition on the functions of the Privy Seal, but to understand Hoccleve's professional life, the office in which he was employed must be briefly considered. It was a branch of administration intimately involved in the functions of English government. When Thomas Hoccleve entered the employ of the Privy Seal office during the reign of Richard II, it had "gone out of court," and was solidly established at Westminster as a department of state, along with, though without the prestige of, the Chancery and the Exchequer. Yet in reality the Privy Seal had become the main secretariat by Hoccleve's day.[2] One of its most important functions was to dispatch warrants from the King to the Chancery for the issue of formal letters by the Chancery under the Great Seal, though the creation of the Signet Seal reduced this operation. Documents bearing the red wax privy seal were used for communications between the English government and foreign courts, communes, and private persons. The Privy Seal office also issued warrants to the Exchequer for payment issues. The Privy Seal, however, had a more important function than merely setting other

201

departments of government in motion. Instruments bearing the privy seal came to be regarded, apart from governmental processes, as valid and constitutional in the conduct of various business functions. A vague distinction was maintained, reserving more important matters for Chancery instruments, and leaving all lesser affairs to the Privy Seal. Great and ordinary Councils were summoned under writs of the Privy Seal, just as Parliaments were called by the Chancery. And the Privy Seal staff was called upon to serve an important role as the secretariat of the King's continuous, executive Council, with the resolutions or ordinances of the Council being executed by writs of Privy Seal. The work of the Privy Seal also developed a judicial aspect during the fourteenth century to ease the work-load of Chancery.

Despite its important functions, the relative status of the office of the Privy Seal remained low. Privy Seal clerks like Hoccleve, though in the thick of governmental activity, did not have the prestige of clerks in the older departments of Chancery and Exchequer, nor could they expect as large financial rewards for their services. Little can be determined of the daily life of the clerks who staffed the Privy Seal. It was their custom to live a corporate life, and it is known that they lived at Chester's Inn on the Strand, the town house of the Bishop of Coventry and Lichfield, just prior to 1381. Hoccleve mentioned living at Chester's Inn, which by his time was regarded as the official residence of the staff. The business of the Seal was conducted at Westminster, and the clerks traveled daily to and from their home at Chester's Inn down the Strand to Westminster.

Almost nothing is known of the physical characteristics of the office in which Hoccleve and his fellows worked, but one certain fact can be learned from the lists of the clerks who served in the Privy Seal office: such clerkship provided one with a lifetime occupation. There was little opportunity for advancement, but there were also few or no instances of dismissal, either for incompetence or for political reasons. Even the royal usurpation of 1399 saw no change either in Keeper or staff of the Privy Seal.

There was one practice in the Privy Seal office that caused Hoccleve to rise up in righteous indignation. As the self-appointed guardian of the well-being of his fellow clerks, he felt compelled to record the abuse they suffered. It had long been customary for any private person coming to the Privy Seal for a letter to leave a gratuity with the clerk drawing up the letter as a remuneration for his services. Hoccleve regarded the practice as standard and quite proper. A difficulty arose, however, from the fact that gentlemen would often send a retainer to the Privy Seal rather than going in person. The retainer would occasionally keep the perquisite intended for the clerk, and report in turn to his master that the clerk had been given his due. Thus both clerk and master were deceived, for the clerk dared not make trouble for the servant since the retainer of a great man would be believed rather than the clerk, and difficulties would then truly be heaped upon the suffering scribe (*Works,* III, 55–56). Such, at least, was Hoccleve's opinion.

Students of the administrative history of England have good reason to be grateful to Hoccleve aside from the mention he made in his poems of working conditions at the Privy Seal. There is a quarto volume deposited in the British Museum that contains in an almost systematic arrangement examples and forms of every type of instrument issued or handled by the Privy Seal office.[3] This manuscript, written largely in Hoccleve's own hand and compiled between 1423 and 1425, is the only formulary that makes possible a detailed study of Privy Seal business.[4] Two other Privy Seal formularies, dating from the late fourteenth century, one an anonymous work and the other compiled by the clerk Robert Fry, do exist, but they are shorter and less complete than Hoccleve's.[5] Though Hoccleve put his formulary together at the end of his career, it would seem to be the work of a still industrious individual. Yet Hoccleve remained an ordinary clerk throughout his long career with the Privy Seal.

Hoccleve described this clerical career as much more difficult than most of his contemporaries thought:

> A writer mot thre thynges to hym knytte,
> And in tho may be no disseuerance;
> Mynde, ee, and hand, non may fro othir flitte,
> But in hem mot be ioynt continuance.
> The mynde al holle with-outen variance
> On the ee and hand awayte moot alway,
> And thei two eek on hym; it is no nay. (*Works,* III, 37)

Artificers could sing and talk while working, but not so the scribe:

> We stowpe and stare vpon the shepes skyn,
> And keepe muste our song and wordes in. (*Idem.*)

The querulous clerk of the Privy Seal, however, was only one aspect of Hoccleve's character. Hoccleve is another example of a citizen of the world of letters who, like Geoffrey Chaucer, devoted the main part of his time to a secular occupation and only his leisure to writing. Hoccleve gained some of his early fame as a poet with his *Letter of Cupid* in 1402,[6] but a more curious poem is the autobiographical *La Male Regle* written in 1406. The poem indicated something of the life open to a young man of Hoccleve's station, for *La Male Regle* (*Works,* I, 25–39) is mainly a lamentation on the dissolute life Hoccleve had led as a youth. He reported being drawn by the lure of Bacchus to his favorite haunts, the wine-houses, except when he was without money. Wine, he wrote, was his greatest lust. He mentioned Paul's Head Tavern where he passed the time with "venus femel lusty children deere." He told of how quickly he squandered his money, and how well known he was among the cooks and taverners at Westminster Gate because he always paid whatever price they asked for their goods. He even mentioned taking an unscheduled holiday from his office for a more enjoyable boat trip.

In other writings Hoccleve added details about himself. He wrote that as a young man it had been his ambition to become a priest, but although he had waited long he received no promotion from the Church. No doubt growing tired of waiting, he drifted into marriage, thereby binding himself to a temporal spouse and ending any chance he might have had of becoming a priest (*Works,* III, 53). Hoccleve assured his readers that he married not for lust or for money, but only for love (*Works,* III, 57). The date of his ultimately childless marriage was about 1410 or 1411, when he was past forty years of age.

The name of the poet's wife is unknown, but those of many of his friends and associates have been discovered. He several times mentions Sir Henry Somer, Keeper of the Privy Seal, who was later promoted to Baron and finally Chancellor of the Exchequer. Other associates were a functionary of the Duke of Bedford named Massey, London's benefactor and town-clerk, John Carpenter, and possibly one T. Marleburgh (*Works,* I, xxxiv-xxxv). Among Hoccleve's fellow Privy Seal clerks were Arundel, Baillay, Fleet, Hethe, Prentys, and Offorde. It is also known that after many years in the Privy Seal, Hoccleve had a junior clerk, John Welde, attached to him, presumably for training.[7] Hoccleve's long official career would have made him an associate of twelve Keepers of the Privy Seal.

Though he remained on the fringes of the royal court, Hoccleve did have some influential patrons. Henry IV was one, as was his son, Henry V, both as Prince of Wales and as King. John, Duke of Bedford, Constable of England and Regent of France; Humphrey, Duke of Gloucester, long a prominent and often a turbulent figure in governmental affairs; and Edward, Duke of York, who died at Agincourt in

1415, were among Hoccleve's noble patrons, as were the Duchess of York; John of Gaunt, Duke of Lancaster; the Countess of Westmorland, a daughter of John of Gaunt by Katheryn Swynford; and Lady Hereford. Other patrons were Robert Chichele, a London merchant, and possibly Sir John Oldcastle, before the latter was accused of heresy. Hoccleve also addressed a poem to his friend John Carpenter.

Hoccleve's life, however, was not all Privy Seal, poetry, and patrons. At least one event of his life gave him a justifiable cause for his frequent lamentations over the infirmities and hardships of mortal existence. Writing in his *Complaint* (*Works*, I, 95–110), to which the date of 1421-2 has been assigned, Hoccleve told of a serious illness that had driven him out of his wits. The illness apparently resulted in a loss of memory for a short period with recovery coming on All Saints' Day, probably in 1416. Hoccleve was shaken by his ill fortune though it resulted in little interruption in his official duties, and he never pursued the cause of his infirmity beyond attributing it to God's will.

Very often Hoccleve's was the voice of troubled man. He had gone mad, and felt his friends had forsaken him. His work as a scribe, the perpetual pushing of quill across parchment, had left his body filled with pain, and his eyes were suffering. As if this were not enough, his pride was so inflated as to keep him even from wearing spectacles. Hoccleve often seems the personification of the shy, retiring clerk, occasionally buying stature from the likes of taverners and boatmen. He revealed himself as something of a coward, and tried to avoid anything rough or violent. So little of the pastoral scene was reflected in his writings that it is a fair assumption that he was a native of London.[8] He stated that he knew nothing of using a plow or harrow nor anything of what sort of land might be suitable for particular crops (*Works*, III, 36).

Hoccleve was completely a son of the Church in accepting fully its teachings as he understood them, and he had a deep and touching devotion to the Virgin Mary, in whose honor he wrote a number of poems. Still, his adult life spanned the Great Schism in the Western Church, but Hoccleve never mentioned it in his poems. It is unthinkable that he was not aware of the Schism, but it certainly did not cause his faith to waver. He was a confirmed traditionalist. After all, conformity, like order and system, is virtue with a bureaucrat. He favored pilgrimages as a virtuous form of devotion, and images as a proper means for visually teaching holy lessons. He spoke out against advocates of such Lollard views as the desirability of apostolic poverty for the Church, saying that since Christ had a purse during His life on earth, the Church should also have property (*Works,* I, 22).

A theme that Hoccleve followed in his writings with more vigor and patronage than even his religious views was his fear and hatred of poverty. Hoccleve was convinced that there was no stability in the world, and that death would soon strike him down as it did every man. At the time he wrote the *Regement of Princes,* he was concerned for his own future. He was afraid that as he grew too old to work he would lose what little he had, and be left to die in poverty without friends or pleasure (*Works,* III, 31). But for all his worry and despair, it was happily not to be his fate to die in poverty. Archives demonstrate that if one type of administrative records were kept with some care by the medieval English monarchy, it was financial records. It is fortunate, therefore, that it is possible to survey in part an aspect of Hoccleve's life that troubled him considerably, and to appraise the income of a medieval bureaucrat.

The incidental sums Hoccleve received from patrons in response to his many poetic appeals and the tips collected in the Privy Seal office must remain unknown, for there are no financial records extant kept by Hoccleve personally. We must rely principally upon official records. In Hoccleve's day it was customary for a competent clerk to earn 7½d. per day for his work, and this was likely the wage Hoccleve began to draw soon after coming to the Privy Seal office. Clerks could also expect to be allotted two robes yearly for their services, a summer robe worth 20s. and a winter one valued at £1 6s. 8d. Other monies came his way also. In 1395 the confiscated goods of an outlaw valued at £40 were turned over to the Privy Seal clerks to be sold for whatever they might bring.[9] Several years later, in 1398, Hoccleve shared £10 with three of his fellow clerks derived from the forfeited possessions of outlaws.[10] Before his marriage, too, Hoccleve obtained his lodging at the King's expense in Chester's Inn. Thus it can be seen that Hoccleve's income for these years was sizeable by the standards of the time. In later years this income was to be increased.

It was customary that after some years of service a clerk would be granted an annuity by the King. It is recorded in a Patent Roll of Henry IV that Hoccleve was granted on 12 November 1399 an annuity of £10 a year for his good service, to be paid annually in two installments of £5, one at Easter and the other at Michaelmas.[11] The annuity was granted for life, or until Hoccleve should receive an ecclesiastical benefice without cure of souls worth £20 per year. A secure ecclesiastical benefice was a plum kept ever dangling before the eyes of hopeful clerks.

Less than three months after the grant of his annuity, Hoccleve resigned a corrody in the convent of Hayling in favor of William Flete and William Gedney. [12] The corrody had been granted to him by Richard II on 22 January 1394, [13] and it is probable that Hoccleve commuted it into a money annuity to supplement his income. When he received his annuity in 1399, he gave up the Hayling corrody.

Hoccleve did not receive the first payment of his annuity until December 1400, more than a year after it was granted. At that, the sum given him was less than the £10 due at Michaelmas: £8 15s. 3d. Such overdue and reduced payments were certainly not rare. England's Exchequer in Henry IV's reign was chronically short of funds, leaving everyone dependent upon its payments in an uneasy state, not the least of these being Thomas Hoccleve. This irregularity of payments provides the key to much of Hoccleve's constant concern with money. Hoccleve had problems with his annuity again in 1402. His Easter payment was £5, but the one for Michaelmas was £4 18s. 9d. Why he was shorted was not recorded (*Works,* I, liii). In the same year, however, Hoccleve acquired a new source of income. Together with John Horston, he assumed suretyship for John Scut in the latter's collection of a £24 tax farm in the city of London. Hoccleve and Horston no doubt received some percentage of Scut's profits from the farm as payment for their mainprise. The arrangement was to last through 1404. [14]

It is to be hoped that Hoccleve's arrangement with Scut supplemented his income well, for the annuity payments due him for 1403 fell far in arrears. No money at all was issued him until October. The sum then was but £9; Hoccleve had to give up £1 in order to get the £9 (*Works,* I, liii). The annuity was paid with fair regularity for the next few years. The annuity payment for Easter 1407 was a bit late, but his Michaelmas payment was far overdue. He sent a short poem to Sir Henry Somer asking him to try to get his clerks paid, so as to make them glad at Christmas time (*Works,* I, 59). The request was only a partial success, and Hoccleve was paid his Michaelmas £5, but not until Feburary 1408.

In May 1409 Hoccleve's annuity was raised by Henry IV from £10 to £13 6s. 8d. per annum. [15] This annuity of twenty marks, which was granted on Hoccleve's completion of over twenty years in government service, was made with the same conditions as the grant of 1399, and it was to remain at twenty marks until his retirement. The first half-yearly payment of his new annuity came just six days after it was granted, and covered the period to Easter 1409. The Michaelmas 1409 payment of £6 13s. 4d. was not made until November (*Works,* I, lviii). Hoccleve's Michaelmas wages for 1410 were even more overdue, not being issued until July 1411. The sums due him for the terms to Easter and to Michaelmas of 1411 were paid at the same time: February 1412 (*Works,* I, lviii). With his annuity falling so much in arrears, it is understandable that Hoccleve should appear distressed in his *Regement of Princes,* written during this period, in which he said:

> My lige lord, the kyng wich that is now,
> I fynde to me gracious ynow;
> God yeld him! he hath for my long seruise
> Guer-douned me in couenable wyse.

> In the schequer, he of his special grace,
> Hath to me grauntid an annuitee
> Of xx^{ti} mark, while I have lyues space.
> Mighte I ay paid ben of that duetee
> It schulde stonde wel ynow with me;
> But paiement is hard to get adayes;
> And that me put in many fould affrayes. (*Works,* III, 30)

The petition had little effect. In the *Regement,* Hoccleve also provided the information that his income in addition to his annuity was about £4 per year (*Works,* III, 34). It seems not at all unjustifiable that he complained of the smallness of that sum, and that, should his annuity fail, 4 could never support him.

The payments of his annuity for 1412 are difficult to determine because of missing and damaged records. The Issue Roll for Easter 1412 has not survived, and he was not mentioned at Michaelmas (*Works,* I, xiii). Henry IV died in March 1413, so Hoccleve was not included in the Easter roll of that year since the new monarch, Henry V, had not yet confirmed the poet's annuity. Henry V did confirm it at twenty marks in September 1413, and on 1 December Hoccleve was paid a full year's annuity to cover the term to Michaelmas 1413 (*Works,* I, lix–lx). It is possible, then, that he received no payment at all for 1412, giving him good reason to complain. There is also no indication that he was paid for the term from Easter to Michaelmas 1414 (*Works,* I, lxi). In a *Balade to King Henry V, for Money,* written about this time, Hoccleve asked for money on behalf of himself and his fellow clerks so that they need not "trotte unto Newgate," the debtors prison (*Works,* I, 62).

His annuity was paid without exception, though often late, for the years beginning with the half-year to Easter 1415 until the term ending at Easter 1422 (*Works,* I, lxi–lxvi). Henry V died on the last day of August 1422, and Hoccleve's annuity was not confirmed in the name of Henry VI until January 1423.[16] His £6 13*s.* 4*d.* for the period to Michaelmas 1422 was paid on 15 February 1423, and his next payment, to Easter 1423, was made on 20 May (*Works,* I, lxvi–lxvii).

On 4 July 1424 Thomas Hoccleve was granted his second corrody, this one to provide for his retirement rather than his income as a clerk. His new corrody was to be the same one as held by the late Nicholas Mokkyng, former master of St. Lawrence Poutney of London, in the priory of Southwick, Hants (*Works,* I, lxviii–lxix). Hoccleve's career as a clerk in the Privy Seal office came to an end in 1424, after more than thirty-five years of service.

The evidence for the financial rewards of that career suggests that he had an adequate and comfortable income, quite enough to satisfy his needs. If he were truly poor, it was because of his own prodigality, not meager earnings. There can, however, be no denial of the worry and insecurity that came from the unsure and irregular payments of the poet's annuity. As the sums due him were issued or withheld, he was faced with veritable feast or relative famine.

How long Hoccleve lived in retirement until his death presents something of a problem since no record of his death has been discovered. The same corrody at Southwick that had been given to Hoccleve was, however, granted to Alice Penford and Thomas Baker in August 1437.[17] It is unlikely that, were Hoccleve still alive, the corrody would have been granted to someone else. It is also impossible to estimate how long the position remained vacant after the poet's demise, but it seems resonable to assume that Hoccleve lived no longer than the summer of 1437.

Thus far Hoccleve has been presented in the context of his work and activities as a functioning bureaucrat, but there is more to be learned from Hoccleve. A significant portion of his writings dealt with subjects that may be called political. His thinking was not profound, but it was the thinking of a man actively engaged in the business of government and thus deserves attention. An outstanding authority on the period of English history in which Hoccleve lived, the late E. F. Jacob, described the era as one of "faction and tension" in the realm of active politics. In the opinion of Professor Jacob, it would be unrealistic to expect writings on constitutional theory to appear under such conditions. The closest thing to such theoretical writings would be to pass moral judgment upon the prince within the context of both the common law and customs of England, and the canon law of the Church. "English speculation about government and society in the fifteenth century was less political than moral and dogmatic." [18] The remarkable extent to which Hoccleve exemplified Jacob's generalization becomes progressively apparent as Hoccleve's ideas are examined.

In his *Balade to King Henry V. on His Accession to the Throne,* Hoccleve's wish is that God would grant that Henry might rule his royal estate virtuously (*Works,* I, 39–40). In the same poem, Hoccleve describes his conception of an ideal monarch. The description resembles a catalog of hagiographic virtues. The prince is to fear and trust God, to be clean in heart, chaste, sober, sad, just, truthful, humble, compassionate, merciful, prudent, sagacious in financial matters, and inclined to hear and follow wise counsel. Hoccleve's ideal prince should also shield and protect his vassals, govern his realm in law and equity, and be ever the devoted champion of Holy Church.

Hoccleve's *opus magnum,* the *Regement of Princes,* was an earlier work also addressed to Henry, who was then Prince of Wales. The *Regement* was composed in 1411–12 to instruct the young man who was destined to be king. The title, *Regement* (i.e., Rule) *of Princes,* or its Latin equivalent, *De Regimine Principum,* was not an uncommon one. Any didactic work written for the benefit of some prince on the art of government might bear the title, and works by that name were written by Thomas Aquinas, Helinand von Froidmont, Engelbert of Admont, Jean de Annosis, Vincent of Beauvais, Giles of Rome, and others. As a book of instruction to the Prince of Wales on how to govern, Hoccleve's *Regement* fits easily into this genre of literature. [19]

The *Regement of Princes* (*Works,* III, 1–197) is a poem of some 5,460 lines, divided into a short prologue, followed by an imaginary conversation between Hoccleve and a beggar, and a brief dedication to Prince Henry. The 468 seven-line stanzas forming the body of the poem are distributed unevenly among the fifteen separate subjects on which Hoccleve chose to give instruction, and are followed by a concluding envoy of three stanzas. It was apparently a popular commentary on the subject of what a prince should be, as more than forty manuscript copies survive. The popularity of the *Regement* seems unwarranted to the modern reader, and one scholar has used some of Hoccleve's writings as fine examples of the "sheer, unabashed, prolonged dullness" that is the vice of much of medieval literature. [20]

The *Regement* was largely derivative in its ideas, and the poet did not attempt to present its content as original. Hoccleve trotted out his sources for all to see, feeling that the prestige of his authorities would add weight to his words. The first of the three major sources Hoccleve mentioned using for the *Regement* was an eighth-century work supposedly written by Aristotle which Hoccleve called "his book of governance." This was the *Secretum Secretorum,* thought in the Middle Ages to be letters of advice to Alexander from his tutor, and many versions and copies of this popular work have survived.[21] The second major source Hoccleve named was the *De Regimine Principum* of Egidio Colonna or Giles of Rome. Hoccleve's *Regement* has been referred to as a translation of the work by Giles,[22] but comparison of the two quickly reveals the falsity of such an assumption. The final prime source cited by Hoccleve was *Chess Moralised (Liber de Ludo Scacchorum)* by Jacob de Cessolis, and it was to this book that Hoccleve was most indebted.[23]

Using these and numerous other occasional sources, Hoccleve commenced his instructions for Prince Henry with words on the dignity that should belong to a monarch. The first thing a king should do to maintain his dignity, wrote Hoccleve, is to love God and hold Him in awe. For Hoccleve, God is the overlord of kings as well as other men. The other elements of conduct necessary for a king in maintaining his dignity are to act justly toward all men, both great and small, and to carefully keep the law of the land. The three themes of fearing God, acting justly, and maintaining the law run all through the *Regement.*

Employing the same sermonizing methodology, Hoccleve made his way from the dignity of a king through the subjects of the keeping of oaths, justice, observing the law, the virtues of pity, mercy, patience, chastity, magnanimity, of not delighting in riches, and generosity, the vice of avarice, the propriety of prudence, the taking of advice, and peace. On all subjects the commentary is moralistic rather than philososophical, blatant as opposed to subtle, and urged with pious and obvious sincerity.

It is quickly obvious to any reader that the *Regement of Princes* is not a clever handbook of practical suggestions for a ruler, and that it is also a failure as a compilation of necessary details that a king might overlook. Hoccleve did not attempt, as Sir John Fortescue, C.J. (d. 1479?), would, to provide a political theory for existing constitutional practice,[24] nor was he a theorist and shrewd observer of the administrative machine of which he was a part like the German Conciliarist, Dietrich of Niem (d. 1418).[25] Much more is made by Hoccleve of the duties of a king than the ways to accomplish his ends. There is more on what an ideal king should be than on what he should do. It is, as such, a general plea for virtue in government that employs many popular sermon themes. As a piece of political writing, the *Regement* falls far short of many theoretical works of previous centuries. However, there are in the *Regement* flashes of genuine concern for the English throne and for Christendom in general. The nearest Hoccleve comes to eloquence is when he is pleading for the end of the war between Christian rulers (though less than three years after the *Regement* was written, the war with France was resumed), and for a return to a golden age in which society would function smoothly, with the clergy, the nobility, and the commons busy about the activities that God and the feudal societal pattern had given them.

The *Regement of Princes* is not, however, the only source for our bureaucrat's political thought. He made significant observations on the Church and the Papacy. God, he said, lent His power to St. Peter and his successors, the popes. Men should turn to the pope for answers about the faith, not to their own wits (*Works*, I, 12). In his *Address to Sir John Oldcastle* (1415), Hoccleve made clear his ideas about the relations of king and pope. A king, he said, is not the prince of priests. The authority of a priest exceeds all earthly power. All men, including kings, must obey their bishops. Spiritual matters are higher in dignity than temporal things, as the soul is more exalted than the body. Hoccleve mustered an old and anachronistic analogy saying that God made two lights to shine in the firmament, a greater and a lesser. The greater light, the sun, denotes the authority of the pope, while the lesser light, the moon, symbolized the kingly power (*Works*, I, 17–18). Hoccleve's idealism transcended reality. The sun and moon analogy had for long been unrealistic. Hoccleve obviously ignored many of the political realities of his own lifetime, and spent his words on other matters.

In references to the papal monarchy, Hoccleve only implied that the Papacy should be supreme over the entire Church. From his other remarks, it is plausible to assume that he considered such a matter so obvious as to need no mention. He would certainly have made the priest the most prestigious and authoritative figure in society.

The poet provides substantive support for the judgment by E. F. Jacob that one could not expect to find a true political theorist in fifteenth-century England. Hoccleve's approach to the problems he perceived in government was consistently moralistic and religiously dogmatic. Though he may have had the innate ability, he assuredly did not have the discipline to mould his ideas into a closely reasoned

political philosophy. At the same time, Hoccleve was sufficiently removed socially and intellectually from the masses of society that he
could not be satisfied with occasional violent attempts to redress immediate wrongs as was the case in 1381. Hoccleve could draw neither
upon the heritage in political thought of the intellectuals, nor upon that
of the masses. Thrown back upon his own resources, he chose the
easiest method available to solve the problems he saw. The very essence
of his proposals for correction in political administration was that men
should lead more virtuous lives, with the prince setting a high example.
Hoccleve tried to be a good man, and he proposed a personal, traditional ethic whereby every man would be good, to the end that society
and government would also be good. Hoccleve's political thinking may
lack appeal because it lacks sophistication, but it remains curious and
significant because Hoccleve rejected his bureaucratic experience
when he approached political problems.

NOTES

1. *Hoccleve's Works*, I, ed. F. J. Furnivall (EETSES) LXI (1892), 119. *Hoccleve's Works*, III, ed. F. J. Furnivall (Early English Text Society, Extra Series), LXXII (1897), 30.
2. T. F. Tout, *Chapters in the Administrative History of Mediaeval England* (6 vols., Manchester, 1920–23), V, 54, 57–64. J. L. Kirby, "Clerks in the Royal Service," *History Today*, VI (1956), 752–53.
3. British Museum, Additional Manuscript 24062.
4. The formulary was edited by E.-J. Y. Bentley in 1965 under the title "The Formu-lary of Thomas Hoccleve" as an Emory University Ph.D. dissertation.
5. A. L. Brown, "The Privy Seal in the Early Fifteenth Century" (Unpublished Oxford D.Phil. thesis, 1954), II, 171–72, 179–80.
6. *The Letter of Cupid* was not, however, strictly Hoccleve's own composition. About three years before it was written, there appeared in France a poem by Christine de Pisan called *Epistre au Dieu D'Amours*. Hoccleve's *Letter* is an abbreviated imitation of Christine's work. P. G. C. Campbell, "Christine de Pisan en Angleter-re," *Revue de Littérature Comparée*, V (1925), 644. On the general problem of Hoccleve's use of sources, see J. Mitchell's *Thomas Hoccleve: A Study in Early Fifteenth-Century English Poetic* (Urbana, 1968), pp. 75–96.
7. H. S. Bennett, *Six Medieval Men and Women* (New York, 1962), p. 77.
8. His name, however, was probably derived from the Bedfordshire village of Hock-liffe.
9. Bennett, *Six Medieval Men and Women*, p. 82.
10. Tout, *Chapters*, V, 91–92.
11. *Calendar of Patent Rolls (1399–1401)*, p. 61.
12. *Calendar of Close Rolls (1399–1402)*, pp. 126–127. The Priory of Hayling was an alien priory of the Benedictine abbey of St. Peter of Jumièges in Normandy that owed to the King the support of two pensioners.
13. *Ibid., (1392–1396)*, p. 249. That Hoccleve had been given this grant was first noted in J. R. Hulbert's "An Hoccleve Item," *Modern Language Notes*, XXXVI (1921), 59.
14. *Calendar of Fine Rolls (1399–1405)*, p. 184.

15. *C.P.R. (1408–1413)*, p. 75.
16. *Ibid., (1422–1429)*, p. 60.
17. H. S. Bennett, "Thomas Hoccleve's Death," *Times* [London] *Literary Supplement* (25 December 1953), p. 833.
18. E. F. Jacob, *The Fifteenth Century, 1399–1485* (Oxford, 1961), p. 305.
19. See L. K. Born, "The Perfect Prince: A Study in 13th and 14th Century Ideals," *Speculum*, III (1928), 470–504. Born devoted some three pages to Hoccleve. A more detailed study of the subject is W. Berges's *Die Fürstenspiegel des hohen und späten Mittelhalters* (Leipzig, 1938). See also A. B. Ferguson, *The Articulate Citizen and the English Renaissance* (Durham, 1965), pp. 88–89.
20. C. S. Lewis, *The Discarded Image: An Introduction to Medieval and Renaissance Literature* (Cambridge, 1964), p. 204. Readers today would likely agree with Lewis, but G. Mathew judged the *Regement* an "accomplished work, with the smooth style prized at the time,. . .a learned poem," belonging "to the new literary movement of the international court culture." *The Court of Richard II* (London, 1968), pp. 57–58.
21. See A. H. Gilbert, "Notes on the Influence of the 'Secretum Secretorum'," *Speculum*, III (1928), 94.
22. Bennett, *Six Medieval Men and Women*, p. 85.
23. F. Aster, *Das Verhältniss des altenglischen Gedichtes 'De Regimine Principum' von Thomas Hoccleve zu seinen Quellen nebst einer Einleitung über Leban und Werke des Dichters* (Leipzig doctoral dissertation, 1888), p. 28. See also Mitchell, pp. 24–31, 84–86, 96.
24. S. B. Chrimes, "Sir John Fortescue and his Theory of Dominion," *Transactions of the Royal Historical Society*, 4th Series, XVII (1934), 147.
25. E. F. Jacob, "Dietrich of Niem," *Essays in the Conciliar Epoch* (3rd ed., Manchester, 1963), pp. 25, 40.

The Rhetoric of Optics in Lord Herbert's Poems to Diana Cecil

Ronald E. McFarland

PERHAPS BECAUSE of its technical nature, the literary response to the flourishing study of optics during the seventeenth century is limited, and what there is tends to be reactionary. Probably the most widely known optical reference in seventeenth-century lyric poetry occurs early in John Donne's "The Extasie": "Our eye-beames twisted, and did thred/ Our eyes, upon one double string." Donne employs the outdated Platonic theory of vision by extramission; that is, a visual ray (species) is emitted from the eye to the object, and then the image is conveyed back to the eye, and thence to the brain. As Plato describes the process in *Timaeus*, the gods "first contrived the eyes to give light," a theory for which he provides a highly poetic rationale. When daylight "surrounds the stream of vision, then like falls upon like" and one sees, but when night falls, the unlike element extinguishes the stream and the eye no longer sees.[1] Among those who accepted the extramittory theory in some form were the Stoics, Empedocles, Euclid, and Ptolemy. A different theory of vision, however, was developed by the Epicureans to some extent and later by Alhazen. Rejecting the Platonic theory, Alhazen holds that light comes from the object to the eye, a process which has been called "intramisison."[2] Aristotle also rejects the notion that vision results from an extramitted ray, but he suggests that vision is caused by a process through the medium between the eye and the object.[3] Roger Bacon, who provides a sort of synthesis of previous optical studies in his *Opus Majus,* insists that Aristotle, like himself, had established a sort of compromise between the active and passive extremes of Plato and Alhazen, for vision "receives the species of the thing seen, and exerts its own force in the medium as far as the visible object."[4] Students of seventeenth-century prose may be aware of these contradictory theories of vision through the passage on basilisks in Sir Thomas Browne's *Pseudodoxia Epidemica* (1646). He observes that, according to Aristotle, Alhazen, and Witelo, "sight is made by Reception, and not by extramission; by receiving the raies of the object into the eye, and not by sending any out."[5]

Professor A. C. Crombie observes that Bacon "asserted that both the extramitted species of vision and the intramitted species of light from the visible object were necessary" for vision. He also indicates Witelo's "adherence to the intramission theory of vision" of Alhazen.[6] The point, then, is that by the early seventeenth century, if not by the mid-thirteenth century, a strictly Platonic theory of vision by extramission was hardly tenable in the serious scientific study of optics. The reason for its continued attraction, however, is not difficult to ascertain. It is, after all, fundamental to the Judaeo-Christian view that man is made in God's image, and as God is the source of light (John 1:4–9) in both a spiritual and physical sense (the sun is the "eye of heaven"), so man is the source of vision in his own microcosm. In all cases involving light there is an emanation, and light is essential to vision. It is consonant with Judaeo-Christian thinking that the human eye, like God and the sun, emits rays or species. In explaining the interest in optics during the thirteenth and fourteenth centuries, Crombie observes that the study of light was "amenable to mathematical treatment" and that "light had been for St. Augustine and other Neoplatonists the analogy of divine grace and of the illumination of the human intellect by divine truth."[7] In his study of Grosseteste and the development of experimental science, Crombie devotes a chapter to the "Metaphysics of Light," which accounts in part for an interest in optics that is not altogether in the realm of physics. Grosseteste, Crombie asserts, perceived an analogy between "the corporeal *lux*" and the "spiritual *lux*," which substantiated his "belief that the study of geometrical optics was the key to knowledge of the natural world."[8] The awareness of both the corporeal (physical) and the spiritual (loosely speaking, metaphysical) ramifications of light are evident, for example, in the opening apostrophe to light in the third book of *Paradise Lost:*

> Hail holy light, ofspring of Heav'n first-born,
> Or of th' Eternal Coeternal beam
> May I express thee unblam'd? since God is light,
> And never but in unapproached light
> Dwelt from Eternitie, dwelt then in thee,
> Bright effluence of bright essence increate.

As Marjorie Hope Nicolson justly observes of this passage in her study of the reception of Newtonian optics in the eighteenth century,

Milton's treatment of light remains "remote, godlike, awful."[9] The poet of the seventeenth century is in fact generally negligent of the terrestrial implications of the physics of light; or, as Nicolson asserts, he is more concerned with the ultimate source than with the immediate. But Milton's use of light, or the familiar references in the poetry of Vaughan or Traherne, does not exhaust the treatment of optics in seventeenth-century poetry.

Perhaps the most effective poetic treatment in the seventeenth century of what I should like to describe as the "physics and metaphysics of optics" is to be found in an unusual and generally neglected series of six poems in celebration of the color black by Edward, Lord Herbert of Cherbury. Lord Herbert's poetic reputation has never been high, in part because his writing pales in comparison with that of his acknowledged mentor, John Donne, and in part because his poetry is syntactically complex and metaphorically abstract.[10] But these poems are among his best accomplishments, and they should be read in an appropriate context. Such a context should account for the apparent tension in the poems between the phenomenal, to which reference to the science of optics is applicable, and the noumenal, to which reference to metaphysics, religion, or possibly mysticism is applicable. Since theories concerning vision, light, and color relate both to the science of optics and to the realm of speculative metaphysics, I shall refer to the use of the physics and metaphysics of optics in these poems. A close examination of the poems will show that Lord Herbert's adherence to the extramittory theory of vision in their composition allows him to emphasize the opposition between the mundane and the transcendental response to experience, which the poems dramatize.

A survey of Lord Herbert's library indicates that he possessed several volumes by scientists who were engaged in revolutionary work in the field of optics. Specifically, he owned copies of Christopher Scheiner's *Rosa Ursina* (1630), Johan Kepler's *Astronomia Nova* (1609) and *De Cometis* (1619), three of Willebrod Snell's works, and, most importantly, Francois D'Aguilon's *Opticorum Libri VI* (1613).[11] Although D'Aguilon is noteworthy in the science of optics for his early description of stereographic principles, his importance to this study is that in this volume he synthesized the known optical theories of the time from the works of Euclid, Alhazen, Witelo, Roger Bacon, and Kepler. Lord Herbert's use of the outdated extramittory theory of vision, therefore, may be supposed to have been quite intentional. Just as Donne, notably in the *Anniversaries* and the *Devotions upon Emergent Occasions*, clings to the Ptolemaic cosmology, or to a Tychonic variation thereof, despite his awareness of developments in the "new philosophy" (see "Meditation XXI"), so Herbert holds to the outmoded optical theory, despite his probable knowledge of more recent findings. While it may be supposed that neither man was willing to assent to the theories and discoveries of the new philosophy, it seems to me that Herbert retains the Platonic theory of vision primarily because he finds it more suitable to his purpose in these poems, for he intends to demonstrate the metaphysical (broadly conceived) growing out of the physical, the concept developing from the experience. In this sense, then, allowing for some poetic license, we might justly argue that Lord Herbert is not being reactionary or unscientific in these poems, but that his movement from empirical evidence to generalization is in the tradition of Francis Bacon's inductions.

Mrs. Diana Cecil, the subject of the poems, is not important as an actual personality any more than Elizabeth Drury is important in Donne's *Anniversaries.* Diana Cecil is a dark beauty; Elizabeth Drury is a recently deceased young virgin. Both serve essentially to supply the poetic occasion, but Diana Cecil also serves in Herbert's poems to provide an essential empirical focus. The opening lines of "To Mrs. Diana Cecyll" suggest that her beauty is not of whiteness, which would imply the reflection of great amounts of light, but of light itself, which Herbert conceives as being "refracted" as from a diamond, or, more figuratively, like "early Morning breaking from the Night." [12] Herbert's use of the word "refracted," in the fifth line, represents a very early appearance of this technical optical term in English. The *Oxford English Dictionary* lists the first appearance of the word "refraction" (in reference to optical matters) in Holland's translation of Plutarch's *Morals* (1603). The verb form, "refract," is first recorded, in an optical context, in 1612, and the word "refracted" is not recorded until the publication of Daniel's *Eclogues* between 1638 and 1648. The use of the term in this poem, although it does not prove Lord Herbert's awareness of recent developments in optics, supplies early evidence that the poems are built upon a metaphorical foundation involving some reference to the science of optics. In this case, Herbert combines the superior value of the diamond with the refracted light, and then elevates that metaphor above the combination of "milk or snow" and "pale and whitely things."

In the second stanza Lord Herbert conveniently ignores his own previous poetic celebrations of blonde beauty, in "A Description" and

218

"Upon Combing Her Hair," and indicates that this traditional Petrarchan convention of light-haired beauty is "the vulgar Poets theme," a theme which he will reject in favor of his adoration of "reverend black." In this stanza the image of morning breaking from night, in the first stanza, is given a religious dimension, as black is served by light in the same way "By which at first night did precede the day" (1.12). The implicit scriptural reference to Genesis 1:3, "And God said, Let there be light: and there was light," is suggestive of a philosophy of light not necessarily pagan or even Neoplatonic, but clearly related in nature to the analogous corporeal and spiritual *lux* of Robert Grosseteste. These multiple implications of light relate directly to the extramittory theory of vision, for it most readily appertains to the active principle of the human soul, the ultimate origin of the visive rays.

In the third stanza Herbert observes that the lady's "symmetry of parts and form divine" are not composed merely "of one vulgar line" any more than her black hair and eyes are common or open to the perception of "vulgar" poets. Rather, this is a new form of beauty, "Like to the Diamond's refracted light," and made "of proportions new," the result of which leads to the recognition of mystery and wonder in the final stanza. Herbert concludes that admirers of Diana's black beauty need not inquire why they so much admire her, for no higher ascent is possible. The question is not why they admire, but precisely what it is that they are admiring. She must not be wooed, therefore, with "common praises," since only that admiration which is based upon understanding is worthwhile. In effect, then, the last lines of "To Mrs. Diana Cecyll" provide a rationale for the following poems. The mystery of Diana's "rare beauty," as it relates both to the phenomenal and to the noumenal range of perception, is to be made understandable. The five poems that follow constitute studies in optics, metaphysics, and, in a way, esthetics. The "anatomy" or analysis of her hair and eyes in the next two poems draws attention away from the actual person who is the subject of the series toward a description of the "perfections in each part," and the two sonnets on black beauty and blackness tend still further away from Diana Cecil herself. But the phenomenal or existential conditions of the opening poem are reasserted somewhat in the concluding poem of the series, "The First Meeting."

"To Her Eyes" opens with an obvious allusion to the Platonic concept of vision by extramission. The beams of the black eyes are described as "deep" and united with the soul. The extramitted "wonders" which proceed from the eyes are likened to the power of the stars, for both may affect the sense, both being "works of light," but her eyes and the stars may also affect the mind (the stars by their astrological "influence"), and that even more significantly than the sense. This rather subtly implied metaphor establishes the base upon which the remainder of the poems builds. As the eyes are related to the soul, so the soul is related to "that first cause" (God) who expresses in her eyes how he broke forth from his "veil of an eternal night." This idea of creation is closely related to the reference in line twelve of "To Mrs. Diana Cecyll," and so the religious texture of the series is reinforced. For purposes of this examination, I shall consider this sort of religious allusion to correspond to the "metaphysical" comment of the poems. Herbert's notion that man has been provided with a "second light," which serves for sight, is again in the tradition of the Platonic theory of extramission. But it is also consistent with Judaeo-Christian tradition, for the first line of the third stanza, "His image then you are," constitutes a restatement of Genesis 1:26. Herbert supposes that, though sight and soul might shine through a "grey, or hasle glass" (1. 29), the true index to the divine light is in the black. That is, a clouded glass, possibly a reference to the tinting of telescopic or helioscopic lenses to protect the eyes, will let through a little light, so obviously a black lens should allow no light to shine through at all. Up to this point, we might regard the observation as a hypothetical experiment in optics. But this is where physics stops and metaphysics begins, for in this instance (Diana Cecil's eyes) light beams do pass through blackness, and so we are to consider such beams not only uncommon, but miraculous, and in fact divine (1. 33).

In "To Her Eyes" the allusions to optics, broadly, with respect to the extramittory theory of vision, and more narrowly, with respect to the use of tinted lenses, are subsumed by the realm of metaphysical speculation. Physics tells us that a certain phenomenon can or cannot occur, or that it will occur only in a certain way, but this particular experience offers evidence to the contrary; in this case, light rays do pass through black lenses. How are we to account for this condition? Clearly the answer rests in the nature of Diana Cecil, and so the problem is ontological, or "metaphysical" in a literal sense. The development of smoked lenses for solar observations sets the limits of vision from the standpoint of optics, but empirical observation provides evidence to the contrary. That phenomenon for which physics cannot offer a satisfactory explanation must be referred to a different mode of comprehension. If a phenomenally grounded understanding is not possible, one must turn to the noumenal.

In "To Her Eyes" Lord Herbert appears to have argued successfully for the divine nature of the mistress, but in "To Her Hair," which follows, he describes a problem that arises in the case of the divine essence of the mistress. The poem begins with a farfetched image in which the hair is envisioned as arising from the extraction of her black eyes, an extraction which is emitted in sleep ("what time her soul retires"). She spins the beams into her hair "destin-like," and then, continuing the comparison with Clotho, the hair shines "as threads of life" or "fatal rays," which meet with a "vulgar light and praise" reminiscent of the uninformed response to beauty in "To Mrs. Diana Cecyll." The appeal of the third stanza, therefore, is for enlightenment, for Herbert perceives that men "are grown blind" in such a way that when their eyebeams should return from the perception of her black beauty with a comprehensible image of its glories, the beams are instead extramitted in vain. Once again, the science of optics tells us that if the eyes are capable of sending out beams (species) and if there is an object for those beams to fall upon, then an image should be returned to the brain. Blindness occurs only when our eyes are incapable of sending out species. How do we account for the fact that, although all the necessary conditions exist, sight does not take place? Again, if we repair to metaphysics, we will see that the blindness is not of the sight but of the understanding, of the "mind's eye."

Faced with the problem of a blindness that is not explicable in simple empirical terms, Herbert turns to more involved optical speculations concerning first the theory of color and then the theory of vision. The fourth and fifth stanzas contain the most explicit optical theorizing in the series of poems as he struggles with the mystery of black beauty.

> Is it, because past black, there is not found
> A fix'd or horizontal bound?
> And so, as it doth terminate the white,
> It may be said all colours to infold,
> And in that kind to hold
> Somewhat of infinite?

The notion of white and black as two extremes of color, and of the other colors as intermediates (combinations of the extremes in varying proportions) is found in Aristotle, and it remains, apparently, an acceptable theory of color until the appearance of Boyle's *Experimental History of Colours* (1664) or Newton's *Optics* (1704). Professor Frank

Warnke suggests that the source of Herbert's relationship of black to infinity may be in the Dionysian concept of "Divine Darkness,"[13] but the terminology of this passage infers that the response is from the realm of physics rather than metaphysics. The last line does suggest an extension beyond the empirically accountable conditions in the reference to infinity, but Herbert does not develop the idea, so there remains an unresolved tension between the physical and the metaphysical implications of blackness.

The next stanza extends the tension between physics and metaphysics from color theory to theory of vision.

> Or is it, that the centre of our sight
>   Being vailed in its proper night
> Discerns your blackness by some other sense,
> Then that by which it doth py'd colours see,
>   Which only therefore be
> Known by their difference?

Other colors are perceived because of their contrasts, both with one another and, incidentally, with the black pupils. While most colors are perceived by difference, which implies color variance, the blackness of Diana Cecil's hair is perceived by the similarity with the center of sight, and that implies unity, which is more proper to her divine nature. Clearly, the special theory devised to account for the perception of Diana Cecil's black hair has nothing to do with the science of optics. Rather, Lord Herbert reverts to somewhat farfetched speculation positing a sort of extrasensory mode of vision.

The poem concludes with a paradoxical plea, which says, in effect, that all would see "shining light in darkness" if they were not blinded by the light of the "Sun beams below." Men, blinded by the light of the sun (by too much light), ironically miss the divine light which breaks out of darkness, the same light that is referred to metaphorically in the first stanza of "To Mrs. Diana Cecyll." That is, Herbert is suggesting that men have become blind to spiritual realities ("upward blind"), and therefore to the essential beauty of Diana Cecil, because they are too thoroughly involved in the commonplace ("sunbeams below"). Or, in terms of the first poem of the series, if we are too impressed by the obvious beauty of "milk or snow," we may miss the rarer and more precious "refracted light" of the diamond, which represents true wisdom or insight. Milton similarly relates bright blackness to wisdom in "Il Penseroso" (1631), where "divinest Melancholy," like Diana Cecil, bears an appearance "too bright," in its own way, "to hit the sense of human sight."

Of the six poems in the series, those least explicitly related to the physics of optics are "Sonnet of Black Beauty" and "Another Sonnet to Black Itself." These poems, however, do bear explicit connections, in addition to the obvious similarity of subject, with the other poems of the series. The essence of blackness itself, now released from any direct personal relationship to Diana Cecil, is examined with reference to day and night. Although there is little direct reference to optics in the "Sonnet of Black Beauty," it is not until the twelfth line that we depart from simple empirical evidence to encounter the recurring paradox of light in darkness, which again introduces the metaphysical realm of noumenal speculation. Black beauty is praised as a power "above that common light," since it can subdue any color which light can renew and because it remains "unvary'd to the sight." Black is black, whether seen in the full light of day or in the deepest darkness of night. The phrase "above that common light," serves as a transition with the last line of "To Her Hair": "With the Sun beams below." It also relates to such phrases as "ordinary sight" ("To Her Eyes," 1. 22) and "common praises" ("To Mrs. Diana Cecyll," 1. 22). The theme of ascent from commonality or vulgarity runs through all the poems of the series and is carried out in various forms of metaphor or allusion: astronomy and astrology, poetry, and optics (of light and color). The colors, both of the spectrum and of figurative language, which "the world call bright" and which "old Poetry" (recalling the "vulgar Poets theme" of the first poem in the group) pursue must yield to the unity of blackness. Moreover, common experience informs us that while night obscures other colors, black maintains its true nature regardless of the light. But this does not mean that blackness is impervious to light, as the physicist might argue, for the poem ends with the paradox which has been restated throughout the series: "blackness is a spark/ Of light inaccessible," and it is men's spiritual blindness that causes them to perceive only the darkness of black.

In "Another Sonnet to Black Itself" the development of a metaphysical (or perhaps mystical) comment on blackness based upon physical considerations of light and color is continued. Echoing the idea that black is the sum of all the colors, which is mentioned in "To Her Hair" (1. 22), Herbert expands the notion to identify black with the beginning and end of all color and with the "colour of the Sun where it doth burn." Black is also related explicitly to the melancholic personality (1. 7), and we are perhaps to recall Robert Burton's observation that students and scholars (including scientists, poets, and metaphysicians) are "more subject to this melancholy than others." To this point, the comments upon blackness might be considered scientific, at least in terms accepted by the age, and the first two observations are clearly within the realm of the physics of optics. In referring to astrology in the tenth line, however, the context shifts to the speculative. During its nightly reign, the stars ("characters of fate," reminiscent of the first two stanzas of "To Her Hair") convey divine messages, but when "Earth's common light" of day "shines to our eyes," all revelation is denied, and we are reminded perhaps of the retreat of Milton's melancholiack before the "flaring beams" of day.

The implications of Diana Cecil's black beauty have obviously extended beyond her actual person, but her person is only incidentally the subject of the poems. It is important to note, too, that the praise of blackness itself does not suddenly begin with this sonnet. The metaphysical and religious implications of "reverend black" have been stated and restated from the first, and in each poem the idea of a dual light, terrestrial and celestial, has been reaffirmed. Lord Herbert uses what he knows of optics, but he is able to move through science, by way of physics, to the soul, by way of metaphysics, as no modern poet could. Back in the second poem of the series, "To her Eyes," Herbert rather casually states that we might imagine a glass through which "sight or soul might shine" (1. 30). What Herbert can do, almost, it seems, without a second thought, is to equate the physical and the spiritual, the phenomenal and the noumenal, in the act of vision, and he can do so in an apparently offhand manner with scarcely a lifted eyebrow from his audience. To this end, the extramittory theory of vision is invaluable, since it alone may potentially link sight and soul. One suspects that T. S. Eliot would have considered this condition typical of an "associated sensibility," both on the part of Lord Herbert and of his audience. That Herbert leaves optical science behind at the conclusions of his sonnets on black beauty would be no more startling to one of his educated contemporaries than would his resumption of scientific allusions in the next poem.

In the final poem of the series, "The First Meeting," Warnke finds a more intense "personal emotional involvement." [14] Indeed, the poem differs from the others in several ways, despite its central image of the woman's black hair and its optical references. The hair, this time, is considered as a "sable Cloud" from which lightning breaks forth in the form of extramitted rays from the lady's eyes. This constitutes a reversal of the opening image in "To Her Hair," in which the eyebeams are transmitted to the hair when the mistress sleeps. Here, she is most certainly awake. Night is not invoked, and although there are allusions to heaven and paradise, the action of the poem is clearly mundane and terrestrial. As the storm clears, the lady sends out her eyebeams (11. 19–20) and changes the speaker's darkness to light. At this point (1. 23) we might fix the climax of the sequence, for darkness is made light, night images have given way to day, understanding is achieved, and the "revelation" denied in the last line of "Another Sonnet to Black Itself" is now at hand. The next two stanzas detail the realization of a love which is both physical and spiritual in nature. An "orient gate" of a smile ravishes his soul, and she infuses her soul into a kiss. Her smile is both "gracious," a term appropriate to theology, and "sweet," a commonplace entry in the dictionary of secular love.

Until this point, four stanzas into the poem (48 lines), "The First Meeting" is similar to most poems on that popular subject, but the fifth stanza involves a rather complicated allusion to the optical theory of extramission.

> But as those bodies which dispense
> Their beams, in parting hence
> Those beams do recollect,
> Until they in themselves resumed have
> The forms they gave,
> So when your gracious aspect
> From me was turned once away,
> Neither could I thy soul retain,
> Nor could you give mine leave to remain,
> To make with you a longer stay
> Or suffer'd ought else to appear
> But your hair, night's hemisphere.

The concept of the bodies dispensing beams would seem to imply a contradictory use of the theory of intramission by Herbert at this point in the poem. More likely, however, he is making use of a combined form of the two theories of vision, for as early as the thirteenth century Roger Bacon had attempted a reconciliation of the theories of extramission and intramission.

> [The species of things] must be aided and excited by the species of
> the eye, which travels in the locality of the visual pyramid, and
> changes the medium and enobles it. . .and so prepares the passage
> of the species itself of the visible object. . . .[And] it is also
> true of the species of vision that it travels altogether along the
> path of the species itself of the visible object. [15]

Herbert turns to this compromise in order to resolve the problems that arise from the physical separation of the lovers. In some ways the dramatic conditions are similar to those of Donne's lovers in the famous "Valediction: Forbidding Mourning." Once the visualized object departs, of course it recollects its species and vision of it no longer occurs. Similarly, the woman has infused her soul into a kiss, but like the visualized object, she recollects that soul when she departs, and she leaves her lover in darkness. In different terms, the "heav'nly grace" (1. 18) that is offered earlier has changed his darkness to light (1. 23), but he now finds that grace is not a permanent condition of men on earth, for she has turned away her "gracious aspect" (1. 54). Now the question occurs whether the revelation in line 23 was real, for if his experience with the mistress is simply transitory, then the darkness he now faces at her departure is not measurably better than the previous darkness of his ignorance.

In the concluding stanza, therefore, Lord Herbert appeals to a metaphoric construct that implies the imparting of a more lasting, permanent condition, and so he turns to the lodestone. Once the magnet imparts its virtue, it "Doth ever in its subject live," so when Herbert and the woman are apart, the power "still abides" to guide his soul by her "magnetique touch inspir'd." Similarly, once an individual has experienced God's grace, the power of it remains to influence him towards the good (virtue). Physics again provides a useful metaphor for the resolution of tension between the phenomenal and the noumenal, but some readers may find the transition from optics to magnetics too abrupt or too convenient. It is obvious, however, that no optical theory is sufficient to bear the new metaphorical burden that arises from the revelation, understanding, and subsequent delight of love. Whether the change of metaphoric vehicles is sufficiently decorous or not, in an esthetic sense, the relationship between the phenomenal and the noumenal, between physics and metaphysics, remains consistent throughout the series.

Lord Herbert's technique of establishing problems or paradoxes in lucid, even concrete terms by reference to scientific or empirical data, and then of resolving or transcending the issues by moving through their physical foundations to metaphysical or religious discourse is used by other more renowned writers of his age. The exchange between Adam and Raphael in Book VIII of *Paradise Lost* proceeds in a comparable fashion. Adam offers his own understanding of the cosmology based upon the Aristotelean-Ptolemaic system of a "sedentarie Earth," but Raphael cautions Adam against such "quaint Opinions" and offers a more recent cosmological theory. The point of the discourse is not to establish the correct cosmological concept any more than Herbert of Cherbury's point is to establish correct optical theories, but to teach Adam that his place is not to understand so much as to admire the works of God. Similarly, in his *Hydriotaphia, Urn-Burial* (1658), Sir Thomas Browne conducts an extensive survey of the recently unearthed Roman burial urns and he ranges broadly over the burial practices of other cultures primarily in order to demonstrate that pyramids and monuments are but vainglory, "there is no antidote against the opium of time," and finally, "there is nothing strictly immortal, but immortality." The scientific discourse is supplanted by religious and metaphysical conclusions. Lord Herbert of Cherbury, therefore, establishes a sort of "rhetoric of optics" in his sequence of poems concerning black beauty, which is similar in nature to what might be called Milton's "rhetoric of cosmology" and Browne's "rhetoric of archaeology."

NOTES

1. Edith Hamilton and Huntington Cairns, eds., *Collected Dialogues of Plate* (Princeton: Princeton University Press, 1969), p. 1173. I gratefully acknowledge the financial support of the Research Council of the University of Idaho in the preparation of this article.
2. A. C. Crombie, *Medieval and Early Modern Science,* Vol. I (Garden City, New York: Doubleday, 1959), p. 102.
3. W. D. Ross, ed., "De Sensu," *Works of Aristotle,* Vol. III (Oxford: Clarendon Press, 1931), 437a–438b.
4. Roger Bacon, *Opus Majus,* Vol. II, tr. Robert B. Burke (New York: Russell and Russell, 1962), p. 470.
5. Geoffrey Keynes, ed., *The Works of Sir Thomas Browne,* Vol. II (London: Faber and Gwyer, 1928), p. 202.
6. A. C. Crombie, *Robert Grosseteste and the Origins of Experimental Science* (Oxford: Clarendon Press, 1953), p. 152.
7. Crombie, *Modern Science,* p. 99.
8. Crombie, *Grosseteste,* p. 131
9. Marjorie Hope Nicolson, *Newton Demands the Muse* (Princeton: Princeton University Press, 1946), p. 20. This account of the poetical response to Newton's *Optics* in the eighteenth century (by Pope, Smart, Thompson, *et al.*) devotes little space to the poetical use of optical theories in the seventeenth century.
10. Frank J. Warnke's unpublished doctoral thesis, "This Metaphysick Lord," *DA,* XIV 1738, is the most complete response to Lord Herbert's poetry in English. The best of the negative responses to Lord Herbert's poetry, in English, is Patrick Cruttwell's in *The Shakespearean Moment* (New York: Random, 1960). A more thorough study of the poetry is available in Robert Ellrodt's *Les Poetes Métaphysique Anglais,* Vol. II (Paris, 1960).
11. C. J. Fordyce and T. M. Knox, *The Library of Jesus College, Oxford* ("Oxford Bibliographical Society," Vol. V, Pt. II; Oxford: Clarendon Press, 1937), pp. 71–115. This catalog does not represent the entire range of Herbert's reading or of his library.

12. G. C. Moore-Smith, *The Poems of Lord Herbert of Cherbury* (Oxford: Clarendon Press, 1923), p. 34. All subsequent allusions to Herbert's poems refer to this edition. Moore-Smith suggests that the poems in this series were composed between 1621 and 1630.

13. C. E. Rolt, ed. and tr., "The Mystical Theology," *Dionysius the Areopagite* (New York: Macmillan, 1920), p. 192.

14. Warnke, p. 108.

15. Bacon, p. 471.

Recent Books About
Medieval Manuscripts

M. L. Colker

Translatio Studii: Manuscripts and Library Studies Honoring Oliver L. Kapsner, O.S.B.,
ed. Julian G. Plante. Collegeville, Minnesota: St. John's University Press, 1973. Pp.
288. $17.50.
Jeanne B. Odier. *La Bibliothèque Vaticane de Sixte IV à Pie XI: Recherches sur l'histoire
des collections de manuscrits* (Studi e Testi 272). Città del Vaticano: Biblioteca Apostolica Vaticana, 1973. Pp. xviii, 477; 78 plates.
Jean Dufour. *La bibliothèque et le scriptorium de Moissac* (Publications du Centre de
Recherches d'Histoire de la IVᵉ section de l'École pratique des Hautes Études, Paris).
Geneva and Paris: Librarie Droz, 1972. Pp. xxii, 184.

AS A TRIBUTE to Oliver L. Kapsner, O.S.B., Director of the Monastic Microfilm Project from 1964 to 1972, *Translatio Studii* offers a wide
variety of manuscript studies, for which fourteen contributors are responsible. Otto Mazal describes the elaborate 14/15th-century French
binding of Vindobonensis 1521; Jean Leclercq discusses, apropos of
Saint Bernard's *Epistola* 87, jongleurs in literature and manuscript art;
A. L. Conde makes known, from two tenth-century Escorial codices,
what seems to be the only extant medieval Spanish quotation from the
Regula Magistri; Jean Glénisson and Odile Grandmottet print selections about legacies of books from the will and codicils of Guillaume
de Chaumont, councillor of Jean le Bon and Charles V (the books are
almost entirely liturgical or canon law works); D. J. Sheerin traces the
early history of the suppression of proper prefaces in missals and
sacramentaries. By keen investigation Bernard Peebles is able to identify the writing of eighteenth-century notes found in many Paris manuscripts of Sulpicius Severus' *Vita Sancti Martini* with the hand of Lau-
rent-Etienne Rondet (1717-1785), who was preparing an edition of the
text. The fifteenth-century collection of letters which I. W. Frank analyzes is of major value for the history of the Dominican cloister at
Vienna, in the absence frequently of other evidence. The collection,
still kept at the cloister (codex 70/291), even reveals internal dissen-
sion: cf. the remark (cited on p. 187) "quasi in horrorem et amaritudi-
nem uersus est michi conuentus meus."

Two writers in *Translatio Studii* give complete *editiones principes*. G. B. Fowler publishes, on the basis of Admont manuscripts, *De consilio uiuendi,* an aphoristic poem of about 1300 by the polymath Engelbert of Admont. Fowler fails, however, to comment on the metrical form and often mispunctuates the verses. For example, at least commas one and three should be eliminated from lines 104–105 (p. 250): "Affectus carnis, preme sub freno racionis, Ne te lex frangat, carnalis condicionis." Also, Fowler ought to have read *remouebis* (not *renouebis*) at line 59 and *sic* (not *sit*) at line 60 (p. 228) as transmitted by his manuscripts A2.3 and A2 respectively; and one suspects that *hoc* (line 78, p. 229) should be *hec*. J. G. Plante edits, from an unnumbered Reichersberg codex, a chronicle concerned with this city and extending to 1250. His use of parentheses for filling out abbreviations and his capitalization and line-division in strict accord with the manuscript both waste space and severely impede perception.

Three authors in the Festschrift take up the history of particular libraries. In an account of the Augustinian Chorherrinstift at St. Pölten, Gerhard Winner declares (p. 66) that the house had approximately two hundred codices at the close of the fifteenth century but that only about eighty of these are preserved. C. R. Rapf, discussing the Irish monastery at Vienna, reports the repeated loss of books there (pp. 6, 11, 14): disastrous for manuscripts were the fire of 1410, the quartering of imperial troops at the monastery in 1529, reckless lending to sixteenth-century humanists, and negligence in the years after 1900— during 1922–1930 no fewer than twelve important codices disappeared, presumably through theft. How one might wish that it had been possible long ago to have a microfilm project like that which Father Kapsner guided.

For a rapid overview of the history of the Vatican Library a reader may turn to Claudia Carlen's nine-page contribution in *Translatio Studii.* For a much fuller treatment he must use Jeanne Odier's book on the subject. Her two preliminary chapters discuss early papal collections, but the book really concentrates upon the Vatican Library since its foundation (1475) to the time of Pope Pius XI, and records its vicissitudes: probably the darkest period was after Napoleon assumed control of St. Peter's (1809) and documents were carried off from the papal archives to Paris. Odier tells about the many renowned scholars who were official or unofficial members of the staff, like Filippo Beroaldo junior, Lucas Holstenius, Jean–Baptiste Pitra, Angelo Mai, Franz Ehrle, Auguste Pelzer, André Wilmart, and Giovanni Mercati.

She also mentions interesting less-known figures such as Roberto de' Nobili, who in 1555 became the cardinal librarian at the age of fourteen, died at nineteen, and happened to be both pious and erudite. She duly notices the principal acquisitions under each pontiff, how the Urbinates, the Palatini, the Reginenses, and many other collections were obtained. An appendix listing administrators of the library from 1475 to 1971, with their respective terms of office, is helpful for reference. On the other hand, the photographs of Louis Valadier's busts of the twenty-four first cardinal librarians could have been omitted: these busts, commissioned in 1783, show little individuality—the faces generally look like those of brothers.

The author presents a dazzling abundance of precise information— Odier worked largely from records in the Vatican archives—and this information is copiously documented: for example, chapter three, consisting of twelve pages, is accompanied by eighteen pages of notes, including the addenda.

Of a like wealth of specific detail is Jean Dufour's work, which probes the history of the Benedictine abbey of Moissac with its scriptorium and library: the abbey, founded about 630, achieved prominence in the second half of the eleventh century but in the twelfth century stagnated and began its disintegration. The abbey was likewise not very fortunate in the preservation of its manuscripts: many of them were destroyed by a fire of 1188; the creation of the post of *custos cartarum* only in 1328 helps to explain why so few early documents survive; in 1678 Raymond de Foulhac stated that the archives of the abbey were in disarray and that a large part of the documents were rat-eaten. Colbert acquired Moissac manuscripts which later entered the Bibliothèque Nationale, as it is now known, and a few manuscripts from Moissac reached other libraries, including the Vatican, British Museum, and Pierpont Morgan. With close attention Dufour examines the codices and documents from the abbey and gives his codicological and palaeographic observations. Virtually each letter and each abbreviation is studied. He finds, for example, eight styles of *g* and seven varieties of caudate *e*. But in this palaeographic section he intermingles manuscripts written in the Moissac scriptorium with manuscripts that may be of other origin before having entered the abbey as the result of purchases, donations, or 'borrowings': Moissac was affiliated with Cluny from 1048 and had connections with Catalan monasteries, especially Ripoll.

Dufour's appendices print early lists of manuscripts once at Moissac and describe 31 documents, 78 codices, and 2 lapidary inscriptions associated with the abbey. At the end of the book are extremely clear photographs representing 78 texts.

Indeed all three new books advance markedly our knowledge about the 'wanderings and homes' of manuscripts and thus merit our gratitude.

Old French Narrative Poetry

SOME RECENT STUDIES

Stephen G. Nichols, Jr.

Joseph J. Duggan. *The Song of Roland: Formulaic Style and Poetic Craft.* Berkeley, Los Angeles, London: University of California Press, 1973. Pp. 226. $8.50.

Karl D. Uitti. *Story, Myth and Celebration in Old French Narrative Poetry 1050-1200.* Princeton: Princeton University Press, 1973. Pp. ix, 256. $11.00.

LIKE CHARLEMAGNE'S ARMY, the two books under consideration constitute an advance and a rear guard of medieval literary criticism and scholarship. Uitti's book is the most interesting and provocative because it ventures into fresh areas of critical concern, while Duggan's conscientiously undertakes to tie up those loose ends left dangling a decade ago when interest in oral-formulaic diction and the Old French epic ran high. If interest in the latter subject has waned in the interim, it is largely that while the *chanson de geste* as a whole, and the Digby version of the Roland in particular, is indubitably the product of an oral tradition, the extant epics reveal a lively interaction with the newer narrative traditions which evolved during the twelfth century, as well as with contemporary cultural and political concerns. It is that dialectic which, for better or for worse, has engaged the energy of most scholars studying the *chanson de geste* in the last ten years.

At first blush, the exclusive concern of Duggan's book with problems of oral-formulaic diction in the Oxford manuscript of the *Roland* seems anachronistic, the final skirmish of a battle long-ended. This assessment is unjust to the extent that interest has continued in the problem of oral-formulaic diction—although not nearly so intensely in Old French as in other medieval literary traditions. Furthermore, Duggan has systematically studied a larger corpus of the *chanson de geste* than any previous scholar working in this domain, and he does modify considerably, if not felicitously, the Parry-Lord methodology in a manner bound to stir up controversy. His study certainly raises questions as to the role which may safely be accorded the computer in literary study above and beyond its now-consecrated use for computer-generated concordances (parenthetically, be it noted that Professor

Duggan's *A Concordance of the Chanson de Roland,* 1970, itself a computer product, is one of the most useful tools for *Roland* scholars to come along in recent years).

Duggan's book consists of six chapters, the first and last of which set forth the rationale and methodology of the study and draw conclusions regarding its "consequences." The four intervening chapters are devoted to exposing the formulaic nature of the Oxford *Roland* and to examining traditional problems, e.g. the Baligant episode, in light of the author's findings. Space does not permit the detailed analysis which the book deserves. One can at best point to some of the questions raised by Duggan's study which will certainly stimulate further discussion and controversy.

In Chapter One, "The Problem and the Method," Duggan reveals a rather ambivalent attitude towards the pioneering studies of Milman Parry and Albert Bates Lord, an ambivalence maintained throughout the book. Heretofore, Parry's definition of the formula has been accepted by most scholars working in the field of oral-formulaic diction with slight variations. (In his book, *Reading the Song of Roland,* 1970, Eugene Vance, while accepting Parry's basic definition of the formula, sought to extend the definition beyond the hemistich to include whole *laisses,* p. 22ff. He thus conflated Parry's quite necessary distinction between formula and theme.) Duggan cites Parry's definition of the formula as "a group of words which is regularly employed under the same metrical conditions to express a given essential idea" in an approving context. Yet he announces on the same page what amounts to a significant modification of Parry's definition: "throughout this work the term 'formula' without qualification refers to semantically stylized hemistiches and not to syntactic formulas" (p. 7, n.17). Later, page 10, he says "by a formula, I mean a hemistich which is found two or more times in substantially the same form within the poem." Whereas Parry respected the poetic nature of the oral text by insisting that a formula was a poetic unit as well as a thought unit (i.e., it possessed a metrical integrity as well as an ideational one), Duggan reduces the definition to purely quantitative linguistic terms. There is neither rigor, nor poetic integrity in Duggan's notion of the formula, confused as it is by his several definitions. It is not difficult to understand why Duggan cannot work with Parry's definition, even though he never openly rejects it. Parry conceived of formula identification as an intellectual effort, an act of cognition. The last two qualifications in Parry's definition require judgment, which is precisely what Duggan cannot allow. For him, the computer is the only tool capable of doing a proper job of formula hunting, and he expresses condescending pity for those predecessors (except, significantly, Rychner), who did their own formula identifying. Duggan never defends nor explains his reduction of formula incidence from Parry's prudent four repetitions ("regularly recurring" meant repeated at least four times) to his own two, but it is in line with the totally quantitative emphasis that pervades the book as a whole and makes it disappointing from a critical standpoint.

Throughout, Duggan is obsessed with the notion that he must prove beyond the shadow of a doubt that the *Roland* is "an oral-dictated text, taken down by a scribe. . .from the lips of a singing poet" (p. 60). To do so, he seeks to show that those passages which have been traditionally adjudged the most moving from a literary standpoint, are precisely those passages which have the highest density of formulas. All well and good, but what about the poetic qualities that make these passages such jewels of the oral formulaic pantheon? Milman Parry, his son, Adam, Lord, Notopoulos, Vance, Rychner, myself, and others all extended their efforts beyond the level of the mere formula to the art of the verse itself, to the use of thematic composition, to the idea of how the poet overcame the constraints of his language; all concepts which, although not susceptible of computerization, played an important role in the oral-formulaic scholar's concern, making of him a literary critic.

Duggan too-often contents himself with giving unnecessary résumés of passages and then passing categorical judgments, e.g. "in these later versions, the majesty of Roland's death is diluted in the maudlin effects of superfluous expansions" (p. 188). The judgment is surprising coming from one so bent on showing oral-formulaic characteristics: it has been shown again and again that expansions are the essential hallmark of the oral poet. Professor Duggan seems to want to have his traditionalism served up with a sauce of individualism.

If Duggan spurned the theoretical underpinnings of the oral-formulaic scholarly tradition in favor of a one-sided emphasis upon technique, Uitti shows how one can build imaginatively upon theoretical foundations to create new critical perspectives and techniques. In this case, he has progressed logically from his earlier book, *Linguistics and Literary Theory* (1969), to elaborate a theory of interaction between literature and culture first outlined in the last chapter of that work. There he argued for "replacing the arbitrary identification of literature with aesthetic by a more stringently defined concept of culture. The 'freeing of poetry' from dependence on language—i.e., the old rhetoric—is simply no longer applicable today. . .'Culture'. . .is a more dynamic concept and is essentially more relevant to literature than either 'semiotic' or 'aesthetic'. It allows for the reincorporation of authentic history into the discussion of literature" (pp. 253–254).

The intellectual antecedents for Uitti's theoretical construct may be found in Roman Jakobson's linguistic theories, particularly his depiction of factors and functions of language which permits a combined analytic and synthetic presentation of the elements of communication and their interaction. Jakobson's theory of binary structures figures prominently in Uitti's concept of "epic binarism" in the chapter which he devotes to the *Roland*. The binary elements depicted by Uitti are not, however, simple structural elements of the epic seen in isolation. They are multi-dimensional, in the sense of De Saussure's concept of *langue et parole*, allowing Uitti to make a very strong case for the *Roland* as at once a poetic construct and a document reflecting authentic historical and cultural concerns. Uitti's approach is closer to Bédier than to F. Lot, in this respect, but differs from both in its success in integrating the cultural and the poetic.

The book is divided into three essays—demonstrating the efficacy of the author's approach on the *Alexis*, the *Roland*, and on the work of Chrétien de Troyes, with a short appendix devoted to Jean Bodel's *Song of the Saxons*. Inasmuch as the exigencies of the different texts require adapting the method to each, the essays are essentially independent of one another. Each contains an introduction with an appropriate review of the scholarship which serves to situate Uitti's own approach. While not strickly necessary for the specialist, the introduction—which in the first two essays contained reasoned résumés of the works in question—will be enormously .helpful to students. The introductions also serve a purpose central to the book: the establish. .ent of the mythic elements referred to in the title. By myth, Uitti intends the cultural and historical resonances which the matter of the individual texts assumed in the imaginations of the medieval public. The concept is not dissimilar to what I have elsewhere called the "Peregrinatio Principle." ("The Interaction of Life and Literature in the *Peregrinationes ad Loca Sancta* and the *Chansons de Geste*," *Speculum*, 44 [1969], 51–77; and "The Spirit of Truth, Epic Modes in Medieval Literature," *New Literary History*, I [1970], 365–386).

In the case of the *Roland*, the myth and celebration concern the person of Charlemagne as historical figure *and* contemporary ideal. Perhaps more than any other *Roland* critic, Uitti insists on the primacy of Charlemagne in every aspect of the work. For him, the text sets up a series of binary associations at once intra-textual and inter-cultural. All of these associations contribute to the authority of Charlemagne and what he represents. By a linguistic-imaginative process of association which he calls "contagion," Uitti shows how the *Roland* develops a coherent dynamics of dialectical rapports between story and idea. To cite examples of these associations baldly in so brief a space would not do justice to Uitti's carefully-reasoned and, with few exceptions, ultimately convincing demonstration.

Ironically, Uitti's essay on the *Roland* stands out as far more sensitive to the language of the poem than Duggan's book. Uitti even makes more imaginative use of Rychner's work, particularly his theory of *laisse* dove-tailing. The comparisons are not meant to be invidious, but only instructive in pointing to the most fruitful direction for medieval literary criticism.

Medieval Economic and Agrarian History

THREE RECENT STUDIES

David Herlihy

M. M. Postan. *Medieval Trade and Finance.* Cambridge: Cambridge University Press, 1973. Pp. vi, 382.

M. M. Postan. *Essays on Medieval Agriculture and General Problems of the Medieval Economy.* Cambridge: Cambridge University Press, 1973. Pp. vi, 302.

Edmund King. *Peterborough Abbey, 1086-1310: A Study in the Land Market.* Cambridge: Cambridge University Press, 1973. Pp. xii, 208.

M. M. POSTAN has over the years been a principal architect of the now current interpretation of the economic history of medieval England and of Europe. He has achieved his high stature through his own research, through the collective scholarly enterprises he has helped organize (most notably, the *Cambridge Economic History*), and through the students he has trained. We have here under review two collections of his short articles, and a volume by one of his most recent students in medieval agrarian history.

Postan has chosen from his numerous publications 22 articles to be reprinted here, and he has divided them into two collections; the first is concerned with "trade and finance" (9 studies) and the other with "agriculture and general problems" (13 studies). These essays illuminate not only medieval economic history but also (since they are reprinted without revisions) the history of medieval economic history over the past half century. As Postan states in his preface to *Trade and Finance,* his earliest interests as a scholar were directed to the "role of capital and the formation of capital" in the medieval world. These interests inspired his studies on credit in medieval trade (1928), on financial instruments (1930), and on the relations of England and the Hansa (1933), to mention only principal studies reprinted here. The culmination of this phase of his research was doubtlessly the lengthy chapter, here occupying 140 pages of text, on the medieval trade of northern Europe. It was originally written for the second volume of the

Cambridge Economic History (1952). Together with Robert Lopez's parallel study of trade in southern Europe, this chapter formed the kernel of that now standard reference volume. Both articles together marked an epoch in the study of medieval economic history, as both advanced in forthright fashion the then novel contention that the late Middle Ages were not a period of "Renaissance prosperity" but of economic contraction and depression.

Agriculture and General Problems, containing Postan's later studies, allows us to trace out the evolution of his thought. His examination of credit and trade in the medieval economy suggested to him that traditional interpretations of economic development, which envisioned an unbroken evolution from a "natural," to a "money," to a "credit" economy, were wrong. Like others of his generation, perhaps influenced by the contemporary crisis in western civilization, he rejected the nineteenth-century notion that social progress was continuous and irreversible. But what then was the pattern of medieval economic change? In search of an answer, Postan in his later career moved deeply into agrarian and manorial history, as agriculture dominated the medieval economy and presumably held the secrets of its movements. *Agriculture and General Problems* contains many of his now classical studies, devoted to the misleading concept of a "money economy," the chronology of labor services, the state of the English economy in the fifteenth century, the evidence in price and wage movements for a declining population in the late Middle Ages, and the evidence of overpopulation on Winchester manors in the thirteenth century.

The same themes appear again and again in his studies. Evolutionary change in the countryside did not move in one direction only; reversals in direction could occur and did occur, as with population movements or the commutation of labor services on the English manors. The late fourteenth and fifteenth centuries were an age of economic crisis and contraction. And the roots of that crisis were in large part Malthusian. In a prior period of growth (tenth through thirteenth centuries), the medieval world had expanded inordinately, and by ca. 1300 its resources could not support its numbers. Terrible famines and plagues inevitably ensued, and recovery came only slowly, not really beginning until the last decades of the fifteenth century.

These ideas are now so well-known (and so widely discussed) that it would be idle in a brief review to offer further comment here. But a reviewer would be ungracious if he did not express admiration for the skill with which Postan develops his arguments. He writes beautifully, and he knows how to strike a delicate balance between factual detail and strong, clear conclusions. There are, to be sure, in the two collections essays which are less impressive. In evaluating, in a negative way, Italian influences on economic development of medieval England, he attacks a straw man; it takes greater effort to prop up the straw opponent than to demolish him. His essay on the reasons for the backwardness of medieval science is filled with the kind of Victorian misconceptions of medieval culture which Postan attacks in his other essays. But in most of the writings presented here, the reader quickly recognizes the hand of a master.

In comparison with Postan's high craftmanship, Edmund King's examination of the land market in the records of Peterborough abbey is a rather weak beverage. It has, to be sure, many merits. Through an exceptional series of sources, he is able to confirm that land trading was much more common in the English countryside, even among peasants, than historians once believed. He also shows effectively how the expansion of settlement, quite visible in his records, affected trading in land. But unlike Postan himself, he is unable to bring his detailed information to a firm and clear conclusion. "The approach is via a family history. . . ," he claims in his preface, "The history of the monastery is itself a family history." The content of such affirmations is never satisfactorily explained (the word "family" is not even referenced in the index). In leaving the work, the reader bears with him the impression that the author has not succeeded in clarifying, for himself or for others, the full import of his study.

In his preface, King thanks the supervisor of his work and gives credit to what he calls the "constant stimulus" of Postan's ideas. This is a sentiment which many economic historians, in many lands, now share.

Medieval Intuition and Seventeenth-Century Dialectic

P. Albert Duhamel

Stanley E. Fish. *Self-Consuming Artifacts: The Experience of Seventeenth-Century Litera-ture.* Berkeley: University of California Press, 1973. Pp. xiv, 432. $12.50.
Russell Fraser. *The Dark Ages and the Age of Gold.* Princeton: Princeton University Press, 1973. Pp. xi, 425. $16.00.

NEITHER OF these books believes in middle terms; both are out to shake the authority of the enthymeme: the first by demonstrating how seventeenth-century literature believed in the superior vision of dialectic, the second by showing how the medieval intuition could reconcile opposites far better than the syllogism.

Self-Consuming Artifacts begins with an analysis of how, in the Platonic tradition, the function of art is to bring the reader to truth and not truth to the reader. His explication of the *Phaedrus* is a much more convincing interpretation of the inter-relations of all its parts that John Wild's lengthy consideration in his *Plato and the Nature of Man.* Professor Fish shows that the subject matter, the end, and the form of Platonic dialogues is dialectic, and that a dialectical presentation succeeds at its own expense. If it succeeds in leading its participants to understanding, it has conveyed them to a point where they are beyond the aid of discursive or rational forms, and it has become the vehicle of its own abandonment.

In the use of the Platonic dialectic in the search for vision, the relationship between the author and his readers is more like that which exists between a physician and his patients, not like that which rhetoric tries to create between a speaker and his hearers. Rhetoric, and its favorite heuristic method, the enthymeme, must be forever at odds, for the end of dialectic is not to clarify the disposition of things in this world, which can be that of rhetoric, but to transform the soul-mind into an instrument capable of seeing the things of this world for the imperfect things they really are.

In his words: "To read the *Phaedrus,* then is to use it up; for the value of any point in it is that it gets *you* (not any sustained argument) to the next point, which is not so much a point (in logical-demonstrative terms) as a level of insight. It is thus a *self-consuming artifact,* a mimetic enactment in the reader's experience of the Platonic ladder in which each rung, as it is negotiated, is kicked away. The final rung, the level of insight that stands. . .because it is the last, is, of course, the rejection of written artifacts. . ."

Continuing in this same tradition, Augustine, most explicitly in his treatise *On Christian Doctrine,* believing that truth was available through divine revelation or could be vouchsafed to man in a vision from God, saw no need for the heuristic topology which had formed the substance of the teaching of the traditional rhetorical *inventio.* The schemes and tropes of *elocutio,* also, were pointless because the truth compels of itself and needs not pleasing words or forceful exhortations.

The ideal sermon in the Augustinian tradition would be forever pointing away from itself, calling attention to what it wasn't doing, in the hope of leading its hearers to a glimpse of the Spirit which animates the preacher. This is why Donne's strategy in his sermons seems so close to that of some medieval sermons described by Th.-M. Charland in his *Artes Praedicandi.* Like the friar preachers, or, for that matter, Hugh Latimer in his sermons on the plough, Donne will begin by asking his hearers to consider a text and then systematically lead them to realize how feeble is their understanding to grasp its implications. This, in turn, leads to a rejection of reliance on the understanding alone and a turning to God for enlightenment. So these sermons achieve their end when they succeed in making their hearers repudiate not only their content but the methods which had discovered their content. Like the missions they fulfill their purpose by making themselves no longer necessary.

The chapters in *Self-Consuming Artifacts* which seem to make most telling use of this insight are those on George Herbert and *Pilgrim's Progress.* Professor Fish shows how "Herbert's poems perform what they require of us, for as they undermine our reliance on discursive forms of thought, and urge us to rest in the immediate apprehension of God's all-effective omnipresence, they become the vehicles of their own abandonment. . .to read Herbert's poems is to experience the dissolution of the distinctions by which all other things are." Of *Pilgrim's Progress,* he argues it is no progress. The only consistent pattern he finds in Christian's journey is cyclical. Whenever a new opportunity to fall into an old error presents itself, he invariably does. The whole is a lesson in the wisdom of distrusting our untutored abilities as well as of all linear configurations in prose or reasoning.

In Bacon, Burton, and Browne, there is this same use of the artifact to create distrust in its relevance—but with a difference. In Donne, Herbert, Bunyan, and Milton, the undermining of discursive forms and the devaluation of rational thought was only the first part of a dialectic which was completed only with the provision of some superior vision. In Bacon's *Essays,* the method is to begin with some generally accepted idea or some respected proverb and then bring in data which question their validity. Bacon wants to call attention to the mind's weaknesses in order to put it on guard against itself. He would develop a method that would make of the mind an unprejudiced reporter. So his induction would reduce all minds to the same level of reliability, whereas the purpose of dialectic is to raise the mind up above itself.

In Burton's *Anatomy of Melancholy* the erosion of the reader's confidence in his mind begins on the first page. He is led on to believe that there must be some way to make sense out of this nonsense, but in the end the only consolation he is offerred is that we are all in the same ship of fools. Browne, in his *Religio Medici,* also begins with commonplaces of belief and constantly shifts away from explaining their implications to call attention to the skill he has in writing about them. With the *Religio Medici,* we are at the end of a tradition of looking upon literature as best when it is self-consuming and reading an artifact which is self-indulgent. Instead of asking its readers to come in search of truth, it seems to say truth is here.

Milton's *Reason of Church Government* is also best understood when it is viewed in the Platonic-Augustinian tradition. Very frequently today's reader who attempts the tract comes to feel that he is getting nowhere. He can think of himself as moving through a series of rooms but always coming back into the same one. The chapter he is reading seems indistinguishable from every other. Professor Fish suggests the reason is that Milton believed that the Presbyterian form of church government had been commanded by God; Episcopacy had not—this was an obvious truth requiring no proof and no proof could make it any more certain. So he will not "club quotations with men whose learning and belief lies in marginal stuffings, who when they have like good sumpters laid ye down their hors load of citations and fathers at your dore, with a rhapsody of who and who were Bishops here or there, ye may take off their packsaddles, their days work is don. . . ."

The Dark Ages and The Age of Gold comes loaded with footnotes and quotations from all the Fathers—from Clement of Alexandria to Marcuse. The purpose of the discussion is "the hypothesizing of an antithetical kind of temperament, which I call medieval" and which is "apt to sponsor a view of life and art that is marked by dubiety, tentativeness, accommodation, and not least of disparate things." This medieval temperament which was blessed with an acceptance of paradox, a belief in the possibility of the coincidence of opposites, was first upset in the Renaissance when man began to brood on the pastness of the past and to reverse the process of decay. The peace of the Salisburyian vision was replaced by the agitations of reason to make all smooth.

Here is a part of his argument: "The impulse to congruity is hopeful, and like so much else in the ambiguous history of Renaissance thought, like the fevered insistence on the value of time, it is a despairing impulse as it communicates revulsion from the world of phenomena in which antinomies jostle endlessly for place. The amorphous world is denied as the regisseur elaborates his decorous ensemble."

Modern man's inheritance from the Renaissance determination to order and regulate has been a reduced vision so that a potentially rich consciousness of creation has been reduced to a mere trickle. Man has invented a series of languages, mathematical, logical, and grammatical to express this reduced awareness. "But," to quote Fraser again, "the characteristic vocabulary or symbology of the Age of Reason victimizes the man who employs it" as it confirms him in the belief that reduced awareness is the only awareness and as it bedevils his sense of reality, so that he is all too apt to take his concepts for data, his words for actual things. "The insistence in this vocabulary on symmetry and sequence destroys the actual things. It sins against the Holy Ghost."

That may be. But sure it is that the medieval mystical writers thought it a gift of the Holy Ghost which gave them the light to perceive the divine mystery of the One and the Many. To convince that the vision, or its approximation, was widespread and lost requires something more than a concatenation of texts, no matter how Byzantine the tesselation.

Culture and Community
in the Italian Renaissance

FOUR RECENT STUDIES

Michael Altschul

Werner L. Gundersheimer. *Ferrara: the Style of a Renaissance Despotism.* Princeton: Princeton University Press, 1973. Pp. xii, 313; 19 plates. $14.00.

Bonner Mitchell. *Rome in the High Renaissance: the Age of Leo X* (Centers of Civilization series, vol. 33). Norman: University of Oklahoma Press, 1973. Pp. xii, 171. $3.50.

Oliver Logan. *Culture and Society in Venice, 1470–1790: the Renaissance and its Heritage* (Studies in Cultural History). New York: Charles Scribner's Sons, 1972. Pp. viii, 344; 26 plates, 1 map. $12.50.

Peter Burke. *Culture and Society in Renaissance Italy, 1420–1540* (Studies in Cultural History). New York: Charles Scribner's Sons, 1972. Pp. x, 342; 19 plates, 1 map. $14.95.

RECENT SCHOLARSHIP on the Italian Renaissance has sought to focus on cities besides Florence, and on the complex interplay between cultural innovation and social-political structures. The range and quality of such work have also encouraged scholars to attempt general syntheses which differ significantly, in approach and in temperament, from the Burckhardtian tradition. Three works on individual communities, plus Peter Burke's general interpretive and methodological survey, are the subject of this review notice.

The key to Professor Gundersheimer's approach in his suggestive book is to be found in a passing remark on page 214: "in a small city like Ferrara. . .the ruler's *persona* had long been one of the few subjects of genuine interest." Gundersheimer has written, not a narrative political history or full-scale institutional study, but a series of profiles of the successive Este rulers of the *Quattrocento,* and through these, a cumulative profile of the social and cultural life of the Ferrarese city and court. The result is a fresh and convincing work. Agreeing with much recent scholarship that sees more similarities than differences between the city-state republic and the city-state despotism, Gundersheimer delineates the basic achievements of Este rule: a government grounded in the kind of popular consent that valued stability more

247

than internal *libertà;* the continuous development of bureaucratic institutions within a traditional polity; and a sharply nuanced but cumulatively enlightened and fruitful cultural patronage. The author does not analyze the courtly poetic culture of Boiardo and Ariosto, preferring to concentrate on earlier periods and less familiar works. In particular, he has used Angelo Decembrio's *De Politia Litteraria* to underscore the classicism and neoplatonism sponsored by Leonello d'Este in mid-century, and the *De Triumphis Religionis* of Giovanni Sabadino degli Arienti to demonstrate significant artistic and urban renewal achievements under Ercole I in the last decades of the *Quattrocento.*

All the Este receive high marks, on grounds and in ways far removed from the unhelpful generalizations of Burckhardt, for their promotion of culture and for a policy of genuine civic concern. Whether "republican" or "despotic," the essential reference point and matrix of Renaissance governance was the city; and Ferrarese civic life was fundamentally grounded in the personalities and priorities of its dynastic rulers. The Este knew their strengths and limitations, and worked within the framework thereby provided. Because Gundersheimer has effectively assembled and presented his profile, his book will be of as great a value to the student of literature as to the historian of Renaissance society and politics.

Professor Mitchell's brief work on Rome is agreeably written and manages to pack a good deal of material into the space at its disposal. It suffers, however, from the editorial limitations of the series, in that there is simply not enough space available to explore topics with the same range and depth that characterize the Gundersheimer and Logan books, or indeed similar works in analogous series, such as Gene Brucker's distinguished *Renaissance Florence* (1969). Mitchell is most effective in discussion of strictly literary subjects, such as the vogue of Ciceronianism; but this cannot sustain the entire work. The chapter on "faith and morals," for example, fails precisely because it is based on impressionistic literary sources and not on documentary and archival evidence. The book makes for enjoyable reading, but lacks the originality and the stimulating integrative quality of the others under review here.

Dr. Logan's study of Venice admirably fills a great gap in the literature. It has one large weakness, however, that must be disposed of at the outset: the quite misleading promise of its title. In truth, Logan has written an immensely detailed and impressive work on Venetian culture to 1630, with only a brief, cursory chapter on the later period. If the date "1630" were substituted for "1790" in the title, and the final chapter retitled to indicate its epilogue character, the reader would have a much fairer indication of the book's scope, value, and interest.

This much said, Logan's achievement is noteworthy. In particular, he has truly entered the social and mental world of the Venetian nobility. Not all cultural figures were patrician, but the social framework certainly was, and the connections are carefully elucidated. Thus Logan is immensely informative on the contributions of the erudite noble to antiquarian scholarship, political and historical thought, and art patronage, both lay and ecclesiastical. His greatest originality lies in the chapter entitled "Patronage and the Collecting of Art" (a chapter more than twice the length of any other), with its related appendix of art patrons (pp. 295–321). Taken together, these form an almost separable monograph of their own, providing a mine of information hitherto scattered or unknown on this topic for the sixteenth and early seventeenth centuries. The connections between the "myth of Venice" and the *gravitas* of the noble life lead to fruitful analyses of the distinctive Venetian tradition in historical and political writing, centered on such figures as Nicolò Contarini, Paruta, and Sarpi. Logan plays down the large claims, especially for Sarpi, that animate the major recent work by William Bouwsma (*Venice and the Defense of Republican Liberty,* 1968), studiously avoiding the temptations to encapsulate generalizations about "Renaissance values." This caution is maintained throughout, so there is little of the daring suggestiveness that characterizes Peter Burke's book in this same series. By the same token, this caution may be said to weaken somewhat the chapters on literary and artistic figures, which are careful and capable but essentially standard critical exercises.

In two areas—science and music—the book is disappointingly brief. Particularly for musical culture, it has failed to explore fully what was not only a glory of Venice in its own day, but what also, in its innovative forms such as opera, was of crucial significance in the larger evolution of Italian (and of European) culture in the seventeenth century, which witnessed the passing of the heyday of classical humanism and of the vitality of the city-state itself. The Venetian Renaissance in its efflorescence coincided with the impact of the Counter Reformation in Italy, and scholars will be indebted to Logan for showing the implications of this fact in certain well-defined areas; that he has slighted other areas, from this as from other points of view, will be all the more keenly regretted. Within these limits, he has written what will become

249

the authoritative study in English of Venetian Renaissance culture and its noble setting.

The publication of Peter Burke's book is an event of signal importance, for it is the most suggestive and stimulating general work to have appeared in the field of Renaissance studies for some time. It is indispensable, not in the sense of having provided a definitive study of "The Renaissance," as concept and as period, but rather in the astonishing range and richness of the questions it asks and the problems it poses. The book is consciously programmatic, in that it constantly challenges our assumptions (or clichés) and maps the ways in which, and the degree to which, such assumptions are verifiable. No student of the Renaissance, however profound or however casual his interest, can afford to neglect it, or can fail to learn from it.

Dr. Burke is particularly concerned to investigate the social history of art and of literature, in two discrete but connected senses: an "internal" or "micro-sociological" sense, addressed to the training and education of cultural figures, the system of patronage, and the social status of the artist; and the "external" or "macrosociological" sense, relating artistic and literary evidence to typical or dominant views, values, and structures of elite society. Burke proposes a complex methodology designed to substitute, as far as possible, empirical and quantifiable conclusions for impressionistic statements; yet he is perfectly aware of those areas in which paucity of data or the inappropriateness of this method preclude this objective. He proceeds in two stages. The first, specifically focussed on the "internal" aspect, is to construct a list of 600 creative figures (artists, writers, musicians, humanists, scientists) and, with the use of a computer, to gather quantifiable information on their origins and provenance, marriage and blood relations, training, and mobility. The fruits of this investigation are presented in the early chapters, to test traditional generalizations and casual terminology: individualism, secularization, artistic autonomy. The second stage is to test, in turn, this fresh range of insights by probing relationships with the larger society. Like Burckhardt—the comparison is inevitable— Burke is concerned to develop a generalized, "static" profile of Italian civilization; but he realizes the need to present a complex, pluralistic picture, so as to minimize the pitfalls of a misleading certitude. Burke's profile is anything but simplistic. It studiously avoids either sentimentalism or anachronism, and incorporates the best recent scholarship on questions Burckhardt never asked, such as the complex manifestations of popular piety, rates and types of economic development, and the nuances of social stratification. Further, he is prepared to use insights derived from sociology and from social psychology to brave forays into forbidding territory, such as the concept of creative drive, and into such familiar *cruces* as the notion of the "Renaissance state." What emerges is not an effort to say something definitive about any one point, but to say something fresh and suggestive about every point. He has thus constructed a "model" that is relativistic, nuanced, and tentative in ways well beyond Burckhardt's work, and therein precisely lies its greatest value.

As with any pioneering effort, there are faults and shortcomings. Bibliographical references are buried in overly compressed and often cryptic notes. The names of the 600 members of the creative elite are presented in bare alphabetical groups in the appendix without any minimal data, such as birth and death dates, or birthplaces, to facilitate the reader's correlation of any given group with a given statement about that group in the text. The few pages of comparison with the Netherlands are interesting, but the comparisons with Japan could have been omitted on the almost certain grounds that no reader will have much ability to assess them. Chapter ten tries to balance emphases on the typical with an analysis of change; but efforts to suggest changes in culture and taste by relating them to clusters of political events by generations, simply does not add up to a convincing exercise in its present form. Some evidence is not exploited fully, in particular what Cellini has to say about patrons and commissions. Most serious of all, Burke occasionally commits the sin of circular reasoning he rightly criticizes in others. An early, tentative suggestion about Florentine achievement orientation is brought forward at the end as a self-evident and self-contained explanation of Tuscan predominance in certain fields. Burke writes that "the art and literature of the age reflects the central values, the world-view of the age, and cannot be fully understood until that value-system or world-view is examined and described" (p. 169); yet often the configurations of the latter are based precisely on evidence derived from the former, notably from such figures as Ariosto and Castiglione.

No work of this magnitude and importance will be perfect; indeed, to adopt a healthy skepticism of any simplistic explanatory system is the basic message of this work, and any weaknesses of method or of substance as it might contain are "understandable" companions, as it were, of the kind of pioneering effort in humanistic scholarship that the book represents. It is possible that this work will achieve a classic

251

status: not, as in Burckhardt's case, as a model of an impressionistic civilizational profile, but as an early specimen of the comparative and quantitative approach to the social history of culture. In the final analysis, Burke's book is not a synthesis, but a case study in how, and in how far, a genuine synthesis that is balanced, pluralistic, and precise, might be achieved. He points scholars on paths of method and of understanding that go well beyond not only Burckhardt, but also beyond himself. That in itself is arguably the very best kind of scholarship.

Review Notices

R. C. van Caenegem. *The Birth of the English Common Law*. Cambridge: Cambridge University Press, 1973. Pp. viii, 160. $8.50.

In 1959 Professor van Caenegem published a study of the origins of the English common law in the twelfth century under the title *Royal Writs in England from the Conquest to Glanvill* (Selden Society, vol. 77). It was a work of meticulous research, brilliant synthesis, and provocative controversy, and it holds a secure and central place in the literature of its subject; but its extreme thoroughness in research and argument brings some weariness to readers who are not specialists in the law. It is the best of good news, therefore, that in *The Birth of the English Common Law* the author has now published a short account of the views that he set forth in *Royal Writs* together with some of the findings of his further studies. The new work is a model of succinctness, grace, and clarity.

The author's leading thesis is that in the century after the Conquest the proliferation in England of diverse laws and jurisdictions—English, Danish, Norman, ecclesiastical, and royal—produced an unmanageable chaos in judicature. Because all else was confusion, parties who had rights to pursue turned to the king, whose judgments were undoubtedly authoritative because he was legally supreme and whose orders were effective because of his great power. For decades the kings reacted in irregular ways to the approaches of these suitors, sometimes ordering lower courts to hear them, sometimes investigating in person or through their justices, often simply taking the petitioners' words for the wrongs they said they had suffered and peremptorily commanding remedies. Then, in the reign of Henry II (1154–1189) and through his genius there came a series of "liberating decisions." The old irregularities ceased. Cases brought to the king's court were generally retained there for decision in a proper judicial manner, and the king's court was equipped, especially by the appointment of travelling justices, to deal steadily with the large volume of business that resulted. For common types of cases standardized judicial procedures were developed; the procedures usually involved the use of juries. Thus were laid the foundations of the English common law: the centralization of justice, the forms of action, the use of the jury. The foundations were neither Roman nor ecclesiastical nor English. The ruling class in twelfth-century England was French, and the bases which it laid for the common law were expressions of twelfth-century French civilization.

Professor van Caenegem has changed very few of the conclusions that he expressed in *Royal Writs* in 1959, and as that book raised much controversy, so this present work continues it: perspicaciously and with graceful wit, the author again and again fends off his critics and sallies out against those whom he wishes to challenge. But the opponents are many and the plan of the present little work hardly allows a thorough settling of differences with any of them, so that readers who have in the past disagreed with Professor van Caenegem on one point or another will usually find that they remain in disagreement. *The Birth of the English Common Law* is an attractive and immensely learned work, but it is by no means definitive.

Donald W. Sutherland
University of Iowa

Hendrik van der Werf. *The Chansons of the Troubadours and Trouvères, A Study of the Melodies and their Relation to the Poems.* Utrecht: A. Oosthoek's Uitgeversmaatschappij NV, 1972. Cloth. Pp. 166. $15.00

Students of Old Provençal and Old French lyric have long felt the need for a rapprochement of the literary and musical aspects of their subject. Avoiding the excessive technicality of previous musicological studies, Hendrik van der Werf makes the music of the troubadours and trouvères accessible to the literary scholar. This is not to suggest that he has written an *oeuvre de vulgarisation.* It is simply that he has concentrated on describing the music as it relates to the literary form, rather than treating it as an adjunct to the general history of music in the Middle Ages. Van der Werf's concise and clear discussions of the technical aspects of the music may be understood by anyone with even the most modest musical training. His book thereby manages that difficult feat of being at once an introduction and an important scholarly study.

Divided in two parts, the book first offers a theoretical exposition of the subject, and then presents fifteen individual texts and melodies. An extremely helpful glossary of musical and literary terms and a bibliography follow part II. There are five chapters in Part I, of which the first two, "Introduction" and "Written and Oral Tradition," constitute a prolegomenon to the central thesis vigorously argued in the three main chapters, "Rhythm and Meter," "Melodic Characteristics," and "Elements of Form."

Van der Werf believes that "the chansons of the troubadours and trouvères were first and foremost poems to be performed to relatively unobtrusive melodies which left the performer ample freedom for a dramatic rendition of the text" (p. 70). The first part of the work, then, constitutes a "défense et illustration" of this position which literary scholars, at any rate, should find very much to their taste.

Van der Werf challenges many of the consecrated shibboleths regarding the performance of medieval chansons, including the time-honored vision of the troubadour with his viol. There is no concrete evidence, he says, for the idea that the chansons were invariably sung to musical accompaniment. Although van der Werf does not mention the *Ensenhamen* of Guiraut de Cabrera, in which the art of playing and singing are coupled, he does mention the many manuscript illuminations showing poets (or jongleurs) with instruments and cites a remark by Colin Muset which has been interpreted as linking singing and instrumental accompaniment. These do not, for van der Werf, constitute documentary evidence sufficient to warrant the rigid assumptions that have been based upon them. Like the courtly love revisionists, van der Werf insists on controlling our assumptions about the performance and mode of existence of medieval chansons by a reexamination of the contemporary evidence available to us. Where, as in most instances, there is no unambiguous evidence for an assumption, he opts for a broad interpretation. Thus, he accepts neither a wholly oral nor a wholly written tradition of textual and melodic transmission for the chansons. In this question, as with others, "each chanson should be studied on its own merits to determine whether there was a written tradition and, if so, whether this included both text and melody" (p. 33).

Van der Werf regards as similarly unsubstantiated the claims of those scholars, increasingly more accepted, who advocate performance of the chansons based upon "regular rhythm and melody strictly measured by long and short notes in regular patterns according to the rhythm of the poetry." Careful examination of medieval treatises of music and metrics reveals no conclusive evidence enabling us to come down firmly for a strictly measured performance or its opposite, free performance. But in accordance with his own bias, van der Werf finds it heartening, and at least an implied support for the free performance theory, that such treatises as Johannes de Grocheo's (ca. 1300) "indicate that not all medieval music was as clearly measured as [medieval theorists] would like it to be" (p. 39).

Particularly irksome to van der Werf is the practice of correcting modern transcriptions of chanson melodies on the assumption that they were based upon the modes of church music as described in medieval treatises. He does not believe this to be the case (again pointing to lack of hard, documentary evidence), but postulates instead an approach to chanson theory based upon the ethnomusicological studies of Curt Sachs' *The Wellsprings of Music.* Rather than classifying the chansons according to melodic characteristics, van der Werf seeks to identify and describe the structural phenomena of the melodies, e.g., "recitation," "step-wise structure," and "scales". Once these organizing and structural characteristics of the melodies have been explained and described, van der Werf turns to the problem of integrating music and text. Chapter Five, "Elements of Form" shows how the forms of the melodies relate (or do not, as is sometimes the case) to those of the poems, and succeeds in laying the foundation for a useful methodology which deserves to be pursued on a much broader scale.

Space does not permit a discussion of the musical transcriptions and texts which constitute the second part of the book. Along with the accompanying discussions of the melodic characteristics of the individual chansons, they should be immensely helpful to students and scholars who want to experience the music and poetry of this tradition.

Stephen G. Nichols, Jr.
Dartmouth College

P.J. Jones. *The Malatesta of Rimini and the Papal State: A Political History.* Cambridge: Cambridge University Press, 1974. Pp. xi, 372. $23.50.

Philip Jones is a scholar of a type now nearly extinct. He has no peer among living historians in his knowledge of the sources and the secondary literature of medieval and Renaissance Italy. He has not limited his interests to a single city or region, or a century, or a Dante or Petrarch; he has read and absorbed it all. His chapter on the agrarian economy of medieval Italy (*Cambridge Economic History of Europe,* I, 2nd ed.) and his piece on Italian despots (*Trans. Royal Hist. Soc.,* 5th ser. XV, 1965) are classics. His first major scholarly enterprise was his doctoral dissertation on the Malatesta of Rimini. That thesis provided material for two articles that appeared in the 1950's. Now, unchanged except for an introductory chapter, he has published the complete work, the only modern, comprehensive account of that dynasty whose "ferocity and bloodthirstiness" had fascinated Burckhardt.

This "political history" of the Malatesta describes the family's rise from obscure origins, "local magnates of the Riminese hinterland" in the thirteenth century, to their domination, first, of the commune of Rimini, and then a large area of southern Romagna and the northern Marches. The fortunes of the Malatesta are thus linked to that of Rimini and other communes (Fano, Pesaro, Cesena, Ascoli, Ancona, Iesi), with neighboring signorial dynasties (Feltreschi, Ordelaffi, Manfredi, Polenta), and with the Papacy, whose efforts to establish control over its temporal possessions is a theme providing a modicum of coherence to the chaotic history of this region. The key dates in their rise to eminence were 1295, when the Malatesta defeated the rival Parcitadi clan for mastery of Rimini; 1335, when their *signoria* was legally recognized by the commune; 1355, when they received a papal vicariate. The key figures were the patriarchal Malatesta da Verucchio (d. 1312), Malatesta Gustafamiglia (d. 1363), and Carlo (d. 1429), who moved beyond local Romagnol politics to a wider world embracing Lombardy and Tuscany, Rome and Constance. Carlo's career also marked the turning point in Malatesta fortunes, which declined rapidly during the lifetime of Pius II's bitter enemy Sigismondo (d. 1468), and reached its ignominious end with Pandolfo, whose expulsion from Rimini in 1500 removed the family from the ranks of Italy's ruling dynasties.

This book, so rich in information and documentation, in perceptions and insights, is not easy to read. Jones does provide contexts and analysis, notably in the introductory chapter and in two concluding chapters on the vicariate and the *signoria,* but the narrative is not integrated effectively into these structures. Occasionally he is overwhelmed by the flood of detail—"the wearisome chronicle continues of war, truces and *cavalcate*" (p. 189)—which could have been condensed without sacrificing meaning or clarity. The story of the Malatesta is most easily grasped on the local level, in Romagna and the Marches, but they intrude regularly into the history of the Papacy and the Papal States, and spasmodically into the wider arena of Italian politics. This shift of focus, from local, to regional, to peninsular experience, is frequently disconcerting. But this book deserves a careful reading, and it offers substantial rewards: for example, in the lucid summary of Romagnol society in the *trecento* (p. 67), in the brilliant portrait of the swashbuckling Pandolfo Malatesta, and in the evidence, on every page, of a rare mastery of the historical craft.

Gene A. Brucker
University of California,
Berkeley

Frederic C. Lane. *Venice: a Maritime Republic.* Baltimore and London: The Johns Hopkins University Press, 1973. Pp. xv, 505. Cloth, $17.50; paper, $6.95.

For well over a generation Frederic Lane has been producing seminal works on the economic and maritime history of Europe, and above all Venice, during the Middle Ages and Renaissance. These have been characterized by precise definition of scope and rigorous analysis of often technically difficult subjects, but just as characteristically they have held implications of considerable breadth. Now, in *Venice, a Maritime Republic,* Lane has written a history of immense scope and vivid interpretation. His *Venice* is a strikingly distinctive history of the Venetian Republic from its beginnings to its fall in 1797. The book is important because it represents the first scholarly interpretation in English of the entire sweep of Venetian history in many decades, and also because it brings to full fruition the special qualities of rigor and command that Lane has displayed in all his work. But its greatest significance seems to me to lie in the unique approach, suggested in the title, that Lane has taken to his subject.

Venice, a Maritime Republic, manages in its 457 pages of text to deal with all the important issues in the Venetian Republic's history. Lane's knowledge of the sources, both primary and secondary, is prodigious— and for the period 1200–1600 probably unequalled among living scholars. (One relative weakness of the book is the somewhat thin account of internal affairs—political, social and cultural—in the seventeenth and eighteenth centuries.) A richly annotated—though not, regrettably, critical—bibliography at the end will, I am certain, be to scholars a valuable part of the book for many years. Lane's style is easy-going yet precise, and permits him to deal with a vast number of complex subjects economically and clearly. Consequently there is no stinting in the coverage; all of the questions that have occupied scholars traditionally and recently come in for scholarly discussion.

And on them Lane writes not only clearly and comprehensively, but interpretatively. Overall, he takes a positive view of the Venetian experience. He is alert to the dangers of over-mythologizing Venice, but he rejects the "countermyth" that depicts Venice's patrician government as a "tyrannical oligarchy" relying on terror to preserve itself (page 89). His position on Venice's controverted role in the Fourth Crusade is dispassionate, but certainly not anti-Venetian (pages 36 *seq.*). He acknowledges that political corruption did exist in Venice, but concludes that "in spite of weaknesses in the Venetian constitution, it provided better government than was generally found elsewhere" (page 271). Regarding Venice's confrontation of big, powerful monarchies in the sixteenth century, he observes that though these posed a mighty challenge to Venetian independence and prosperity, Venice could claim to have survived the challenge with its republican institutions intact at a time when elsewhere republicanism had all but disappeared (page 251). While admitting the problems posed by what he calls the "oceanic challenge," symbolized by Columbus' discoveries, he argues that far from being destroyed by them, Venice adjusted, and indeed "was certainly more populous. . .and probably wealthier in the sixteenth century than it had been in the fifteenth" (page 305).

It is necessary to make some extended mention of the one concern that dominates Lane's entire characterization of Venetian history, and that gives the book its special significance—the sea.

In the Preface, Lane writes that all authors emphasize what they know best. But he adds, "I have put nautical affairs in the center of my story not only for that reason but also because I believe they were important in determining Venetian social structure and the city's fortunes" (page *v*). Those familiar with Lane's other work know his interest in Venice's maritime activities; here, more than any other author I know, he has made these activities the backbone of his interpretative scheme of Venetian history.

It is not only that maritime dominance is viewed as the source of Venice's power and wealth, nor only that the sea—above all the Adriatic—fills a dramatic role in certain crucial moments of Venice's history, such as the fifteenth century "turn westward." Lane goes further, to associate the Venetians' maritime capacities—or lack of them—with every important point in the Venetian experience, often in precise detail. Thus after the Fourth Crusade Venice's dominance in the eastern Mediterranean was "solidly based on Venetian efficiency in shipbuilding and in the operation of both warships and merchantmen" (page 45). Thus an important stimulus to preserving Venice's island and coastal empire in the Mediterranean was the need for seamen from Dalmatia and Greece (pages 197, 356, and *passim*). Thus an explanation for Venice's naval reverses in the sixteenth century lies in the political practice of giving naval commands not to seasoned sea dogs but to politically prominent men who sometimes lacked all naval experience (pages 359, 361).

This overwhelming emphasis on maritime affairs—I count ten of the thirty chapters devoted specifically to such topics as nautical technology, manning and arming fleets, naval organization, and so on—amounts to a redressing of an imbalance in Venetian historiography. Venice was a sea power and Venetian history has long needed the refocusing on the sea that Lane has now provided. Yet, particularly in the second half of the book, the sheer mass of nautical information tends to drown the coverage of other, non-maritime issues. Lane's treatment of internal developments in Venice's last centuries, earlier referred to as sketchy, only seems so in contrast with his full and extensive discussion of nautical matters. On balance, the price is worth paying, but there are points in the later sections of the book when the reader may want to spend a bit more time on dry land surveying in a bit more detail what was going on in Venice and its mainland domain.

But all things considered, this is a comment more on the richness of Lane's maritime material than on the sparseness of his attention to other concerns. There is no question that *Venice: a Maritime Republic* is a work of major importance to the specialist and the general reader alike. A fitting climax to a career of exemplary scholarship, it now takes its place as the foremost survey of Venetian history in any language, and a successful restoration to that history of the maritime perspective from which it cannot rightfully be separated.

Stanley Chojnacki
Michigan State University

P. D. King. *Law and Society in the Visigothic Kingdom* (Cambridge Studies in Medieval Life and Thought, Third Series, no. 5). Cambridge: Cambridge University Press, 1972. Pp. xiv, 318. $21.00.

R. B. Dobson. *Durham Priory, 1400–1450* (Cambridge Studies in Medieval Life and Thought, Third Series, no. 6). Cambridge: Cambridge University Press, 1973. Pp. xiv, 428; 5 maps. $22.50.

The monographic series, Cambridge Studies in Medieval Life and Thought, was founded in 1920 by G. G. Coulton, under whose aegis fourteen volumes were published in the subsequent decade and a half. After World War II, the series was revived under the editorship of Dom David Knowles, and a new set of fourteen books appeared between 1951 and 1969. Professor Walter Ullmann then assumed responsibility for a third series; besides the works under review here, this series includes Alan Cobban, *The King's Hall within the University of Cambridge in the Later Middle Ages* (1969); A. J. Black, *Monarchy and Community* (1970); J. A. Watt, *The Church and the Two Nations in*

Medieval Ireland (1970); and Peter Linehan, *The Spanish Church and the Papacy in the Thirteenth Century* (1971). All of these works have been warmly received by medievalists as individual monographs; insofar as they form part of an integral collection, they maintain those qualities of distinguished scholarship and of wide appeal to historians in many fields that characterize the original works of the successive general editors themselves. In this regard, while there is a certain balance geographically between English and continental topics, the majority of the works can be classified under the rubric of ecclesiastical history in its broadest sense, including clerically-oriented cultural and intellectual history. There is nothing rigidly confining about this pattern, however, as the subject matter of Dr. King's study, as well as some others in earlier series, indicates; the basic editorial aim is to provide a vehicle for the publication of important work by English-trained medieval historians, and it is in this sense that the two under consideration here, wholly disparate in all respects save as the two most recent publications in the series, must be evaluated.

Dr. King's study, *Law and Society in the Visigothic Kingdom,* is a welcome addition to the limited amount of scholarly work on the Visigoths available in English. The book essentially is a careful summary of, and commentary on, the last major statement of the impressive Visigothic legal tradition, the code issued by King Ervig in 681. The author credits Visigothic rulers with a realistic, comprehensive, and constructive blending of Germanic legal elements with those derived from Roman jurisprudence and Christian principles; there is little evidence in the codes of the supposed "decadence" of the Visigothic kingdom on the eve of its destruction by the Muslim conquerors of Spain. Dr. King traces his theme through successive sections on the legislative authority of the king, the institutions of government, legal procedure, the legal characteristics of nobility and of slavery, and the laws governing property, family, and marriage. The sections on slavery, pp. 160–182, and on seventh-century anti-Jewish legislation, pp. 130–145, are particularly valuable, insofar as these formed much more crucial elements in Visigothic society than in the other Germanic Mediterranean kingdoms. The book is not a dry catalogue of legal rules and prescriptions; Dr. King is well aware of social and political realities, and stresses the limited ability of rulers to impose their authority on nobles and clergy, much less the general population. Nonetheless, and despite its abrupt termination, the Visigothic kingdom bore witness to the possibility of constructive synthesis of Germanic, Roman, and

Christian elements, not least in the jurisprudential tradition. The work thus makes a vital (and readable) contribution to our understanding not only of Visigothic Spain, but in a larger sense, of the entire Germanic Mediterranean world of the early middle ages.

Durham Priory 1400-1450 by Dr. R. E. Dobson takes us into an entirely different, but no less fascinating, world. It is a splendid example of monographic study at its very best. Its chief virtue is an unfailingly lucid and sympathetic appreciation of what can be known about monastic organization, and about the wider problem of the quality of spiritual life, in the late middle ages. The major figure in the story is prior John Wessington (1416-res. 1446, d. 1451), through whose career the problems of administrative and economic policy, the nature of ecclesiastical and of lay patronage, and the nature of cultural interests, are minutely examined. Much of the design of the book is structured around the paradox that a religious community is "always in part a product of the society from which it is trying to escape" (p. 388); Dr. Dobson convincingly demonstrates the force of this paradox by showing how Durham drew the basic sources of its vitality in the fifteenth century from its constructive relationships with the city of Durham, and, in a wider national sense, from Durham College, Oxford (founded 1381), the essential training-ground for many of the monks of his period. The author's conclusion is that the Priory maintained a generally high level of personal and collective moral commitment, and, in Wessington's hands, a vigorous if traditional intellectual activity. Only the Durham cells, poor in human and fiscal resources, show evidence of a clear decline in monastic energy and ability. The cells, however, are only a small part of the entire story; the basic impression to come from the pages of this book is that of a large and respected community, not content to live off past glories, but resolutely and intelligently addressing itself to the problems and quality of monastic life in its own day. The book, then, is indispensable for its patient and sensitive probing, not only of Durham Priory itself, but of the entire phenomenon of late medieval monasticism. No student of medieval culture and society can fail to profit from a careful reading of this work.

The qualities of historical interest and scrupulous scholarship that have consistently marked the Cambridge series are amply maintained by the two works most recently published in it. Scholars are indebted to Professor Ullmann and to Cambridge Press for ensuring the continuation of the vitality, distinction, and importance of this series of studies.

Michael Altschul
Case Western Reserve University

BOOKS RECEIVED

This list was compiled from the books received between 25 April 1973 and 30 April 1974. The publishers and the editorial board would appreciate your mentioning *Medievalia et Humanistica* when ordering.

Brandt, William J. *The Shape of Medieval History: Studies in Modes of Perception.* New York: Schocken Books, 1973. Pp. xix, 177. $2.95 paper.

Burke, Peter. *Culture and Society in Renaissance Italy, 1420–1540.* New York: Charles Scribner's Sons, 1972. Pp. x, 342; 19 plates, 1 map. $14.95.

Chazan, Robert. *Medieval Jewry in Northern France: A Political and Social History.* Baltimore and London: The John Hopkins University Press, 1973. Pp. xiv, 238. $12.50.

Clemoes, Peter, ed. *Anglo-Saxon England,* 2. Cambridge: Cambridge University Press, 1973. Pp. x, 333. $19.50.

Cohen, Kathleen. *Metamorphosis of a Death Symbol: The Transi Tomb in the Late Middle Ages and the Renaissance.* Berkeley, Los Angeles, London: University of California Press, 1974. Pp. xviii, 215; 122 plates. $30.00.

Dobson, R. B. *Durham Priory, 1400–1450.* (Cambridge Studies in Medieval Life and Thought, Third Series, no. 6.) Cambridge: Cambridge University Press, 1973. Pp. xiv, 428; 5 maps. $22.50.

Dufour, Jean. *La bibliothèque et le scriptorium de Moissac.* (Publications du Centre de Recherches d'Histoire de la IVᵉ section de l'École pratique des Hautes Études, Paris.) Geneva and Paris: Librarie Droz, 1972. Pp. xxii, 184; 78 plates.

Duggan, Joseph J. *The Song of Roland: Formulaic Style and Poetic Craft.* Berkeley, Los Angeles, London: University of California Press, 1973. Pp. 226. $8.50.

Guido delle Colonne. *Historia Destructionis Troiae,* trans. Mary E.

Meek. Bloomington: Indiana University Press, 1974. Pp. xxxiv, 324. $12.50.

Gundersheimer, Werner L. *Ferrara: The Style of a Renaissance Despotism.* Princeton: Princeton University Press, 1973. Pp. xii, 313; 19 plates. $14.00.

Hartung, Albert E., ed. *A Manual of the Writings in Middle English, 1050–1500.* New Haven, Conn.: The Connecticut Academy of Arts and Sciences, 1973. Vol. 4. Pp. x, 961–1313. $16.50.

Jones, P. J. *The Malatesta of Rimini and the Papal State: A Political History.* Cambridge: Cambridge University Press, 1974. Pp. xi, 372. $23.50.

Kim, H. C., ed. *The Gospel of Nicodemus: Gesta Salvatoris.* Toronto: Pontifical Institute of Mediaeval Studies, 1973. Pp. 54. $2.75 paper.

King, Edmund. *Peterborough Abbey, 1086–1310: A Study in the Land Market.* Cambridge: Cambridge University Press, 1973. Pp. xii, 208.

Lane, Frederic C. *Venice: A Maritime Republic.* Baltimore: The Johns Hopkins University Press, 1973. Pp. xv, 505. Cloth $17.50, paper $6.95.

Lieb, Michael, John T. Shawcross, edd. *Achievements of the Left Hand: Essays on the Prose of John Milton.* Amherst, Mass.: University of Massachusetts Press, 1974. Pp. x, 396. $12.50.

Logan, Oliver. *Culture and Society in Venice, 1470–1790.* New York: Charles Scribner's Sons, 1972. Pp. viii, 344; 26 plates, 1 map. $12.50.

McNeil, John T. *The Celtic Churches: A History, A.D. 200 to 1200.* Chicago and London: University of Chicago Press, 1974. Pp. xiv, 289. $10.00.

Miller, Joseph M., Michael H. Prosser, Thomas W. Benson, edd. *Readings in Medieval Rhetoric.* Bloomington: Indiana University Press, 1973. Pp. xx, 299. Cloth $12.95, paper $4.50.

Mills, Maldwyn, ed. *Six Middle English Romances.* London: Dent, 1973. Pp. xxxiii, 224. Cloth $7.50, paper $3.50.

Mitchell, Bonner. *Rome in the High Renaissance: The Age of Leo X.* (Centers of Civilization Series, vol. 33.) Norman: University of Oklahoma Press, 1973. Pp. xii, 171. $3.50.

Nelson, William. *Fact or Fiction: The Dilemma of the Renaissance Story-teller.* Cambridge, Mass.: Harvard University Press, 1973. Pp. x, 121. $5.95.

Odier, Jeanne B. *La Bibliothèque Vaticane de Sixte IV à Pie XI: Recherches sur l'Histoire des collections de manuscrits* (Studi e Testi 272). Città del Vaticano: Biblioteca Apostolica Vaticana, 1973. Pp. xviii, 477; 78 plates.

Peter of Spain (Petrus Hispanus Portugalensis). *Tractatus (Summule Logicales).* Ed. L. M. De Rijk. Van Gorcum & Comp. B. V. Assen, 1972. Pp. cxxix, 303. $27.50.

Postan, M. M. *Medieval Trade and Finance.* Cambridge: Cambridge University Press, 1973. Pp. vi, 382.

Postan, M. M. *Essays on Medieval Agriculture and General Problems of the Medieval Economy.* Cambridge: Cambridge University Press, 1973. Pp. vi, 302.

Sanderlin, David. *The Mediaeval Statutes of the College of Autun at the University of Paris.* (Texts and Studies in the History of Mediaeval Education, No. XIII.) Notre Dame: The Mediaeval Institute, 1971. Pp. 117.

Société Internationale pour l'Étude de la Philosophie Médiévale, ed. *Bulletin de Philosophie Médiévale,* No. 14. Louvain: Secretariat de la S.I.E.P.M., 1972. Pp. 215.

Synan, Edward A. *The Fountain of Philosophy: A Translation of the Twelfth-Century Fons Philosophiae of Godfrey of Saint Victor.* Toronto: Pontifical Institute of Mediaeval Studies, 1972. Pp. 89.

Translatio Studii: Manuscripts and Library Studies Honoring Oliver L. Kapsner, O.S.B. Ed. Julian G. Plante. Collegeville, Minn.: St. John's University Press, 1973. Pp. 288, $17.50.

Travis, James. *Early Celtic Versecraft: Origin, Development, Diffusion.* Ithaca: Cornell University Press, 1973. Pp. x, 166. $12.75.

Van Caenegem, R. C. *The Birth of the English Common Law.* Cambridge: Cambridge University Press, 1973. Pp. viii, 160. $8.50.

Vessey, David. *Statius & the Thebaid.* Cambridge: Cambridge University Press, 1973. Pp. viii, 357. $23.50.

Zacour, Norman P. *Petrarch's Book without a Name.* A translation of the *Liber sine nomine.* Toronto: Pontifical Institute of Mediaeval Studies, 1973. Pp. 128. $3.00 paper.